AFRICA

MAPS AND CHARTS BY
CATHRYN L. LOMBARDI

PHOTOGRAPHIC SELECTION BY
MARY JOY PIGOZZI

EDITED BY

PHYLLIS M. MARTIN
and
PATRICK O'MEARA

RICA

INDIANA UNIVERSITY PRESS   *Bloomington & London*

PUBLISHED IN CANADA BY FITZHENRY & WHITESIDE LIMITED, DON MILLS,
ONTARIO

MANUFACTURED IN THE UNITED STATES OF AMERICA

Library of Congress Cataloging in Publication Data
Main entry under title:
Africa.
    Bibliography: p.
    Includes index.
    1.   Africa—Addresses, essays, lectures.
I.   Martin, Phyllis.   II.   O'Meara, Patrick.
DT3.A23   1977   960   77-74450
ISBN 0-253-30210-2   1 2 3 4 5 81 80 79 78 77

CONTENTS

IV.   The Forces of Modernization

MAPS

FIGURES

PLATES

PREFACE

African Studies programs in the United States in the 1960s were primarily concerned with graduate studies and advanced undergraduate courses in specialized fields. In the 1970s, however, there has been an increased awareness of the need to educate a wider segment of the student population, and the general public as well, about Africa. In response to an interest shown by undergraduates, an introductory interdisciplinary course on Africa was introduced at Indiana University in 1972 and has been offered each semester since. This book is a direct outgrowth of the experience gained through teaching the course and from student responses to it.

It does not attempt to be comprehensive in the sense of providing a detailed account of social, political, economic, and historical developments for all of Africa; that would be an impossible task given the size and diversity of the continent. This overview can only focus on significant themes that relate to the continent as a whole, such as the development of Early Man, social change, colonialism, industrialization, or on problems which, although primarily concerned with specific regions and peoples, such as the impact of Islam in the northern third of the continent or of race conflict in southern Africa, have wide ramifications.

By its very nature, this book does not have the overall uniformity of a volume written by a single author. All the contributors have lived and worked on the African continent, but they vary in their individual interpretations, insights, and disciplinary perspectives. Each contribution reflects the academic training, personal experience, and, at times, the ideological perspective of the writer.

This is not intended as a collection of disparate essays, however; all the chapters are Africa-focused, and comparison and interdisciplinary linkages may be easily made. For example, there are obvious linkages between the Sieber and Bravmann chapters, which deal with African art, and between those by Merriam and Kaemmer, which deal with the dynamics of African music through time. The Bravmann and Kaemmer chapters may in turn be read in conjunction with the Armer and Snyder chapters, which deal with social change in contemporary Africa. Other chapters also have interconnected themes which can be usefully related. The Vaughan and Schneider essays include discussions of the rise of states in Africa from an anthropological perspective, and the Lamphear chapter on themes in African history deals with the same problem in a time perspective. Another example is in the South African context, where Lamphear, Brooks, and Carter all have material related to important developments in the nineteenth century.

What are some of the specific factors that have influenced the interpretations of the contributors? In the first instance this is a mid-1970s approach to the study of Africa; thus the essays reflect the period in which they are written and may differ substantially from earlier interpretations. Whereas scholars a decade or two ago had relatively few sources on which to base their research, there is now a growing body of new data available. Historians, for example, can now at least attempt to answer some of the fundamental questions of early periods of African history which until recently were thought to be unanswerable. Improved techniques in archaeology and linguistics, the collecting of oral history, the preservation of documents, and systematic archival research have all opened up new possibilities and directions.

Theoretical changes within particular disciplines also take place over time and affect the way in which new data are analyzed and examined. The contributors are writing from the points of view of their respective disciplines—economics, political science, anthropology, and so on—and thus their research and writing are influenced by prevailing interpretations and theoretical approaches within their own fields. However, this is intended as an introductory text and hence the authors have as their primary goal the conveying of a clear and basic statement and not the presentation of specialized academic arguments. The focus of research also changes as a result of contemporary issues and interests. Thus, a decade or two ago, when colonialism was of immediate concern, the colonial period was considered an all-important era. Now there is a tendency to de-emphasize the dramatic nature of the changes introduced during this time and to underscore continuities from the African past. Similarly, with the coming of independence in the 1960s, the issue of the transition from colonial rule to self-determination was a major focus. Today the emphasis is increasingly on questions of development, the nature of political institutions in independent Africa, military rule, and neocolonialism.

Two conferences organized with the Indiana Consortium for International Programs (ICIP) brought together a number of college teachers whose criticism and comments were most helpful to individual contributors and to the editors. In part, the impetus for holding these conferences by the African Studies Program, an NDEA VI Language and Area Center, was due to the emphasis placed on outreach activities by the Division of International Education of the Office of Education. In particular we should like to thank John Stabler and David Waas of ICIP for helping to organize the meetings. The staff of the African Studies Program, Anne Fraker, Alice Young, Sue Myers, Rhonda Bastin, and Rebecca Riley, has given invaluable assistance with the production of the book. Finally we are indebted to our contributors for their cooperation and insights. They have provided us with a stimulating experience and have widened our knowledge and understanding of Africa.

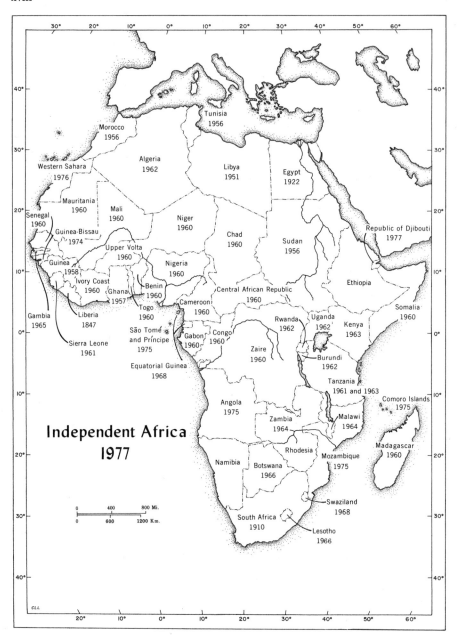

Independent Africa
1977

MAP 1

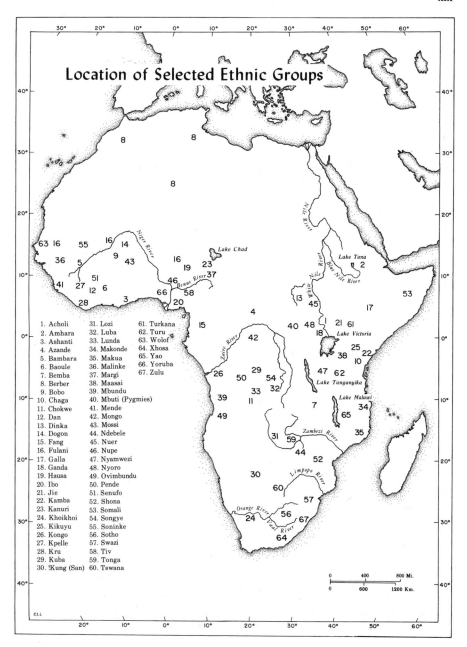

Location of Selected Ethnic Groups

1. Acholi
2. Amhara
3. Ashanti
4. Azande
5. Bambara
6. Baoule
7. Bemba
8. Berber
9. Bobo
10. Chaga
11. Chokwe
12. Dan
13. Dinka
14. Dogon
15. Fang
16. Fulani
17. Galla
18. Ganda
19. Hausa
20. Ibo
21. Jie
22. Kamba
23. Kanuri
24. Khoikhoi
25. Kikuyu
26. Kongo
27. Kpelle
28. Kru
29. Kuba
30. !Kung (San)

31. Lozi
32. Luba
33. Lunda
34. Makonde
35. Makua
36. Malinke
37. Margi
38. Maasai
39. Mbundu
40. Mbuti (Pygmies)
41. Mende
42. Mongo
43. Mossi
44. Ndebele
45. Nuer
46. Nupe
47. Nyamwezi
48. Nyoro
49. Ovimbundu
50. Pende
51. Senufo
52. Shona
53. Somali
54. Songye
55. Soninke
56. Sotho
57. Swazi
58. Tiv
59. Tonga
60. Tswana

61. Turkana
62. Turu
63. Wolof
64. Xhosa
65. Yao
66. Yoruba
67. Zulu

MAP 2

FIGURE 1

Basic Information

Country (Independence)	Former Name	Former Colonial Power	Capital (and Former Name)
Algeria (1962)	Algeria	France	Algiers
Angola (1975)	Angola	Portugal	Luanda
Benin (1960)	Dahomey	France	Porto-Novo and Cotonou
Botswana (1966)	Bechuanaland	Britain	Gaborone
Burundi (1962)	Part of Ruanda-Urundi	Germany; Belgium under League Mandate and UN Trust Territory	Bujumbura
Cameroon (1960)	French Cameroun and British Cameroons	Germany; France and Britain UN Trust Territories	Yaoundé
Cape Verde (1975)	Cape Verde Islands	Portugal	Praia
Central African Republic (1960)	Ubangi-Shari	France	Bangui
Chad (1960)	Chad	France	Ndjamena (Fort-Lamy)
Comoro Islands (1975)	Comoro Islands	France	Moroni
Congo (1960)	Middle Congo	France	Brazzaville
Djibouti (1977)	French Somaliland; Afars and Issas	France	Djibouti
Egypt (1922)	United Arab Republic	Britain	Cairo
Equatorial Guinea (1968)	Spanish Guinea, Rio Muni (mainland) and Fernando Póo	Spain	Malabo (Santa Isabel)
Ethiopia	Abyssinia	Independent (Italian occupation 1935-41)	Addis Ababa
Gabon (1960)	Gabon	France	Libreville
The Gambia (1965)	The Gambia	Britain	Banjul (Bathurst)

Ghana (1957)	Gold Coast	Britain	Accra
Guinea (1958)	Guinea	France	Conakry
Guinea-Bissau (1974)	Portuguese Guinea	Portugal	Bissau
Ivory Coast (1960)	Ivory Coast	France	Abidjan
Kenya (1963)	Kenya	Britain	Nairobi
Lesotho (1966)	Basutoland	Britain	Maseru
Liberia (1847)	Liberia	Independent	Monrovia
Libya (1951)	Former colonies of Cyrenaica, Tripolitania, Fezzan	Italy and UN Trust Territory	Tripoli
Madagascar (1960)	Malagasy Republic	France	Tananarive
Malawi (1964)	Nyasaland	Britain	Lilongwe
Mali (1960)	Soudan	France	Bamako
Mauritania (1960)	Mauritania	France	Nouakchott
Mauritius (1968)	Mauritius	Britain	Port Louis
Morocco (1956)	Morocco	France and Spain	Rabat
Mozambique (1975)	Mozambique	Portugal	Maputo (Lourenço Marques)
Namibia	South-West Africa	Germany; South Africa League of Nations Mandate and UN Trust Territory	Windhoek
Niger (1960)	Niger	France	Niamey
Nigeria (1960)	Nigeria	Britain	Lagos
Réunion	Réunion	French colony	Saint-Denis
Rhodesia	Southern Rhodesia	Britain (Unilateral Declaration of Independence 1965)	Salisbury
Rwanda (1962)	Part of Ruanda-Urundi	Germany; Belgium under League Mandate and UN Trust Territory	Kigali
São Tomé and Príncipe (1975)	São Tomé and Príncipe	Portugal	São Tomé
Senegal (1960)	Senegal	France	Dakar
Seychelles (1976)	Seychelles	France; Britain	Victoria
Sierra Leone (1961)	Sierra Leone	Britain	Freetown

FIGURE 1 (continued)

Country (Independence)	Former Name	Former Colonial Power	Capital (and Former Name)
Somalia (1960)	British and Italian Somalia(s)	Britain, Italy and UN Trust Territory	Mogadishu
South Africa	South Africa	Britain	Pretoria and Cape Town
Sudan (1956)	Anglo-Egyptian Sudan	Britain and Egypt	Khartoum
Swaziland (1968)	Swaziland	Britain	Mbabane
Tanzania (1961 and 1963, with Unification in 1964)	Tanganyika and Zanzibar	Tanganyika: Germany; Britain under League Mandate and UN Trust Territory. Zanzibar: Britain	Dar-es-Salaam
Togo (1960)	Togoland	Germany; France and Britain. League of Nations Mandate and UN Trust Territory	Lomé
Tunisia (1956)	Tunisia	France	Tunis
Uganda (1962)	Uganda	Britain	Kampala
Upper Volta (1960)	Upper Volta	France	Ouagadougou
Western Sahara (1976)	Spanish Sahara	Spain	El Aaiún
Zaire (1960)	Belgian Congo; Congo-Leopoldville; Congo-Kinshasa	Belgium	Kinshasa (Leopoldville)
Zambia (1964)	Northern Rhodesia	Britain	Lusaka

AFRICA

INTRODUCTION

I

Phyllis M. Martin and Patrick O'Meara
Africa: Problems and Perspectives

1 What are the factors which contribute to the diversity of the African continent, and what are the integrative forces which draw together different peoples and cultures? Are there common experiences derived from a deep awareness of a shared past and from a concern for future objectives? Or is Africa only a geographic entity? Has Africa participated in the major developments of world history, or has it really been a "Dark Continent"? In what sense are continuities from the past, often termed traditional, relevant for individuals and societies today? How have Africans been affected by experiences such as colonialism, independence, and the priorities of modern governments? And how have these developments shaped the contemporary map of Africa? These are some of the general questions that are considered in the introductory section of this book. Together they provide a broad framework for an understanding of the issues and problems of African societies.

Size and Diversity

The size and diversity of Africa are striking. More than three times the size of the continental United States, and including over fifty countries and at least three hundred million people, Africa is divided not only by the boundaries of nation-states but also by ethnic differences, geographic barriers, and vast distances.

The character of individual African countries is also diverse. Population can range from Botswana's 700,000, the size of a modest American city, to Nigeria's

75 million. In terms of area, the Gambia (4,261 square miles) is less than half the size of New Hampshire, while Sudan (967,498 square miles) is almost four times the size of Texas. Life-styles within nations can vary dramatically because of environmental factors and because the impact of industrialization and urbanization is usually more intense in one part of a country than another.

Since the late nineteenth century the peoples of Africa have experienced diverse patterns of colonial rule. All countries on the continent, except for Ethiopia and Liberia, were subject to foreign domination and control, an important ingredient in a shared African past. Colonialism also created other levels of diversity; it caused new language divisions, such as those between francophone, anglophone, and lusophone countries, and imposed norms and values which continue today despite the end of the colonial era. While colonialism created blocs of peoples and countries with the common background of the same colonial ruler, it also created profound political problems with which independent governments now have to grapple. In certain cases colonial boundaries cut across particular ethnic groups; for example, the Somali people can be found today not only in Somalia but also in the neighboring countries, and this not only produces border conflicts but also gives rise to the emergence of irredentist movements. Very few countries such as Somalia, Swaziland, and Lesotho have only one dominant ethnic group and most include within their boundaries many different peoples. In some instances nations have to reconcile profound cleavages such as those between the Hausa, Yoruba, and Ibo in Nigeria and the Kongo, Mbundu, and Ovimbundu in Angola. Thus, historical experience, language, and cultural traditions, often rooted in the distant past, remain the base for contemporary problems within individual African countries.

The most significant division on the continent at present derives from continuing white minority rule in southern Africa, in the countries of Rhodesia (which will be renamed Zimbabwe when it becomes independent), Namibia, and the Republic of South Africa. This last vestige of white privilege and power causes both internal conflict and continent-wide division along black-white lines. When Ghana became independent in 1957, Kwame Nkrumah, its prime minister and later its first president, said that the liberation of Ghana was meaningless without the liberation of the whole continent. And this sentiment, twenty years later, prevails.

Questions of diversity and integration are highly complex. Diversity does not necessarily imply division and indeed can make for a richer human experience. Division, which frequently does occur, however, can cause major disagreement, conflict, and even bloodshed. While the Organization of African Unity (OAU) and other supranational organizations, such as OCAMM (*Organisa-*

tion commune africaine, malgache, et mauricienne), which loosely joins most of the French-speaking territories in Africa, and the East African Community, which consists of the English-speaking states of East Africa, attempt to promote united action, there is no unified African approach. National sovereignty involves varying political systems ranging from radical to conservative, although differences can be sometimes overcome in continent-wide or regional cooperation for specific common goals.

An apparent division between North Africa and the rest of the continent, often referred to as Black Africa, sub-Saharan Africa, or Tropical Africa, is seen as another point of diversity. There is some substance to this perception since North Africa has been more heavily influenced by the forces of Islam, which pervades all aspects of life, political, social, and ideological. Historical and cultural influences and the use of Arabic have been all-important factors integrating countries such as Mauritania, Morocco, Algeria, Tunisia, Libya, and Egypt, and to some extent Sudan and Somalia, with the Arab countries of the Middle East. Since 1948 conflicts with Israel have further served to solidify ties within the Arab world. Thus, the countries of North Africa are linked to each other and to peoples across the Red Sea and the Mediterranean as much as to the rest of the African continent.

Yet the historical chapters clearly show that for centuries there have been direct and continuous linkages between North Africa and the rest of the continent and that the division of the continent by the Sahara can be overemphasized. A majority of the population of the whole northern third of the continent are Muslim, and the forces of Islam are strongly present elsewhere. Trade, diplomacy, the transmission of skills and techniques across the continent from north to south and south to north are all evidence of continuing continent-wide interaction. "One cannot allow the mind to be dominated by such conventional divisions as Tropical Africa or North Africa, but rather one must seek to achieve a vision of the whole in which the Sahara appears not as a barrier, but rather as a filter or as a sea that unites as well as divides."[1] In the period of decolonization, Nasser of Egypt, Ben Bella of Algeria, Sekou Touré of Guinea, and Nkrumah of Ghana all closely cooperated to bring an end to colonialism, and today the Organization of African Unity includes all Arab countries on the African continent.

Africa in World Perspective

There is an all too frequent misconception of Africa as a Dark Continent, and a recurring notion that Africans have been isolated from the rest of the world. The emphasis placed on the "discovery" of the continent by white explorers from Prince Henry the Navigator in the fifteenth century to David Livingstone in the nineteenth century, and a continuing ignorance of its cultures and heritage by non-Africans all contribute to this false impression.

Africa has simply never been cut off from the cross-currents of world history. It is the "Cradle of Mankind," the source of Man's earliest biological and cultural development, and therefore the point from which some of the most essential elements of human society and growth were derived. Africa also drew from other continents for fundamental developments in agriculture and material technology: food crops such as maize, manioc, and yams from the Americas and East Asia, and the knowledge of iron probably from the Middle East. As early as the first millennium A.D., Africa was part of a busy Indian Ocean trading system dealing with distant places in Arabia, India, Persia, and China. At the same time, the Middle East and Europe were in contact with Africa across the Sahara exchanging scholars and ideas with important centers of learning in the Arabic-speaking world, while West Africa exported gold and other commodities to Europe. Thus before the better-known contacts between Europe and Africa associated with the "Age of Exploration" in the fifteenth century, parts of Africa had interacted continuously with other world areas over centuries.

With the beginnings of the transatlantic slave trade in the sixteenth century, Africa's interaction with the Americas became an important strand of world history. About ten million people were forcibly taken to the Carribean, North America, and Latin America. In the course of the twentieth century many black Americans have become increasingly aware of their African ancestry, as dramatically portrayed in Alex Haley's book, *Roots*. The African element in the making of America has clearly been as important as that of immigrant groups such as the Poles, the Italians, the Irish, and the Jews.

As already noted, the interaction of Europe and Africa took on a new dimension at the end of the nineteenth century with the subjugation of the continent under white colonial rule. From the African's point of view the colonial period was characterized by land alienation, the exploitation of raw materials, forced labor, and racism, as well as by the advent of Western education and technology. The full impact of this period, which only lasted some eighty years, a short time in the total span of history, cannot yet be finally assessed. However, this was another important factor linking Africans with other peoples who experienced Western domination in the last century. Interests common to the Third World (a term used loosely to describe countries not aligned with Western or with communist countries) provide a further element in the continuing linkages between Africa and the rest of the world.

Traditional and Modern

The terms "traditional" and "modern" are frequently misused and can mask a clear understanding of the continent. The popular view regards traditional Africa not only as isolated from the outside world but also as static, and emphasizes an unchanging life style and value system. Contrasted with this is the popular view of modern Africa as much more progressive and dynamic, due largely to the impetus of Western ideas and technology. Implicit in the concept of traditional and modern is the idea of evolution or progression over centuries from an inferior to a superior state of being. The traditional in Africa is seen as anachronistic, inevitably to be superseded by the modern, and since the former is thought to be incapable of adapting to either internal or external forces, its decline is usually applauded. There is also a tendency to see a sharp dichotomy between the traditional and the modern, to perceive them as closed systems irreconcilably separated from each other. Individuals who try to bridge the "gap" are often portrayed as being caught between two worlds, and whole societies are seen to be under stress because of these conflicting pressures.

These terms, traditional and modern, are clearly invalid and do not reflect reality if they are used to describe separable parts of individual or group experience; they are not absolute categories into which individuals, institutions, and societies can be neatly categorized. While the division of the African experience into such dichotomies is misleading, the terms continue in use as simple, convenient, almost unavoidable concepts which can provide an initial though limited understanding of the world. If they are to be used, however, they should not be seen as counterbalancing or opposing forces but rather as interdependent. They are a useful way of identifying *relative* differences in values and life-styles, but they do need qualification and explanation.

Tradition implies time-depth, the continuity of ideals, values, and institutions transmitted over generations; but the process also involves continuous borrowing, invention, rejection, and adaptation on all levels, individual, local, and regional. The emphasis is always on continuity *and* change for all societies. In attempting to differentiate modern Africa from traditional, it should be noted that while change occurred in traditional societies it was not as rapid as in the twentieth century. This increase in the rate of change has been a worldwide phenomenon, resulting from a period of radical technological growth in the Western world in particular. With the coming of colonialism to Africa, the impact of new forces and values was most pronounced. In the colonial period the principal agents of change, who penetrated African societies at the local level, were traders, missionaries, and petty bureaucrats. These were followed by other purveyors of change. Their interaction with Africans resulted in the introduction of new expectations and value systems which diminished the significance of local ties, emphasized the importance of the individual over the group, encouraged the development of universal norms, and led to an increased emphasis on status resulting from achievement rather than birth. New national political authorities, integration into regional, national, and world capitalist economies, and the introduction of services such as highly developed transportation systems and formal Western education all contributed to this period of intensive change.

The terms traditional and modern are often used to differentiate between rural and urban societies in contemporary Africa. Here again the distinction can be far too sharply drawn, since parts of the continent, especially West Africa, had large-scale urban complexes such as the cities of Kano and Timbuktu long before the twentieth century. On an individual level, the most remote rural villager is not left untouched by modern influences; for example, the transistor radio reaches the most inaccessible areas. In the cities workers and professionals alike are still influenced by traditional ties at least on certain levels, as with their extended family loyalties and responsibilities. Modern and traditional elements often interact beyond the level of daily life within many institutional aspects of society. For example, in contemporary politics, both on the local and national levels, rulers and elites recognize the significance and legitimacy of traditional influences. Thus the African experience is an integrated whole, fusing traditional and modern at different levels according to individual or group experiences, situations, and needs.

Africa's diversity and integration, its continuous interaction with other parts of the world, and the complex notions of tradition and modernity have been highlighted because they are crucial to an understanding of the continent and are recurring ideas throughout this book. There is a danger that such discussion may reduce these and other themes to a level of abstraction removed from the struggles, vitality, and excitement of daily life. Every day people have to make choices, solve problems, and create new options for the future.

NOTE

1. See Robin Hallett's "Introduction" to E. W. Bovill, *The Golden Trade of the Moors*, 2d ed. (London: Oxford University Press, 1970), p. xii.

James H. Vaughan
Environment, Population, and Traditional Society

2 There are two problems in attempting to discuss African societies in general terms: their heterogeneity and their changing nature. The total number of named African societies is very high, probably in excess of two thousand, although this number may overemphasize their diversity since many of them differ only slightly. Linguistic diveristy may afford a more accurate picture. Map 3 shows four broad language families which differ from one another as much as Indo-European differs from Sino-Tibetan. On a more particular level, however, considering differences such as those between English and German, there are perhaps as many as a thousand African languages. In this chapter an effort is made to overcome the problem of social heterogeneity by drawing generalizations from a sample of 277 sub-Saharan societies.[1]

The changing nature of African societies presents a more difficult problem, for they, like all societies, are never static. This is partly a result of internally generated growth and partly due to external forces such as additions through contact with other peoples. It is difficult to generalize about any African society since changes have taken place within each from time to time. Changes, however, are never random; there is always a continuity with the past. At any moment a society is a combination of the new and the traditional—not as unrelated parts but as a mixture, the new often shaped and interpreted in terms of the traditional.

In this chapter, the phrase "traditional society" is used in the sense of that which is historically and integrally African as opposed to non-African. For ex-

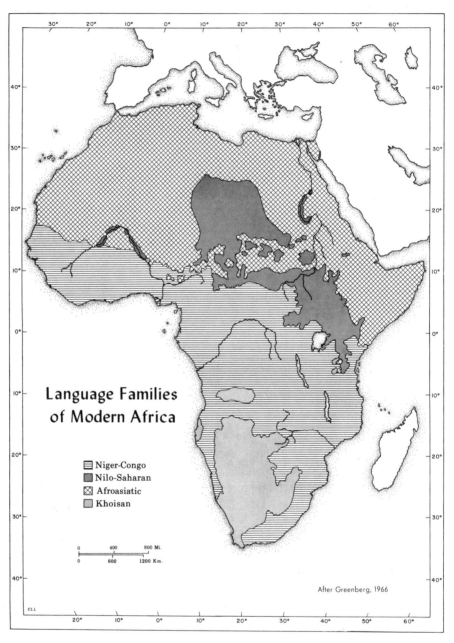

Language Families
of Modern Africa

▤ Niger-Congo
■ Nilo-Saharan
⊠ Afroasiatic
▨ Khoisan

| 0 | 400 | 800 Mi. |
| 0 | 600 | 1200 Km. |

After Greenberg, 1966

MAP 3

ample, Africans plowing their fields or attending Christian church services are unquestionably functioning parts of contemporary society, but these customs are not traditional; each is a consequence of colonialism and of the changes which it has produced. Furthermore, there are African alternatives in each case; much is known about traditional African religions and techniques of farming. Africa has interacted with the rest of the world over a long period of time and, to be sure, institutions or customs have been imported. Some of these "imports" are now considered parts of traditional society—agriculture and metallurgy, to mention two revolutionary concepts. Such ideas were integrated harmoniously and thoroughly centuries ago and hence are of a different order from more recent influences.

All societies reflect their environmental settings and the human resources of their populations. An understanding of African social and cultural behavior requires that the peculiarities of the African habitat and the characteristics of the African population be examined. In many ways the interaction of these two variables explains not only the shape that a society takes but its conservatism and change through time.

Environment

The African environment is in itself a very broad topic which will here be treated only to the extent of emphasizing those aspects which have had important consequences for the development of African societies. Topographically the continent is marked by a general absence of impediments to migration. Even the great Rift Valley, the Sahara Desert, and the mountains of East Africa do not seem to have blocked significant movement. The desert is, of course, a topographic feature only as a consequence of climatic conditions, and, in fact, climate has very significantly shaped African societies. Unquestionably, the most important ingredient in African climate is water. Whether in the form of rainfall, river-flow, or humidity, water has a profound impact upon African life.

Rainfall (see map 4) must be viewed in both seasonal and annual contexts. Total annual rainfall shows marked variation on the African continent, with very high amounts being characteristic of the equatorial areas and very low amounts in regions near the deserts. Seasonally, rainfall in Africa is distributed into wet and dry seasons which correspond roughly with the temperate seasons of summer and winter. (It should be remembered that seasons are reversed on either side of the Equator.) In many parts of Africa this means that virtually all rain, certainly all useful rain, falls during the five or six months of the rainy

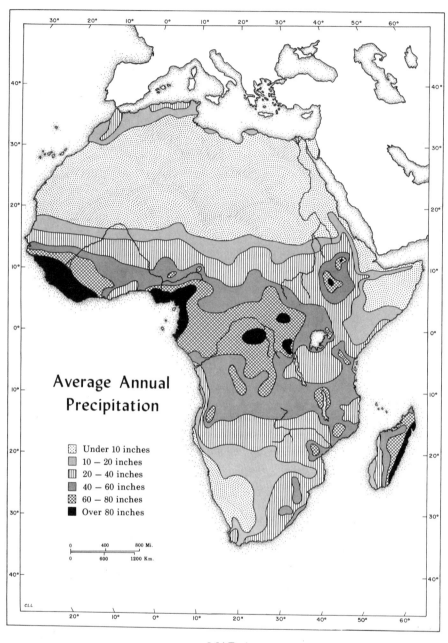

Average Annual
Precipitation

- ▨ Under 10 inches
- ▦ 10 – 20 inches
- ▥ 20 – 40 inches
- ▨ 40 – 60 inches
- ▨ 60 – 80 inches
- ■ Over 80 inches

MAP 4

season, while none, or almost none, falls during the dry season. Obviously this severely limits agricultural production, animal pasturing, and general human activity. It is this seasonal characteristic which makes the African climate so markedly different from that of more temperate continents. For example, the city of Chicago has slightly less rainfall *annually* than does the West African city of Kano, but the Chicago rainfall is distributed relatively evenly throughout the year while the Kano rainfall occurs in only six months (figure 2). The con-

AVERAGE ANNUAL RAINFALL
BY MONTH

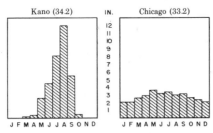

FIGURE 2

trast is remarkable: Kano looks like near-desert in comparison to Chicago. But the difference goes beyond mere appearances, for northern Illinois has much more productive farm land than does northern Nigeria.

A consequence of this rainfall distribution is a very pronounced vegetational pattern in Africa (map 5). The tropical rainforest is far less characteristic of Africa than is the savanna grasslands, and most African societies have a grasslands environment rather than the forest environment so popularized in motion pictures. These vegetational zones reflect contrasting environmental conditions, but they have cultural consequences as well, for different crops are suited to different environments. Africa has had two agricultural revolutions (see chapter 5), each associated with a different vegetational zone. The first, based on cereal grains, was adapted to the savanna regions and the second, which had to await the spread of tuberous crops from Malaysia, was suited to the more humid tropical forest regions. Agriculture, except in the very arid desert and sub-desert regions, swept across the continent replacing the earlier food-gathering activities, and by the fifteenth century African societies were very largely agricultural. In the sample of sub-Saharan societies, agriculture was absent in less than 3 percent. The general pattern was that societies located in savanna regions had

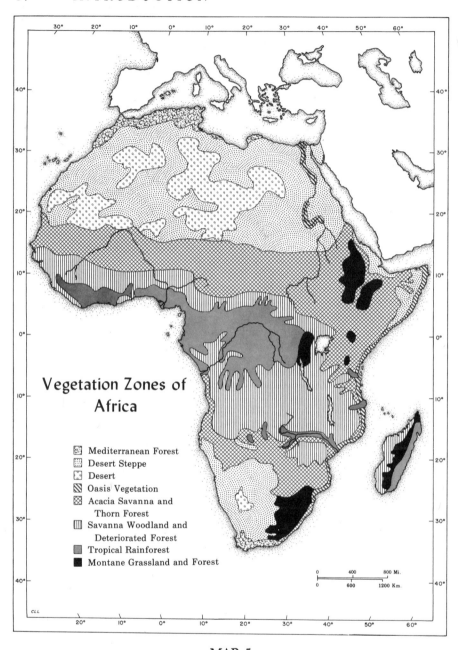

Vegetation Zones of
Africa

Mediterranean Forest
Desert Steppe
Desert
Oasis Vegetation
Acacia Savanna and
  Thorn Forest
Savanna Woodland and
  Deteriorated Forest
Tropical Rainforest
Montane Grassland and Forest

MAP 5

1. Cattle grazing in the savanna grasslands of East Africa.
Photo courtesy United Nations/ Magata/ jr.

cereal crops as staples, principally sorghum, millet, and eleusine, while societies in the forest areas relied upon tuberous crops such as yams and taro. The pattern was slightly altered by the importation of two crops from the New World after the fifteenth century: maize (or corn) and manioc (or cassava). These crops, the former a grain and the latter a tuber, are less moisture sensitive than are the traditional African crops, and they grow in both savanna and tropical forest zones. Today, each has supplanted indigenous African crops as staples in many societies.

The distribution of large domesticated animals is also related to water in the environment. The tse-tse fly, which is devastating to cattle, requires a very humid habitat and is generally limited to areas with more than 40 inches of rainfall annually, though its seasonal distribution may vary. Consequently, areas inhabited by the tse-tse are not regions in which livestock such as horses and cattle are usually found. The fly does not affect smaller domesticated animals such as chickens, sheep, and goats, or a rare dwarf breed of cow, nor does it affect wild animals.

The diseases of the African environment are legendary; they range from exotic new discoveries like Lassa and green monkey fevers to one of the world's great killers, malaria. The importance of diseases for African development will be discussed in chapter 3, but their impact upon traditional society should not be overlooked. It is not unusual even today to find societies in which 50 percent of the children born never reach adulthood. A less dramatic consequence of high disease rates but perhaps of greater importance is the loss of energy and vitality which a society suffers through illnesses, even those which are nonfatal. Malaria is, of course, a terrible killer, but it also causes periodic fevers and general sickness among such high percentages of the population that the ability of a society to use its human resources is seriously impaired and its culture may come to reflect special attitudes toward illness and death.

2. Tropical rainforest in the Cameroon Republic.
Photo courtesy United Nations/ jt.

Characteristics of Population

Two aspects of population must be considered, though their cultural significance is unequal. First are those characteristics intrinsic to the human animal as a species, such as its needs, potentialities, limitations, and genetic characteristics. Second, and of greater cultural significance, are the demographic char-

3. Woman pounding grain into flour, Ivory Coast.
Photo courtesy United Nations/ AP/ ab.

acteristics of populations: size, density, growth, age distribution, disease rates, and so on.

Since all human societies for the past 100,000 years or so have been composed of the same species, *Homo sapiens sapiens*, it is highly improbable that biological characteristics alone account for variations between societies. Such characteristics do determine, however, the general structures of all societies. Thus human societies, no matter where they are found, will sustain themselves nutritionally, will reproduce sexually, and will be bound by countless limitations which afflict the human animal.

Historically and culturally one of the most important of these limitations comes from dependence upon learning and its cumulative nature. Consequently, a post-Neolithic society may be vastly different from its pre-Neolithic stage, not because the population is substantially different or even more intelligent, but because it is the beneficiary of accumulated knowledge. The cumulate nature of human learning is a major source of social and cultural development and accounts for the apparent progress in many aspects of human culture. One reservation must be offered concerning the cumulative nature of learning, however. In the Euramerican world it has been possible, through writing, to accumulate knowledge more readily, disseminate it more widely, and thereby greatly accelerate the rate of change. With the partial exception of Islamic areas, Africa was until recently lacking in this ability. Under nonliterate conditions, the rate of accumulation of knowledge was more restricted, and so also was the rate of change.

It must also be recognized that the human animal is capable of invention and discovery and thereby of initiating cultural forms which are new and novel. Frequently mentioned in discussions of the arts, this human potential for creativity is also an important source of cultural variation and change. Though all societies are in some ways limited by the characteristics of the human animal, each society has potential for creative and independent development.

Physical type is another element in the discussion of Man in Africa. What follows is only a brief introduction to this very complex subject. Undeniably, mankind is genetically heterogeneous; there are many, many more genes in the human pool than there can be in any individual. This genetic heterogeneity has two important consequences: first, there are differences from individual to individual (polymorphism), and secondly, largely through isolation and adaptation, genetic differences tend to cluster into relatively contrasting types or races (polytypism). These facts are not in dispute, but arguments arise over attempts to delimit the types. Briefly, there are two major problems: the greater the number of genetic criteria which are considered, the more complex and variable the classification will become; conversely, if too few criteria are chosen, the typology may be hopelessly simple. Perhaps the greater problem lies in the tendency to classify populations largely or solely by visible rather than genetic characteristics (phenotypic versus genotypic classification). In all cases the classifications vary according to the criteria used and have an arbitrary or inconsistent appearance. The reader therefore should be aware of the imprecision of any racial typologies.

There are four African populations which show significantly different physical characteristics: these are usually referred to as Negroid, Pygmoid (or Negrillo), Khoisan (or Bushmanoid), and Caucasoid. The Negroid population is by far the most numerous. It shows a great deal of regional variation, but the following may be listed as general characteristics: medium height (approximately 5 feet 8 inches), relatively long limbs, considerable prognathism, broad nose, black very curly hair, dark skin color, and thick often everted lips. The Pygmoid peoples seem to have been limited to Central Africa and have been supplanted largely by Negroid population. They are very short (approximately 4 feet 6 inches), have short trunks and legs but relatively long arms, very broad noses, Negroid hair, protuberant eyes, very dark skin color but with considerable variation, and downy body hair. The Khoisan peoples once inhabited most of eastern and southern Africa but are restricted today to the arid areas in and around the Kalahari Desert. They have short stature (approximately 5 feet), slight build, broad and flat faces, very broad noses, orthoganous skulls, extremely curly hair, yellowish-brown to reddish-brown skin, and marked tendencies to wrinkly skin even in fairly young individuals. Indigenous African Caucasoids, as opposed to those principally of European origin who have migrated there since 1500, are found mostly in North Africa. They are of medium height (approximately 5 feet 8 inches), have long heads, straight to convex and narrow noses, light skin color (though darker than Caucasians native to Europe), straight black hair, and thin lips.

These descriptions are extremely general, and each population shows considerable variation. In addition, individuals and some populations reveal the effects of crossbreeding. For example, the pastoral Fulani of West Africa show so many North African features that they are often classified as Caucasian.

Having portrayed the predominant African physical types, it is critical now to indicate that the best scientific knowledge available at this time reveals no causal relationship between race and society or culture. The detailing of African physical types above is for descriptive purposes only.

In contrast to physical appearance, the demographic features of a population are intimately related to its life-style. Numbers and density have considerable relationship to matters of social control; growth rate affects the allocation of resources; age distribution influences the size of the labor force, the allocation of time to caring for the immature, even attitudes toward the aged; and disease and morbidity rates affect not only the vitality of the population but its ritual life and its religious system as well.

High birth rates and high death rates have been prevalent in African traditional societies. As a result, a very high percentage of any population is quite young, a correspondingly low percentage is aged, and life expectancy is very short, only about twenty-five years. In contrast, Western society has low birth rates as well as low death rates. This leads to very different age distributions in the two types of societies, as illustrated by the population pyramids in figure 3.

REPRESENTATIVE AGE-SEX PYRAMIDS

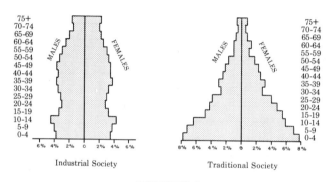

FIGURE 3

Growth rates in traditional societies tend to fluctuate widely, however, but over very long periods of time they show very slight positive growth trends. This fluctuation is due to unchecked disease and famines; however, both of these have been greatly controlled through scientific technology in the recent past. Fluctuating population size and very slow growth rates lead to two of the most pervasive characteristics of traditional societies: their tendency toward communal organization (see chapter 11), and their apparent slow rate of change. The slowness of change can be related to two characteristics of African population. The slow rate of population growth associated with the precolonial period (less than .1 percent per year) did not produce pressures for change, and, as noted, the absence of writing restricted change, particularly technological change, which is so dependent upon accumulated knowledge.

The Interaction of Population and Environment

Humans are not indifferent to their environment; they act upon it, they use it, and if necessary they exploit it. This mastery is achieved through culture, and, as a result, humans overcome environmental limitations and are able to live all over the globe. Environmental manipulation has already been alluded to in the discussion of agriculture in Africa, for by virtue of the knowledge of the techniques of agriculture man can live a more sedentary life, overcome scarcity, and generally support larger populations. In Africa agriculture was supplemented significantly by widespread knowledge of metallurgical techniques. Iron technology, both smelting and smithing, had spread throughout the continent, with the exception of the Khoisan areas of southern Africa, by the end of the fifteenth century. Iron hoes, axes, and sickles made Africans relatively efficient farmers from early times.

Africans in traditional societies are more than farmers, however; they also hunt, gather wild foods, fish, and practice animal husbandry. No society relies entirely on any one of these means of subsistence and the vast majority use several. The survey of 277 sub-Saharan societies suggests that approximately 86 percent depend largely upon agriculture, 6 percent upon animal husbandry, and in 3 percent agriculture and animal husbandry are co-dominant; 2 percent rely primarily upon fishing, 1 percent fishing and agriculture equally, and slightly more than 2 percent upon hunting and gathering. There figures do not reflect the extent to which minority activities supplement the predominant technique, and it is important to note that the agriculturalists of the tse-tse-free regions of western, eastern, and southern Africa obtain approximately 25 percent of their subsistence from animal husbandry.

One dimension of the African environment over which traditional societies exercise only limited control is disease. As noted earlier, the populations of traditional societies have grown at very slow rates and only over very long periods of time. However, since early in the twentieth century Western medical practices and public health procedures have steadily made an impact upon the population of even the most remote societies, through health education, mass inoculations, and vastly improved health delivery techniques. The population of Africa today is increasing at almost thirty times its traditional growth rate.

Figure 4 represents an estimate of the population's growth of sub-Saharan Africa between A.D. 1000 and 1967.

Several important points are to be noted. First, the early population was in fact extremely high when compared to an area like the New World. In 1500 the African population was approximately 79 million while the North American population, in a comparably sized area, was no more than 9 million. This large

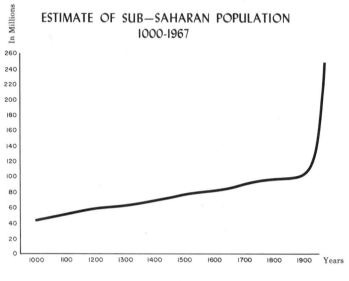

FIGURE 4

These new estimates are derived from my research on the subject and reflect a projection based upon current population, estimated rates of growth for various periods, and the most recent estimates of slave losses.

African population with its comparatively high density, is a major factor in explaining the relatively complex traditional societies of Africa. Secondly, the period from near the beginning of the seventeenth century until almost the end of the nineteenth century is marked by a flattening of the curve as a result of the slave trade. This would have been even more devastating if the population had not been so large initially. Finally, the dramatic increase in population in this century is striking. Prior to 1500, the African population increased about 10 percent in a century, but by the second quarter of the twentieth century it took only six years to increase by 10 percent, and in the last quarter of the century it will increase by that amount in no more than three and one-half years.

Social and cultural changes inevitably result from this growth. These, combined with borrowings resulting from recent contact with other peoples, make African traditional society the foundation for some of the most exciting social dynamics the world may ever know.

NOTE

1. George P. Murdock, "Ethnographic Atlas: A Summary" (*Ethnology*: VI, April 1967), presents in coded form characteristics on 862 societies of the world. Of this number, 277 may be said to be from sub-Saharan Africa. This figure differs from the 239 which Murdock claims. Included in this discussion, however, are Ethiopia and the Horn and certain Muslim societies located south of the Sahara which Murdock did not classify as "sub-Saharan Africa."

Michael L. McNulty
The Contemporary Map of Africa

3 Few students or faculty in American universities would be able to name more than a handful of the African countries in map 6 (identified by number in figure 5). The ability to accurately name and locate such a large number of countries may not be particularly important in itself, yet the inability to do so often reflects a more profound lack of knowledge concerning important events and processes which influence contemporary Africa. Ignorance of Africa is not a new phenomenon. A general lack of knowledge and frequent misunderstanding characterized most European thought for centuries. In many of the early accounts and accompanying maps of Africa, scholars employed an ingenious cartographic device in an attempt to cover up gaps in their knowledge (see plate 4). This practice is characterized in a rhyme by Swift, written in the early eighteenth century:

> So geographers in Afric maps
> With savage pictures fill the gaps
> And o'r unhabitable downs
> Placed elephants for want of towns.

While there is clearly a growing interest in Africa at the university and secondary school levels in the United States, the popular image of Africa is still based on exotic pictures and concepts.

As noted in chapter 1, Africa is characterized by marked patterns of contrast and diversity, and this must be reemphasized if the contemporary map is to be understood. This variety is reflected in the regional distribution of human and

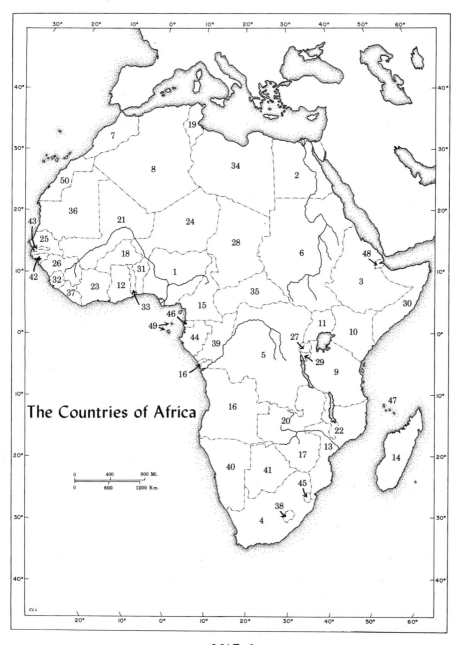

The Countries of Africa

19

7

8

34

2

50

36

21

24

28

6

43

25

26

18

31

1

48

42

32

23

12

35

3

37

33

15

30

46

49

44

39

11

10

27

5

29

9

47

16

16

20

14

22

13

17

45

40

41

38

4

0   400   800 Mi.

0   600   1200 Km.

CLL

20° 10° 0° 10° 20° 30° 40° 50° 60°

MAP 6

FIGURE 5
Countries and Resources

No. (See Map 6)	Country	Population Est. (1975) (thousands)	Area (Square miles)	GNP($) at market prices (1973)	GNP($) per capita (1973)
1	Nigeria	75,597	357,000	15 billion	210
2	Egypt	39,183	386,100	8.8 billion	250
3	Ethiopia	27,993	455,000	2.3 billion	90
4	South Africa	24,305	471,982	25 billion (includes Namibia)	1,050
5	Zaire	19,712	905,063	3.2 billion	140
6	Sudan	18,543	967,498	2.2 billion	130**
7	Morocco	17,647	171,953	5 billion	320
8	Algeria	16,611	920,000	8.3 billion	570
9	Tanzania***	15,150	362,821	1.8 billion	130
10	Kenya	13,176	225,000	2.1 billion	170
11	Uganda	11,196	91,452	1.6 billion	150
12	Ghana	10,052	92,100	2.7 billion	300
13	Mozambique	9,227	302,328	3.1 billion	380**
14	Madagascar	7,993	228,000	1.3 billion	150
15	Cameroon	6,484	183,568	1.5 billion	250
16	Angola	6,353	481,351	2.8 billion	490
17	Rhodesia	6,008	150,333	2.5 billion	430
18	Upper Volta	6,008	106,000	410 million	70
19	Tunisia	5,965	63,378	2.5 billion	460
20	Zambia	5,874	290,724	2 billion	430
21	Mali	5,764	464,873	370 million	70
22	Malawi	5,068	45,747	530 million	110
23	Ivory Coast	4,885	124,500	2.3 billion	380
24	Niger	4,486	490,000	450 million	100
25	Senegal	4,452	76,000	1.2 billion	280
26	Guinea	4,418	94,925	570 million	110
27	Rwanda	4,325	10,169	290 million	70**
28	Chad	4,194	496,000	320 million	80
29	Burundi	4,070	10,739	270 million	80**
30	Somalia	3,213	246,155	250 million	80**
31	Benin	3,077	44,472	330 million	110**
32	Sierra Leone	2,982	27,925	460 million	160
33	Togo	2,240	21,853	380 million	180
34	Libya	2,202	679,360	7.6 billion	3,530
35	Central African Republic	1,713	241,000	280 million	160
36	Mauritania	1,321	419,229	250 million	200
37	Liberia	1,298	43,000	450 million	310
38	Lesotho	1,150	11,716	120 million	100**
39	Congo	1,055	135,000	410 million	340
	Mauritius*	976	720	360 million	410

FIGURE 5 (continued)

No. (See Map 6)	Country	Population Est. (1975) (thousands)	Area (Square miles)	GNP($) at market prices (1973)	GNP($) per capita (1973)
40	Namibia	702	318,261	Not available (included in South African data)	
41	Botswana	700	231,805	150 million	230**
42	Guinea-Bissau	596	13,948	170 million	330
	Réunion*	542	969	570 million	1,210**
43	The Gambia	514	4,261	60 million	130
44	Gabon	505	102,317	680 million	1,310
45	Swaziland	490	6,705	150 million	330**
46	Equatorial Guinea	308	10,820	80 million	260
47	Comoro Islands	292	863	40 million	170**
	Cape Verde*	270	1,517	90 million	340**
48	Djibouti	104	9,000	160 million	1,580**
	Seychelles*	62	107	20 million	370**
49	São Tomé Príncipe	61	375	40 million	470**
50	Western Sahara	48	102,703	Not available	

*Not shown on map
**Tentative figures
***Mainland Tanzania only

Sources: Colin Legum, ed. Africa Contemporary Record—Annual Survey and Documents, New York: Africana Publishing Company, 1976.
Helen Kitchen, ed. Africa from Mystery to Maze, Lexington, Mass.: Lexington Books, D.C. Heath and Company, 1976.
Roger D. Hansen and the Staff of the Overseas Development Council, The U.S. and World Development: Agenda for Action, 1976, New York: Praeger, 1976.
World Bank Atlas: Population, Per Capita Product and Growth Rates, Washington, D.C.: The World Bank, 1975.

natural resources, in the nature of urban and rural environments, and in the contrasting life-styles of a small but growing urban elite and a mass of small-scale farmers. It is also seen in the wide spectrum of social and political institutions, influenced by indigenous, colonial, and now national ideas. Despite this tremendous diversity, there are strong elements of commonality among and between the diverse peoples that make up the countries of Africa. This chapter attempts to identify and discuss the significance of these similarities and to provide a broad framework within which the problems of contemporary African development may be understood.

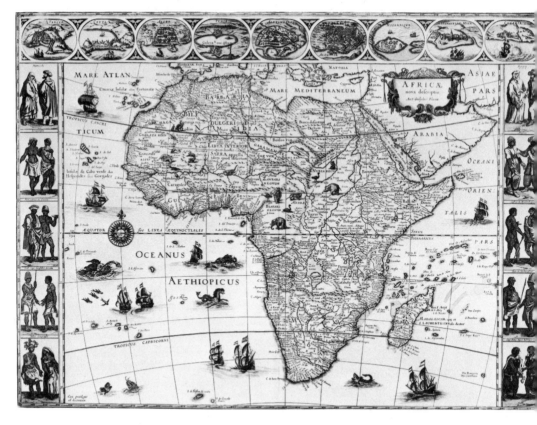

4. Seventeenth-century map of Africa from G. and I. Blaeu, *Atlas*, 1648.
Photo courtesy Lilly Library of Rare Books and Manuscripts, Indiana University.

The Geographical Pattern of Development in Africa

The countries of Africa are among some of the poorest and least developed
in the world. They constitute an important part of what has been called the
"commonwealth of poverty." Yet, within this general pattern of underdevelopment there are conspicuous differences (see figure 5). This is evident at the
national level, but it is even more pronounced within particular countries and
on regional levels.

The distribution of population presented in map 7 reflects the high degree
of regional diversity. Large areas of the continent are virtually uninhabited,
while others, particularly urban centers, exhibit a high degree of concentration.
Some of the highest densities occur along the coast, most notably in West

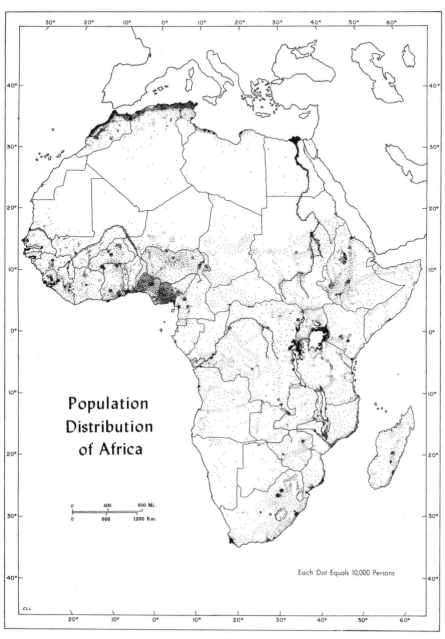

Population
Distribution
of Africa

0   400   800 Mi.

0   600   1200 Km.

Each Dot Equals 10,000 Persons

CLL

MAP 7

Africa, with occasional clusters further inland, as on the shores of Lake Victoria in East Africa.

Comparison of population distribution (map 7) with the distribution of major commercial production (represented in map 8) indicates similarities in the two patterns. While there are a number of exceptions, it is clear that the distribution of population and the areas of major commercial production are closely associated. A map illustrating the distribution of railways in Africa (map 9) shows the tendency for transportation networks to coincide with these same areas of population concentration and commercial production. Indeed, if individual elements of African development were overlaid as though they were a series of transparencies, a growing and intensifying distribution of regional inequality would be evident. This series of maps would thus distinguish "development islands" surrounded by a large "sea" of underdevelopment (map 10). As has been noted,

> Development has so far taken place, and in all probability will continue to take place, within a framework of social and economic islands—and their growing tributary areas—which have already left an indelible imprint on the African continent. It is this common factor, this established pattern of advance, which is the key to the analysis so urgently needed. That pattern is, and in the foreseeable future will remain, essentially nodal; with social and economic growth focusing on a number of dominant centers and their expanding territorial spheres of influence.[1]

There has been a remarkable stability in the pattern of these elements of development since at least the turn of the century. Areas which stand out today as major "development islands" would seldom have appeared on a map of underdevelopment drawn at the turn of this century. Modern focal points of development occur in areas which also showed the earliest signs of growth. At the beginning of the twentieth century, commercial production was even more highly concentrated. Essentially it was limited to a few areas along the coast, to some interior centers of mining, and to isolated patches of commercial agriculture, most notably in the highland regions of East Africa.

Areas of major commercial production account for only about 4 percent of the total area of Africa, yet they include nearly all the urban population and more than three quarters of the value of African produce sold on world markets. Thus much of Africa's wealth is concentrated in a relatively small part of the continent. However, the influence of these "development islands" extends far beyond that limited area which they occupy. They have an important impact on surrounding regions, and by attracting migrant labor they provide linkages to rural areas often far removed from the actual sites of commercial production.

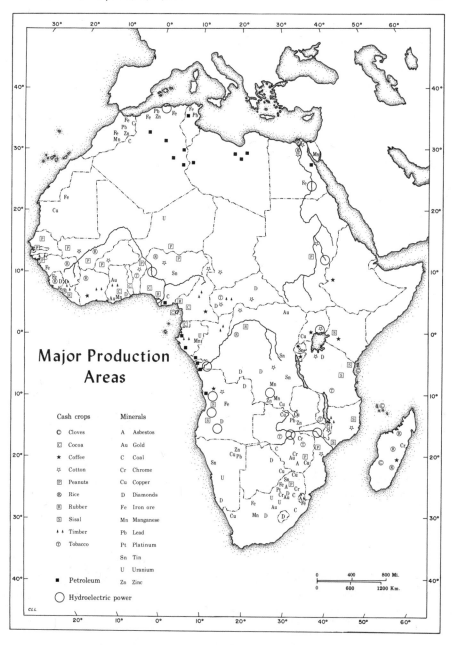

Major Production
Areas

Cash crops		Minerals	
©	Cloves	A	Asbestos
©	Cocoa	Au	Gold
★	Coffee	C	Coal
✿	Cotton	Cr	Chrome
Ⓟ	Peanuts	Cu	Copper
®	Rice	D	Diamonds
Ⓡ	Rubber	Fe	Iron ore
Ⓢ	Sisal	Mn	Manganese
▲▲	Timber	Pb	Lead
Ⓣ	Tobacco	Pt	Platinum
		Sn	Tin
		U	Uranium
■	Petroleum	Zn	Zinc
◯	Hydroelectric power		

MAP 8

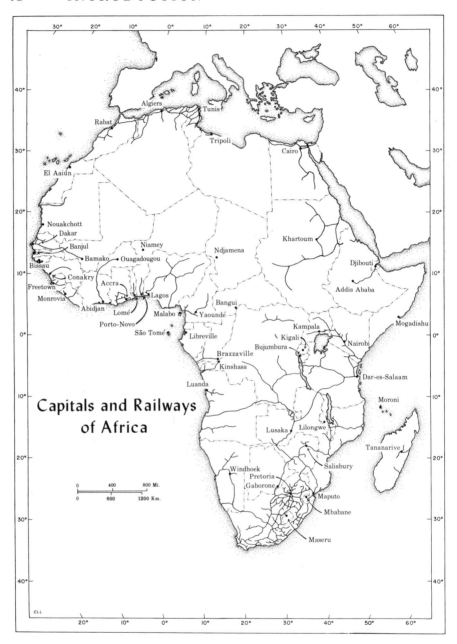

Capitals and Railways of Africa

MAP 9

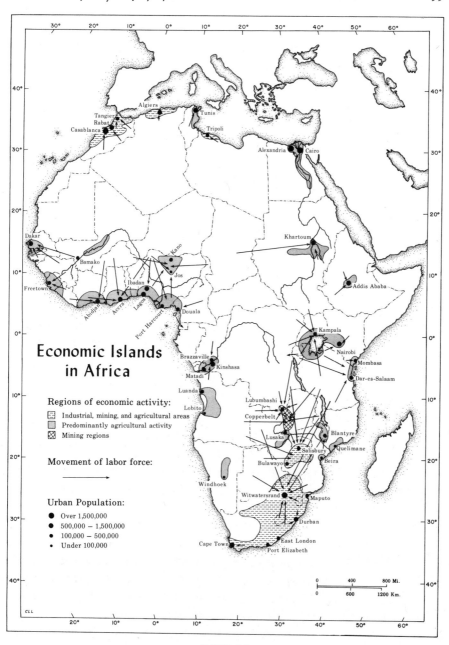

Economic Islands
in Africa

Regions of economic activity:

Industrial, mining, and agricultural areas

Predominantly agricultural activity

Mining regions

Movement of labor force:

Urban Population:

● Over 1,500,000

● 500,000 – 1,500,000

● 100,000 – 500,000

• Under 100,000

MAP 10

5. View of Abidjan, capital of Ivory Coast.
Photo courtesy United Nations/ AP/ ab.

These development islands have also influenced the local economies, social institutions, and cultures of still other areas. Thus, although relatively few in number, the major areas of urban concentration and commercial production play an important role in articulating the overall pattern of African development. This phenomenon has remained relatively unchanged over the past seventy years, and the dominance of these centers in economic and political terms has been accelerating. The data in figure 6 illustrate the dominant role played by some capital cities as centers of manufacturing.

What accounts for this highly inequitable pattern of development? What processes have brought about increasing concentration within relatively few areas? What accounts for the fact that these few islands contain most of the

FIGURE 6

Share of Manufacturing in Selected Capital Cities[2]

City	Percentage	City	Percentage
Abidjan	62.50	Kampala	27.78
Accra	30.43	Khartoum	60.00
Addis Ababa	47.09	Kinshasa	30.28
Banjul	100.00	Lagos	35.00
Brazzaville	33.30	Libreville	100.00
Bujumbura	80.00	Lusaka	35.00
Conakry	50.00	Monrovia	100.00
Dakar	81.48	Nairobi	41.67
Dar-es-Salaam	62.50		

wealth, the highest standards of living, the greatest concentration of educated and talented individuals? Why do these centers generate the flow of goods, peoples, and ideas?

In order to understand the origin of these development islands and the reasons for their continued growth, we must examine a number of important processes which have contributed to their continued existence: these include the initial distribution of natural resources and the elements of the natural environment; the historical pattern of development in precolonial Africa; the impact of colonial domination; and the efforts of the now independent African countries to achieve higher levels of development.

The contemporary map may be characterized in terms of physical and activity patterns. Physical forms are represented by those features such as towns, highways, dams, agricultural regions, and other elements of the landscape which are physically present at particular locations. Activity patterns refer to the flow of goods, people, and information between and among the elements of the physical pattern. Together, the physical and activity patterns define the geographic structure of contemporary Africa.

Elements of the Natural Environment

The unevenness of African development is often thought to result from the nature of the physical environment and the distribution of natural resources. Until recently textbooks often overemphasized the importance of the physical environment in an effort to explain the underdevelopment of Africa. For example, climate and soil were seen as "obstacles" which made development difficult or impossible in certain areas of the continent. Although an understanding of the physical environment is important, it cannot be viewed as the only, or

6. Goods being unloaded at Tema Harbor, Ghana.
Photo courtesy United Nations/ PR/ mh.

even the most important, reason for Africa's underdevelopment at the present time. Elements of the natural environment must be viewed within the context of particular periods of history and corresponding levels of technology. An assortment of isolated facts regarding the natural environment, the landscape, and the climate cannot in themselves give the reader a clear understanding of why or how such elements are significant. Nothing could be more tedious than learning that the mean annual temperature in Navrongo, Ghana is 83° and that the total precipitation is 43.1 inches per year. Such information is important only in relation to other factors, as is suggested in this and the previous chapter.

Physiographic Features

Africa is frequently viewed as a rather compact continent. Its periphery is marked by a shoreline with few natural inlets or harbors. Along most of the coast there is a notable absence of extensive coastal plains and the land often

7. Valuable tropical hardwoods being transported to the coast for export.
Photo courtesy United Nations/ PJ/ db.

rises to a plateau within a few miles of the shore. Indeed Africa may be viewed as a large plateau area, broken up by a series of basins (map 11). While the consequences of this physiographic structure are numerous, two aspects have been discussed frequently by authors concerned with development in Africa. First, a rather smooth coastline (map 12) afforded little opportunity for gaining entrance to the interior for those Europeans who wanted to tap inland resources. In addition to lacking natural harbors, the coast was often inhospitable due to desert-like conditions or the presence of lagoons and swamps at the mouths of major rivers. Secondly, the plateau-like structure also meant that rivers draining from the interior generally have a series of rapids which rendered navigation difficult or impossible and reduced their use as avenues into the interior. All of these features limited contacts between peoples of the interior and European merchants, soldiers, and other agents who were attempting to penetrate Africa from the coast. Access from the north was also difficult, although never impossible, because of the vast expanse of the Sahara. Furthermore, the Nile, the only

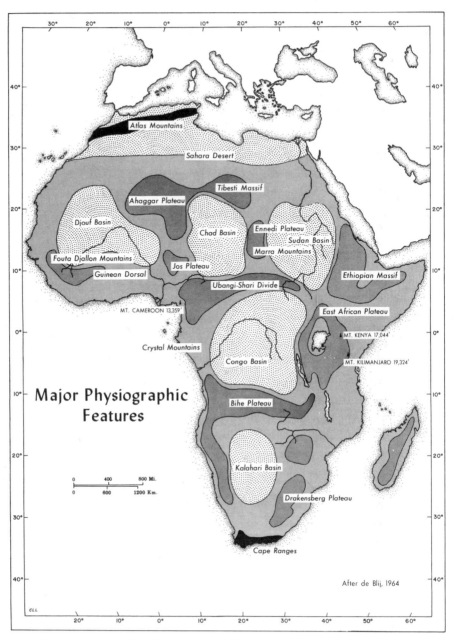

Major Physiographic
Features

Atlas Mountains

Sahara Desert

Tibesti Massif

Ahaggar Plateau

Djouf Basin

Chad Basin

Ennedi Plateau

Sudan Basin

Fouta Djallon Mountains

Marra Mountains

Jos Plateau

Guinean Dorsal

Ethiopian Massif

Ubangi-Shari Divide

MT. CAMEROON 13,359'

East African Plateau

MT. KENYA 17,044'

Crystal Mountains

Congo Basin

MT. KILIMANJARO 19,324'

Bihe Plateau

Kalahari Basin

Drakensberg Plateau

0   400   800 Mi.
0   600   1200 Km.

After de Blij, 1964

Cape Ranges

CLL

MAP 11

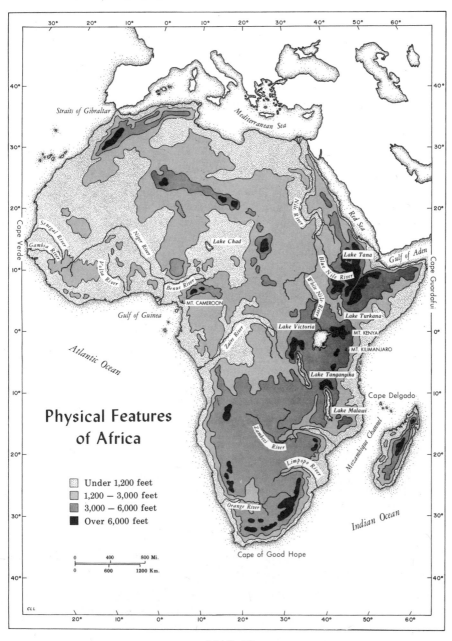

Physical Features of Africa

Under 1,200 feet
1,200 – 3,000 feet
3,000 – 6,000 feet
Over 6,000 feet

Straits of Gibraltar

Mediterranean Sea

Cape Verde

Senegal River

Gambia River

Volta River

Niger River

Benue River

Gulf of Guinea

MT. CAMEROON

Lake Chad

Nile River

Red Sea

Blue Nile River

Lake Tana

Gulf of Aden

Cape Guardafui

White Nile River

Lake Turkana

Lake Victoria

MT. KENYA

MT. KILIMANJARO

Zaire River

Atlantic Ocean

Lake Tanganyika

Cape Delgado

Lake Malawi

Zambezi River

Limpopo River

Mozambique Channel

Orange River

Indian Ocean

Cape of Good Hope

0   400   800 Mi.
0   600   1200 Km.

CLL

MAP 12

river connecting the Mediterranean coast with areas to the south, was a poor communication channel. It flowed through a basin known as the Sudd which was marked by extensive areas of floating vegetation that made early navigation difficult.

Another important feature of this physiographic structure is its effect upon precipitation. Particularly along the west coast, the prevailing onshore wind, carrying moist maritime air, rises over the plateau, resulting in a high level of precipitation. This heavy annual rainfall produces dense tropical forests, which further impede transport developments from the coast.

Development and Climatic Patterns

Africa, due to its shape and location astride the Equator, exhibits a classic climatic pattern which ranges from tropical climates near the Equator to more temperate ones to the north and south. Of the total land area of some 11.7 million square miles, more than 9 million lie in the tropics (defined as between 23½°N and 23½°S latitudes). Despite its having been characterized as the most tropical of continents, Africa has relatively few areas of tropical rainforest; savannas constitute approximately one-third of tropical Africa; and approximately three-fifths of the continent, or two-fifths of tropical Africa, is desert or steppe (see map 13).

The transition from one climatic type to another is usually gradual. In moving from the coast in West Africa toward the north, one encounters a series of ecological zones—the rainforest of the coast gives way to a mixed environment of savanna, trees, and grasses; gradually the trees become more infrequent and grasslands predominate; finally, the grasslands merge into areas of steppe. The boundary between each of these zones tends to shift as changes occur either in the amount and timing of rainfall or through the action of men as they remove trees from agricultural land and burn off the grasses in order to prepare their fields and graze livestock. Man plays an important role in the ecology of Africa and has been a prime agent in changing the nature of the ecological zones. In some areas people have developed ingenious methods of agriculture to make the best use of the tropical soils and meager rainfall and to protect against deterioration of the land. In other areas, however, the increasing human and animal populations have had deleterious effects upon the landscape and have contributed to soil erosion and accelerated the pace of desertification.

The combined effects of inadequate rainfall and poor conservation methods are most dramatically evident in the area known as the Sahel. This area, which includes parts of Chad, Niger, Mali, Upper Volta, and Senegal, was brought to

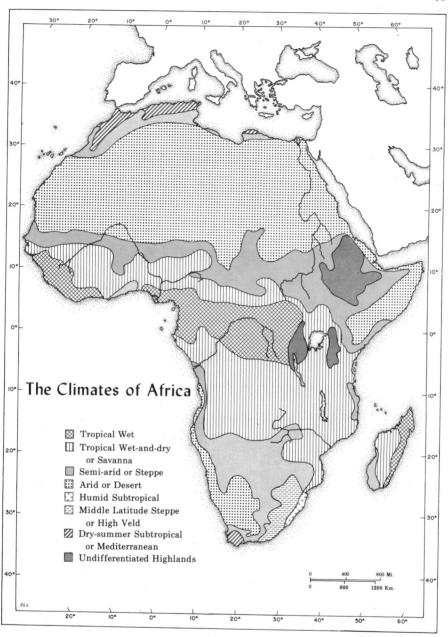

The Climates of Africa

⊠ Tropical Wet
▥ Tropical Wet-and-dry
   or Savanna
▨ Semi-arid or Steppe
▦ Arid or Desert
▥ Humid Subtropical
▤ Middle Latitude Steppe
   or High Veld
▧ Dry-summer Subtropical
   or Mediterranean
▓ Undifferentiated Highlands

MAP 13

the world's attention in the early 1970s when reports of widespread starvation resulted in an international effort to provide some degree of relief to the people in the region. It was said at the time that the starvation and suffering in the area, which had already caused numerous deaths among the human and animal populations, were the results of a drought which had destroyed crops and upset the delicate ecological balance which characterized daily life along the southern margins of the Sahara. This was true, but this was in fact only the most recent

8. Toureg and his family in the Sahel of West Africa.
Photo courtesy United Nations/ Cida/ w.

in a series of droughts affecting the area during the past decade. Some scientists suggest that these events are evidence of a gradual climatic change which is causing the Sahara to extend southward. But the problem of the Sahel is not a matter of climate only. Man contributed significantly by overgrazing and by agricultural practices which destroyed the natural vegetation and increased erosion. Thus, the impact of the drought was much more severe than might otherwise have been the case. Here is evidence of the way in which climate can interact with social and economic institutions to create severe problems which contribute to the underdevelopment of a region.

Presently, the countries of the Sahel are among the poorest of the poor in Africa. They lie at the periphery of the area dominated by the major areas of development along the coast. It is tempting to interpret this pattern solely as a result of climatic differences. However, this has not always been the case in West Africa. For centuries, some of these same Sahelian areas were centers for African kingdoms and urban centers which dominated politics and commerce in West Africa (see chapters 6 and 7). These kingdoms were at that time focal points of economic and political activity, while the southern coastal regions were at the periphery.

Thus the development pattern of the contemporary map represents a complete and dramatic reversal of the spatial structure of West Africa. This cannot be explained solely by climate, but must be understood in terms of changing economic and political conditions as well. There is indeed some evidence that the climate in this area has been changing and that conditions were less severe during the period when trans-Saharan trade was flourishing. But what dramatically changed the situation was the decline of the ancient kingdoms occasioned by political strife related to control of the trans-Saharan trade and to the impact of colonial penetration along the coast.

Understanding the nature of climatic variations together with the nature of social and economic institutions aids in interpreting many features in this West African region. The climatic differences between the northern and southern areas have directly contributed to one of the most significant features of West Africa—seasonal migration.

Rainfall decreases as one moves from south to north in West Africa, with 80 inches or more annually along some parts of the coast and less than 35 inches in areas just a few hundred miles further inland. Aside from being drier, the northern areas of West Africa also have a marked seasonality in the distribution of rainfall. West Africa is affected by the movement of the Intertropical Convergence Zone (ITCZ), which marks the boundary between a moist, maritime airmass and a drier, continental airmass (see maps 14 and 15). As the ITCZ moves north and south it results in a highly seasonal distribution of rainfall, alternately characterized as the "rainy season" and the "dry season." Agricultural practices are related to the distribution of rainfall, and in the north, where the distinction between the seasons is most marked, little can be grown during the dry season. Because of the lack of adequate storage facilities, the dry season is a period of food shortage referred to in some areas as the "hungry season." During this time many northerners migrate to the south, where employment is sought on farms. Just before the rains return to the north, many of these men go back to prepare their fields for planting. This seasonal pattern of migration

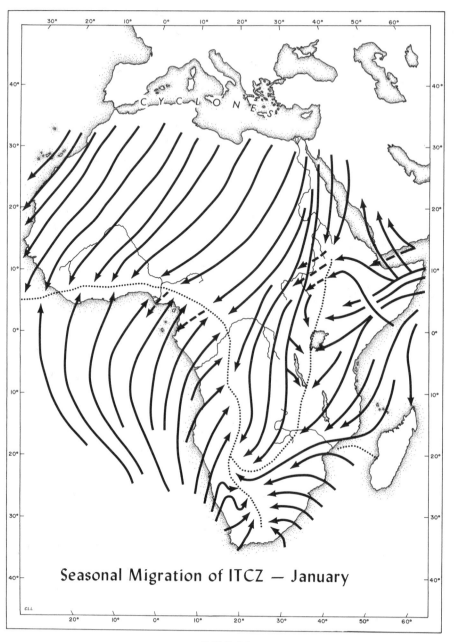

Seasonal Migration of ITCZ — January

MAP 14

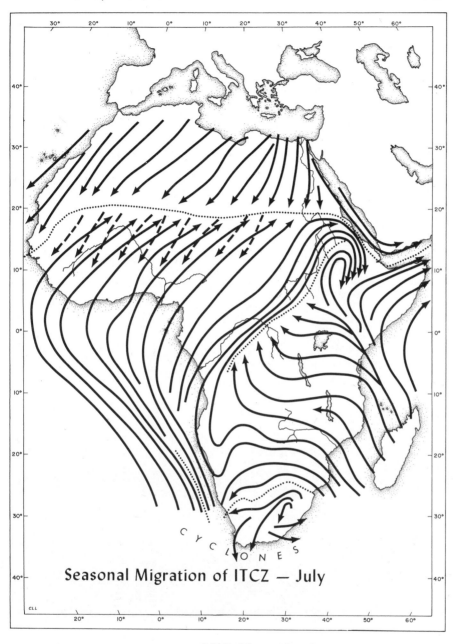

Seasonal Migration of ITCZ — July

CYCLONES

MAP 15

is an important feature of West African life and has had a significant effect upon social and economic conditions in both the north and the south.

The difference in climate, then, strongly affects the organization of economic and social life. Many other examples of this interrelationship between the natural environment and social and economic institutions could also be provided to help explain certain important features of development in other parts of the continent.

Environmental Elements and Health

The impact of environment is particularly evident in terms of health. The conditions of tropical Africa contribute to a host of health-related problems, which are aggravated by a lack of research, insufficient health facilities, and in-

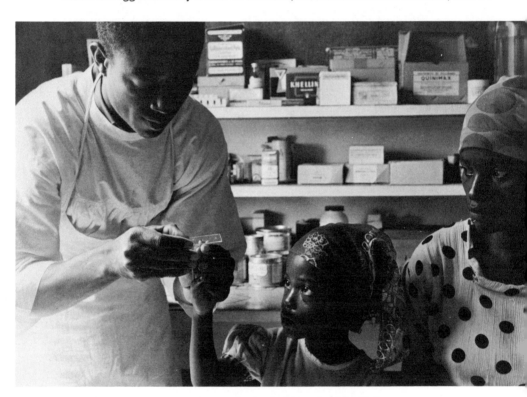

9. Testing for malaria in a health clinic.
Photo courtesy United Nations/ BZ/ ara.

adequate resources to control or eradicate certain diseases endemic to the region. Large areas of the continent are still affected by the tse-tse fly, which impairs the health of both human and animal populations. Malaria, despite current levels of medical technology, still adversely affects large segments of the population and results in a waste of human resources. These and a number of other health-related environmental factors seriously limit the full use of Africa's human and natural resources and affect the pattern of their development. At the local level, this problem may be seen in the occurrence of a disease known as river blindness (the technical term is *onchocerciasis*). The disease results in an incalculable loss of human resources every year; its victims suffer serious physical debilitation and eventual blindness. It is spread by the small blackfly and affects an estimated 20 million people throughout the world. In West Africa, one of the areas most affected, an estimated 1 million people suffer from the disease in the Volta basin alone. The blackfly survives in areas close to rivers and most seriously affects populations living near or on the riverbanks. The effects of this disease are clearly evident in the settlement pattern in affected regions. "Stemming the River of Darkness," a pamphlet describing the joint efforts of the United Nations, the World Bank, and seven West African countries to eradicate or control the disease, describes its effects:

> On the ground, the disease spreads in zones. The blackfly seeks the nearest source of blood. The closer a village is to a river where the blackfly breeds, the heavier the likely degree of infection. In addition, a small village runs a much greater risk than a town in a similar position. If there are only a few people, they are bitten more often.
>
> The human tragedy is coupled with an economic one. If you fly over the worst onchocerciasis regions, you see green, well-watered land that looks ideal for agriculture and animal raising. But you see little sign of man. When you do, it will be a deserted village, grass-roofing collapsed and mud walls crumbling. Along the White Volta alone, some 50 villages are abandoned.
>
> Having been forced to surrender their fertile land to the blackfly, people crowd on to the plateau, where uncertain rains and thin soils produce violent fluctuations in crop yields. Much of the plateau land should not be farmed at all, but retained as forest reserve. Soil exhaustion, and then erosion, often follow. These less-favoured areas often lack roads, clinics, or even markets. Listless and undernourished communities drift along, vulnerable to disease and to the vagaries of weather. This the Governments are determined must end.[3]

Control of the blackfly would also aid in reclaiming vast areas of potentially fertile agricultural land which could contribute to the development of the affected areas. However, such an effort will require careful planning and a deliberate reallocation of resources.

The Impact of Colonialism

A knowledge of the physical environment is insufficient to account for the continued uneven pattern of development. In order to fully understand the situation, it is necessary to examine economic and political institutions which have determined how natural resources have been used. Why have some areas continued to be underdeveloped while others have experienced development? Why has development focused on relatively few areas of the map while large areas continue to be neglected? It is important to recognize that the contemporary map reflects some of the elements of physical and activity patterns of the past which still affect the present to some degree. In many ways the current map of the continent is a colonial map. This is reflected in existing national boundaries, which bear little relation to natural divisions (mountains, rivers, etc.) or to indigenous concepts of space (ethnic areas, traditional kingdoms, etc.). Urban centers and transportation systems were also designed for the purpose of colonial administration and economic exploitation. As part of an export-oriented, primary producing economy, they connected coastal areas and ports to important sources of raw materials and agricultural production but afforded little opportunity for internal circulation of goods or people. Until recently it was difficult at best, and indeed nearly impossible, to travel overland along the coast in West Africa between neighboring countries. This colonial pattern of transportation has important implications for interregional economic exchange and severely hampers the realization of the often stated goals of closer African unity.

Can such spatial configurations, designed for essentially colonial ends, serve the purposes of now independent African nations? As in so many other areas of economic and social life, there is a clear need for the decolonialization of the map of Africa. In the future, new patterns of social order, political institutions, and economic systems more consistent with the objectives of independence will be developed. The map of Africa must be redrawn, and this is the challenge which now faces the African people.

NOTES

1. Green, L. P., and T. J. D. Fair, *Development in Africa* (Johannesburg: Witwatersrand University Press, 1962), p. 11.

2. This table is based on A. L. Mabogunje, "Manufacturing and the Geography

of Development in Tropical Africa," *Economic Geography*, vol. 49, no. 1 (1973), p. 11, Table 3.

3. United Nations, Development Programme, *Stemming the River of Darkness: The International Campaign Against River Blindness* (New York, 1974?), 20pp.

SUGGESTIONS FOR FURTHER READING

Amin, Samir. "Underdevelopment and Dependence in Black Africa." *Social and Economic Studies*, 22 (March 1973), 177–196.

Boville, E. W. *Golden Trade of the Moors*. London: Oxford University Press, 1968.

Brookfield, H. *Interdependent Development*. Pittsburgh: University of Pittsburgh Press, 1975.

de Souza, Anthony R., and Philip W. Porter. *The Underdevelopment and Modernization of the Third World*. Washington, D.C.: Association of American Geographers, Commission on College Geography, Resource Paper No. 28, 1974.

Hance, Wm. *Population, Migration and Urbanization in Africa*. New York: Columbia University Press, 1970.

Hopkins, A. G. *An Economic History of West Africa*. London: Longman, 1975.

Mabogunje, A. L. "Manufacturing and the Geography of Development in Tropical Africa." *Economic Geography*, 49, No. 1 (January 1973).

McNulty, M. L. "West African Urbanization," in B. J. L. Berry, ed., *Patterns of Urbanization and Counterurbanization, Vol. 11 Urban Affairs Annual*, 1976.

THE AFRICAN PAST

II

John Lamphear
Reconstructing the African Past

4 In attempting to reconstruct the African past, historians have come to rely on a variety of "tools." Since many African peoples have had preliterate traditions enduring until recent times, the usual tool of the historian of Europe or Asia, the written record, is of very limited value for vast portions of Africa. Therefore, many historians have begun to make extensive use of the rich oral traditions which exist in most African societies. They have also looked beyond their own discipline for help in unraveling the complexities of the African past. This chapter discusses several of these sources, and some of the following chapters consider the themes which scholars have begun to investigate using these tools.

Sources of African History

Africa was not entirely devoid of written sources prior to the nineteenth century. In some areas a literature tradition does indeed exist, and is sometimes of considerable antiquity. One of the earliest forms of literacy in the world, the writing of ancient Egypt, was invented in Africa by Africans by about 3000 B.C., and gives us a vivid and intimate picture of this great African civilization during the nearly three millennia of its existence. South of Egypt, the Kushitic civilization, focused on the ancient city of Meroë, had its own form of writing five centuries or more before the birth of Christ, and in neighboring Ethiopia, Ge'ez, the classical language of ancient Axum, was being expressed in a unique written form by the fourth century A.D.

10. Remains of Meroë, center of the Kushitic civilization.
Photo courtesy Ruth Hidore.

Other literate traditions were brought into Africa by outsiders. In Mediterranean Africa literacy in a variety of languages, including Greek, Latin, and Arabic, dates back many centuries. Literacy in Arabic also penetrated to the western Sudanic belt, where important centers of learning, such as Timbuktu and Jenne, existed during the fifteenth and sixteenth centuries. The same tradition was also found in the Swahili city-states of the East African coast. Later, with the arrival of Europeans, along the coast of sub-Saharan Africa in the fifteenth century, came the written accounts of Portuguese, Dutch, English, French, and other visitors. With the end of the nineteenth century and the imposition of European colonial rule, a veritable flood of written documents began to appear.

Nevertheless, many parts of the continent, especially the interior of Africa south of the Equator, remained largely without any written sources before the colonial period. In these areas, oral history becomes a vital methodological tool. During the past two decades historians have made increasing use of oral sources, and they have found that a great many African societies have surprisingly rich and detailed oral histories going back hundreds of years.

In some societies, especially the more politically centralized with powerful

11. Nyama Suso, a *griot* from the Gambia, reciting with *kora* accompaniment.

Photo courtesy Roderick Knight.

dynasties of hereditary kings, selected individuals were entrusted with the memorization, recitation, and passing on of oral history from one generation to the next. The *griots* of West Africa were such men, and they often accompanied their recitations with the music of stringed instruments. In these centralized states with professional court historians, great care was taken to ensure that the traditions were recited in a precise, verbatim way. Such traditions have been termed "fixed texts."[1]

In other societies, including those without centralized political systems based on hereditary rule, oral traditions tended to be "free texts." Here the traditions were not the concern of any professional class but could be rendered by any member of the society, though most often by the elders. Unlike the fixed texts, these free texts were not recited verbatim from one telling to the next. Frequently the personality of the individual telling them would be reflected to some degree in the manner in which they were told.

Both types of oral text have proved useful to the historian of Africa, and often provide a very reliable means of reconstructing the past. Of course, oral materials like written materials, must be thoroughly scrutinized and systematically analyzed. One of the first things any historian must realize is that there can be no absolute historical truth. Rather, any source is "a mirage of reality."[2] This is certainly true for the written sources pertaining to Africa. Many of the narratives written by Europeans during the colonial era, for example, were fraught with misinformation, biases, distortions, and misinterpretations. Any semblance of objectivity is frequently lacking. Such sources, though potentially very valuable, must be treated with the utmost care.

Thus oral information must also be handled carefully. Over the past two decades, historians of Africa have begun to develop systematic methodological approaches for its collection and use. Very basic questions must be asked when beginning the analysis of a tradition. With the fixed text of a centralized kingdom, for instance, an historian immediately has to determine if it was an "official version" of a particular event, perhaps existing mainly to underscore and support the claims of a royal dynasty. One useful means by which the historian might begin to determine the reliability of such a tradition would be to pay close attention to the parallel traditions of "commoner" clans; many of these "common" traditions are free texts, where fallacies in the royal traditions are often clearly indicated. The free texts of decentralized societies seldom are the same sort of "official versions"; they often are more likely to be etiological accounts invented after the event to "explain" a given existing situation. The historian must also determine whether the tradition has been "polluted," either through omission of pertinent information or by the addition of extraneous information. In some extreme cases, highly truncated or embellished versions might even combine two or more quite separate traditions.

In general, traditions which pertain to the individual historical experience of a particular clan or smaller kinship group in a society tend to be more reliable than traditions which purport to tell about the historical experience of the society as a whole. Usually the former traditions, often called "local" or "family" traditions, are known only by the individual group to which they pertain, unlike the "general" traditions which are known widely throughout the entire society. Frequently these "general" traditions supposedly tell about the origin of the whole society. In most cases, however, an entire society would not have had any single origin but would have been formed through a complex process of interaction and assimilation of different peoples, from different places, over a considerable period of time. These widely known traditions often are of the "pleasing story" variety and are told more to entertain than to instruct.

A good example of this is provided from the traditions of the Jie, a decentralized people of northeastern Uganda. Among them there is an almost universally known tradition which undertakes to explain why a small group of clans, known as the Kadokini, migrated from one part of the Jie country to another:

> Long ago the Kadokini came from Rengen.
> The Rengen [people] had a feast in which
> a tortoise was slaughtered. When it came
> time to divide the liver of the tortoise,
> they found there was not enough to go
> around, and the leader of the Kadokini
> was given none. He grew very angry
> and took his people away to Panyangara.
> That is why they are now called "Kadokini"
> [from *adokini*, to go away in anger].

The Jie never tire of this story, and the thought of dividing such a tiny thing as the liver of a tortoise is always accompanied by gales of laughter. Compare it, however, with another version of the story, known only to the Kadokini themselves:

> Before the time of [the age set] Ngisiroi,
> no-one lived here in this part of Panyangara . . .
> Our people [ancestors] lived in Rengen, in the area north-west
> of Lokatap Rock. Most of our pastures, therefore,
> were west of the Dopeth River. But each time
> our people took their cattle west of the river to
> graze, they were attacked by the Dodos [a neighbouring
> people] and many of their cattle were stolen. Our
> people grew angry at this, and so they decided
> they must leave Rengen and come to this part
> of Panyangara for safety.[3]

Clearly this account is far more factual and useful but far less amusing than the "liver of the tortoise" tale invented by the non-Kadokini Jie, who had little reason to care when or why the Kadokini migrated.

Another concern of the historian working with oral traditions is to establish a chronology for the events described. This is especially important since many peoples in Africa (and other parts of the world) do not share the Western concept of linear time. Some people, for instance, have a cyclical notion of time in which alternate generations are seen to replace one another quite literally. In the centralized states, traditions are frequently told with regard to the reign of a particular ruler. Here the historian must try to assemble a reliable king list and determine the approximate lengths of the reigns of individual rulers. Several formulas for determining the lengths of dynastic generations in various African kingdoms have been painstakingly worked out by historians. In some societies, genealogical generations, that is, the span of time between the birth of a man and that of his eldest surviving son, also are of use in establishing a chronology. However, it must be remembered that this length can vary tremendously from one society to the next, and sometimes within the same society from one generation to the next.

With the decentralized societies, there are neither the king lists nor the deep genealogical memories to aid the historian. Fortunately, many of them do have age-set systems (see chapter 11), and historical events often are told with regard to a particular named set, as was the case with the Kadokini tradition above. By very carefully analyzing the dynamics of these systems and collecting lists of remembered sets, the time spanned by individual sets can be gauged and the historian gains some reliable chronological pegs by which events can be approximately dated.

Another problem is the possibility of chronological "telescoping." This sometimes happens when events which occurred over a considerable span of time are lumped together in a single tradition with a single chronological reference. At other times, intervening events can be forgotten and an incident which took place in the remote past may be consigned to a relatively recent period.

When an oral tradition makes reference to a natural phenomenon, such as an eclipse, or when it refers to an event also recorded in a written source, it sometimes becomes possible to establish a precise date. Recently several historians have been exploring the use of the annual flow records of the Nile, which date back to the seventh century, as a means of establishing dates for extended periods of drought and resulting famine mentioned in the traditions of many East African peoples. When historians conduct research in adjacent societies they often find that the same event is described in the oral history of each society. Working independently, they try to determine a date for the event through their own chronological reconstruction, and then they compare their work with that of their colleagues in order to find added corroboration.

A serious limitation of oral traditions appears to be their fairly shallow chronologies, which usually do not go back further than about three hundred years. There are exceptions to this: for example, the Sundiata epic, still widely recited by West African *griots*, includes a detailed account of the battle of Karina, fought in about 1235. Recently, oral traditions from East Africa were at least indirectly responsible for the discovery of archaeological sites some two thousand years old.[4] But most oral traditions do not have a reliable chronological depth of more than two or three centuries. Often some cataclysmic event, such as a war, famine, or migration, will mark the "beginning" of oral history. All the remembered events which took place prior to that time are frequently lumped together into a shadowy and often mythological epoch "when sky and earth were one" or "when gods and men walked together." The traditions of this epoch are difficult to analyze and usually impossible to date.

Therefore, historians have turned to other disciplines for help in gaining a glimpse of the remoter past. Archaeology is one of the most important of these disciplines, since it can provide valuable insights into early material culture. The nature of an early society's economy, its technology, and something of its artistic development can often be understood through archaeological studies. By the use of a process such as the radiocarbon dating method, it is possible to date with some accuracy artifacts from as much as 60,000 years ago. It is very difficult, however, to establish definite links between a civilization known exclusively through the archaeological record and later civilizations about which something is known through oral or written historical sources or through linguistic evidence. Nevertheless, in such cases as the identification of prehistoric Dhar Tichitt peoples with the modern Niger branch of the Niger-Congo language family in West Africa, the Stone Age Wilton complex with speakers of proto-Khoisan in eastern Africa, and the early Khartoum Neolithic peoples with ancestral Nilotic-speakers, scholars have been able to establish probable linkages (see chapter 5). However, many parts of Africa have as yet received little or no archaeological attention, and thus the full potential value of archaeology to historians still lies in the future.

Linguistics is another discipline to which historians have turned for help. Through such methods as lexicostatistics and glottochronology, linguists can determine how and when, and sometimes even where, a language underwent changes. Sometimes changes which occurred even in the pre-Christian era are discernible. In some cases, contact between two different linguistic groups are clearly indicated. Where linguistic data can be compared with the existing archaeological record and these are found to be mutually corroborative, both disciplines become even more important to historians.[5] Great care must be exercised in such comparisons, of course, and historians must be careful not to draw too hasty inferences from incomplete or only partially corroborative data. Archaeology cannot tell us anything about the language of a particular culture (except, of course, where writing existed, as in ancient Egypt), and, conversely, the inferences drawn by linguists about the material culture of a given language group at a particular time in its history require definite archaeological confirmation.

Other disciplines, such as botany and genetics, can also make useful contributions to historical reconstruction—the former, for example, by measuring pollen counts in the ground to reveal long-term climatic change and by providing data on plant domestication, and the latter by discerning the genetic development of both human and domestic animal populations. As yet, little use has been made of these and other potentially valuable disciplines, but they will surely provide important methodological approaches for future research.

Another discipline which has been extensively employed by historians is anthropology. By helping the historian to understand the values, institutions, and ideas of a society, anthropology becomes a vital tool in the historical analysis of oral tradition. It can instruct the historian in concepts of time, the dynamics of political institutions, the nature of kinship and other social groups, and the whole complex process of social change. The historian must understand all these if he is satisfactorily and effectively to interpret and utilize oral tradition.

Of course, it is difficult enough for a person to master one discipline, let alone three or four. Some historians have managed to work effectively with two disciplines, but such cases are exceptional. In the future, therefore, research must increasingly be carried out by multidisciplinary teams of scholars, bringing the special expertise and perspective of each discipline to bear on the common problem of reconstructing the African past.

NOTES

1. See Jan Vansina, *Oral Tradition: A Study of Historical Methodology* (Chicago: Aldine, 1965).

2. Vansina, *Oral Tradition*, pp. 76ff. See also Daniel F. McCall, *Africa in Time-Perspective* (Boston: Boston University Press, 1964), especially pp. 1–28.

3. From John Lamphear, *The Traditional History of the Jie of Uganda* (Oxford: Clarendon Press, 1976), p.29.

4. J. E. G. Sutton, "New Radiocarbon Dates for Eastern and Southern Africa," *Journal of African History*, XIII, 1 (1972), p.9.

5. For an example of such a comparison see Robert Soper, "A General Review of the Early Iron Age of the Southern Half of Africa," *Azania*, VI (1971), pp.5–37.

SUGGESTIONS FOR FURTHER READING

Gabel, Creighton, and Norman Bennett, eds. *Reconstructing African Culture History.* Brookline: Boston University Press, 1967.
Lamphear, John. "Reconstructing Jie History: The Transmission and Collection of Oral Traditions," Chapter II in *The Traditional History of the Jie of Uganda.* Oxford: Clarendon Press, 1976.
McCall, Daniel F. *Africa in Time Perspective: A Discussion of Historical Reconstruction from Unwritten Sources.* New York: Oxford University Press, 1969.
Vansina, Jan. *Oral Tradition: A Study of Historical Methodology.* Chicago: Aldine, 1965.
————. "Once Upon a Time: Oral Traditions as History in Africa." *Daedalus,* 100, 2 (Spring 1971), 442–468.
————. "Recording the Oral History of the Bakuba." *Journal of African History,* I,1 (1960), 43–51, and I, 2 (1960), 257–270.

Patrick J. Munson
Africa's Prehistoric Past

5 The African continent, and particularly sub-Saharan Africa, has an extremely lengthy period of human prehistory. Over one hundred years ago Charles Darwin hypothesized, on the basis of the limited evidence available at that time, that Africa would prove to be the center of origin of the human species. Archaeological and paleontological research in the last fifty years, together with the development during the last twenty-five years of a variety of techniques for dating the past, has frequently and emphatically proven Darwin's position.

It has now been documented that early forms of man, or "proto-man," were making and using stone tools in eastern Africa as early as two and one-half million years ago. Unequivocal evidence for similar cultural behavior in areas outside Africa does not appear until almost two million years later. The earliest known fossils of creatures that might be called man or proto-man also come from eastern Africa, with an antiquity of some five and one-half million years, almost five million years earlier than evidence for man in areas other than Africa. Thus the first five million years of man's prehistoric record in Africa are not just the prehistory of Africa but rather the prehistory of humanity.

The Earliest Men

To understand the reasons that sub-Saharan Africa came to be the cradle of mankind it is necessary to look some fifteen million years into the past, during the Miocene Epoch. At that time the earth's surface was much warmer and a tropical climate not only existed in Africa and Southeast Asia but also extended as far north as what is now Germany and Central China. Throughout this broad tropical zone, according to fossil finds, a creature existed which had already separated from the evolutionary line leading to the modern great apes, a creature which already exhibited a number of human-like characteristics. Members of the genus *Ramapithecus*, as this form has been named, were apparently adapted to a tropical mixed forest-grassland environment. They could stand and probably run in an upright position, the shape of the teeth and jaws was very similar to that of man, and there is some suggestion (based, unfortunately, only on indirect evidence) that they could make and use very simple tools and weapons.

By about ten million years ago, the beginning of the Pliocene Epoch, the earth's surface began to cool, restricting the zone of tropical environment. The *Ramapithecus* population, which biologically adapted to this tropical environment, became isolated in one of the remaining portions of its habitat, the savanna zone of eastern and southern Africa. Within a very "short" period of time (on the geological time scale), perhaps four million years or so, *Ramapithecus* had evolved into a much more advanced form, the Australopithecines. The earliest Australopithecine fossils discovered so far date to the period from five and one-half million and three million years ago and come from sites in southern Ethiopia, northern Kenya, and the Transvaal region of South Africa. At this early period there is still no direct evidence of tool manufacture, but biologically the Australopithecines show numerous human characteristics: they were totally upright in posture, which freed the hands for carrying and manipulating things; they apparently had considerable dexterity of the hands; and their teeth were essentially identical to ours in shape.

The next major development was cultural, as opposed to biological, and had momentous consequences. About two and one-half million years ago, approximately coinciding with the beginning of the Pleistocene Epoch, the Australopithecines "invented" stone tools. The earliest ones were extremely crude and simple by later standards, consisting only of large pebbles or small cobbles which had been fractured, intentionally, along one side to form a sharp edge. These are referred to as Pebble Tools, or the Oldowan Lithic Industry. Simple as these implements were, they gave their makers tremendous advantages. These early men, like their ancestors for over ten million years before them, and like modern man, totally lacked the biological "equipment" with which to cut and tear. Without the means of tearing through hide and cutting meat into bite-sized pieces, man's early ancestors were unable to utilize animals larger than those which could be torn apart with the fingers and teeth. Probably, much like modern wild chimpanzees, their diet consisted of fruits, berries, edible tubers, insects, birds' eggs, immature birds, and other animals no larger than a rabbit.

With a cutting tool, however, a new and vast resource of food became available: the large mammals of the African savanna. The tool-bearing Australopithecines were quick to utilize this resource; at Olduvai Gorge near the Kenya-Tanzania border (map 16), at several sites near Lake Turkana (formerly Lake Rudolf) in northern Kenya and southern Ethiopia, and elsewhere in eastern Africa, bones of animals ranging from gazelles to elephants have been found at Australopithecine campsites. Whether these early men were able to kill animals of this size or whether they were scavenging the remains of animals that had died or been killed by larger predators is not yet resolved. The important point is that they were eating meat from animals this large.

Following this major breakthrough there was a relatively long period, about one million years, of slow or little cultural or biological change. However, beginning about one and one-half million years ago certain modifications and elaborations appear in Oldowan tool kits: more flakes were removed from the pebbles, producing somewhat different and varied shapes. This "Developed

12. Olduvai Gorge, near the Kenya-Tanzania border, site of excavations of Early Man.
Photo courtesy Boyce Rensberger.

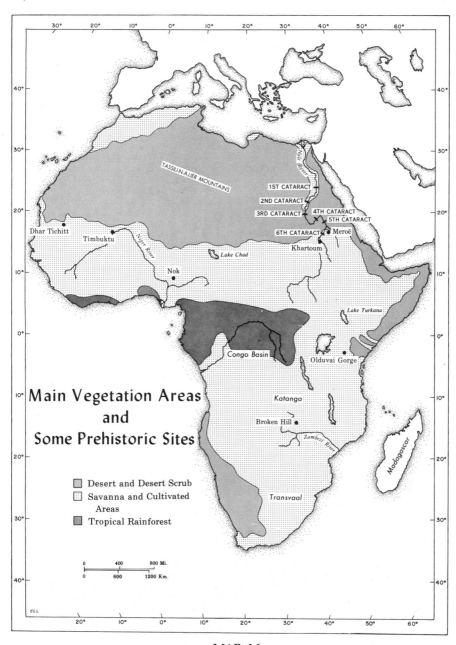

30° 20° 10° 0° 10° 20° 30° 40° 50° 60°

TASSILIN-AJER MOUNTAINS

Nile River

1ST CATARACT
2ND CATARACT
3RD CATARACT   4TH CATARACT
                5TH CATARACT
6TH CATARACT   Meroë
               Khartoum

Dhar Tichitt
Timbuktu
Niger River
Lake Chad
Nok

Lake Turkana

Congo Basin   Olduvai Gorge

Main Vegetation Areas
and
Some Prehistoric Sites

Katanga

Broken Hill

Zambezi River

Madagascar

Transvaal

Desert and Desert Scrub
Savanna and Cultivated
  Areas
Tropical Rainforest

0   400   800 Mi.
0   600   1200 Km.

CLL

MAP 16

Oldowan Industry" tool kit can be considered a transitional stage between the simple Pebble-Tool–Oldowan Industry and the next and relatively much more sophisticated tool kit: the Hand-Ax complex or Acheulian Industry.

While the tool kit was undergoing modification, biological changes were also occurring in the makers of these tools. Although there is still some controversy concerning specific details, some or all of the Australopithecines who occupied the savannas of eastern and southern Africa began evolving toward a relatively much more advanced form of man. *Homo erectus*, who had "emerged" at least one million years ago, was essentially identical to modern man from the neck down. The skull, face, and jaw still exhibited some "primitive" characteristics and the brain was still somewhat smaller than that of modern man, but this was clearly a form that could be called man.

The tool kit of *Homo erectus*, the Acheulian Industry, was much more sophisticated and varied than the preceding Pebble-Tool complex. Large, bifacially flaked, pointed implements which are called hand axes apparently were used to perform a variety of piercing, cutting, and perhaps digging activities. Large, heavy implements with a straight cutting edge, assumed to be cleavers, were used in butchering. A variety of stone knife forms was used for different cutting tasks. Scrapers, made of large flakes, were probably used to prepare hides for clothing or "tents" and to shape wooden implements and utensils. Long, slender picks of flaked stone were probably used for digging up edible tubers and small burrowing animals.

Campsites of these people have been found throughout the African savannas, usually along the banks of lakes and rivers where there would have been drinking water and a concentration of animals and edible plants. From the size of the campsites it seems as if the *Homo erectus* peoples lived together in small bands, perhaps groups of several families. The great abundance of bones of large animals associated with these camps leaves little doubt that these people were effective hunters and that hunting played a major role in their subsistence patterns. Furthermore, by analogy with modern hunting peoples, it can be assumed that much of the hunting, at least of the larger animals, involved the cooperative efforts of several members of the group. In turn, this suggests that some rudimentary communication system (language) was present.

The complexity and sophistication of the tools, skills, and other cultural mechanisms of the *Homo erectus* peoples, relative to those of the preceding Australopithecine/Oldowan stage, allowed them to occupy the entire African savannas, including parts of what is now the Sahara Desert, which at that time received much more rainfall than at present. Also, with superior cultural mechanisms for obtaining food and for staying warm with clothes and shelters, man was able for the first time to expand into the cooler subtropical and temperate zones of the Middle East, southern Europe, and southern Asia. Significantly, the forest portions of Central and western Africa remained uninhabited; *Homo erectus*, like his ancestors for over 10 million years before, had adapted only to the savanna. It was not until about 125,000 years ago that tools and techniques were developed for the effective utilization and occupation of the forest environment.

Regional Diversifications

About 125,000 years ago there occurred another major inflection point in the course of man's cultural and biological evolution, not only in Africa but throughout most of the area of the occupied world. Perhaps as early as 200,000 years ago a new technique of manufacturing stone tools was developed, called Levalloisian. Very special kinds of flakes could be produced, and with only a slight amount of additional modification these flakes could be shaped into a variety of specialized tools and weapons. Archaeological evidence indicates that this technique was first developed on the African continent, probably somewhere in the northern or northwestern region. The idea spread and was adopted, eventually modifying and replacing the earlier Acheulian Industry with a variety of regionally distinct tool kits.

In northern Africa, the Middle East, and southern Europe a Levalloisian technique-using complex called Mousterian appeared by 125,000 years ago. In the savanna regions of eastern and southern Africa there developed, at about the same time, a somewhat similar complex called Developed Acheulian or Middle Stone Age. People with this tool kit, like their Acheulian ancestors, were culturally adapted to the savanna habitat, subsisting by hunting and gathering wild animals and plants. However, some of the Final Acheulian peoples who had been living in those portions of the savanna which bordered the eastern and southern fringes of the Central African forests did not modify their tool kit in this direction. Rather, these forest-fringe peoples began to develop tools, weapons, strategies, and other adaptations which allowed them, for the first time in man's prehistory, to occupy the tropical forest environment.

This new complex, called the Sangoan Industry, is characterized by particular kinds of large, heavy chopping tools (core axes), scrapers (core scrapers), and push planes. All of these were probably used primarily for cutting and shaping wood, which would have existed in abundance in the forests and which was the raw material for most of the basic implements of the Sangoan peoples. Another characteristic to the Sangoan Industry is the abundance of stone picks,

Suggested Continuities of African Prehistoric Complexes

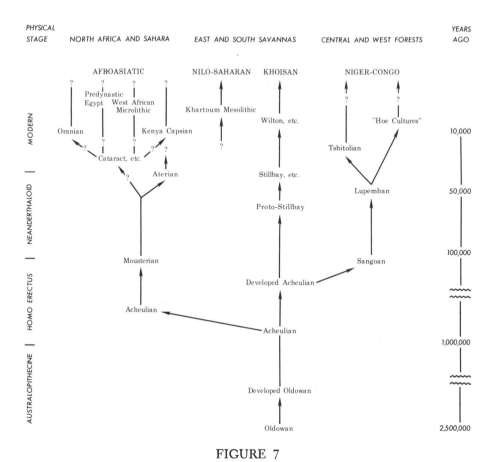

FIGURE 7

apparently for digging numerous edible wild roots and tubers which exist in the African forest zone. Once this pattern was "perfected" on the forest fringe, the Sangoan peoples soon spread throughout the tropical forests of Central and western Africa.

At approximately the same time all of these changes were occurring in tool kits and adaptations, changes were also taking place in the biological characteristics of man. By 125,000 years ago the earlier *Homo erectus* population had evolved into a group of human beings called Neanderthals or Neanderthaloids. This population, although still exhibiting certain rugged, somewhat "primitive"

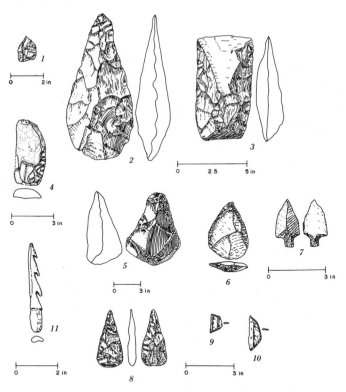

TOOLS: *1 pebble tool; 2 hand axe; 3 cleaver; 4 scraper; 5 core-axe; 6 Mousterian point; 7 Aterian point; 8 Stillbay point; 9-10 geometric microliths; 11 bone harpoon.*

FIGURE 8

characteristics of the skull and face, is similar enough to modern man to be placed in the same species, namely *Homo sapiens.* The best known fossil representatives of this form from Africa are the famous "Rhodesia Man" skull from the site of Broken Hill (associated with a transitional Final Acheulian–early Sangoan tool kit), the Saldanha skull from South Africa (associated with Final Acheulian artifacts), and a recently discovered partial skeleton from northwestern Kenya (associated with Sangoan tools).

The three major cultural traditions of Africa which had developed and diverged by 125,000 years ago continued to evolve and change within their respective geographical regions, and by about 45,000 years ago the tool kits and adaptations had become sufficiently altered that new names are applied. The Mousterian of North Africa had become the Aterian, which is most easily recognized by large, stemmed projectile points. The early Middle Stone Age of the eastern and southern savannas developed into a complex called Stillbay with a particular kind of flake industry and triangular projectile points. The Sangoan of the forests changed into Lupemban, which is characterized by very long, slender projectile points. Soon after the appearance of these new technologies, the last major change in man's biological history occurred; about 35,000 years ago the Neanderthaloids developed into a population which was essentially like that of modern man.

The Later Stone Age

The next major cultural development on the African continent occurred between 20,000 B.C. and 10,000 B.C., and again the three basic geographical regions exhibit their own flavor in terms of cultural characteristics. In the Central Nile region, in northern Sudan and southern Egypt, there appears, by 18,000 B.C., a group of related cultural complexes, of which the Cataract Tradition is one, which made very small flake tools that are called microliths. These people had also developed specialized techniques and implements for utilizing fish and other aquatic resources, a variety of wild seeds, and a wide range of animals. Unfortunately, how or from what this complex developed is not precisely known. However, it precedes by several thousand years comparable cultural developments outside this area (technologically similar and later patterns in the Middle East and Europe are called Mesolithic). Also it retains certain technical vestiges of the earlier Mousterian Industry of this area. Consequently it might be assumed that this Central Nile culture was an indigenous development.

Within a few thousand years, tool kits and adaptations similar to the Central Nile pattern appeared in a number of adjacent parts of Africa. Perhaps as early as 14,000 B.C., and definitely by 12,000 B.C., a complex called Oranian was established along the Mediterranean coastal plain where it evolved into a more developed cultural complex called Capsian by 6000 B.C. In western sub-Saharan Africa, along lakes and rivers from the Lake Chad–northern Nigeria area to the Central Niger valley, a microlithic complex which may be called the "West African Microlithic Industry" appeared by at least 9000 B.C. and seems to have had a subsistence pattern similar to that of the Central Nile complexes. Perhaps as early as 15,000 B.C., definitely by 10,000 B.C., a complex called Kenya Capsian, with a somewhat similar microlithic industry and a strong subsistence orientation toward aquatic resources, appeared in the lakes region of Uganda and northwestern Kenya (see map 17).

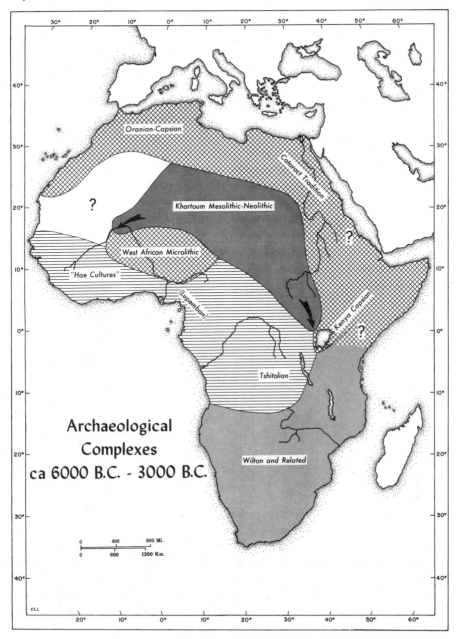

Oranian-Capsian

Cataract Tradition

Khartoum Mesolithic-Neolithic

?

West African Microlithic

?

"Hoe Cultures"

(Lupemban)

Kenya Capsian

?

Tshitolian

Archaeological
Complexes
ca 6000 B.C. - 3000 B.C.

Wilton and Related

0   400   800 Mi.
0   600   1200 Km.

MAP 17

Although it is largely speculative, and is not an opinion shared by all archaeologists, all of the above cultural complexes or adaptations may be viewed as related. Thus their appearance in widely spread areas might have resulted from the expansion of Central Nile peoples, with their more efficient tool kit and subsistence pattern, into adjacent and somewhat similar environments.

In the savanna zones of southern Africa and much of eastern Africa, the local Stillbay and related cultural complexes also began undergoing modifications in their tool kits and adaptations. Perhaps as early as 14,000 B.C., definitely by 10,000 B.C., microlithic tools were added and a particular hunting and gathering subsistence pattern, oriented primarily toward land animals and plants, was developed. This resulting complex, referred to as the Wilton Industry, is very similar to that of many of the San and similar hunting and gathering peoples which existed historically in the savanna and semidesert areas of southern and eastern Africa. Consequently it would seem safe to assume that the Wilton and related complexes of southern and eastern Africa represented the prehistoric ancestoral pattern of the modern San (the San have pejoratively been called Bushmen) and their relatives.

In the forest zone of Central and western Africa at approximately the same time (15,000 to 10,000 B.C.), the indigenous Lupemban Industry was modified into complexes called Tshitolian in Central Africa and the "Hoe Cultures" in the West Africa forest zone. Characteristic implements include relatively small leaf-shaped projectile points and a variety of digging tools, including broad, flat, stone hoes.

Prior to 10,000 B.C., sub-Saharan Africa had been a major center of cultural innovations, "exporting" these innovations, in a sense, to the remainder of the inhabited world. After 10,000 B.C., however, many of the major cultural developments that occurred in man's prehistoric past appeared earliest in areas outside of Africa. Foremost among these developments are food production and metallurgy. Based on what seems overwhelming archaeological evidence, both of these developments occurred much earlier in the general area of the Middle East than in sub-Saharan Africa. The sequence and, to some extent, the time-scale of appearance of these innovations in sub-Saharan Africa are very comparable to their appearance in western Europe, and in both cases this apparent "lag" in development can largely be explained on the basis of geography.

By 10,000 B.C. almost all of the inhabitable world was occupied by man. Viewing the Old World as a whole, the Middle East occupies a "crossroads" position; movement of ideas or techniques between eastern Asia, western Europe, and the African continent would very likely pass through this area. Given this and the fact that most of what is called invention or innovation is simply the combining of two or more preexisting ideas or techniques, the peoples of the Middle East occupied a unique position. They were most likely to obtain the greatest number of new ideas and techniques before other areas. Sub-Saharan Africa, like western Europe, represented at that time the extreme margins of the inhabited world and, by the simple fact of distance, participated least and latest in this cultural interaction. Furthermore, by 10,000 B.C. climatic conditions were such that the Sahara was almost as inhospitable as it is at present, with the result that interaction across it was very difficult.

An additional factor, particularly relevant to the development and adoption of food-producing subsistence patterns, is that much of sub-Saharan Africa, again like much of western Europe and quite unlike much of the Middle East, was an area with a great wealth of game and edible wild plants. Man in Africa had for millions of years been adapting and perfecting methods to exploit these abundant wild resources and had developed a very efficient and satisfying hunting and gathering subsistence pattern. There therefore was little initial pressure to change these well-tried methods and patterns.

Appearances of Food Production

There are some indirect and not too convincing hints that food production was developed in the forest zone of Africa at a relatively early date. Early food production in this area, if it existed, would undoubtedly have emphasized a number of root and tree crops. Indigenous African plants that might have been used include the oil palm, cowpeas, the Guinea yam, and the "Kaffir potato." Unfortunately, few of these would leave recognizable remains in the archaeological record except under the most rare and unusual circumstances, and if remains of such plants do exist from an early date, this evidence has not yet been discovered. There are, however, certain suggestions from oral traditions, linguistic analysis, and modern cultural practices that the cultivation of several of these plants has some antiquity in the forest zone. But there is no way of knowing if the time period is only a few thousand years or ten thousand years. Were the Guinea Neolithic peoples of the West African forest root-crop cultivators by 3000 B.C. or earlier? Or was food production practiced at a still earlier date by their "Hoe Culture" ancestors or the Tshitolian people of the Congo basin? All this is simply unknown as yet.

The earliest "hard" and irrefutable evidence of food production on the African continent comes from the Lower Nile region of Egypt and immediately adjacent areas. Here, by 5000 B.C., there are bones of domesticated cattle, sheep, and goats and preserved grains of wheat and barley. All of these species have a long history of domestication in the Middle East, going back to about 7000–8000 B.C. Since it is only a few hundred miles from areas in the Middle East where these species were first domesticated to where they were found at this early date in Egypt, it is assumed that they diffused from the Middle East to northeastern Africa.

During the period between 5500 B.C. and 2000 B.C., the region which is presently the Sahara Desert began to receive substantially more rainfall than it does at present. Huge, shallow lakes formed particularly in the southern half, and lush grassland-scrub vegetation extended over most of the area. This environment presented considerable potential for both hunters-gatherers-fishers and pastoral peoples with their herds. Somewhere within what is now the southeastern portion of the Sahara there developed a cultural pattern highly adapted to fishing and the taking of other forms of aquatic animals. This cultural complex is called the Khartoum Mesolithic, named for the first site where it was discovered. It is easily recognized by its distinctive pottery decorated by "wavy line" incisions, its finely-made bone harpoons, and its distinctive stone gouges. This compelx had apparently developed by 6000 B.C., and with the moister conditions that began shortly thereafter and which transformed the Sahara into an area of lakes and grasslands, these people began expanding until they eventually occupied the entirety of the central, south central, and southeastern Sahara (see map 17).

Along what is now the southwestern margin of the Sahara, another cultural group or groups, with technologies which blended some of the earlier "Hoe Cultures" and "Western African Microlithic" characteristics, also began to expand northward into the Sahara about this time. Simultaneously, North African peoples who may have practiced some cultivation of grains began expanding southward into the grass-covered Sahara along with their recently acquired herds of cattle, sheep, and goats.

All of these groups seem to have met in the central Sahara, and through these contacts food production, particularly herding, was adopted by many of the sub-Saharan Africans who had expanded into this region. By 3500 B.C. the cultural and probably biological heirs of the Khartoum Mesolithic (now called Khartoum Neolithic) were practicing a mixed herding-fishing subsistence pattern from Khartoum on the Central Nile to the Tassili-n-Ajjer Mountains of southeastern Algeria. Presumably, although it is not as well documented archaeologically, similar developments were occurring in what is now the western portion of the Sahara, with peoples ultimately from the savanna zone of West Africa. With a return to more arid conditions, which began by 2500 B.C. and which were comparable to present-day conditions by 2000 B.C., these food-producing peoples of the Sahara were forced back toward the margins of the desert. It is at this point, for the first time, that actual evidence of food production in sub-Saharan Africa is found.

At the moment the best archaeological documentation of the appearance of food production along the southern margins of the Sahara comes from the Dhar Tichitt region of south central Mauritania. Presently the climate and vegetation of this area is transitional between true desert and dry steppe (Sahel), but prior to 2000 B.C. rainfall was more than double that of today. The subsistence pattern of the indigenous peoples prior to 2000 B.C. was oriented toward fishing in the then-existing broad shallow lakes, hunting, and the gathering of certain wild food plants. After 2000 B.C., however, with the onset of much drier conditions and consequent environmental stress, this pattern was replaced by one which strongly emphasized the herding of cattle and goats, although fishing continued to play an important role, and some hunting and plant-collecting was still practiced. The climate, however, continued to deteriorate, and by 1000 B.C. the lakes had totally dried up, thus eliminating the potential for fishing. It was at this time, presumably in response to the stress factor, that the people turned to cultivation, emphasizing bulrush millet.

With the adoption of full-scale food production, a tremendous jump in population occurred. This in turn led to the emergence of a relatively complex cultural pattern, which included, among other things, the construction of large stone-masonry villages. Substantial evidence suggests that these prehistoric farmers of the Tichitt region may be identified as black Africans. They were almost certainly the ancestors of some of the modern speakers of the Niger branch of the Niger-Congo language family, very possibly being the proto-Soninke or proto-Mande peoples.

At approximately the same time (2000 to 1000 B.C.), in the northern portion of East Africa, people who appear to have been the heirs of the Khartoum Neolithic cultural tradition, and very probably the ancestors of the modern speakers of the Nilotic branch of the Nilo-Saharan language family, introduced the same complex of animals and the techniques of herding them. Although the evidence is less conclusive than in the Tichitt area, it would seem that cultivation was also present in this area by about 1000 B.C. From the northern savanna portions of West and East Africa, about 1000 B.C., the complexes of herding and grain-crop cultivation spread to the remainder of sub-Saharan Africa.

The Appearance of Iron

The next major development in Africa's prehistory was the introduction of metallurgy, specifically the manufacture and use of iron. The technology of smelting iron was discovered by the Hittites of Asia Minor, about 1200 B.C. The knowledge of this technique originally was spread primarily by the military conquests of the Hittites. The technology first appeared on the African continent about 700–600 B.C., with the Assyrian invasion of Egypt and the Phoenician colonization of the North African coast. From Egypt the technology spread up the Nile to the Meroitic kingdom of Kush in central Sudan, probably by 300 B.C. The first evidence of the use of iron in sub-Saharan Africa occurs well after its appearance in the Middle East and there can be little doubt that the technology in sub-Saharan Africa, as in all other parts of the world, derived from this source. The precise route or routes and date of introduction are, however, the subject of some controversy.

The earliest known occurrences of iron in sub-Saharan Africa come from central Nigeria, dating at least from 250 B.C., perhaps 400 B.C. Iron also may have occurred in the Rwanda–Uganda–northwestern Tanzania area about the same time, but this is not as well documented. For many years it had been assumed by most archaeologists that Meroë was the source of introduction of ironworking technology into sub-Saharan Africa. If iron indeed occurred at an early date in northern East Africa, then Meroë would seem to be a reasonable source. Our present state of knowledge, however, makes it increasingly difficult to argue that Meroë was the source for the spread of iron in West Africa.

Greek historical documents indicate that by 500 B.C. some contacts were occurring across the Sahara between the metal-using peoples of the Mediterranean coast, such as the Phoenicians and their neighbors, and the peoples of the savanna zone of West Africa. Archaeologists have also demonstrated two ancient routes across the desert. One ran from the Mediterranean coast across the center of the Sahara and is marked on exposures of rocks by a line of engraved and painted pictures of horse-drawn chariots. The other consists of a line of engravings of ox-drawn carts across the western Sahara. Both routes seem to date about 500 B.C. and both terminate on the Central Niger in the vicinity of Timbuktu. Recent archaeological investigations in western Mauritania, near the western cart-route, have also revealed considerable evidence of the mining and smelting of metals in that area by this date. Hence it would seem most likely that ironworking in West Africa, which first appeared in the 400–250 B.C. period, diffused to that area from northwestern Africa.

The peoples of the Nok culture of central Nigeria were among the earliest known iron-users of West Africa. Unfortunately little is known about their lifestyle, although their artwork has attracted considerable attention, as noted in chapter 14. This consists of well-made, highly naturalistic terra-cotta (baked clay) sculptures of human heads, assumed to be portraits of individuals. The Nok culture, or at least its art tradition, was probably the ancestral source of subsequent art traditions in this area, specifically the fine terra-cottas and cast bronzes of Ife and the cast bronzes of Benin. Although artwork comparable to that of prehistoric Nigeria was not typical of the remainder of West Africa (or if it existed was in such mediums as wood, which have not survived in the archaeological record), it does appear that ironworking technology had spread throughout West Africa by A.D. 1 and that people throughout the area were practicing various forms of food production on a fairly extensive scale.

It is about this date, or a few hundred years later, that the first signs of iron appear in the southern portions of Africa. This evidence comes from sites along the southeastern margin of the central forests in southeastern Zaire, in Zambia, and in eastern Angola. Associated with this earliest iron is pottery of a very particular design called Channel Decorated. This pottery and later derivatives from it are assumed to be the product of peoples who spoke an early or proto form of the Bantu language. The origin, spread, and characteristics of the early Bantu-speaking peoples have been a subject of considerable interest to scholars and have generated much controversy among archaeologists, historians, linguists, and ethnologists.

Bantu is a major branch of the Niger-Congo language family. Its speakers are today found throughout the Congo basin and most of eastern and southern Africa, but it is related to the languages of the West African forest and savanna regions. Precisely when and where the Bantu branch diverged from its West African linguistic relatives are questions not satisfactorily answered. Linguistic analysis has, however, clearly demonstrated that the speakers of the earliest form of Bantu, prior to its divergence into its present numerous dialects, lived in or along the margins of the African forests. Several very convincing studies have indicated that the Bantu originated at this time in the southeastern margin of the Congo forest—almost exactly the area where archaeologists have found an iron-using and Channel-Decorated pottery-making complex. It is very tempting, therefore, to assume that this material culture is representative of the early Bantu.

Linguistic analysis also indicates that iron, livestock, and cultivation were all known to the early proto-Bantu peoples, and this also corresponds well with archaeological knowledge. Characteristics which seem to derive from this early Katanga complex are found elsewhere in southern and eastern Africa but occur at a later date, suggesting that peoples expanded from this area.

To summarize on the question of Bantu origins, most scholars are in agreement that the earliest Bantu peoples occupied an area somewhere within the central forest zones (or at its margins), and that they had knowledge of ironworking, livestock, and cultivation of both indigenous African plants and Southeast Asian root and tree crops. From the forests, with their superior technology and subsistence patterns, they then expanded throughout the remainder of the central forest zone and into the savanna portions of eastern and southern Africa. Here they practiced various combinations of seed-root-tree crop cultivation and the herding of livestock. Questions still remain regarding the sources from which the early Bantu acquired livestock, the Southeast Asian crops, and the knowledge of ironworking.

The source of livestock is readily answered by linguistic analysis. A large portion of the proto-Bantu vocabulary concerning livestock consists of loan words from the Nilotic languages, and it is assumed that the first animals, as well as the words for them, were acquired through contacts with early Nilotic peoples. As already noted, prehistoric herding groups that were probably Nilotes had expanded into the lakes region of eastern Africa prior to 1000 B.C.

Most scholars have assumed that iron technology spread to the early Bantu either across the central forests from West Africa, or southward through the East African savannas from the general area of Meroë. Neither of these presumed routes has yet been proven, and if a proto-Bantu origin at the southeastern margin of the central forests is assumed, still another source for this technology may be suggested. Historical records show that by A.D. 1 seagoing Arab traders were plying the Indian Ocean between Southeast Asia, Yemen, and the east coast of Africa. Also, sometime after this date, the island of Madagascar, only 250 miles off the coast of southeastern Africa, was colonized by Malayo-Polynesian speaking peoples. The presumed place of origin of the proto-Bantu at the southeastern margin of the central forests is only about 500 miles from the coast opposite Madagascar. Could it not be that contacts with the Arab traders or Malayo-Polynesians in this area were the proto-Bantu source for the knowledge of ironworking? Assuming this is the case, it would also explain the source of such species as the banana, the cocoyam, and chickens, all of which were known to the proto-Bantu peoples and all of which were domesticated in Southeast Asia.

Correlations of Archaeology and African Languages

Various references have been made throughout this survey of Africa's prehistory regarding possible correlations of prehistoric archaeological complexes with existing African language groups. At this juncture it would seem desirable to summarize these, as well as to suggest certain others. Proto-Bantu peoples seem clearly to have originated within or along the margins of the Central African forest zone, and only subsequently began to expand into the savanna portions of eastern and southern Africa. This language group is related to a

variety of others spoken by peoples in the West African forests and the savannas to the north. Collectively they are referred to as the Niger-Congo family.
Since the speakers of related languages probably share a common cultural ancestor somewhere in their past, and since most of the Niger-Congo peoples live
in or near the African forests, it would seem reasonable to search for an ancestral complex there. In this forest zone there is, archaeologically, a long cultural
tradition: Sangoan-Lupemban-Tshitolian and "Hoe Cultures." Could there
be a correlation between this tradition and proto-Niger-Congo? This seems a
reasonable assumption.

Prior to the expansion of the Bantu, which began about A.D. 1, the savanna
and semidesert portions of eastern and southern Africa were inhabited by
peoples of the Wilton complex. Because of its characteristics and its continuity
in some areas into the historic present, this can with some certainty be identified as the material remains of the proto-Khoisan speakers. Remnant modern
groups, most of whom are still hunters and gatherers, include the Hadsa and
Sandawe of eastern Africa and the San of southern Africa. A correlation of
Wilton with proto-Khoisan speakers, and a continuity from Wilton back to
Stillbay and the still earlier developed Acheulian, would suggest tremendous
time-depth for this language family in the area (see map 18).

There is increasing acceptance among scholars of a correlation between
proto-Nilotic speakers and the herding-fishing Khartoum Neolithic peoples. At
an earlier level, however, prior to the adoption of livestock herding by about
5000 B.C., the ancestral Khartoum Mesolithic peoples, with a strong emphasis
on fishing, had an even wider distribution within the general southeastern
Sahara area. This correlates very closely with the modern distribution of the
combined languages of the entire Nilo-Saharan family: that is, the Nilotic
branch, the Saharan branch, and the Songhaic branch (compare maps 17 and
18). Interestingly, the subsistence patterns of many of the modern speakers of
this family emphasize herding and fishing (Nuer), herding (Maasai, Teda), or
fishing (Songhai).

The remaining major African language to be considered is Afro-Asiatic. The
Arabic sub-branch of this family, which is an historically recent intrusion into
northern Africa, and the expansion of Berber-speaking peoples into the central
and western Sahara about 500 B.C. may be disregarded, since they are too late
to be relevant. The distribution in Africa of the remaining branches of this
language is then Berber in North Africa, Ancient Egyptian and Cushitic in
northeastern Africa, and Chadic (for example, Hausa) in and around northern
Nigeria. To find a possible archaeological correlation with this language distri-

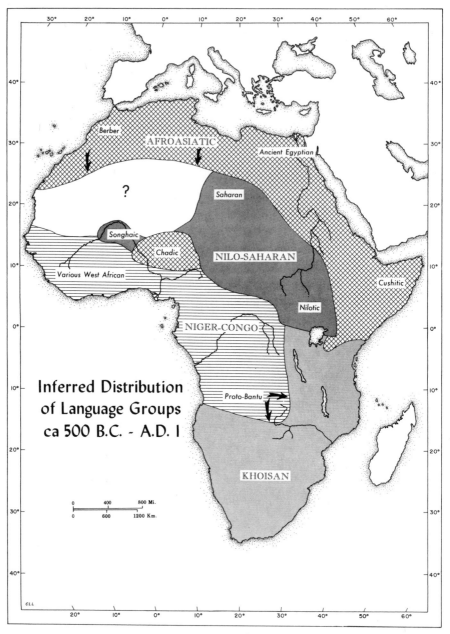

MAP 18

bution it is necessary to search back into the past, prior to 10,000 B.C. As already suggested, there appeared by 18,000 B.C. a particular microlithic industry and subsistence pattern in the Central Nile region: the Cataract Tradition and related complexes. By 12,000 B.C., a similar cultural complex appeared in adjacent North Africa (Oranian-Capsian); by 10,000 B.C., similar complexes appeared in the lakes region of northern East Africa (Kenya Capsian), and in the Central Niger valley area ("West African Microlithic"). After their appearance in these regions these complexes can each be traced until 6000-3000 B.C., and the correlation between their distribution at that time and the inferred distribution of Afro-Asiatic languages about 500 B.C. is extremely close (compare maps 17 and 18).

There is more certainty about the movements of peoples speaking languages of the major groups after 500 B.C. The expansion of the Berber-speaking peoples into the Sahara beginning about this date, and the much later expansion of Arabic-speaking peoples into North Africa, are fairly well documented by historical documents. It is presumed that some peoples speaking various early languages of the Niger branch of Niger-Congo and the Songhaic branch of Nilo-Saharan were pushed southward from the southwestern fringe of the Sahara by the combined pressure of expanding Berber populations and the increasing desiccation of the Sahara after 500 B.C. Some southward migration of the Nilotic speakers of the Nilo-Saharan language family continued to occur after 500 B.C., but this seems to be minor compared to migrations prior to this date. The major movement of peoples after 500 B.C. involved the speakers of the Bantu branch of Niger-Congo who began expanding into the savanna portions of eastern and southern Africa, eventually replacing or surrounding the indigenous Khoisan peoples.

By the first century A.D. almost all of the major traditional African language patterns had been established. Except for some minor shifts, the distribution of the speakers of the major language families was more or less as it is today (see map 3). Food production, employing most of the animals and plants still used in Africa, was being practiced by the majority of Africans. The manufacture and use of iron, with all of its technological implications, was already widespread.

The stage was thus set for the final major cultural development in Africa's prehistoric past. This was the emergence of large and complex political organizations of the kind that are referred to as states, kingdoms, or empires. The initial appearance of such organizations occurred during the last stages of Africa's prehistory. Their appearance, development, and characteristics are discussed in the following chapter.

SUGGESTIONS FOR FURTHER READING

Clark, J. Desmond. *The Prehistory of Africa.* New York: Praeger, 1970.
————. "Africa in Prehistory: Peripheral or Paramount?" *Man* (n.s.) 10 (1975),
  175–198.
Collins, Robert O., ed. *Problems in African History.* Englewood Cliffs, New Jersey:
  Prentice-Hall, 1968.
Fage, J. D., and R. A. Oliver, eds. *Papers in African Prehistory.* London: Cambridge
  University Press, 1970.
Oliver, Roland, and Brian M. Fagan. *Africa in the Iron Age.* London: Cambridge
  University Press, 1975.
Sampson, C. Garth. *Stone Age Archaeology of South Africa.* New York: Academic
  Press, 1974.

John Lamphear
Two Basic Themes in African History: Migration and State Formation

6 To capture the essence of the African historical experience in a single volume, let alone a few chapters, is extremely difficult. Even a concise outline of the major emerging themes of the past two millennia of African history would require rather more space than is available here. It has been decided in this chapter to focus on two important African historical themes: migration and state formation.

These two themes have been selected for several reasons. In the first place, African initiative is perhaps more readily obvious in these two instances than in some other major developments, such as the impact of Islam, the effect of the Atlantic slave trade, or the advent of European imperialism (dealt with in other chapters). Moreover, the themes of migration and state formation are often closely intertwined in African history. Internal population movements in Africa typically led to the formation of new societies, linguistic groups, and states. Indeed, state formation in Africa was most often a process of the coming together of different peoples and their subsequent interaction and assimilation, from which new ideas, approaches, and political forms emerged. In their studies of migration and state formation, historians of Africa increasingly have begun to make use of the "tools" described in chapter 4: oral history, archaeology, anthropology, and linguistics.

State Development in Africa

In many cases, the origins of African states lie in the remote prehistoric past, about which information can be gleaned only from the archaeological record.

For some regions, such as the Sudanic belt of West Africa or the Swahili coast of East Africa, written sources, often in Arabic, concerning African states exist from about the ninth century A.D. Throughout the continent, oral tradition is of vital importance in reconstructing the histories of various states. This becomes especially true for those areas where little archaeological work has been done or where pre-nineteenth-century written records do not exist.

In Africa there were two basic kinds of traditional political organization: centralized states, with political authority vested in the hands of hereditary rulers, and the more egalitarian decentralized communities, where political power was regulated by interactions between kinship groups such as clans or lineages, or maintained by a congregation of elders whose status was determined by their "rank" in an age-set system. These types of political organizations are further discussed in chapters 11 and 12.

Although recent research increasingly has begun to show that decentralized societies have far more complex and sophisticated political institutions than was at first commonly supposed, one fundamental, though rather arbitrary, yardstick employed by Western observers to guage relative "levels of civilization" continues to be the existence of centralized political systems. Contrary to widespread myths, more current earlier in this century, but often still accepted today, powerful and highly developed centralized states have existed in Africa from very remote times. Obviously surprised by the high level of political development of the various African kingdoms and empires, some earlier observers tended to believe that African political institutions must have been "imported" from outside the continent. This gave rise to such infamous theories as the "Hamitic complex" (the idea that statehood was introduced to the continent by an Hamitic master race), which bedeviled historiography earlier in this century, or to the ludicrous attempts to credit the Phoenicians or the Portuguese with the establishment of the Zimbabwe state in southern Africa between the Zambezi and Limpopo rivers. Because of a growing body of evidence, however, it is becoming increasingly clear that the development of African political institutions owed relatively little to any direct outside infusion, but was basically a product of the African historical experience.

This is not to say that the growth of many African states was not stimulated by outside commercial, cultural, and religious contacts. Nor is it to say that certain ideas or even specific institutions were not borrowed internally from one part of Africa to another. Rather, the formation of an African society, whether centralized or not, typically came about through a long period of interaction and assimilation between different peoples, each contributing its own particular skills, technologies, and ideas to the emerging community.

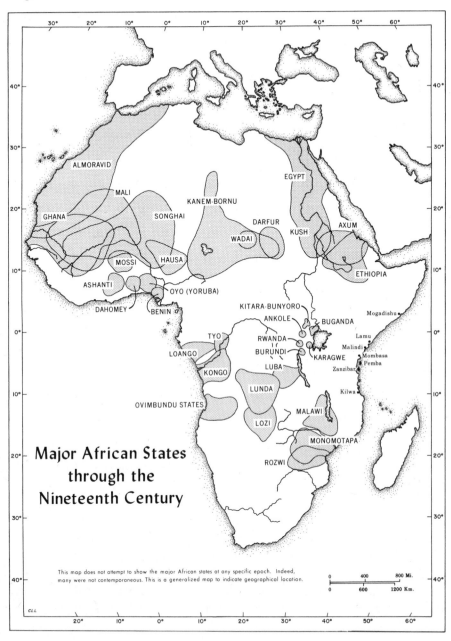

Major African States through the Nineteenth Century

This map does not attempt to show the major African states at any specific epoch. Indeed, many were not contemporaneous. This is a generalized map to indicate geographical location.

MAP 19

In investigating state formation in Africa, it is convenient to focus attention on two internal migrations: the first took place in West Africa, and the second, that of the Bantu-speakers, took place in Africa south of the Equator.

Migration and States

West Africa

The first of these migrations was occasioned by the steady desiccation of the Sahara. In the face of progressively drier conditions, the cultivators and herdsmen of the region were forced into its peripheries, carrying the idea of food production with them into the Sudanic regions at least by the end of the second millennium B.C. It seems likely, however, that considerable agricultural experimentation, as well as the use of wild grains for food, was taking place in Nubia, and possibly in other sub-Saharan areas, well before the dispersal of the Saharan food producers.[1] These movements out of the Sahara caused new cultural centers to develop in the grasslands beyond the edge of the desert. The development of these communities took place well beyond the range of oral tradition and long before the appearance of any written record in this area, and it is necessary to look to archaeology for some insights.

At Daima and other locations in northern Nigeria, excavations have shown that pastoral societies, with perhaps some grain agriculture, flourished as early as the first millennium B.C. Also, as noted in the previous chapter, to the west, at Dhar Tichitt in Mauritania, there is evidence of an even earlier food-producing society where a population herding domestic animals lived in stone villages by 1200 B.C. Within two centuries these people had begun to cultivate millet and their population increased substantially. By 800 B.C. they had reached their peak, with an even greater population settled in large, well-constructed towns. Perhaps they had commercial contacts with the Garamantes of the Fezzan region of Libya, or with some other trading people who used wheeled chariots to cross the Sahara. By three centuries later, however, this thriving population was gone, forced by continued desiccation to migrate to more fertile areas further south.

Archaeological evidence indicates that some form of state system, linked to the agricultural economy of the inhabitants, existed in these large stone towns. Indeed, the impact of food-production on the development of any society is tremendous. A food-producing population, especially one engaged in agriculture, has to become more sedentary than a food-gathering population, so that farmers can remain close to their fields. As agricultural technology develops and production intensifies, farmers often begin to produce more food than their own families can consume. This surplus not only brings about dramatic and rapid population explosions, but also enables some of the population to become involved in non-food-producing activities. Such people can devote their energies exclusively to religious, political, or military activities, or they can become full-time artisans, craftsmen, or traders. Such specialization and the expansion of populations ultimately lead to a clustering together of sedentary agricultural communities.

Archaeological findings indicate that this process probably occurred in the Sudanic regions, as the food-producing revolution introduced by Saharan migrants triggered rapid population increases, the development of non-agricultural specialization, and the roots of urbanization. It was probably the need for some overall regulation of the agricultural cycle which occasioned the appearance of political centralization. Additional stimuli, in the form of pressures from hardy Saharan pastoralists, who represented the last populations to be driven from the steady encroachment of the desert, probably intensified the process, which was also aided by long-distance commercial contacts. At any rate, it is safe to conclude that the roots of political centralization in sub-Saharan Africa extend at least into the first millennium B.C.

The steady movements of people southward from the expanding desert appear to have continued into the first millennium A.D. From this point the archaeological record is augmented to some extent by West African oral traditions which vaguely recollect early migrations of certain clans from the places far to the north or northeast. As the food-producing revolution spread to the south, two groups in the West Central Sudan, the Mande-speakers of the Upper Niger and the Kanuric-speakers driven south by the desiccation north and west of Lake Chad, became the leading cultivators. It would seem that these and other groups of food producers transmitted ideas and techniques, rudimentary urbanization, and the beginning of centralized government throughout a wide area. The growing Sudanic populations were probably further swelled by incoming Saharan pastoralists in search of new grazing lands and watering places. There was considerable interaction between the agriculturalists and the pastoralists, with some of the latter assimilated into the agricultural communities and others employed as mercenaries or military allies to check the encroachment of other pastoral bands following hard behind.

It has been suggested that an important stimulation to the process of centralization appeared with the increase of trans-Saharan trade in the third century A.D., brought about by the introduction of the camel into North Africa.[2] The importance of this commerce to the formation of Sudanic trading cities from which sprawling empires would grow, and the significance of the spread of metalworking to the political development of the region have also been emphasized.[3]

By perhaps as early as the fifth century A.D., the first of the great Sudanic empires, Ghana, was formed. The picture of Ghana is far more complete than that of any earlier Sudanic civilization, for the archaeological record and oral sources are augmented with written accounts of Arab and North African visitors from about the ninth century. All the evidence shows that the Soninke inhabitants of Ghana developed their state into a large and powerful empire, which dominated vassal states in every direction and controlled, as middlemen, the lucrative trade in salt and gold which spanned western Africa from the Mediterranean coast in the north to the Guinea forests in the south. It is also possible to discern the existence of highly developed political institutions, lavish and wealthy courts, and well-organized and well-equipped armies. Ghana was succeeded in the western Sudan by Mali, and then Songhai, each larger and more powerful than the last, while in the east the Lake Chad region was dominated by Kanem-Bornu, in some respects the grandest of them all. A host of smaller states, the Mossi kingdom, the Tukolor state, and the Hausa city-states, to name but a few, existed as well. Again, fairly detailed pictures of many of these states can be derived from archaeological data, oral traditions, and written records.

With few exceptions, these Sudanic states, large and small, displayed remarkably similar political institutions. Their rulers were divine kings, entrusted with important religious functions, and with whose personal vigor the well-being of the state was closely identified. They kept magnificent courts, and appointed the high officials of state, who frequently served as a council of ministers. In most cases, hereditary office did not exist outside the royal clan, and thus the danger of factionalism so prevalent in the federal structures of Europe and other parts of the world was usually avoided. Such institutions were also present in the political systems of the large states that developed in the forested lands along the Guinea coast of West Africa—Benin, Oyo, Ashanti, and Dahomey—encountered by Europeans from the sixteenth century. In the case of these kingdoms some of the art associated with their traditional rulers remains (see chapter 14). These divine kings and bureaucratic structures were a "typically African conception" and seem to reflect a widespread cultural unity which had been an important feature of the much earlier African past.[4]

13. A seventeeth-century European depiction of the court of the ruler
of Loango, from D. O. Dapper, *Description de L'Afrique*, 1698.
Photo courtesy Lilly Library of Rare Books and Manuscripts, Indiana
University.

Bantu Africa

A second migration, that of the Bantu-speakers, was also of great importance
in the formation and development of African states. The problem of Bantu
origins has been discussed in the previous chapter. Here, some of the actual
migrations of Bantu-speaking peoples into Africa south of the Equator is examined, as well as some additional population movements in eastern Africa
which also played a role in state development in "Bantu Africa" (map 20), as
the southern subcontinent is often called.

In briefly examining the actual migrations of Bantu-speakers, two key features need special emphasis. First, these movements were, for the most part,
carried out very slowly and over very short distances. Although linguists can
speak of these migrations being very rapid in the sense that no Bantu language
seems to have been derived from a parent tongue more than 2,000 years ago, the
actual movement of the peoples speaking these languages was very gradual indeed. It was usually small kinship groups or small bands of associates that carried out a particular move. Oral tradition is a valuable source of information

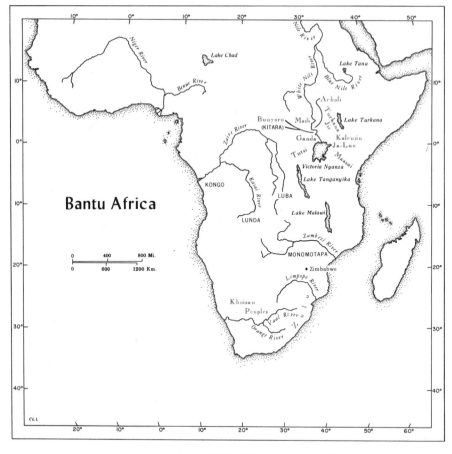

MAP 20

in examining these migrations. Yet, it is often very difficult to discern any definite pattern or even any given direction to the overall movement from these traditions; it is as if "the whole drifted almost as unconsciously and as slowly as a glacier drifts from its mountain top."[5] In some cases a migration would be undertaken for economic reasons. Where shifting cultivation was the basis of subsistence, migration often would take the form of a move from one place, where perhaps population pressures had developed or the soil was being leached of nutrients, to another site a mile or two away. Where pastoralism was important, many traditions speak of young herdsmen driving animals into new grazing lands beyond the range of the society's normal transhumant pattern and thus effecting a short-distance migration. There were countless other reasons for a migration: family quarrels, disease, misfortunes thought to be caused by the supernatural, succession and inheritance disputes, famines, feuds, or even simply the love of adventure—each would be sufficient cause for setting a group in motion.

The second feature in need of emphasis concerns the considerable amount of interaction which went on between the Bantu and other inhabitants of the subcontinent as the migrations progressed. Most of this interaction apparently was peaceful: assimilation rather than extermination was the rule. It would be very wrong to picture any but a very few of the Bantu migrations as being military invasions. These interactions were not just in one direction, with influences passing only from Bantu to non-Bantu. While Bantu speech usually predominated, it did not always do so and people whose ancestors were once Bantu-speaking can now be found, for example, among the Cushitic-speaking Iraqw and the Nilotic-speaking Maasai in East Africa. In southern Africa, the distinctive click sounds of San-speaking hunters were incorporated into several Bantu languages. If in some instances Bantu-speakers were responsible for introducing new political, economic, and technological concepts to non-Bantu speakers, the reverse also happened. Several varieties of food production and possibly iron technology may have been introduced to Bantu-speakers by others in sub-Equatorial Africa. In the same way, many Bantu-speaking societies adopted patrilineal kinship organizations of various neighbors, and in some parts of East Africa took over political organizatons based on the age-grade systems of Cushitic- and Nilotic-speakers. Throughout their migrations, the Bantu-speakers proved themselves capable of adapting smoothly to new areas, new concepts, and new situations. The proof of this outstanding adaptability can be seen in the surprising variety now to be found among the diverse societies of Bantu Africa: from forest cultivators, to grain-producing empire builders, to politically decentralized pastoralists.

There are probably a number of reasons, depending on the time and the region in question, why Bantu speech has predominated in sub-Equatorial Africa. There is no question that in many parts of southern Africa the Bantu-speakers were technologically far superior to the Khoisan hunters and pastoralists they encountered, especially after the advent of the Later Iron Age. Many of the Khoisan peoples were probably quickly assimilated by the Bantu, though others, especially some bands of hunters, preserved their language and their economy, and established symbiotic relationships, valuable to both peoples, in which the assimilation process took place much more slowly. In other instances, where the technology of the Bantu was matched or even surpassed by those with whom they interacted, other factors were at work. Some observers have seen in the original matrilineal kinship system of the Bantu-speakers a means for the wide expansion of Bantu lineages during the early stages of the migrations. It has also been maintained that "Bantuization" was closely tied to urbanization.[6] The Bantu usually lived in more compact settlements than their more widely dispersed neighbors, who came into the Bantu towns to trade, and eventually intermarried and began speaking Bantu languages. In others instances, the diffusion of Bantu speech seems to have been a facet of political processes. With the Lunda of the Upper Kasai, for example, a gradual process took place by which small groups of migrants pushed out from the core area setting up new Lunda-speaking chiefdoms further and further afield.

In some instances, Bantu urbanization grew into large and complex centralized kingdoms, in many ways reminiscent of the states of West Africa. The earliest about which there is certain knowledge was Zimbabwe in Central Africa. Unlike the situation in other parts of Bantu Africa, it is archaeology rather than oral tradition that gives the clearest glimpse of this civilization. At the site of

14. The ruins of Zimbabwe.
Department of Information, Rhodesia.

Zimbabwe are stone ruins of impressive size indicating considerable techno-logical expertise. By as early as the fourth century A.D., the people of this area were skilled metalworkers, smelting iron and extracting gold from extensive mines. Written accounts of traders at the busy Swahili ports of East Africa's coast refer to a thriving inland kingdom existing in the Zimbabwe area by the tenth century. Indeed, the very existence of these ports came to depend heavily on the flow of gold from this region, and they vied with one another to control its export to the Indian Ocean world. In a situation very similar to that of the West African commercial empires, Zimbabwe, and, by the fifteenth century its successor state, Monomotapa, derived considerable stimulus from this long-distance trade and were transformed into powerful and far-reaching empires. Other great states, including the kingdoms of Kongo, Luba, and Lunda, also developed in various parts of Central Africa. Their development, and even their specific political institutions, bore a striking resemblance to the West African empires.

In southern Africa, large politically centralized states developed consider-ably later and in a somewhat different manner. In many parts of this area, apparently one of the last to be penetrated by Bantu pioneers, ecological condi-tions were not as conducive to the same intense buildups of population as they were in the fertile Central African grasslands. Until the nineteenth century, these areas tended to be rather sparsely settled, and there was always room for further migration to alleviate localized demographic pressures. Here, then, the political process tended to be one of fission rather than imperial fusion, with the dominant political structure being that of the small, independent chiefdom. By the beginning of the nineteenth century, however, population pressures, at least in many parts of this area, had begun to grow. The situation was exacer-bated by the appearance of another migration, which pushed into the region from the south: that of the land-hungry *trekboers*, descendants of seventeenth-century Dutch settlers who had established themselves at Africa's southern tip (see chapter 8). With the previous processes of peaceful migration thus cur-tailed, one Bantu people, the Nguni-speaking Zulu, sought a radical solution. Under the leadership of Shaka, one of Africa's true military geniuses and inno-vators, the Zulu transformed themselves into an efficient and powerful military empire. In a process quite unlike those which had typically taken place in Bantu Africa, the Zulu mobilized large armies which assimilated, crushed, or displaced vast numbers of other Bantu peoples. The process, known in southern Africa as the *Mfecane* (a Zulu word meaning "Time of Troubles"), set off a series of chain reactions which had wide repercussions through much of East Central Africa, as far north as the area of modern Tanzania.

In much of East Africa, in ecological conditions similar to those in southern Africa, political organization of Bantu peoples either tended to be decentralized or else took the form of small chiefdoms. Only in the more fertile interlacustrine region did large centralized states similar to those of the Sudanic region and Central Africa develop. But here the process of political consolidation was more complex. East Africa experienced not only the immigrations of Bantu-speaking peoples but also equally important immigrations of other peoples from the north. Nowhere in Africa is the historical process of interaction and assimilation between various peoples more vividly to be seen than in this region.

Considerable interaction took place many centuries before the arrival of the first Bantu-speakers. The earliest discernible inhabitants of East Africa were several different groups of food gatherers, including some who spoke Khoisan languages. Sometime well before the first century A.D., immigrants from the north entered the region. In the Rift Valley, and its adjacent highland and plains areas of present-day Kenya and Tanzania, settled southern Cushitic-speakers from Ethiopia, who the archaeological records shows may have been responsible for introducing both domestic livestock and cereal crops into East Africa. A second possible intrusion from the north was by Central Sudanic-speakers, into Uganda, west of the Rift Cushites.[7] The next group to enter the area were southern Nilotic-speakers, ancestors of the Dodog and the Kalenjin-speaking groups which now inhabit northern Tanzania and southern Kenya. Here, linguistics becomes a valuable research tool, and linguistic indications are that these immigrants arrived at the beginning the first century A.D. It seems likely that these Southern Nilotes experienced close contacts with the Rift Cushites and that considerable intermingling took place.

By the end of the first millennium A.D., Bantu-speakers had begun to appear in the eastern parts of the region. Typically, the Bantu did not sweep boldly into East Africa, but rather it was a gradual process. They, too, intermingled with the earlier inhabitants. In most cases, Bantu speech seems to have prevailed in the new societies born of this interaction, but in some instances the cultural, political, or economic outlooks of the non-Bantu were retained.

The next major group of immigrants were again northerners, another branch of the Nilotic language family variously termed "Plains Nilotes," "Eastern Nilotes," or "Paranilotes" (formerly and very incorrectly called "Nilo-Hamites"). The vanguard of this group were the ancestors of the modern pastoral Maasai, whose oral traditions tell of them pushing their way as far south as central Tanzania by the seventeenth century. In their wake came others, including the Iteso, Turkana, and Jie. These people, especially the vanguard, became more pastoral as they moved to the south. Here they encountered Bantu,

Southern Nilotes, and the last remnants of the Southern Cushites, and the process of interaction was again repeated. Some observers believe that there was also considerable intermingling between these northern immigrants and the Central Sudanic populations in the west, lending to the ultimate assimilation of the latter.

While there were some instances of conflict between groups, for the most part these various migrations and assimilations were carried out peacefully. The antagonisms between communities of pastoralists and agriculturalists which may have been a feature of other parts of Africa were generally not found in most of East Africa. Rather, agricultural and pastoral societies seem to have coexisted (frequently the farmers occupy the wetter hills, with the herders ranging the plains below) and entered into symbiotic relationships. Assimilation went on, but only very gradually. When conflict did develop it was usually between groups with the same economic outlook and often with the same linguistic affiliation.

Perhaps the earliest penetration of Bantu-speakers into East Africa occurred in the interlacustrine region. It seems likely that communities of Bantu agriculturalists had settled in this area during the first millennium A.D. Their occupation of the land was greatly facilitated by the Southeast Asian food crops, especially bananas, which thrived in many parts of the area, and a rapid population buildup seems indicated from archaeological and oral sources. Again, the great centralized states which grew up in the region were probably rooted in this early period. However, there also seem to have been external influences at work. The oral traditions of the Bantu-speakers of the area remember an early dynasty of god-kings, called the Abatembuzi, who are associated with the very time of Creation and who were responsible for a large centralized state called Kitara in Uganda. Scholars have very different theories concerning this dynasty. They have been seen as Central Sudanic-speaking Madi,[8] as a group produced by contacts between Bantu agriculturalists and Hima pastoralists in response to pressures from further north,[9] and it has even been suggested that they never existed at all but were simply expressions of deeply held cultural values.[10]

At any rate, the Abatembuzi were closely associated with a second dynasty known as the Abachwezi, who established themselves as a pastoral aristocracy over Bantu-speaking agriculturalists. The original linguistic and ethnic derivation of the Abachwezi (also known by several other names, including "Hima," and today represented by the Tutsi of Rwanda and Burundi) is unknown, but many have theorized that they were Cushitic-speakers before adopting Bantu languages. By the fourteenth century they had established a political hegemony over the Kitara area, and are credited with constructing large earthwork enclosures.

Still, it would almost certainly be incorrect to picture the Abachwezi as having introduced the concept of political centralization to the Bantu-speaking agriculturalists. The roots of centralization probably predate this period by several centuries and grew out of a process set in motion by intensive food production.

The final major influx of migrants into East Africa was yet another group of Nilotic-speakers from the north, the Lwoo. Pushing into Uganda around 1450, the Lwoo supplanted the Abachwezi with their own Babito dynasty. The coming of the Lwoo caused the disintegration of the sprawling Kitara state into a number of new, yet still highly centralized, kingdoms, such as Bunyoro and Buganda. Like the Abachwezi before them, the Babito kings quickly abandoned their Nilotic languages in favour of Bantu speech.

Elsewhere, the Lwoo established smaller and less strongly centralized states. In the north, for example, the Acholi were organized into small kingdoms and even smaller chiefdoms, while to the south, on the northeastern shores of Victoria Nyanza (Lake Victoria), the Ja-luo were politically decentralized. In both of these areas, the Lwoo experienced very close interactions with their neighbors, although there were periods of conflict as well. In the Nyanza area, especially, there was a great intermixing of Lwoo, Nilotic-speakers and Bantu-speakers. In the north, Paranilotic-speakers, such as the ancestral Langi, were much influenced by the culture and economic outlook of the Acholi, and ultimately adopted Lwoo speech. Others, such as the Jie, although retaining their Paranilotic language, were greatly influenced by Acholi culture and political features. Once again, however, the process was by no means only in one direction. Some Lwoo-speaking clans were absorbed by their neighbors, and several of the features of the Paranilotic-speaking societies, notably their military and age-grade systems, were taken over by many of the Lwoo, once again demonstrating that migration in Africa was largely a gradual process of cultural, political, economic, and linguistic interaction.

NOTES

1. See E. Jefferson Murphy, *History of African Civilizations* (New York: Dell, 1972), p.20.
2. A. Adu Boahen, "Kingdoms of West Africa," in *The Horizon History of Africa*, ed. Alvin M. Josephy (New York: American Heritage, 1971), pp.180–81.
3. Basil Davidson, *A History of West Africa* (Garden City, New York: Doubleday Anchor, 1966), pp.27ff.
4. A. Adu Boahen, "Kingdoms of West Africa," p.181.

5. Jan Vansina, "Traditions of Genesis," *Journal of African History*, XV, 2 (1974), 319.

6. Jan Vansina, "Inner Africa," in *The Horizon History of Africa*, pp.263ff.

7. See Christopher Ehret, *Southern Nilotic History* (Evanston, Illinois: Northwestern University Press, 1971) for his pioneering linguistic approach to the reconstruction of early East African history. Also J. E. G. Sutton, "The Settlement of East Africa," in B. A. Ogot and J. A. Kieran, eds., *Zamani* (Nairobi: East African Publishing House and Longmans, 1968, pp.70–97) is a concise summary incorporating much of the archaeological data which existed in the late 1960s.

8. J. P. Crazzolara, *The Lwoo* (Verona: Instituto Missioni Africane, 1950), pp.449–50, and also his "Notes on the Lango-Omiru and the Labwoor and Nyakwai," *Anthropos*, IV (1960), 117ff.

9. David William Cohen, *The Historical Tradition of Busoga* (Oxford: Clarendon, 1972), pp.78–9.

10. C. Wrigley, "Rukidi," *Africa*, XLIII, 3 (1973), 219–34.

SUGGESTIONS FOR FURTHER READING

Davidson, Basil. *A History of West Africa*. Garden City, New York: Doubleday Anchor, 1966.

————. *A History of East and Central Africa*. Garden City, New York: Doubleday Anchor, 1969.

————. *African Kingdoms* (Time-Life). New York: Time Inc., 1966.

Fagan, Brian M., and Roland Oliver. *Africa in the Iron Age*. Cambridge: Cambridge University Press, 1975.

Josephy, Alvin M., ed. *The Horizon History of Africa*. New York: American Heritage Publishing Co. Inc., 1971.

Kieran, J. A., and B. A. Ogot, eds. *Zamani*. Nairobi: East African Publishing House and Longmans, 1968.

Mair, Lucy. *Primitive Government*. Harmondswoth, Middlesex: Penguin books, 1962.

Murphy, E. Jefferson. *History of African Civilizations*. New York: Dell, 1972.

Vansina, Jan. *Kingdoms of the Savanna*. Madison: University of Wisconsin Press, 1966.

Periodicals such as the *Journal of African History* and the *International Journal of African Historical Studies* should also be used to keep abreast of new data and of new interpretations of African history.

B.G. Martin
The Spread of Islam

Introduction

7 Islam is a culture, a religion, a state, or a vast economic complex, a common market. Founded by the Prophet Muhammad (c. A.D. 570–632), Islam spread quickly over the Arabian Peninsula and beyond, into Iran (Persia) and Iraq, into Palestine and Syria, into parts of Central Asia and into Africa. Thus, in the eastern and western Mediterranean basins, and in Western Asia almost as far as the Chinese frontiers, the spread of Islam was nearly complete by A.D. 750. In this earliest phase of its expansion, Islam was spread by Arabs: first soldiers, then settlers and traders. In Ethiopia, it was first introduced by Muslim ("those who accept Islam") refugees from the Arabian side of the Red Sea. Despite its rapid expansion, Islam was soon deeply rooted, answering to the spiritual and cultural needs of millions of Arabs, Iranians, Turks, and, within a few centuries, large numbers of Africans. These were not only North African Berbers, but also populations further south across the Sahara, or along the East Africa coast.

By the time the first universal Muslim state, the Umayyad Caliphate, was functioning from its capital, Damascus, in the last half of the seventh century, very large areas of North Africa and parts of the Horn and East Africa were already incorporated into this new Muslim world community and the common market associated with it. The Arab take-over had integrated huge areas, far larger than the domains of the Greeks and Romans, for the first time in many centuries. In a striking manner, the spread of Islam realized the dream of Alexander the Great: the unification of the known world. With its new-found political stability under Islam, commerce in North Africa, throughout the Mediterranean basin, in the Indian Ocean region with later extensions to Russia and China and Southeast Asia, was now linked together. The trade of the Islamic world expanded in spectacular fashion. By the time of the second universal Muslim state, under the Abbasids of Baghdad (750–c. 1000), this economic revival had moved forward on an even broader base. To the new prosperity of Islam, Africa contributed its share.

Egypt and North Africa

Although it is on the African continent, some Africanists omit Egypt from their discussions, as it seems to them to belong to the "Near" or "Middle East" or the "Mediterranean World." In the case of Islam, however, the continent must be regarded as a whole. Indeed, Egypt was the first major political province taken over by the Muslims. It was controlled by two successive caliphates, then by a series of militarized hierarchies which were originally composed of imported slaves (*Mamluks*). Egypt later came under consecutive foreign occupations, for example, Ottoman Turks, the Albanian dynasty of Muhammad 'Ali, and a British colonial regime. It only gained its full independence in the mid-1950s. Throughout this long period, Egypt exercised a certain cultural and political influence over parts of eastern Libya, along the Nile into Nubia and the eastern Sudan (from *bilad al-Sudan*, "Land of the Blacks"), as well as down the Red Sea in the direction of Somalia and East Africa.

In the seventh century, Egypt was a most important Muslim acquisition. It served as a springboard for the Arab conquest of the rest of North Africa—the present-day areas of Libya, Algeria, Tunisia, Morocco, and the northern borderlands of Mauritania. As the Arabs moved westward along the Mediterranean shore, eventually reaching the Atlantic coast of Morocco and there dividing, some turned northward into Spain, others faced southward toward the Sahara. Domination through military conquest was paralleled by conversion to Islam; it affected the indigenous Berbers of the coastal ranges in Algeria and eastern Tunisia, and also some of the people of the mountainous regions of Morocco. These phenomena, invasion and conversion, were the results of the first great wave of Arabization and Islamization in the Maghrib ("the place of the setting sun," a general Islamic term for all of North Africa except Egypt). The newly converted Berbers of this region, from about A.D. 800, now started to bear Islam across the southern deserts, following trade routes which were already well-established. New commercial towns, like Kairouan (Qairawan) in Tunisia, Murzuk in the Fezzan, and the centers of Tahert in the mountains of central Algeria and Sijilmasa in southern Morocco, began to flourish.

Shortly after the start of the ninth century, the trans-Saharan trade from the headwaters of the Senegal and Niger rivers was already beginning to make an indispensable contribution to the stability and continued well-being of the Islamic common market. The new West African contribution took the form of a growing trade in gold. These mines had been unknown and inaccessible when the Greeks and Romans had occupied North Africa, but increased production later enabled a series of North African states to expand and prosper, as the traffic moved by caravan across the Sahara to the cities of Egypt and elsewhere in the East. Muslim gold coinage of this period was widely accepted: Islamic *dinars* have been found in archaeological sites from Zanzibar to northern Russia. Other Muslim coins (silver *dirhams*) have turned up in medieval hoards and coin caches all over western Europe.

Like the civilizations of the Greek and Romans, the Islamic economy not only ran on a stable currency but also functioned through slave labor. Domestic and industrial slavery was prevalent—yet by all accounts it was never as harsh as nineteenth-century black slavery in North America. Manumission was frequent—often dictated by pious considerations—and many slaves virtually became members of Muslim families. Even so, thousands of Africans perished on the arid routes of the Sahara, just as thousands of Slavs from Eastern Europe and Russia were forced to travel the routes to Baghdad or Cairo. Central Asian Turks, Germans, and even French or English captives contributed to this commerce. Often these slaves passed through the hands of Christian monks (in Nubia, or Egypt) or Jewish traders (in southern France and elsewhere) who added to the total of the casualties among these unfortunate people by turning many of the male captives into eunuchs (a practice forbidden to Muslims by Islamic law), highly valued in the courts and rich households of the East. Although it gradually diminished, the slave trade from Africa into the Islamic world continued into the early twentieth century.

In return for slaves and gold, and perhaps ivory, the towns of Tahert and Sijilmasa, Fez and Marrakech, Tunis and Kairouan dispatched south across the Sahara camel-loads of textiles, metal bars and rods, steel weapons, knives, ceramics, and other manufactured goods derived from Muslim countries, or occasionally from Europe. Rock salt in slabs was another staple export from the northern fringes of the desert or from mid-Saharan towns. Hence, in addition to local trade and agriculture, the long-distance commerce of the western Sudan was the economic mainstay of many successive North African states. In medieval times it was usually far more significant than North African trade to the Iberian Peninsula or elsewhere in Europe.

During the brief era of the Almoravids of Morocco (c. 1065–1145), these mercantile links to West Africa continued to flourish. In the time of their successors, the Almohads (c. 1125–1260), the western Maghrib enjoyed a period of high prosperity, political unity, and artistic creation, which found expression in remarkable palaces and mosques. By 1300, the political and commercial focus of North Africa shifted to the east, to Tunisia, where the Hafsid dynasty continued to hold power into the sixteenth century. First at Algiers, then at Tripoli and Tunis, the Hafsids and other local rulers were supplanted by Ottoman Turks, compelled by their ongoing conflict with Spain to expand westward along the western littoral of the Maghrib. Further west, in Morocco, two successive dynasties came to power in the sixteenth and seventeenth centuries, forming the so-called Sharifian state. Its rise was rooted in new political factors, concurrent invasions of Morocco by Spain and Portugal, which triggered a Moroccan reaction and the resurgence of a powerful clerical class.

By the beginning of the seventeenth century, Islam in North Africa had

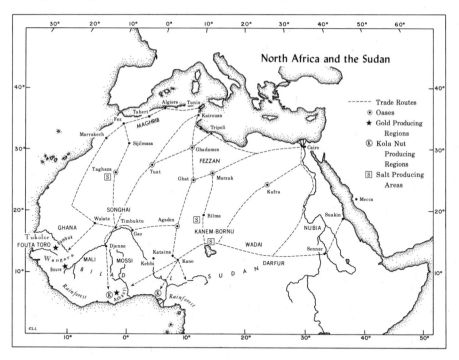

MAP 21

been firmly established for many centuries, with a population that was about 90 percent or more Muslim; the only exceptions were perhaps some of the remote desert Tuareg nomads, living on the southern fringes of the Maghrib. In the Maghrib itself, the eastern section (Libya, Algeria, and Tunisia) came under Ottoman Turkish rule, which in some places lasted for nearly three hundred years. The Turkish era was followed by French colonial control: in Algeria from the 1830s, in Tunisia from 1881, and in Morocco from 1912. Under the new European colonial circumstances, Islam was hard pressed, particularly in Libya where an Italian invasion in 1911 created a coercive colonial state. Islam was perhaps least affected in Morocco. In the other areas of the Maghrib, French or Italian culture was forced on the population through the colonial system of education. Any education which was available was tightly controlled by the European power and offered only in the language of the occupier. Yet, in spite of the years of European occupation, the states of North Africa survived the colonial period with their cultures and languages largely intact, and remain that part of Africa where Islamic influences are the most pervasive.

West Africa

It is logical to follow a discussion of Islam in North Africa, the parent, by a discussion of West African Islam, its child. Admitting minor influences from Egypt and other areas, West African Islam has a broad family resemblance to its Maghribi ancestor. Once the North African shore had been occupied by the Arabs, converted Berber Muslims, who had already been trading across the Sahara for many centuries (probably since about the third century A.D., when the camel was introduced to North Africa), began to take the new religion and culture southward. Nomadism and trade were key elements here. The traffic moved from North Africa over the well-known routes, pioneered and guarded— even monopolized—by Berbers and their relatives, the Saharan Tuaregs. These caravan tracks, furnished at appropriate intervals with supply towns and wells, carried the products of North Africa and the Muslim East to West Africa. After 1300, slaves and ivory, as well as gold and kola nuts, traveled in the opposite direction.

As the scope of trade widened, so did conversion to Islam, or at least accommodation to outward Islamic practice. The use of Arabic and literacy in Arabic became more common. Perhaps by 1400 or so, certain African languages may have been written in an Arabic script, doubtless slightly modified. Islam also advanced in the Saharan and trans-Saharan regions because of its medical ideas and theories, and through Islamic magic, particularly medical magic. In the absence of organized medical services, any new techniques had value and could be absorbed by local non-Muslims. Whether or not Islam came in at the grass roots, as in the case of medicine and magic, or as an "imperial cult" in West Africa is uncertain. However, it is obvious that a whole spectrum of Islamic belief and practice existed in West Africa from an early date, with full acceptance or orthodoxy at one end and superficial accommodation and integration at the other. This diversity became a political issue in certain places in the sixteenth century and again by the mid-eighteenth century.

As was noted in the previous chapter, several large states—the most notable being Ghana, Mali, and Songhai—developed in the western Sudan, partly as a result of the gold and slave trade. Many of these political units became increasingly Islamized as time advanced. Mali, flourishing by 1250, was considerably attracted to Islam, and numerous Malian rulers went on the pilgrimage to Mecca. On the way, they passed through Cairo, where their abun-

15. Modern-day Muslims at prayer in front of the Mopti Mosque in Mali.
Photo courtesy United Nations/ AP/ ab.

dant supplies of gold dazzled and pleased contemporary Egyptians. In its turn, Mali was supplanted about 1450 by Songhai, a state in which the Muslim learned class held appreciable power: about 1490 a clash broke out over the incomplete, syncretic beliefs of a ruler named Sonni 'Ali. Songhai, on the Upper Niger, passed through a number of political oscillations and phases of expansion from 1510 to 1530. Its capital, Timbuktu, was taken by the Moroccans in 1590–91. By the start of the seventeenth century, Songhai also had disappeared from the scene.

In the area of Senegal and the Gambia, Mali had a number of successor states. Even before the fall of Mali, Malinke (or Manding) traders were active over much of West Africa. These Dyula ("merchant," in the Mande language) traders were able to pass everywhere because of the desirability of their goods, even when there were local wars. Some, but by no means all of them, were Muslims by the fifteenth and sixteenth centuries. Of these, the Muslim Wangara from the Senegal River district were probably the best known. They contributed greatly to the spread of Islam in present-day Guinea, Sierra Leone, northern Nigeria, Ivory Coast, Togo, Benin (Dahomey), and modern Ghana.

Another center of Muslim culture, with several Muslim institutions and an Islamic political facade, was the Kanem-Bornu region near Lake Chad. For centuries it sponsored a lively slave trade into Libya via the Fezzan, a route which occasionally served for other products, including gold. Kanem had ties to the rulers of Tunis, and at one time claimed parts of the southern Fezzan. After about 1475, Bornu, led by a number of energetic kings, or *mais*, superseded Kanem. Bornu expanded south and east of Lake Chad by making raids on its neighbors, and during the sixteenth century had close relations with foreign powers such as Ottoman Turkey and Sharifian Morocco. It lasted as an independent state until the end of the nineteenth century, when it was incorporated by the British into their Nigerian colony.

Between Bornu and the coast of West Africa lay a number of states, or city-states, which came into prominence about the turn of the sixteenth century. These included the independent states of Kebbi, Kano, Katsina, and Fouta Toro.

About 1750, with the arrival of many Muslim Fulani cattle nomads from Senegal and coastal Guinea in the pastureland belt of northern Nigeria, already occupied by populations of semi-Islamized Hausas, the relative number of Muslims in the population became larger than ever before. Syncretism and religious accommodation again became vital political questions. The result was the Fulani *jihad* (often translated as "holy war"), which brought the Muslim nomads to power under Usuman dan Fodio in 1804. This Fulani revolution was widely imitated by other local Muslim leaders within a radius of several hundred miles, contributing further to the speed of Islam through West Africa during the nineteenth century.

When the colonial powers—Britain, France, Germany, Spain, and Portugal—took over West Africa, they generally developed their possessions from coastal trading centers into sizable holdings. Certain of these powers, for example France and Portugal, manifested some official dislike or fear of Islam and Muslims. Others, like Britain and Germany, were either neutral, admired Muslims and their culture at the personal level, or decided for political reasons to interfere with them as little as possible. Thus the colonial era in West Africa was by no means a period in which Islam stopped growing or lost influence. Broadly, it would seem that the reverse was the case, even when political Islam was in abeyance. Thus contemporary West African states such as Guinea, Nigeria, Cameroon, Togo, Benin, Ghana, and Ivory Coast contain large Muslim populations. Some of these are organized as political groups while others are not, although even the latter continue to exercise considerable religious influence and to enjoy cultural autonomy.

Islam in the Eastern Sudan

Islam came to the eastern Sudan from two directions: north, from Egypt, down the Nile, and from the east, across the Red Sea from Arabia. For centuries after Islam had first entered Egypt, about A.D. 643, it made no progress to the south, for its route was blocked by a number of Christian Nubian kingdoms. They resisted Arab armies and other encroachments, such as an Arab "gold rush" in the ninth century to the Red Sea hills, until the fourteenth century. At that time, Arab nomads breached Nubian resistance and made a breakthrough. These were slow movements, a mixing and remixing of nomadic elements with settled cultivators, a creeping Arabization which moved up the Nile. By the time of the fall of the town of 'Alwa, near Khartoum about 1500, Islam began to spread out into what is now the Sudan Republic, aided by teachers and missionaries from Iraq and various parts of Arabia. As in areas in the Congo and East Africa in the nineteenth century, many of the teachers were themselves Muslim mystics (*sufis*) who were attached to certain of the major Islamic mystical organizations (*tariqas*, such as the Qadiriya and Shadhiliya). The progress of Islam with the help of such men took many centuries, but by 1900 the vast majority in the eastern Sudan was Muslim.

After the Ottoman Turkish conquest of Egypt in 1517, Sultan Selim I tried to exercise closer control over the Upper Nile valley. To the Sudanese-Egyptian borderlands he sent garrisons of Turkish Balkan troops, who settled and inter-married with the local people. Not long after, a new Sudanese Muslim state came into being here, the kingdom of Sennar. Although it was defeated by these Balkan troops and moved southward, it survived into the early nineteenth century. As in other Sudanese states before it, the people of Sennar welcomed Muslim travelers and teachers. Under such favorable conditions, Islam spread westward to the region between the Nile and Lake Chad, into kingdoms such as Darfur and Wadai, as well as up and down navigable sections of the White and Blue Niles.

During the nineteenth century, the major episodes of Sudanese history con-cern an Egyptian invasion, set in motion by Muhammad 'Ali Pasha in 1820, which led to an Egyptian, then an Anglo-Egyptian occupation. Simultaneously, slaving and ivory raiding grew to large dimensions. When the slaving and devas-tation became general, about 1880, the social and economic dislocation of the Sudan was almost total. The people looked for radical social and political change—which assumed the form of a millennial figure, the Sudanese *Mahdi* ("Messiah"). This popular movement (1881–1898) temporarily ejected the British and Egyptians from the country but did little to alleviate the poverty of the nomads, peasants, and urban-dwellers. The colonial power returned and set up a new regime, which lasted into the mid-1950s. The era saw the growth of nationalism and big religious orders (*sufi* organizations like the Mirghaniya), and also the revival of the Mahdiya—a brotherhood that originated with the *Mahdi*—as a modified mystical organization with some minor political aims. With the coming of Sudanese independence in 1953, some sections of these sufi orders served as the nuclei for political parties.

East Africa

Islam in East Africa built on old foundations. They were laid by pre-Islamic Arabs from South Arabia and the Persian Gulf region, who had been trading in slaves and ivory down the East African coast for centuries. These mariners knew the prevailing monsoon winds, blowing in a southerly direction from Novem-ber to March and northward from April to August, which aided their sailing ships. Greeks and Indians had likewise participated in this coastal trade. They vied with the Arabs to find harbors and islands, offshore bases with good water supplies, where they could trade with the local Africans or repair their vessels for the return voyage northward. Occasionally merchants from the Malabar Coast (West India) took advantage of the monsoons to sail to Arabia, then south to East Africa. Later, this seaborne traffic in goods, persons, and ideas

16. Arab sailing ships, called *dhows*, which are used by traders across the Indian Ocean.
Photo courtesy Ministry of Information and Broadcasting, Kenya.

acquired more permanence, with lasting settlements at major trading points and harbors. Such places, most of them only archaeological sites now, may be found along the shore of the Red Sea, around the Horn of Africa, and on the East African coast as far south as central or even southern Mozambique.

In the seventh century, Muslim refugees, fugitives from Mecca, were welcomed by the ruler of Ethiopia. This group returned to Arabia after a few years. Other Muslims followed to settle on the Sudanese and Eritrean shores and on the coasts of Somalia. Slavery became an important element in the situation: the purchase of slaves for resale in Arabia had been going on for centuries. From Arabia the slaves were taken to Syria, or to the head of the Persian Gulf where, about 800, there were sizable slave contingents working on the salt pans and sugarcane plantations in the Tigris-Euphrates deltas. About 860 they rebelled against their masters, a landmark in East African–Arab relations. The word "Zanj" or "Zinj" (etymologically related to Zanzibar), usually applied to these slaves by Arab poets and historians, suggests that they might have been taken from the Kenyan or Tanganyikan coastal areas for shipment to the Muslim world. Coastal slave-taking seems to correspond to the progress of Muslim settlements southward: to the Lamu Archipelago, the islands of Pemba and Zanzibar, the ports of Mombasa and Kilwa, and the Comoro Islands and Mafia, all of which certainly saw Muslim sailors and settlers by 950.

By this time or earlier, Islam had moved westward from the shores of the Red Sea into the highlands of Ethiopia, creating a series of small states and trading towns. Ultimately these were overrun by the expansion of a unitary Ethiopian state in the thirteenth century, and by the end of the fourteenth century the Muslims were in retreat to the lowlands from where they had come. The final episode of Muslim activity in Ethiopia took place in the mid-sixteenth century, when another attempt to take the highlands was defeated.

After A.D. 1000 the Islamic coastal settlements on the shores of Kenya, Tanganyika, and northern Mozambique grew in size and economic significance. For the next four hundred years, they carried on a coastal trade based on commercial links from one city-state to another. Whether, or rather how far, they may have traded into the interior for ivory and other products is uncertain. There was also an exchange of animal skins, of birds and beasts of the smaller varieties, of musk from civet cats, and of useful ores and rock crystal. Around the beginning of the thirteenth century, Kilwa, on the southern Tanganyikan coast, acquired control of the gold trade coming from the mines between the Zambezi and Limpopo, mines that were later controlled by the Monomotapa. The gold was shipped northward to the Red Sea, to Egypt, or to the Persian Gulf and Iran. This export, like the others, integrated the East African coasts (the *sawahil*) firmly into the Islamic common market. Although the East African gold trade never rivaled that of West Africa in value or volume, it made a large contribution to the economies of the Muslim East and the Indian Ocean region. Following demand and price, other East African products moved, like gold, up the Red Sea or along the Persian Gulf and from there into the eastern Mediterranean regions. Extensive trade in textiles existed, mostly from India, transshipped in South Arabia or on the Somali coast and then taken southward. East Africa also absorbed a large number of Chinese luxury products: porcelains, celadons, and other costly ceramics. Occasionally Chinese coins are also found in archaeological sites.

Although Islam appears to have penetrated very little into the regions behind the coasts in this period (1000–1500), it saw the start of a significant cultural change: the growth of an indigenous East African blend of Arab and Bantu elements, most obvious perhaps in the growth of a new language, Swahili ("coastal"), a *lingua franca*, and in trade. Swahili probably started in the Lamu region on the coast of Kenya, then spread to Zanzibar, Mombasa, Pemba, and elsewhere. Its roots doubtless go back before 1500: it appeared in written form in a modified Arabic script by 1700 but had probably existed before that. Accompanying the new language, its verse, and then its prose (in order of their emergence), was an independent Swahili culture with strong Islamic influences. Soon well rooted on the coasts and islands, this culture spread inland in the late nineteenth century and can now be found as far west as parts of Zaire; Swahili is now the official language of Tanzania.

Just before 1500, Portuguese mariners sailed around the East African coasts, having navigated the Cape of Good Hope. Because of their better-armed and more seaworthy vessels, they were able to make the Indian Ocean, or large parts of it, a Portuguese sea. They did their best to destroy the flourishing Muslim commerce of the Indian Ocean and to take over the pepper and spice routes. Here they used aggressive tactics against the "Moors" (*Moros* being their definition for any sort of Muslim) as a matter of state policy, seemingly a carry-over from wars against the Muslims of Morocco. By these measures, Portugal was able to assert a partial control over the Indian Ocean trade for about two centuries, one of its most important bases being in Mozambique. Just before 1700, their now antiquated ships, their overextended lines of communication, and the pursuit of mistaken policies toward Africans, Indians, Arabs, and even other Europeans caused them to lose many ports and harbors, such as Mombasa. After these defeats, they retreated to their strongholds in Mozambique and on the west coast of India. Thus East Africa, South Arabia, and the Persian Gulf and the Red Sea became a backwater for European activities, a scene of peripheral naval warfare and conquest, and there was a revival of Arab power. Here the leader was the state of Oman ('Uman) in southeastern Arabia, whose rulers had the will to extend their rule to East Africa.

By the early eighteenth century, Mombasa, Zanzibar, Pemba, Mafia Island, and Kilwa were all under local Arab governors, themselves often ruled from Oman in southern Arabia. In this way, parts of the old trading network of the pre-1500 period were restored, and Islam began again to expand. It seems likely that it started to penetrate the hinterland of the coast where it had not been seen before.

The ruler of Oman moved his capital and court to Zanzibar in 1840, which shortly afterwards led to an expansion of commerce. Financed by great Indian merchant houses and financiers at Bombay and elsewhere, Arab caravans pushed inland, looking for slaves and ivory to sell in the Middle East, Zanzibar, or other parts of East Africa. Slave and ivory raiding, lasting until the arrival of European colonial rule in the 1880s and 90s in Tanganyika and the Congo, meant much disruption for African societies, a topic further discussed in the next chapter. For Islam, this had an unforeseen result: altered social and personal values allowed many persons in such disrupted societies to embrace the religion. Many others were also converted by proselytizers from Somalia, Zanzibar, or the Comoro Islands. These *sufis*, or mystical teachers, were religious figures of a type new to East Africa and were usually associated with Muslim religious orders whose work spread through Tanganyika, parts of Uganda and Kenya, Malawi, Mozambique, and eastern Congo.

British and German colonial rule in East Africa did little to slow the spread of Islam. The colonial rulers generally allowed it to pursue its own development, although this is not entirely true of the Belgians in the Congo. At present, in the independent states of East Africa Islam still forms a large cultural and religious bloc, and it continues to spread and to attract adherents there, as it also does in Malawi, Zaire, and in parts of Mozambique.

South Africa

As a postscript, it is worth mentioning Islam in South Africa. In the late seventeenth century, the Dutch Cape Colony served as a place of forced exile for nationalists, religious leaders, or "rebels" from Java, Sumatra, and elsewhere in Indonesia, many of whom were Muslim. One of these political exiles, Shaykh Yusuf of Macassar, died at the Cape in 1699. His tomb at Sandvliet near Cape Town, quickly became a shrine for local Muslims, largely his fellow-Indonesians. Muslims from India came to South Africa in the late nineteenth century and their religion spread throughout the country. At present Islam holds the religious allegiance of several hundred thousand people in South Africa.

Islam and African Societies: Spread and Interaction

What factors encouraged the spread of Islam in Africa? In certain North African areas—Egypt, Libya, Algeria, Tunisia, and Morocco—Islam spread through military conquest. Although some of the Berber population in the Maghrib accepted orthodox (Sunni) Islam, many others embraced an unorthodox variety because it agreed with their own egalitarian social ideas and expressed their rejection of the central authority of the Umayyads of Damascus or the Abbasids of Baghdad. There are other examples, particularly in nineteenth-century West Africa, where Islam took root through conquest.

Generally, however, Islam was adopted through personal acceptance, without any sense of compulsion. There was an awareness on an individual level of another civilization which an African might want to learn about, be a part of, identify with, even if it were remote and intangible. If it had a superior technology, style of government, wealth, a different mode of education or learning with methods of writing and calculating unknown in his own society, it could exercise great power over him. Peer pressures might be conclusive here, or even a sense of superiority or exclusivity derived from being a member of a special community different from this original one. Easy acceptance, simplicity of doctrines and rituals, and, more recently, emphasis on equality and rejection of racism are attractive features. In the colonial era, Islam frequently drew adherents because it appeared and spread through the efforts of African proselytizers, not through whites or other foreigners as in the case of Christianity.

Islam also reached Africans through population movements, even through nomadism among populations having no previous contacts with Muslims. The movement of East African peoples toward or into coastal regions, thus coming in contact with Muslim traders, is an example. In the Maghrib, nomadism by Arabs had its effects on sedentary Berbers, cultivators, and seminomads who took up Islam.

Another factor favoring conversion is trade. Muhammad supposedly said, "The merchant is the favorite of God." Islamic culture and ethics are compatible with commerce, reflecting the fact that early Islam was often the religion of urban Arabian merchant classes. Thus long-distance trade, seaborne trade, or trade across the Sahara must have brought many Africans into touch with Islam, permanently or temporarily. It has also been said that there are "no missionaries" in Islam, that each Muslim can and should be a missionary. Hence any merchant or trader in his off-hours can proselytize: many have done so. But there have been professional proselytizers at times, too. Among them, for instance, were the teachers of mystical orders, *sufi* masters whose spiritual gifts and standing impressed Africans and caused them to accept their teachings, values, and attitudes. They were particularly effective in East and West Africa in the nineteenth century.

Certain scholars have described African Islam as an "imperial cult," a religion first accepted by a ruler and his court, or by an elite, then spreading downward through society. In some cases this may be so; in others, no doubt Islam made converts in the lowest social ranks, and Muslim beliefs then moved upward until they reached the top. In some places, magic, charms, and spells may have accelerated the acceptance of Islam. Magic, attempts to influence everyday events by supernatural forces, may also become mixed with medical ideas and practices and hence be attractive to non-Muslims wanting to supple-

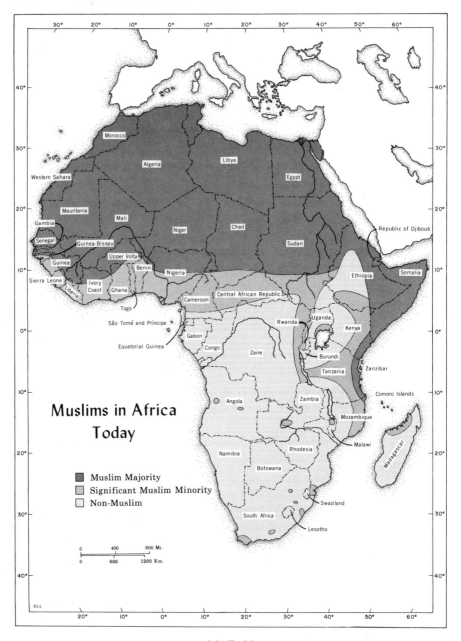

Muslims in Africa
Today

■ Muslim Majority
▨ Significant Muslim Minority
☐ Non-Muslim

MAP 22

ment their own armories of magical and medical techniques. Through this means, the persons or societies touched may have been more ready to accept Islam.

Muslims with special skills, like literacy, had great advantages and may have impelled some of their non-Muslim contemporaries to convert. Many Islamic teachers served as part-time secretaries, negotiators, or advisers in situations where African leaders or groups dealt with foreigners; or they had influential positions in the entourages of African rulers. Occasionally a non-Muslim ruler would employ Muslim bodyguards or troops who could be used for special duties, or as emissaries, or to exercise other delicate functions, sometimes in the ruler's own family. Literate Muslims could also fill administrative or organizational roles better than those without such training. The rulers of the African states of Buganda and Ashanti, for example, employed Muslim officials in the nineteenth century.

Islam and African societies could also interact in the domain of legal matters and procedure. Here traditional custom might agree with or conflict with Muslim law. Whatever the situation, the two sides might come to know each other's procedures and legal attitudes and values, perhaps with different courts functioning side by side. Property, including land and slaves, and marriage are two of the more obvious areas for such legal interaction.

Finally, indigenous African religions, doctrines, beliefs, and opinions could and did come into touch with Islam. In West Africa in particular, there was much interaction of beliefs, ideas, and rituals. This might occasionally have been objectionable in the eyes of Muslim purists, who might denigrate it as syncretism or "mixing," but such objections mean little with the existence of an entire spectrum of accommodation and interpenetration.

SUGGESTIONS FOR FURTHER READING

Lewis, I. M. *Islam in Tropical Africa.* London: Oxford University Press, 1966.

Lewis, W. H., and Kritzeck, J. *Islam in Africa.* New York: Van Nostrand-Reinhold Co., 1969.

Lombard, M. *The Golden Age of Islam,* trans. Joan Spencer. New York: American Elsevier, 1975.

Martin, B. G. *Muslim Brotherhoods in 19th Century Africa.* Cambridge: Cambridge University Press, 1976.

Trimingham, J. S. *The Influence of Islam Upon Africa.* Harlow: Longmans, 1968.

————. *Islam in the Sudan.* New York: Barnes and Noble, 1965.

————. *Islam in Ethiopia.* New York: Barnes and Noble, 1965.

————. *Islam in East Africa.* Oxford: Clarendon Press, 1964.

George E. Brooks
European Relations with Africa before 1870

8 The history of relations between Europeans and Africans from the earliest Portuguese voyages in the mid-fifteenth century to the Partition of Africa during the last quarter of the nineteenth century involves numerous interactions. Their interpretation has caused much debate among scholars. The following discussion highlights some of the most important themes of these relationships, at the same time stressing ongoing processes characteristic of African societies and cultures.

Three themes may be stated at the outset. First, until the nineteenth century, African exchanges with other parts of the world—Europe, the Middle East, the Indian Ocean trading complex, and the Americas—served chiefly to obtain luxury commodities for a few commercial and political elites. At the same time, such contacts caused the diffusion of a wide spectrum of social and cultural influences: food crops, endemic diseases, religious practices, musical instruments, and art styles. Second, European commerce and cultural influences along the periphery of the continent from the fifteenth century resulted in cumulative and far-reaching disruptions for African societies. These intensified during the eighteenth and early nineteenth centuries as a consequence of the rapid expansion of slave trading, across the Atlantic, the Sahara, and the Indian Ocean. Third, by the end of the eighteenth century, the production of agricultural and forest crops for export had begun, while intra- and extra-continental slaving continued and even increased. This exacerbated the far-reaching changes already under way as Africans were progressively linked to, and made dependent upon, world markets. The imposition of colonial rule accelerated these developments and served to control or redirect them for the benefit of Europeans.

African Commercial Networks before the Fifteenth Century

Commerce was the principal stimulant for the interaction of African societies and an important catalyst for state building. As noted in chapters 6 and 7, long before Portuguese caravels ventured southward along the African coasts to initiate direct contact, numerous African societies had for centuries engaged in commercial and cultural exchanges with other parts of the world. They were linked by long-established routes connecting markets, sources of raw materials, and political and religious centers. Traders, artisans, envoys between states, and pilgrims were among the travelers who used these routes.

The most highly developed trading system was in West Africa. Here riverine and caravan networks, notably those developed by the Mande- and Hausa-speaking peoples, expedited the exchange of products from the Sahel, savannas, rainforests, and coastlands. These exchanges between neighboring ecological zones involved a wide range of products, including cloth, iron and iron utensils, captives, leather goods, salt, livestock, pots, baskets, rice, millet, kola nuts, dried fish, and numerous other foodstuffs, condiments, and medicinal substances. These commodities, together with African luxury products such as gold, beads, and prestige cloth, and the expensive items exchanged across the Sahara were transported along the expanding trade routes.

Thus, long before Europeans arrived, West African societies were linked by extensive and growing trading patterns which connected areas from the Atlantic to Lake Chad and from the Gulf of Guinea to the Sahara. These commercial networks testify to the viability of the social and political institutions which ensured the safe movement of travelers and merchandise. A French priest who visited Senegal in 1686 described what he had learned of West African travel. He could not know that his account merely repeated what Muslims from North Africa had reported centuries before.

> Some [Senegalese] go to Mecca to visit Mahomet's tomb, although they are eleven or twelve hundred leagues distant from it; and as they go there on foot and through the deserts one can well imagine that they are very often exposed to suffer both hunger and thirst; this they might avoid if they made a few preparations when setting out from their homes. What prevents them from doing this is their knowledge that hospitality reigns so truly among their people that passing travellers, whether on a journey or on

business, are always well received, and on departing settle their accounts by blessing; "Farewell and peace be with you; I pray God to preserve and keep you always."[1]

Similar patterns of commerce and hospitality existed in other parts of Africa. In West Central Africa, notably in the Kongo state south of the Zaire River, salt, fish, palm cloth, and seashells used as a medium of exchange were bartered for ivory, iron, copper, foodstuffs, and other commodities produced in the interior, and a relay coastal trade may have connected the Zaire basin with the Gulf of Guinea. In East Africa, the Swahili settlements extending from Somalia to Mozambique linked coastal peoples and the inhabitants of the Monomotapa Empire.

All these trading complexes were in operation when Portuguese caravels first arrived on the African coasts. It is against this background that Portuguese voyages of "discovery" must be discussed. Portuguese mariners encountered numerous communities prepared to engage in commerce for mutual benefit but ready, at the same time, to bar Europeans from penetrating the interior or from trade that was inimical to their middleman interests.

European and African Commercial Relations from the Fifteenth to the Seventeenth Centuries

Historical accounts which identify India as the goal of Prince Henry the Navigator (1394–1460) and his associates greatly distort their short-range objectives. They were instead largely preoccupied with the possibility of diverting the West African gold trade. European interest in West African gold had been heightened in the previous century by reports from the Muslim world of the fabulous quantities of gold disbursed by the ruler of Mali, Mansa Musa, on his pilgrimage to Mecca in 1324–25; news quickly spread to Europe, and Mansa Musa was depicted on a map of Africa drafted in 1339.

Another major objective was the establishment of sugar plantations on the Atlantic islands off the coast of Africa. Slaves were used as the labor force for these plantations. Thus, Africans were transported from the Senegambia and Upper Guinea coasts to plantations on the Cape Verde Islands; from the Gulf of Guinea and the Kongo-Angola area to São Tomé and Príncipe. From the sixteenth century, African captives supplied the labor for sugar cultivation, a process which had been transplanted to the Americas, with profound consequences for Africa, Europe, and the Americas alike.

Meanwhile, Portuguese traders were relatively successful in diverting gold from trans-Saharan trade routes, and established a considerable commerce on

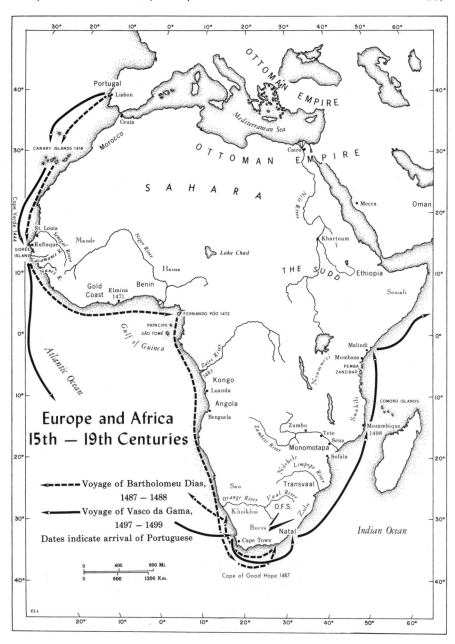

Europe and Africa
15th — 19th Centuries

- - - - Voyage of Bartholomeu Dias,
1487 — 1488
——— Voyage of Vasco da Gama,
1497 — 1499
Dates indicate arrival of Portuguese

MAP 23

the West and West Central African coasts, exchanging horses, spirits, cloth, iron, copper, hardware, and other European and North African commodities for gold, ivory, captives, malaguetta pepper, dyewoods, and other African products.

In East Africa, Portuguese naval power quickly subdued the Swahili settlements, but the Monomotapa Empire lay far beyond the range of naval gunnery, and Portuguese missionary and commercial initiatives were effectively thwarted by African rulers and Swahili traders. Portugal's advances in the Indian Ocean and the Arabian Sea brought a counterresponse from the Ottoman Turks, who provided firearms to Somalis to reignite their dormant *jihad* against Christian Ethiopia. Somalis overran Ethiopia in the 1520s, to be driven out in the 1540s with the assistance of a Portuguese expeditionary force. Portuguese and Spanish priests were successful in converting some of the Amhara elite to European Christian practices, but traditionalists ultimately triumphed and drove European priests from Ethiopia in the 1630s. Ethiopia's rulers thereafter followed an isolationist policy toward Europeans until the late nineteenth century.

African commercial exchanges with Portuguese traders established economic, social, and political patterns which in many areas continued well into the nineteenth century. The first Portuguese mariners to visit West Africa raided local communities, as they had done earlier along the coasts of Morocco and Mauritania. This policy of violence was soon abandoned as too dangerous and unprofitable. Instead, Portuguese traders accommodated themselves to African patterns of commerce and diplomacy; for example, they had to initiate trade by paying tolls, endure frustrating delays before obtaining returns, reside where Africans directed, and negotiate rents and taxes for land leased for "factories" (trading posts) and forts. These forts were constructed to defend African-granted trading privileges from European rivals, not to coerce Africans. African societies for their part guaranteed Europeans privileges traditionally accorded to "stranger" Africans: security of persons and goods; forbearance for transgressions stemming from ignorance of local social and religious customs; and mediation in disputes and conflicts caused by disagreements over trade. When a European transgressed, Africans convened a judicial process, a *palaver*, levied fines payable in trade goods, and, if the infraction was sufficiently serious, expelled the European from the society. These reciprocities and "ground rules" in West Africa were a part of what is termed the "landlord-stranger" relationship. This type of interaction characterized African-European relations elsewhere on the continent.

For a long period European trade was of marginal consequence for African societies, especially those in the interior of the continent. African traders added or rejected European imports and transported them varying distances, depending on their competitiveness with local equivalents such as cloth, iron, and salt, or, in the case of luxuries, the tastes of African elite groups. Africans and Europeans alike recognized that most European imports could be dispensed with, since African artisans and cultivators produced high-quality cloth, iron, spirits, and tobacco (after the latter had been introduced from the Americas). These items, together with guns, which had to be imported, were the staples of European trade until the twentieth century. That is, in spite of local equivalents, large quantities of these commodities were imported whenever they could be obtained from Europeans at more advantageous prices than from African suppliers—such was the competitiveness of African economic systems and the freedom of action permitted traders almost everywhere on the continent. Except for weapons and horses, which rulers sought to monopolize, Afri-

17. Unloading surf boats at Accra Harbor.
Photo courtesy United Nations/ TW/ vmb.

can traders were allowed to deal in any commodities they wished, subject only to established tolls and duties which went to rulers and their entourages, thereby reinforcing ties between traders and political elites.

Little noticed at the time, but undoubtedly the most valuable imports introduced to Africa by Portuguese and subsequent European visitors, were seeds and cuttings from the Americas which were brought to European forts and factories on the coast. Maize, manioc, pineapples, peanuts, tobacco, and numerous other plants and useful trees were quickly adopted and spread rapidly from one people to another. Europeans likewise aided the diffusion of Asian and European plants to parts of Africa where they had not previously been introduced.

Shifting Balances: The Era of the Slave Trade

The seventeenth century was a watershed in African relations with Europeans. Portugal's commercial hegemony was supplanted by rival European states in West and West Central Africa, and in East Africa by the reassertion of Swahili and Arab trading interests. At the same time, there was an enormous growth in slave trading, principally across the Atlantic but also across the Sahara and in the Indian Ocean.

During the seventeenth and eighteenth centuries, Holland, England, France, and several lesser European states established plantation economies in the Americas and looked to Africa for an adequate labor supply. Portugal's commercial networks in Africa were thus quickly destroyed. By the mid-seventeenth century France dominated European commerce in the Senegal River, and England that of the Gambia River; England and Holland were the chief rivals for the trade of the Gold Coast, and England, Holland, and France competed with Portugal on the Kongo-Angola coast. In East Africa, Arabs from Oman, together with Swahili, took advantage of Portugal's declining naval power to drive Portuguese vessels and traders from the coasts, except for Mozambique. By the close of the seventeenth century Portuguese and Luso-African traders retained their commercial position only between the Casamance and Nunez rivers, on the Angola coast, and in the Zambezi River valley.

The reasons for the participation of African societies in the divisive and destructive slave trade involve complex issues as yet unsatisfactorily understood by historians. Clearly, one of the crucial factors was the independence of action afforded African traders, who could engage in commercial activities detrimental to their own societies. A second and closely related factor was the self-serving collusion of political elites. Rulers and elites were often so attracted by foreign luxuries, especially spirits, that they were induced to wage war on neighboring societies to obtain captives and, in some instances, even sold their own people as slaves. Sometimes military elites became uncontrollable and subsisted off slave-raiding of agricultural and pastoral groups.

An important factor everywhere was the success of Europeans, Eurafricans, and other "stranger" groups in collaborating with African elites and merchants. Successful individuals exploited African social ties, at the same time collecting bands of armed retainers which made them effectively independent of traditional social controls and sanctions. In East Africa, Swahili, Arabs, and Indians worked toward the same ends.

Spurred by rising demands for labor from the plantation economies of the Americas and North African, Middle East, and Indian Ocean markets, slaving spread through Africa, sparing virtually no area of the continent by the nineteenth century. Many societies disintegrated, survivors taking refuge in remote areas—reversing centuries-old patterns of progressive commercial and cultural interchanges among peoples.

How many Africans were enslaved, perished as a consequence of wars and raids, died en route to markets or while awaiting shipment can never be known. The side effects are even more difficult to assess: peoples stricken by deprivation, reduced food production resulting from losses of young adults, diseases and illnesses exacerbated by reduced diets, and, as the result, social malaise and psychological disorientation.

A recent statistical survey of the transatlantic trade has calculated that some 11 million Africans were shipped across the Atlantic from the sixteenth to the nineteenth centuries, nearly all of them from West and West Central Africa. Of these, an estimated 9.5 million arrived in the Americas; of these some 350,000 came to the United States. About 80 percent of the total were transported between 1701 and 1850, suggesting that African societies must have experienced immense stresses during the peak years of the slave trade.[2] These calculations do not include West Africans taken across the Sahara to North Africa and the Middle East.

One of the earliest areas to be affected by slave trading was the kingdom of Kongo. Here, the supplying of captives to the plantations of São Tomé and the transatlantic markets, the breakaway of provinces as royal authority declined, and attacks by African enemies combined to fragment the kingdom by the end of the seventeenth century. West Central Africa continued to be a source of slaves for two centuries more, providing captives to both the Atlantic and the Indian Ocean trades.

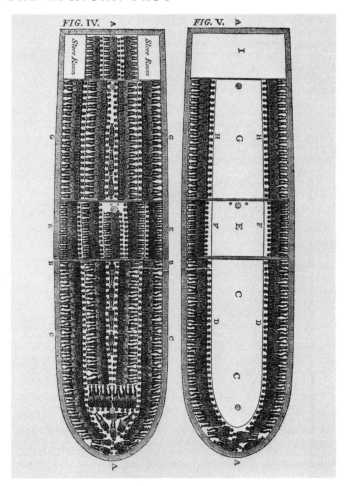

18. Diagram of a slave ship showing how slaves were transported across the Atlantic Ocean. From An Abstract of the Evidence delivered before a select committee of the House of Commons in the years 1790 and 1791, on the Part of the Petitioners for the Abolition of the Slave Trade.
Photo courtesy Lilly Library of Rare Books and Manuscripts, Indiana University.

In West Africa, the continuing slave trade across the Sahara, together with the progressive intensification of the Atlantic trade from the latter part of the seventeenth century, created a demand for people which many societies found impossible to resist or control. In certain areas large proportions of the population were enslaved, some to be sold immediately into the Sahara or Atlantic trades, others to be grouped in slave villages where their labor might be used until they were sold.

Estimates of the number of Africans enslaved in East and East Central Africa and sold in Indian Ocean markets vary widely. The devastation of African societies in the interior dates principally from the eighteenth century, after the Omani Arabs had displaced the Portuguese on the northern part of the coast. Arabs collaborated with the Swahili and Nyamwezi to develop caravan routes across East Africa, supplanting the relay trade of earlier times. Slaves and ivory were the major commodities of this long distance traffic, and by the early nineteenth century both were brought to the coast from as far away as the eastern Congo basin and from the area of present-day Uganda. Some of the slaves were shipped to the Middle East, others were used on the clove plantations on Zanzibar and Pemba islands and on French and British sugar plantations on the Mascarene Islands.

To the north, the peoples of the Upper Nile valley were ravaged by Sudanese and Egyptian slavers. Ivory traders and slavers first breached the Sudd

19. An old drawing of Fort Jesus, the Portuguese castle of Mombassa. From W. F. W. Owen, *Narrative of Voyages to Explore the Shores of Africa, Arabia and Madagascar*, 1833.
Photo courtesy Lilly Library of Rare Books and Manuscripts, Indiana University.

in the 1840s, and progressively raided and enslaved the peoples to the south in the decades following.

Recent studies on East Africa in the nineteenth century indicate that one of the most significant consequences of caravans penetrating the interior was the introduction of diseases such as smallpox and cholera. These spread from society to society in epidemics which may have caused more deaths and disruption of social patterns than did the export of slaves to Indian Ocean markets. Indeed, the population decrease caused by disease among Africans encouraged slave raiding and slave trading as a means to recruit new members for their societies.[3]

Southern Africa was another area where the introduction of epidemic diseases had enormous consequences for indigenous peoples. It is unique in that it was the only part of the continent where there was significant European settlement prior to the nineteenth century. In 1652, the Dutch East India Company founded a "refreshment station" at the Cape of Good Hope to supply vessels. Dutch, German, and French colonists who settled there in the half-century following served as intermediaries for ship-borne diseases which decimated the Cape's sparse populations of pastoral Khoikhoi (pejoratively called Hottentots) and San hunters. European frontiersmen, or trekboers, moved progressively inland, each generation seeking new land and incorporating as "bondsmen" the remnants of Khoikhoi societies. The scattered San hunting groups were driven deeper and deeper into the interior, or exterminated by "commandos" of Boer horsemen accompanied by their Khoikhoi servants.

A new phase in the history of southern Africa began in the latter part of the eighteenth century, when the expanding trekboers came increasingly into conflict with the southward migrations of Bantu societies. By the 1770s the two groups confronted each other along a frontier roughly demarcated by the Fish River.

The Great Trek was the culmination of Boer settlement in South Africa. Between 1835 and 1843, an estimated 12,000 Afrikaners moved away from the Cape to free themselves from British rule and to seek new land. Following the defeat of the Ndebele in 1836 and the Zulu army at the close of 1838, the majority of the Trekkers settled in the area of present-day Transvaal and Orange Free State. While the Afrikaners gradually expanded their holdings in the interior, British colonists settled the Cape and Natal provinces in circumstances that changed little until the last quarter of the nineteenth century when the exploitation of diamonds and gold transformed southern Africa. These later developments are discussed in chapter 23 in the context of how they affected the evolution of race relations.

The Nineteenth Century: Changing Relationships between Europe and Africa

The beginning of the nineteenth century marked an important transitional phase in relations between Europe and Africa. Changes were notable in three spheres of interaction. Firstly, the suppression of the slave trade in the Atlantic and Indian oceans began, and there was a gradual transition to "legitimate," non-slave commerce. Secondly, there was a rapid growth in European scientific interest in Africa. Thirdly, there was a remarkable growth of interest in Christian missionary endeavor. All three were interconnected, since members of the scientific community and missionaries shared merchants' interests in commercial prospects and potential areas of mineral wealth. Separately and together, these three spheres of interest revolutionized European-African relations during the first three-quarters of the nineteenth century.

European scientific interest concerning the African continent grew rapidly from the latter part of the eighteenth century. The research of geographers, botanists, zoologists, and other scholars was world-wide, but for many Africa had a special fascination. For geographers, locating the sources of the Nile and of the Niger had presented a special challenge from the time of Herodotus in the fifth century B.C. Individuals recruited to investigate the two rivers included some of the most famous names in African exploration: for the Niger, Mungo Park, René Caillié, Hugh Clapperton, and the Lander brothers; and in East Africa, Richard Burton, John Hanning Speke, David Livingstone, and Henry Morton Stanley. But to put their achievements into proper perspective, several points must be appreciated.

First of all, such men did not "discover" anything, to use a word highly pejorative to Africans: they generally followed well-worn trade routes and were dependent on African societies for intelligence, good will, supplies, and acts of charity and assistance, without which their expeditions would have ended in disaster. All of these testify to the persistence of patterns of hospitality and assistance to strangers even in troubled times. There were exceptions, of course: Muslims often resented European intrusions, whether as Christians or as potential competitors; and many African societies deflected Europeans from certain objectives or denied them information.

Africans safeguarded their interests with remarkable tenacity. For example, societies living along the outlets of the long-sought Niger River were determined to preserve their middleman trading position in relation to interior peoples. The Niger's course was not learned by Europeans until 1830, when John and Richard Lander traveled overland to reach the middle stretch of the river and followed it hundreds of miles to the sea. Their "discovery" came some 350 years after the first Portuguese navigators sailed along the coast and 50 years after the beginning of concerted efforts on the part of European scientific societies.

A good insight into the nature of the interactions between African societies and European travelers is provided by the following statement:

> Looking at the matter from the point of view of the large number of small separate societies in a state of hostility, or, at best, of armed neutrality towards their neighbours, and with no civic obligations outside their own small group, it seems at first sight almost culpable negligence on their part that . . . [so few] Europeans were killed. The strangers often came to a tribe straight from the headquarters of its bitterest enemies. They were generally unable to give any intelligible reason for their presence. . . . Their behaviour was generally unaccountable and often menacing and improper. They made sinister attempts to reach places that were profitless or forbidden. They were possessed of novel and exciting possessions which were a standing temptation to robbery, and, finally, they had powers and weapons that made them a mystery and a danger. Yet these men, utterly dependent and sometimes destitute, were allowed to pass chief after chief and tribe after tribe at the cost here of some restraint upon their impatient purposes and there of a persecution for presents nearly always stopping short of the violence which was well within the power of these chiefs. They were, on the contrary, not infrequently assisted at the cost of their hosts.[4]

Some of these observations concerning European explorers apply equally to missionaries, many of whom made notable scientific contributions in geography, biology, medicine, and especially linguistics; regarding the latter, missionaries compiled dictionaries, grammars, and texts in hundreds of African languages. David Livingstone was an ardent and effective advocate for the relationship between European Christianity and materialistic Western culture. In his famous lecture at Cambridge University in December 1857, Livingstone asserted concerning East Central Africa:

> In going back to that country my object is to open up traffic along the banks of the Zambesi, and also to preach the Gospel. The natives of Central Africa are very desirous of trading, but their only traffic is at present in slaves, of which the poorer people have an unmitigated horror: it is therefore most desirable to encourage the former principle, and thus open a way for the consumption of free productions, and the introduction of Christianity and commerce. By encouraging the native propensity for trade, the advantages that might be derived in a commercial point of view are incalculable; nor should we lose sight of the inestimable blessings it is in our power to bestow upon the unenlightened African, by giving him the light of Christianity. Those two pioneers of civilization—Christianity and commerce—should ever be inseparable.[5]

Protestants and Catholics were both acutely aware of the fact that nineteenth century missionary activity represented a "second" attempt to evangelize the peoples of Africa, and that the first effort made by the Portuguese in the fifteenth and sixteenth centuries had failed due to lack of personnel and resources and because of the great resiliency and eclecticism of traditional African religious practices. Wherever nineteenth-century European missionaries evangelized Africans, therefore, the latter were expected to adhere to European standards of behavior as an outward manifestation of their conversion to Christianity.

Except for southern Africa, European missionary activities were usually restricted to the perimeter of the continent until the period of colonial rule. Even so, certain patterns were already established by the last quarter of the nineteenth century. Generally speaking, missionaries were most successful in areas where there was no competition from Muslims, where there had been a breakdown in the structure of society, and where they could organize and discipline African communities. After the Partition of Africa in the last quarter of the nineteenth century, mission groups acquired additional influence over Africans through collaboration with colonial authorities.

Although the slave trade continued, the beginning of the nineteenth century also saw the initial stages of the transition to commerce in forest, agricultural, and mineral products. This first began in West Africa in response to Europe's growing requirements for vegetable oils for use in soap, candles, cooking oil, and other industrial and domestic purposes. Palm-oil trade dates from the 1790s, while the commercialization of peanuts began in the 1830s. Meanwhile, the slave trade was gradually suppressed during the half century after 1808, the year that Britain and the United States made the trade illegal for their citizens. In many areas of Africa slaving and legitimate commerce coexisted for decades, and African societies weighed the advantages of selling captives to slave ships or using their labor to produce palm oil, peanuts, gum copal, timber, cloves, or other export commodities.

The suppression of the slave trade and the development of legitimate trade frequently encouraged significant economic and social changes in African societies. As traditional elites found their income from the slave trade reduced they sought to exploit the wealth of the new commerce by levying taxes. These were resisted by producers, carriers, and trading groups, who resented these exactions as not sanctioned by tradition, and because they had come in many cases to regard rulers and their military entourages as parasitic and oppressive. An area where growing alienation between traditional elites and the productive members of society was most pronounced was in the Senegambia, where Islam provided an alternative ethos. Islam spread rapidly among peanut cultivators and migrant laborers during the nineteenth century, and Muslim spiritual leaders (*marabouts*), encouraged the supplanting of traditional authorities in many areas of the Senegambia during the "Soninke-Marabout" Wars, lasting from midcentury until the colonial take-over. There were similar conflicts during the same period between oppressed slave groups and the leaders of the palm-oil exporting city-states in the Niger delta and Cross River areas.

In many areas of Africa "outsider" groups which had previously profited from the slave trade were among the principal beneficiaries of the new commerce in primary products. In West Africa, Eurafricans from the Senegambia promoted the commercialization of peanuts along the coast to the south: likewise, Eurafricans, together with former African slavers living along the Gold and Slave coasts, became increasingly involved in palm-oil commerce. Eurafricans in West Central Africa long continued in the more remunerative slave trade, before gradually turning to legitimate commerce after midcentury. In East Africa, Swahili, Arabs, Indians, and the Luso-Africans living in the Zambezi River valley also continued in the slave trade, at the same time expanding their commerce in ivory, gum copal, cloves, and other commodities.

On another level of participation, African coastal groups which had been associated over a long period with Europeans in slave trading found employment in legitimate commerce as boat-pullers and seamen in coastal and riverine trade, and as clerks and laborers in trading establishments. The most important groups were Lebou, Wolof, Kru, and Fante in West Africa and Cabindans from West Central Africa, thousands of whom came to be employed in factories and aboard European trading vessels. Paralleling the labor migrations in West Africa, Comoro Islanders sought employment with commercial firms the length of the East African coast and also in South Africa.

After midcentury, European commerce with sub-Saharan Africa underwent distinct changes. The period from the 1860s onward was marked by sharply declining prices for primary products, fostering ruthless competition and resulting in numerous business failures among European, Eurafrican, and African firms. African and Eurafrican middlemen were squeezed out as independent traders and were reduced to taking employment as agents for European companies. Though their former economic position was destroyed and many were forced to live in reduced circumstances, these same individuals realized that there would be no turning back, and astutely recognized the educational opportunities provided by incoming European missionaries. By sending their children to mission schools, they ensured that their descendants would obtain preference in European mercantile, administrative, educational, and religious employment

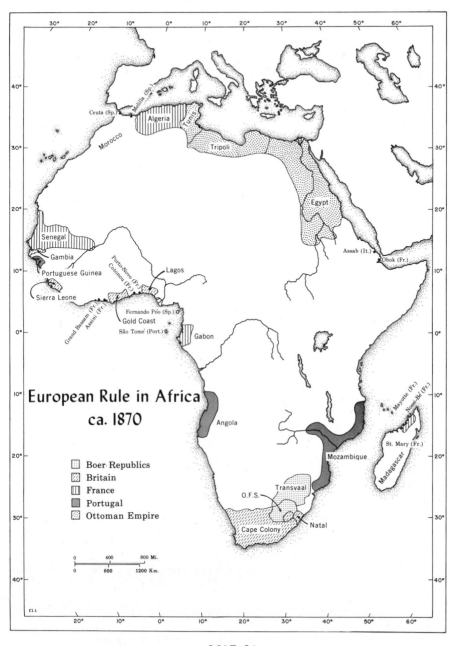

European Rule in Africa
ca. 1870

- Boer Republics
- Britain
- France
- Portugal
- Ottoman Empire

Ceuta (Sp.)
Melilla (Sp.)
Morocco
Algeria
Tunis
Tripoli
Egypt
Assab (It.)
Obok (Fr.)
Senegal
Gambia
Portuguese Guinea
Sierra Leone
Porto-Novo (Fr.)
Cotonou (Fr.)
Lagos
Grand Bassam (Fr.)
Assini (Fr.)
Gold Coast
Fernando Póo (Sp.)
São Tomé (Port.)
Gabon
Angola
Mayotte (Fr.)
Nossi-Bé (Fr.)
St. Mary (Fr.)
Madagascar
Mozambique
Transvaal
O.F.S.
Cape Colony
Natal

0   400   800 Mi.
0   600   1200 Km.

MAP 24

during the colonial era. East and East Central Africa, still largely tied to Indian Ocean trading patterns, was less affected by the European economic depression. Arabs and Indians in particular proved tenacious competitors for European firms, and ably protected their commercial interests.

Conclusion

Conventional history textbooks frequently emphasize the rapidity of the European military conquest of Africa in the last two decades of the nineteenth century. Such a presentation is correct in that the European colonial take-over of the continent was rapid; yet it is also misleading, for it stresses the over-whelming military superiority Europeans had at their disposal by the last quarter of the nineteenth century (summed up aptly in Belloc's couplet: "Whatever happens we have got the Maxim gun and they have not"). Thus the imperial-istic flag-waving during the Partition is overemphasized whereas the processes of change which were already under way are not sufficiently elucidated. As this chapter has emphasized, changes in African societies, particularly in coastal areas, were already so pervasive and fundamental that for them the European take-over in the 1880s and 1890s represents more a period of transition than a sharp break with the past. In the interior regions less affected by such changes, resistance to European conquest and the imposition of European rule was often longer sustained than in coastal areas, sometimes continuing for decades. Con-trasting responses to European conquest and administration are discussed in the following chapter.

NOTES

1. J. B. Gaby, *Relation de la Nigritie* (Paris: Chez E. Couterot, 1689), trans-lated and quoted in John D. Hargreaves, ed., *France and West Africa: An Anthology of Historical Documents* (London: Macmillan, 1969), p.33.
2. Philip D. Curtin, *The Atlantic Slave Trade: A Census* (Madison: University of Wisconsin Press, 1969), pp.265–69.
3. Gerald W. Hartwig, "Economic Consequences of Long-Distance Trade in East Africa: The Disease Factor," *African Studies Review*, Vol. 18, No. 2 (Sept. 1975), 63–73.
4. Margery Perham and J. Simmons, *African Discovery*, 2d. ed. (London: Faber and Faber, 1961), p.20.
5. Livingstone, David, *Cambridge Lectures*, notes and appendix edited by Wil-liam Monk (Cambridge: Deighton Bell and Co., 1858; reprinted, Farnborough: Gregg International Pub. Ltd., 1968), p. 21.

SUGGESTIONS FOR FURTHER READING

Bennett, Norman R. *Africa and Europe from Roman Times to the Present*. New York: Africana Publishing Company, 1975.

Bovill, E. W. *The Golden Trade of the Moors*. London: Oxford University Press, 2d. ed., 1968.

Davidson, Basil. *Africa: History of a Continent*. New York: Macmillan, 1972.

Hopkins, A. G. *An Economic History of West Africa*. London: Longman, rev.ed., 1975.

Oliver, Roland, and Anthony Atmore, *Africa Since 1800*. London: Cambridge University Press, 2d. ed., 1972.

Wallerstein, Immanuel. "The Three Stages of African Development in the World-Economy," in Peter C. W. Gutkind and Immanuel Wallerstein, eds., *The Political Economy of Contemporary Africa*, Sage Series on African Modernization and Development, vol. 1 (Beverley Hills, California: Sage, 1976).

Sheldon Gellar
The Colonial Era

9 While often depicted as a progressive and modernizing force, colonialism in fact was based on autocratic and often oppressive foreign rule. Ironically, the conquest and Partition of the African continent took place at a time when major European powers like Britain and France were moving toward greater implementation of democratic principles at home.

Although the European occupation of Africa was well under way by 1870, the year 1885 is a useful date to mark the beginning of the colonial era because of the historic importance of the Berlin Conference of 1884–1885, which legitimized the "Scramble for Africa" by formally sanctioning the Partition of the continent among several European powers. This chapter is primarily concerned with the impact of colonial institutions and policies on African societies during the autocratic phases of colonial rule (1885–1945) when Africans had few political and civil rights.

European Imperialism and the Partition of Africa

As noted in chapter 8, the nature of the relationships between Europe and Africa began to change with the abolition of the slave trade and the advance of "legitimate" commerce. The Industrial Revolution spurred Britain and other European countries to intensify their trade with the non-Western world. The requirements of an expanding world capitalist system dominated by the major industrial nations, led at that time by Britain, were major factors underlying the subjugation of Africa and other parts of what has come to be known as the Third World.

While superior technological and military strength allowed Europe to conquer and occupy the African continent, the primary causes for colonization were essentially political and economic.[1] Political factors such as nationalist rivalries and balance of power politics among the leading European nations, and a quest for national glory, heightened the desire for colonies. Imperialism was also stimulated by the need of the major industrial powers to acquire and control new markets and sources of raw materials in the so-called "backward" areas of the globe. In many instances, Africa was not as highly valued an economic prize as were other parts of the world. Britain, for example, was at first more concerned with maintaining and developing its Asian possessions than in acquiring an African empire. Thus, the military intervention and occupation of Egypt in 1882 began primarily as a measure to protect sea routes to the Middle East and Asia by insuring British control over the Suez Canal.

As the leading military and industrial nation in Europe, Britain obtained the most valuable colonial possessions in Africa. Encouraged by Germany, France also acquired a large number of colonies on the continent, to compensate for the provinces of Alsace and Lorraine lost to Germany during the Franco-Prussian War of 1870–71. Germany became an imperial power by establishing colonies in German East Africa, South-West Africa, Togo, and in Cameroon. All these were lost following Germany's defeat in World War I. Portugal, a close ally of Britain and the European nation with the longest historical ties to Africa, acquired more territory in Angola, Mozambique, and Portuguese Guinea. Belgium emerged as a colonial power largely through the efforts of King Leopold II, who established the Congo Free State, which became the Belgian Congo in 1908. Italy gained colonies in Libya and Somalia, and Spain acquired holdings in the Spanish Sahara and in Equatorial Africa. The only two African states to retain their sovereignty during the colonial era were Ethiopia and Liberia, the latter founded in 1821 by freed Afro-American slaves.

Much of the rationale justifying the conquest and colonization of Africa was based on evolutionary theories of history influenced by the ideas of Darwin, Spencer, Morgan, and Marx. Such theories maintained that societies organized within the framework of the nation-state and industrial capitalism represented the most advanced forms of human organization. Apologists for European colonialism and imperialism argued that it was the right, indeed the duty, of the "higher" civilizations to conquer the "lower" civilizations in order to bring prosperity and "Progress" to all parts of the world. Such claims, often expressed in terms of the "White Man's Burden," or what the French referred

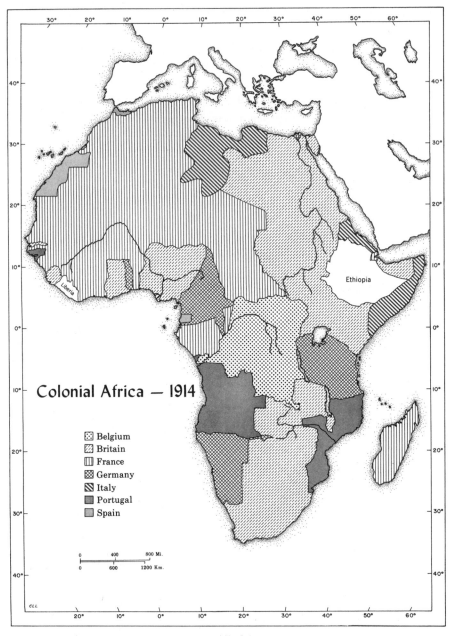

Colonial Africa — 1914

Liberia

Ethiopia

Belgium
Britain
France
Germany
Italy
Portugal
Spain

0   400   800 Mi.
0   600   1200 Km.

CLL

MAP 25

to as their "civilizing mission," were reinforced by racial theories which asserted the biological superiority of the "white race."

During the late nineteenth century, the popular image of Africa held by Europeans was that of a "Dark Continent" inhabited by "savage, war-like tribes." Africa was regarded as further down the scale of evolution than Asia and therefore in greater need of European guidance. In order to bring "civilization" to Africa, many also thought it their duty to propagate Christianity. The activities of dedicated and daring missionaries like David Livingstone who explored the continent and established missions to serve and convert the "heathen" captured the imagination of large segments of American and European public opinion and provided another powerful moral argument for those advocating the colonization of Africa.

Colonial Conquest and African Resistance

With the exception of Algeria, Senegal, Portuguese enclaves in Angola, Mozambique, and Portuguese Guinea, and South Africa, where the Afrikaners had pushed inland from the British-controlled Cape Colony to establish their own autonomous republics, most of the continent remained under African control until the last two decades of the nineteenth century.

At the time of the colonial conquest the African continent was in a state of flux. Morocco, Tunisia, and Egypt in North Africa were Muslim states whose monarchs had begun to modernize their countries before the occupation by France and Britain. In West Africa, Europeans had to deal with highly structured traditional states such as Dahomey, Ashanti, and the Mossi empire as well as with numerous Muslim states like the Emirates of Northern Nigeria, Futa Djallon, and newly created empires built by nineteenth-century Islamic reformers and military leaders such as Umar Tall and Samori Touré. Among the more prominent states in northeast and East Africa were the ancient Christian kingdom of Ethiopia, Buganda, and the Arab sultanate of Zanzibar. The great diversity of peoples and political units scattered throughout the continent at the time of the colonial conquest included not only large-scale states but also smaller chiefdoms and stateless societies, reflecting different levels of political, social, and economic development.

The military conquest of Africa was precipitated by the terms of the Berlin Conference, which insisted that European powers had to "effectively occupy" a territory before they could claim sovereignty over it. Although Europeans portrayed themselves as liberators, the process of occupation was often brutal and conducted by mercenaries primarily concerned with enriching themselves and their employers. Perhaps the most notorious case of brutality and greed occurred in the Congo Free State, which came under the personal control of Leopold II after the Berlin Conference. Under Leopold's rule the pillaging and abuses of the indigenous populations reached such proportions that the pressure of world opinion obliged him to transfer control of the colony to the Belgian government. With the tacit support of their governments, empire builders and adventurers such as Cecil Rhodes, George Goldie, and Sir Harry Johnston (all British), Carl Peters (German), and DeBrazza (French) organized their own personal armies and expeditions which brought large areas under European rule. France relied primarily upon its regular military forces to carve out a vast African empire in West and Equatorial Africa and Madagascar, while military conquest was also the principal means used by Germany, Portugal, and Italy in acquiring colonies.

Although resistance to colonial conquest was widespread throughout the continent, Menelik II's successful effort to preserve Ethiopian independence in the face of European imperialism proved to be the exception rather than the rule. Samori Touré organized one of the most spectacular examples of resistance to the imposition of European rule, using guerrilla tactics which delayed the completion of France's occupation of French West Africa for nearly two decades before his defeat and capture in 1898. Armed resistance was also fierce in other Muslim-controlled areas of West Africa, among the desert peoples of the Sahara, the Baoule of the forest zones of the Ivory Coast, the Hehe, who kept the Germans at bay for seven years in German East Africa, and the Yao, who fought the Portuguese in Mozambique. After brief periods of resistance, other African states and peoples capitulated, realizing that European technological superiority gave the invaders a decisive edge over conventional African armies whose traditional tactics and weaponry were ill-suited to modern warfare.

Not all African leaders saw Europeans as enemies. In some instances weaker rulers allied themselves with Europeans to escape the hegemony of more powerful neighbors. Moreover, European military forces often included large numbers of African troops recruited from conquered territories or provided by their African allies. In retrospect, it is clear that the strategy of "Divide and Conquer," taking advantage of traditional African political and ethnic rivalries, proved to be extremely successful in undermining African efforts to form effective alliances for the common purpose of resisting the invader.

The colonial conquest proved to be a shattering experience for many Africans. Although the imposition of colonial rule eventually led to the abolition of slavery and the establishment of peace, it also meant the end of African political, economic, and cultural autonomy, the transformation of Africa's elites and masses alike into colonial subjects with few political and civil rights, foreign economic domination, and the decline and denigration of traditional authority and values.

Racial and Cultural Domination under Colonialism

Notwithstanding different patterns of European rule throughout the continent, colonialism was essentially a system of political, economic, and cultural *domination* forcibly imposed by a technologically advanced foreign minority on an indigenous majority. As a system, colonialism justified itself largely through ideologies which asserted the superiority of the colonizer and the inferiority of the colonized.

The dogma of the innate moral inferiority of the indigenous populations was widely shared by many Europeans living in colonial Africa and was used to rationalize the master-servant relationships between Europeans and Africans. The demeaning concept of the "native" implied that Africans, as inferior crea-

20. "District Officer on Tour." Thomas Ona's carving—an African's view of a colonial officer.
Photo courtesy Mr. and Mrs. William Bascom, Berkeley, California.

tures, were not fit to rule themselves. In his powerful polemic against colonial-ism, Frantz Fanon, the author of *The Wretched of the Earth*, bitterly described the image of the "native" held by the colonizer:

> As if to show the totalitarian character of colonial exploitation the settler paints the native as the quintessence of evil. . . . The native is declared insensible to ethics; he represents not only the absence of values, but also the negation of value. . . .[2]

Although the viewpoint depicted by Fanon is based on his experiences in Al-geria and is obviously an extreme one, it was by no means uncommon in areas with large white settler populations, who used such arguments to justify their brutal repression of African uprisings.

The racial character of the colonial system was not only reflected in the ideologies of the day; it was also reflected in colonial social structures. Thus, in most colonies, European officials, businessmen, farmers, and missionaries con-stituted a privileged ruling caste open only to those of European birth. The principle of racial hierarchy was most developed in South Africa, particularly after 1910 when Britain transferred all of its prerogatives as a colonial power to a white settler minority government. One interesting feature of the colonial caste system was the relatively privileged but ambigious status of the Eurafri-cans, who constituted a small westernized elite midway between the European rulers and the African masses in the colonial racial hierarchy. In the rare in-stances when political and civil rights were accorded to "nonwhites," these were generally granted to Eurafricans such as the Creoles in Sierre Leone, the *métis* in Senegal, and the *asimilados* in Portuguese Africa.

Although the colonial system was often justified in terms of its "civilizing" mission, few colonial regimes were willing or able to provide the Western education deemed necessary to transform the "native" into a "civilized" person. Until the end of World War II, Western education was made available to less than 5 percent of the school-age population. During the early phases of colonial rule, Catholic and Protestant mission schools were the main source of Western education for Africans. In government and mission schools, African children learned that European culture and civilization were superior to their own, and they were taught to reject their former religious practices and cultural tradi-tions. The limited Western education offered to a small minority of Africans did not attempt to make the African the equal of the European; it only pre-pared the African to occupy subordinate positions within the colonial system in what have been called "auxiliary" elites.

While Eurafricans and Western-educated African "auxiliary" elites sought political and social equality for themselves, they often regarded the indigenous African masses as backward and not ready for full political and civil rights until they acquired a modicum of Western education and values. Liberal European colonizers also rejected the doctrine of the African's innate racial inferiority and, unlike most colonizers, were willing to grant some rights to *westernized* Africans. The greatest resistance to African equality came from the relatively large white settler populations of South Africa, Kenya, Southern Rhodesia, Portuguese Africa, and Algeria, where relationships between Europeans and Africans most closely approximated the master-slave model of the colonial system depicted by Fanon.

Metropolitan Policies

The broad outlines of colonial policy were formulated in London, Paris, Brussels, and Lisbon, primarily in terms of the needs of the metropole. Colonial policies were affected more by the political climate at home and by international events than by what was taking place in Africa. For example, because of France's numerical inferiority in relation to Germany, the French government adopted a colonial policy which treated the African territories as a reservoir of troops for the French army. Germany ceased to be a colonial power not because of revolutions in its African colonies but because it was the loser in World War I. During the interwar period (1919–39) the triumph of fascism in Portugal perpetuated repressive colonial policies in Portuguese Africa while the victory of the left-wing Popular Front in France in 1936 led to significant colonial reforms.

Metropolitan governments and public opinion were generally indifferent to colonial matters, which they regarded as less important than domestic issues and foreign policy. Although colonial questions were significant in British politics because of the vast size of the empire, Britain was generally more concerned with events taking place in Asia; for example, with the rise of Indian independence movements under the leadership of Gandhi and the emergence of Japan as a world power. Smaller European colonial powers such as Belgium and Portugal were more involved with their African possessions than were Britain, France, Italy, and Germany, which were preoccupied with big power politics in Europe. Portugal looked to her African colonies as a means of restoring some of the grandeur of the past. The "renewal" of Portugal through its empire in Africa became an important part of the ideology of the Salazar regime and the *Estado Novo* which came into existence following the overthrow of the Portuguese Republic in 1926. Despite the fact that Portugal was a fascist state while Belgium was a bourgeois parliamentary democracy with a constitutional monarch, both nations pursued similar, paternalistic colonial policies which stressed the spiritual and "civilizing mission" of the colonizer, centralized decision-making in the metropole, and denied political representation to both Europeans and Africans in the colonies.

While some commentators on French and British colonial policy have contrasted French "Cartesianism" with British "Empiricism,"[3] these differences may have been overstated. "Cartesianism" implies a uniform approach based on a clear-cut set of rules which are universally applied; yet, French colonial policies and practices were far from being uniform, since France, like Britain, responded pragmatically to the various political, economic, and cultural realities in different parts of Africa. Thus, French colonial policy in North Africa bore little resemblance to that practiced in Black Africa. In North Africa, the French regarded Algeria as an integral part of the metropole and totally destroyed traditional political structures. On the other hand, in Morocco and Tunisia, which were governed as protectorates, the French maintained traditional political and social structures, particularly in Morocco where the sultan remained a prominent political figure throughout the colonial period. Colonies in Black Africa were organized within a highly centralized federal framework— French West Africa and French Equatorial Africa—headed by a governor-general who supervised and coordinated the activities of the territorial colonial governors. Although France practiced a policy of Direct Rule which insisted upon the legitimacy of only one sovereign authority in a colony—that of France —its colonial policy in Black Africa was nonetheless flexible enough to preserve and work through traditional political structures in territories like Mauritania, Upper Volta, and Niger; in those areas the limited French presence necessitated a greater use of traditional indigenous authorities.

Britain's reputation as a "liberal" colonial power was based largely on its policies in West Africa whereby a small number of Africans could vote and participate in modern representative institutions even during the earlier phases of colonial rule. Each British colony in West Africa was divided into a "colony," whose inhabitants were governed by British law and granted political representation in municipal councils, and a "protectorate." Unlike the "colonies" centered on coastal towns such as Bathurst, Freetown, Lagos, and Accra, the "protectorates" in the interior were administered through traditional African leaders and institutions or through newly constituted "native administrations," often organized along ethnic lines and headed by traditional chiefs. The absence of a white settler population and the opportunities for African farmers to be integrated into the colonial export economy on relatively favorable terms made British colonial rule in West Africa less heavy-handed and oppressive than in East and Central Africa, where white settlers expropriated large tracts of African communal lands and denied Africans political representation.

Colonial Government and Chiefly Authority

Although colonial rule has often been described as a "School for Democracy," this image did not reflect accurately the realities of political life in Africa. Before 1945 less than 1 percent of the African population had full political and civil rights or access to modern democratic institutions. Instead, most Africans were ruled by autocratic bureaucracies which demonstrated little interest in promoting democratic ideals.

While European colonial governments were obviously new factors affecting African societies, the impact of colonial rule on political life at the local level should not be exaggerated. The European presence in many territories was limited to small numbers of administrators, merchants, and missionaries concentrated primarily in the colonial capital and in the major trading centers. In many areas of rural colonial Africa, the people rarely came into direct contact with European officials. For example, as late as the mid-1920s there was only one British administrator for every 100,000 persons in northern Nigeria. Because of the small number of European personnel, limited financial resources, and an undeveloped communications infrastructure, the colonial state had to rely heavily upon traditional African rulers, chiefs, and religious authorities to help govern the vast areas and populations under its control. The system of Indirect Rule permitted traditional rulers and chiefs to govern certain areas under the careful supervision of the European authorities. The survival of traditional authority, however, did not alter the fact that traditional rulers and chiefs were clearly subordinate to the colonial power structure and could be deposed if they did not follow the dictates of the colonial administration. The ideal chief under the colonial system was loyal, accepted the hegemony and superiority of the colonizer, maintained order, collected taxes for the colonial regime, encouraged his people to produce cash crops for the colonial export economy, and provided forced labor for public works projects and cheap wage labor for European enterprises.

As long as they complied with the demands of the colonial authorities, traditional rulers and chiefs retained a privileged position within the colonial system. Thus, because of his collaboration with the Belgian colonial administration, a traditional chief like the father of Moise Tschombe—the leader of the unsuccessful Katanga secession movement after independence and Prime Minister of Congo Leopoldville (Zaire) in the early 1960s—could become a millionaire in his own right. In other instances, the colonizer permitted traditional rulers and certain ethnic groups to preserve their hegemony over other peoples, as was the case in Rwanda where the Tutsi continued their feudal domination of the Hutu, a situation which eventually led to bloody genocidal conflict after independence in the 1960s. Thus many of the ethnic and regional cleavages which plague contemporary Africa had their roots in the administrative politics of the colonial era which favored certain traditional authorities, regions, and ethnic groups over others.

The integration of traditional chiefs as subordinate cogs in the colonial bureaucracy performing unpopular tasks like collecting taxes and recruiting labor for the colonial regime undermined chiefly authority throughout much of colonial Africa. The people came to regard them as agents of the colonizer rather than as spokesmen for African interests. This was particularly true in France's Black African colonies and in the Belgian Congo where the *chefferies* were clearly creations of the colonial state and had few roots in African tradition. On the other hand, traditional authority tended to persist in colonial areas under Indirect Rule or in regions like eastern and western Nigeria, where the British successfully modernized traditional authority structures while reinforcing the prestige of chiefly authority.

White Settler Politics

White settler politics consisted primarily of efforts by Europeans to perpetuate their political and economic supremacy over colonial populations. In the multiracial colonial societies of Kenya, the Rhodesias, and Tanganyika, white settlers fought to restrict the suffrage of the Asian and Arab populations and to restrict their representation in the legislative councils which were set up by the British after World War I. In Kenya, white settlers not only expropriated the best farmlands in the colony from the Kikuyu, but also won their battle to prevent Asians from obtaining equal political, economic, and social rights during the 1920s. The white settlers of Southern Rhodesia gained the right to govern themselves in 1923 and used their power to maintain white supremacy. Settler influence on colonial administrative power was not as great in Nyasaland (Malawi) and Tanganyika (Tanzania), where climatic conditions and fewer economic opportunities attracted much smaller European populations. Despite the presence of significant numbers of settlers, European political life was less intense in Belgian and Portuguese Africa, which had no representative political institutions. Colonial administrators generally had a freer hand in colonies with small European populations.

An unusual blend of democratic and totalitarian politics emerged in South Africa. For the Europeans there was a highly competitive and democratic form of electoral politics which pitted a predominantly English-speaking party against a predominantly Afrikaner-speaking party; for the Cape Coloureds and the Asians there was limited representation and an inferior political, social, and economic status; for Africans there was almost no representation and, over the years, a steady deterioration of their civil rights. In Algeria, the sizable French population enjoyed all the political prerogatives of metropolitan citizens, including representation in the French Parliament, which they used to prevent the passage of colonial reforms aimed at enfranchising Muslims. Ironically, white settler tyranny over the indigenous populations was often greatest in territories such as Algeria, South Africa, Southern Rhodesia, and Kenya, where Europeans insisted upon exercising all the rights of citizens living in democratic societies while denying these same rights to Africans. Hence, it was not surprising that African hostility to colonial rule and European domination tended to be most intense in these territories. The Mau Mau Rebellion in Kenya, the Algerian Revolution, and the wars of national liberation undertaken in Portuguese and southern Africa during the 1960s and 1970s were to a large extent the fruits of the master-servant relationships which developed during the colonial era.

African Participation in Democratic Politics

Before World War II, the main centers of modern African political activity could be found in colonial protectorates like Morocco, Tunisia, and Egypt and in West Africa, where colonial policies permitted limited African participation in electoral politics.

In North Africa radical nationalist parties emerged, such as the Neo-Destour Party in Tunisia led by Habib Bourguiba, as well as more traditionalist nationalist movements which rallied around the banner of Islam in Egypt and Libya or around the person of the monarch as in Morocco with Muhammad V. The French severely repressed North African nationalist movements which challenged French sovereignty, especially in Algeria, which was considered to be an integral part of France. The British continued to occupy Egypt, despite its nominal independence, until 1936 and intervened frequently to protect pro-British monarchs and governments from being overthrown by nationalist opponents.

Unlike the mass nationalist politics practiced in North Africa, African political activity in West Africa during the colonial era was restricted to a minuscule Western-educated African elite. This elite was primarily concerned with gaining full political, economic, and social rights for educated Africans, increasing the power of representative political bodies in the colony, and widening the scope of African participation in the political process. In British West Africa, the elite sought to improve their position by constitutional means. This meant petitioning for more African representation on the legislative councils and demanding less representation by chiefs appointed by the colonial administration or by European officials themselves, who often constituted a majority of the members. The elite of British West Africa resented the system of Indirect Rule practiced in the "protectorates" which treated the chiefs as the authentic spokesmen of the people and encouraged the modernization of traditional authority structures. The establishment of "native administrations" and the preservation of precolonial entities such as the Emirates of Northern Nigeria often frustrated the aspirations of the new elite to provide leadership in the colony. Yet the modern elite and the chiefs were not always in conflict; blood and marriage ties often bound them together, and some of the chiefs were themselves highly educated by colonial standards. Moreover, the modern elite defended the prerogatives of the chiefs on many occasions, especially on questions concerning the expropriation of communal land by the colonial administration.

African participation in French West Africa was largely confined to Senegal's so-called "Four Communes" of Dakar, Gorée, Rufisque, and Saint Louis, where Africans enjoyed the rights and privileges of "citizens." Senegal was the only Black African colony where the French ideal of "assimilation" was actually practiced. The principle of assimilation called for giving the overseas colonial populations the same kind of education and rights as were extended to Frenchmen, representation in metropolitan assemblies, and local political institutions patterned on those found in France. Senegal was perhaps the only colony in Tropical Africa during this period in which Africans and Europeans competed and worked together in politics on an equal and integrated basis. Like their counterparts in British West Africa, the African elite of "citizens," led by men such as Blaise Diagne and Galandou Diouf, were more concerned with asserting the rights and prerogatives of the "citizens" in the "Four Communes" than with extending these rights to the "subject" populations of the interior, who constituted more than 95 percent of Senegal's total population. Elsewhere in French West and Equatorial Africa and in Madagascar, Western-educated Africans resented their "subject" status and sought to gain the same rights enjoyed by Senegal's "citizens." Despite France's assimilationist ideals, French colonial officials resisted efforts to increase African participation in democratic institutions and made it extremely difficult for even well-educated African "subjects" to become naturalized French citizens.

In other parts of colonial Africa, the westernized African elite—the *asimilados* of Portuguese Africa, the *évolués* in the Belgian Congo, and the mission-educated elite of British East and Central Africa—were not permitted to engage in electoral politics. In these territories, Africans learned most of their modern political skills through their activities in various ethnic, cultural, and religious associations sanctioned by the colonial authorities.

Other Forms of Political Expression

Although less than 1 percent of the African population directly participated in the limited democratic politics of the colonial era, there were other ways in which Africans could express their political views. These responses to colonial rule and policies varied from violent rebellions and protest to accommodation and collaboration.

During the early colonial period, rebellions were frequent throughout the continent, often touched off by repressive land, labor, and tax policies. Thus, in South Africa, the Zulus in Natal rebelled in 1906 after the imposition of oppressive poll taxes; in Tanganyika, the Maji-Maji insurrection against German rule in 1905 was put down only after a bitter struggle in which tens of thousands of Africans lost their lives; in Liberia, the Kru revolted against the black American-Liberian government; and in the Sahara, desert nomads refused to accept French authority. With the consolidation of colonial rule, large-scale rebellions became far less frequent during the interwar period (1919–1939).

In areas where Africans had few formal political outlets to express themselves collectively, political responses to colonial rule were often organized within the framework of millenarian religious movements and separatist churches which reaffirmed traditional African values and world views. Many of these movements and churches directly challenged the political and moral authority of the colonizer. Kimbanguism in the Belgian Congo, the Watchtower movement in British Central Africa, the Black Zionist churches in South Africa, and the Muslim Hamallist movement in French Soudan represent some of the more prominent examples of mass dissatisfaction with European rule expressed in a religious form.

Despite their exclusion from the political process, African peasants and workers did not remain passive in voicing their sentiments about colonial economic policies and employment practices. Miners in South Africa and Northern Rhodesia, for example, on several occasions launched illegal strikes to protest low pay and poor working conditions, while the railway workers in West Africa were among the first group of African wage earners to organize trade unions. Ashanti cocoa farmers initiated the Cocoa Holdup of 1939 to protest the low prices they were getting for their crops. In the rural areas, tax evasion was widespread, particularly among herdsmen, who moved frequently to avoid paying the cattle tax.

Although expressions of discontent with various aspects of European rule prevailed throughout colonial Africa, most Africans demonstrated their passive acceptance of colonial rule by recognizing the authority of the colonial regime. Indeed, some African leaders and ethnic groups collaborated very closely with the colonizer in exchange for certain privileges within the colonial system, while others were grateful to the colonizer for liberating them from slavery and rule by other ethnic and religious groups. And many westernized Africans saw colonialism in Africa as a progressive and civilizing force which, despite its many abuses, had eliminated slavery, human sacrifice, and internecine warfare while providing opportunities for Africans with modern skills to rise socially and economically regardless of previous low traditional social status.

The Economics of Colonialism

As an economic system, colonialism bound the peoples of Africa more closely to the international capitalist system in general and to the metropolitan economy in particular. The colonial situation gave the metropole the power to monopolize economic policy and impose a system of "enforced bilateralism." In practical terms, this meant that trade was generally oriented toward the metropole, that nationals of the metropolitan power controlled the most important sectors of the colonial export economy, and that colonial development policies reflected the interests of metropolitan banks, import-export houses, shipping firms engaged in colonial trade, mining companies (exploiting the mineral resources of the colonies), and the white settler population. The colonial system provided the metropole with outlets for its manufactured goods, raw materials for its industries, and tropical products for metropolitan consumers on terms which were advantageous to the colonizers.

Although colonial economic policies clearly stimulated economic growth, this growth was often achieved at the expense of indigenous populations. From the point of view of Africans, colonial rule meant the expropriation of traditional communal lands, the transformation of countless numbers of Africans into an uprooted and poorly paid rural and urban proletariat, and a labor system which kept urban Africans at the bottom of the economic scale and prevented rural Africans from effectively competing with European farmers. Economic exploitation, like political oppression, was most pronounced in territories containing relatively large numbers of white settlers in need of cheap African labor.

The degree to which Africans were subordinated to European economic interests was directly related to the size of the European community. During the colonial era, the white settler population was primarily concerned with acquiring land and access to cheap labor. Economic exploitation was most systematic in South Africa. There, Europeans took the best land and established a Native Reserve system and an economic "Color Bar" which forced Africans to work for low wages while legally preventing them from holding the same jobs as whites. Appropriation of vast tracts of land by European settlers was also widespread in Kenya, Southern Rhodesia, Portuguese Africa, the Belgian Congo, and Algeria, and carried out on a smaller scale in the Ivory Coast, Tunisia, Libya, and Cameroon. The development of mining and the rapid expansion of plantation agriculture stimulated an enormous demand for cheap African labor, which was generally supplied from the poorer and usually more densely populated regions in the territory or else imported from neighboring colonies. In most instances, the labor-supplying region had no solid economic base of its own and lacked a source of cash income to pay the taxes levied by the colonial government. Thus, to pay taxes, it was necessary for Africans in Mozambique and Nyasaland, for example, to seek work in the mines of South Africa and the farms of Southern Rhodesia. In West Africa, Upper Volta became a major reservoir of labor for cocoa plantations in the Ivory Coast and the Gold Coast.

The subordinate position of Africans within the colonial economic system was also maintained by discouraging African competitors in the modern capitalist sectors of the colonial economy. Thus, European import-export companies and banks thwarted the development of a modern African entrepreneurial class in places like Senegal by withholding credit from what had been a flourishing class of African traders and middlemen before 1900. European firms and the colonial administration further discouraged African competition in the modern sectors of the economy by using nonindigenous groups as middlemen, for example, the Lebanese in West Africa and the Asians in East Africa. Colonial economic policies also made it difficult for Africans to compete with Europeans in agriculture. Thus, the British in Kenya did not permit African farmers to grow coffee and other cash crops produced by the white settlers, while the French administration in the Ivory Coast clearly discriminated against African cocoa producers by offering higher prices to French planters.

European economic oppression was less intense outside of South Africa and the major white settler colonies. In West Africa and Uganda, where colonial policies precluded large-scale European settlement and seizure of African communal lands, rural Africans, though increasingly vulnerable to fluctuating world market conditions, nevertheless enjoyed greater economic opportunities as cash crop farmers producing cocoa, coffee, cotton, peanuts, and palm oil for European markets. The main beneficiaries of economic growth in the rural areas tended to be notables, chiefs, and religious leaders who could transform their traditional prerogatives over the allocation of communal land and local labor into wealth derived from cash crops. In the urban areas, Western-educated Africans who occupied modern economic roles—bookkeepers, clerks, civil servants and school teachers—also profited materially from the patterns of change fostered by the colonizer.

Many regions and territories in colonial Africa were only partially integrated into the international capitalist system through colonialism and therefore continued to remain largely untouched by modern economic forces and modes of production. This was particularly true of the desert, Sahelian, and forest zones which lacked modern roads and railways to facilitate the evacuation of tropical products. In territories like Mauritania and northern Nigeria, precapitalist modes of production and exchange continued to persist as most of the people remained largely outside the colonial economic system. In areas where the colonial economy did not replace traditional African products with European imports, African artisans and merchants continued to supply most of the needs of the local populations in goods and services and to control the traditional long-distance trade in cattle, dried fish, and other products.

The results of the export-oriented pattern of economic growth during the colonial period seem to support the contention that the integration of colonial African economies fostered what some have called the "development of underdevelopment."[4] Thus, critics have argued that the development of the European-dominated colonial export economy and the advantages which accrued to the metropole were achieved primarily at the expense of most of the indigenous populations, who were obliged to remain in a state of chronic underdevelopment in order to sustain the system. At any rate, it seems that the colonial situation clearly made it more difficult for Africans to enjoy the fruits of whatever economic growth took place during the colonial era. The diverse patterns of colonial economic development and their consequences for Africa, especially as they relate to the economic problems of the post-independence period, will be discussed further in chapter 16.

Conclusion

The Second World War marked the beginning of the end of the colonial era and its autocratic rule. The war discredited the racist ideologies which had served as the original rationale for European colonization, heightened African aspirations for self-government, and seriously weakened the capacity and the will of the major colonial powers to maintain their overseas empires, thereby setting the stage for the era of political decolonization which was to follow.

NOTES

1. There are two contending interpretations as to the principal causes and motivations underlying modern European imperialism. One school of thought, associated with the names of such historians as Brunschwig and Gallagher and Robinson, gives the primacy to political factors, while the other school of thought, associated with such names as Hobson and Lenin, gives the primacy to economic factors. For a useful discussion of these schools of thought and excerpts from their main proponents, see George H. Nadel and Perry Curtis, *Imperialism and Colonialism* (New York: The Macmillan Company, 1964).

2. Frantz Fanon, *The Wretched of the Earth* (New York: Grove Press, Inc., 1968), p.41.

3. See, for example, Thomas Hodgkin, *Nationalism in Colonial Africa* (New York: New York University Press, 1957).

4. For two interesting samples of this approach, see Walter Rodney, *How Europe Underdeveloped Africa* (Dar-es-Salaam: Tanzania Publishing House, 1972) and E. A. Brett, *Colonialism and Underdevelopment in East Africa* (New York: Nok Publishers, Ltd., 1973). For a more sympathetic interpretation of colonial economic development, see Allan McPhee, *The Economic Revolution in West Africa* (New York: Negro Universities Press, 1970).

SUGGESTIONS FOR FURTHER READING

Balandier, Georges. "The Colonial Situation," in Pierre Van Den Berghe, ed. *Africa: Social Problems of Change and Conflict.* San Francisco: Chandler Publishing Company, 1965, pp.36–57.

Crowder, Michael. *West Africa Under Colonial Rule.* London: Hutchinson, 1968.

Curtis, Perry, and George H. Nadel. *Imperialism and Colonialism.* New York: Macmillan, 1964.

Delavignette, Robert. *Freedom and Authority in French West Africa.* London: Oxford University Press, 1950.

Duffy, James. *Portugal in Africa.* Baltimore: Penguin, 1963.

Fanon, Frantz. *The Wretched of the Earth.* New York: Grove Press, Inc., 1968.

Gallagher, John, and Ronald Robinson. *Africa and the Victorians.* New York: Anchor Books, 1968.

Gellar, Sheldon. *Structural Changes and Colonial Dependency: Senegal, 1885–1945.* Beverly Hills, California: Sage, 1976.

Hodgkin, Thomas. *Nationalism in Colonial Africa.* New York: New York University Press, 1957.

Maquet, Jacques. *Power and Society in Africa.* New York: McGraw-Hill, 1971.

Edmond J. Keller
Decolonization and the Struggle for Independence

10 The independence period in African political history began in 1957 with the independence of Ghana, formerly the Gold Coast, and by 1977 virtually the whole of Black Africa was again in the hands of black rulers. The only unliberated areas remaining are a few minor possessions of Spain and France, and the territories controlled by the white minority regimes of Rhodesia (Zimbabwe), South Africa (Azania), and Namibia. In these areas, African liberation movements are actively struggling to reverse the balance of power and to return the whole of Africa to Africans.

In studying colonial rule, a great deal of attention is often paid to the structure of colonial administration and government. Britain is usually associated with Indirect Rule and respect for the "noble savage"; France, Portugal, and Belgium are associated with Direct Rule and a variety of schemes for African assimilation. Just as no colonial power followed a uniform pattern of administration, so too, patterns of decolonization also varied from one colony to the next. This was particularly the case with British and French colonies, where multiple factors influenced the process.

What were the factors which determined the timing of African nationalist movements? Was the beneficence of the imperial powers a significant variable? Or was the desire to be free simply irresistible? Were factors internal to Africa more relevant than international forces in determining the rate and pattern of the demise of colonialism?

There are no easy answers to these questions, but two things are reasonably apparent. Perhaps of *least* importance was the goodwill of the colonial powers; and *most* important were the changes taking place in the international political and economic order, shifts in public opinion with respect to the colonies in the metropolitan countries at the close of World War II, and the emergence of a vocal, educated, and sometimes militant indigenous elite which fed the fires of African independence. Understanding the significance of each of these factors is essential in order to comprehend the total process called the African Independence Movement.

A close examination of the process of decolonization reveals that although there was a typical British or French "way" of disengaging from a colonial possession, there were atypical cases as well. And in some instances, special features of certain colonies, whether they were controlled by Britain, France, Belgium, or Portugal, forced them into similar molds. For example, the movement toward decolonization in Algeria, Angola, Mozambique, Guinea-Bissau, and to a certain extent in Kenya and Zaire, was a much more violent and traumatic process than that in Ivory Coast, Upper Volta, Tanzania, or the Central African Republic. In the former cases, the presence of European settler interests greatly influenced the nature of the nationalist struggle, while in the latter, settler interests were of little consequence. The nature and organizational abilities of the indigenous leadership class also contributed to certain important variations.

Before exploring the factors that determined the timing and nature of the African independence movement, it is necessary to examine the historical and intellectual underpinnings of the nationalist period in Africa.

Decolonization and Nationalism in Historical Perspective

World War II was a critical period in recent African history and influenced fundamentally the relationships that existed between African colonies and the colonial powers. During the war, the colonies, which in some cases were virtually cut off from their respective metropolitan countries, were mobilized to play an important role in the war effort. The emphasis was upon developing local productive capacity. For example, forced labor was increasingly utilized in French, Belgian, and British colonies such as the Ivory Coast, the Congo, and Kenya in order to extract record volumes of agricultural and mineral resources. Furthermore, these commodities were now processed in the colonies themselves. Before the war the practice had been to ship raw materials to Europe for processing, but during the war this became difficult because of military pressures applied by the Nazis. Moreover, it was a problem to ship finished products from Europe to the colonies for consumption by white settlers and bureaucrats. In addition to stressing the local production of consumer items, colonial administrators were also responsible for mobilizing their subjects to provide military and strategic nonmilitary products, such as copper and uranium in the case of Belgian Congo. These were used to conduct the war effort and to keep money in European treasuries.

Many Africans were also drafted into the armies of the colonial powers, where they served in various capacities: some were combatants, fighting alongside Europeans on the battlefield; others served in noncombat roles as porters, servants, and drivers. The war experience enabled these African soldiers to see another side of their European masters, who had always appeared to be dominant, self-assured individuals in the colonial setting, but who were now revealed to be as human as anyone else. There were rich and poor Europeans. At home, they lived in slums as well as on luxurious estates. Moreover, in the heat of battle they displayed emotions, fears, and weaknesses as all humans do; they were not invincible, as some Africans had been led to believe. For many African soldiers World War II had a tremendous formative impact. The war expanded their world view to the extent that they were no longer satisfied with being subjects who relied upon the goodwill of paternalistic overlords for their welfare. They gained confidence that they could determine their own destinies—if they were willing to take action, to struggle and sacrifice for what they wanted. These men added a militant character to the social, political, and economic movements which arose after the war, especially in the Gold Coast and Kenya. Ex-soldiers in the Gold Coast played central roles in Kwame Nkrumah's "Positive Action Campaign," and in Kenya they were heavily represented among the Mau Mau forest fighters.

By the end of the war the colonies were experiencing an economic boom. Urban centers were expanding on an unprecedented scale, and Africans were beginning to earn money over and above what they needed to pay taxes. This was particularly true in the mineral-rich colonies of Northern Rhodesia and Belgian Congo. It was during this period that the colonial powers began to put forward plans which called for rapid industrialization in some territories and expanded agricultural production in others. Dams, factories, roads, and communication networks were elevated to highest priority.

Up to this point, African peasant farmers had been restricted in the amount and type of cash crops they could produce. Postwar development plans, however, generally called for an increase in the amount of land under cash crop cultivation by Africans. In some cases new crops were introduced, and efforts were made to teach farmers to adopt improved methods of agriculture and thereby to increase the productivity of small farms. Where they resisted, peasants were forced to become involved in these development programs.

After 1945 a significant number of Africans began to demand more formal education and a fuller role in the economy. This was particularly so among the urbanized, who had high expectations after their significant contributions during the war years. At the end of the war, most African schools were still either traditional Muslim Koranic schools or mission schools. Formal schooling was usually only up to the primary level under the old colonial arrangements, since Africans were assumed to need only a basic facility in the language of the dominant colonial power and some skill in writing and numbers. Too much education, it was felt, could result in rising expectations which in turn might lead to incipient protests and this was the last thing that colonial governments wanted. Only a few members of the African elites, such as Kwame Nkrumah of the Gold Coast and Jomo Kenyatta of Kenya, left the colonies and traveled to Europe and the United States in order to secure advanced education before World War II. It was not a conscious policy of any of the colonial powers to educate Africans to fill bureaucratic and technical roles.

During the course of the war, however, and at a time when the colonies were being asked to increase their productivity, the number of European personnel who staffed posts in the colonies was severely depleted. The pressures placed on colonial economies to expand served to highlight the paucity of semiskilled, skilled, and professional African manpower. Attempts were made in some instances to utilize European technicians on private contracts, but this proved to be costly and created apprehensions among Africans about the growing entrenchment of Europeans. Educated and urbanized Africans were making demands and now appeared ready to engage in active protest to secure what they wanted. After the war, the colonial powers had no choice but to train Africans to fill bureaucratic and technical roles.

In the postwar plans adopted by the colonial powers, an emphasis was placed on the expansion of secondary and university opportunities for Africans. Britain trained new African elites in high schools and universities mostly on the African continent, at Fourah Bay College in Sierra Leone, for example. However, African administrators and technicians from French colonies were trained primarily in France, and African teachers were educated most frequently at William Ponty School in Senegal. Although these institutions accommodated a relatively small number of students, efforts were made to provide them with much more education than had been the case in previous years. With the demand for economic and political reforms, the growth of increased opportunities for formal education influenced the development of nationalist movements which emerged after the war.

In addition to change originating on the African continent, independence movements were greatly influenced by events in other parts of the world. After the war, European powers came to be dominated by more liberal, anticolonial points of view. Young administrators and missionaries from the major colonial powers began to express doubts about the policies their countries had adopted. And although decolonization was not part of a well-laid plan for any colonial power, immediately after the war programs were set in motion which accelerated the rate at which the colonies moved toward self-government. Independence for most countries thus became not only inevitable but also imminent. France was confronted with increasing pressures in Indochina and in North Africa; Britain was beset with demonstrations for national independence on the Indian subcontinent and in the Middle East; Belgium was in the midst of internal political squabbles between liberals and conservatives, clerics and anticlerics, in which Belgian Congo was the central issue. Throughout Europe, very serious questions were being raised about continued European involvement on the African continent.

The Intellectual Roots of African Nationalism

Africans played as important a role in the demise of colonialism as did the European powers. As already noted, many aspiring Africans had gone to Europe and the United States before and immediately following World War II. This was the first opportunity for such men as Nkrumah, Kenyatta, and Obote of Uganda to come together and to exchange ideas about how Africans should relate to the colonial situation. Several of those who led the struggle for independence could trace their formative experiences to such contacts with Africans from other parts of the continent who were also experiencing colonialism. These new political activists were greatly influenced in their ideas by the writings and teachings of pan-Africanists, such as W. E. B. DuBois, Marcus Garvey, and George Padmore from the Americas, and also by the ideas of Marxists, socialists, and communists they met in Europe. Few Africans committed themselves completely to the communist cause, but they were open to using it as a mechanism for the liberation of their people if it proved to have some merit. For example, African elites from the French colonies, upon achieving representation in the French National Assembly of the Fourth Republic, utilized their ties with the French Left to secure laws which led to the abolition of forced labor in the colonies as well as to an expansion of African political rights.

Later, when it became clear that France was going through a period of reaction against the communists, some Africans broke ranks and formed new coalitions.

One of the most significant convocations of Africans and pan-Africanists from throughout the world, the Fifth Pan-African Congress, took place in Manchester, England in 1945. The Congress was chaired by W. E. B. DuBois, and Africans from all over the continent were represented. The Congress adopted a strongly worded resolution condemning colonialism and calling for various social and economic reforms in the colonies. The delegates at the conference also demanded full independence for Black Africa, and it was resolved that no price was too great to pay for total African independence. Several notable African nationalists, including Jomo Kenyatta and Kwame Nkrumah, were at the conference. Nkrumah worked closely with Obote and Kenyatta and also developed important relationships with Leopold Senghor of Senegal and Sekou Touré of Guinea.

At this time most of the political activity among Africans was in London and Paris and not in Africa itself. By the late 1940s, however, these African intellectuals had returned to their own countries and had begun to mobilize their own campaigns for African independence. The tactics adopted were dependent upon local situations and also on the type of leadership which emerged. In francophone Africa the pattern was usually for African elites to secure political offices which allowed them to represent their territories either at the national level in Paris or at the federal level within their own geographic areas, whereas in anglophone Africa mass parties led the struggle for independence.

African Nationalism and Independence

Generally in British and French colonies where there were no European settlers the colonial powers looked more favorably upon the idea of internal self-government by Africans. Where there were settlers, however, the process of decolonization was less certain. A good example of typical British colonial disinvolvement in the absence of complicating settler interest was the case of the Gold Coast. This was the first colony in Black Africa to cast out British colonialism, and the struggle was led by Kwame Nkrumah, a man whose name became synonymous with African independence. Nkrumah returned to the Gold Coast in 1947 after completing his education in the United States, where he had studied the socialist, communist, and black nationalist thought of the day. Upon his return to West Africa, he began to pursue an active policy designed to seize political initiative from the colonial government. Nkrumah had been invited by some older African leaders to become the secretary of the

21. Kwame Nkrumah, the first president of Ghana.
Photo courtesy United Nations/ MB/ vb.

United Gold Coast Convention (UGCC) and in this role he was able to fashion a strategy for total independence. He called upon the people to join him in a "Positive Action Campaign" against colonialism. Through his organizational abilities Nkrumah was able to expand the cadre of UGCC members until it had branches in five hundred locations throughout the colony.

The Gold Coast had no significant European population at that time and Nkrumah's efforts were aimed for the most part at the colonial administration itself. In the early days the activities of the United Gold Coast Convention were confined to peaceful demonstrations growing out of specific economic or political grievances, but as time went on the organization became more militant and riots were not uncommon. Perhaps the most significant of these protests occurred in 1949 and centered around the high price of commodities made available to Africans in the capital city of Accra. What had started out as passive resistance by the UGCC ended in violence, and the top leadership of the organization, including Nkrumah himself, was arrested.

From this point on, the colonial regime succeeded in splitting the movement by courting the more cautious and moderate African leaders. The colonial government set up a commission on constitutional reform, and this had the effect of convincing the more conservative elements in the UGCC that they were at least gaining some political recognition and should allow Britain to work out a final solution at its own pace. Nkrumah rejected this rationale, contending the struggle should continue. He broke away from the UGCC and in 1949 organized his own political party, the Convention People's Party (CPP), calling for "Self-Government Now." The British government subsequently accepted the commission's recommendations for a constitutional government patterned on British parliamentary democracy.

Nkrumah, on the other hand, continued to build a power base for himself and his organization so that he and the CPP would be ready, when the time came, to take over the government. He agitated and protested and was even arrested again while the independence settlement was being worked out. In February 1951, during a period when Nkrumah was in jail, general elections were held in which the UGCC was opposed by the CPP. In these elections, the CPP was the overwhelming victor, outpolling the UGCC by a margin of more than ten to one, thus winning 34 of 38 municipal and rural council seats. Nkrumah's party had demonstrated its strength and he was subsequently released from jail and asked to form an interim government. Many around him began to see Nkrumah as a messiah, a redeemer, *Osagyefo!* Over the next four and a half years, Nkrumah, both as an elected executive and as the charismatic leader of a dynamic political party, began to lay the groundwork for independence. Finally, on March 6, 1957, Ghana became the first Black African independent state from among the British territories.

Similar patterns of development could be observed in other anglophone countries. In Tanganyika, in the early 1950s, Julius Nyerere founded a mass party, the Tanganyika African National Union (TANU), which succeeded in outmaneuvering all other political parties and eventually led Tanganyika to independence in 1961. Settler interests were few in Tanganyika, and Britain bequeathed the same constitutional framework to that East African nation as it had to Ghana in West Africa. In places such as Uganda and Nigeria, which also had only limited settler involvement, political competition took place according to the traditions of British parliamentary democracy, and, although one party did not dominate, the drive to independence was on the whole orderly and peaceful.

Kenya, on the other hand, was characterized by extensive settler involvement. From as early as the first decade of the twentieth century Britain had encouraged European settlement in this "White Man's Country," which was known for its cool and fertile highlands not unlike the British countryside. A conscious effort was made to attract only the elite of British society in order to construct a clearly white-dominated colony with subservient blacks. Lower-class whites were not encouraged to settle in Kenya; it was felt that miscegenation might take place, thus creating a coloured class as in South Africa and lusophone Africa.

Europeans flocked to Kenya between 1904 and the 1950s, with periods of intensive immigration in the interwar years and immediately following World War II. As the settlers arrived and became entrenched, laws were enacted to protect their rights and to otherwise give them the advantage over Africans. African land was alienated, and measures such as hut and poll taxes were introduced to compel peasants to work on European farms and plantations. Robbed of their land, Africans were forced onto overcrowded and overcultivated reserves, and a pass system, similar to that in South Africa, was introduced to regulate African population movements.

As early as the 1920s Africans attempted to make the relationship with the Europeans in Kenya one of partnership, but the trend was consistently toward settler dominance over the indigenous population, who, as a matter of course and a fact of law, were denied social advancement. Racial discrimination and segregation became a fact of life. Africans, through labor unions and other types of interest organizations, pushed for fairer treatment, but with only limited success. Eventually, in 1952, protests exploded into a full-scale uprising, the Mau Mau Rebellion. Intense open conflict between Mau Mau guerrillas and the colonial regime continued until 1954. More than 12,000 rebels were killed and over 2,000 loyalist Africans were listed as fatalities of the struggle. Europeans, the designated enemy, suffered comparatively few casualties: only 32 died as a result of Mau Mau assaults. Although this struggle did not lead to immediate political independence for Kenya, it did set the wheels in motion for total independence. Settler interests began to lose ground, and Kenya finally achieved independence on December 13, 1963, with Jomo Kenyatta as its leader.

French colonies in Africa, with the exception of Algeria, were not characterized to any great degree by European settlement. France viewed Algeria not so much as a colony but as a province of the metropole. By the 1950s more than one million Europeans had settled there and, as in Kenya, the settler presence was accompanied by the alienation of land. Although Europeans constituted only 8 percent of the population in Algeria, they came to possess approximately 85 percent of the arable land.

In spite of the protests of such Arab nationalists as Farhat Abbas, France had no intention of turning over the government to the indigenous popula-

22. Kenya achieves independence, December 13, 1963.
Photo courtesy Ministry of Information and Broadcasting, Kenya.

tion. Algerians had no alternative, therefore, but to confront France in a revolutionary struggle. The fighting began in November 1954 and lasted for more than seven years. At its height France committed more than a half-million troops to the war. The Algerian revolutionaries were organized into seven military districts, six inside the country and one outside (the Army of National Liberation in Tunisia). Most of the actual combat took place in Algeria between French soldiers and Arab guerrillas, but a terrorist campaign was also waged in France. Thousands of Algerians and Frenchmen were casualties of this protracted and bitter struggle, until finally, in 1962, France agreed to a political settlement with the National Liberation Front in which thousands of French settlers lost their businesses, estates, and extensive farms and vineyards.

This, however, was not the typical scenario for decolonization in French colonies. Independence became a real possibility for most of the French colonies in West Africa and Equatorial Africa when a referendum was held in these territories in 1958. As a result of the Algerian Revolution, France's Fourth Republic had collapsed. General Charles DeGaulle, who took over power in an effort to restore the country to stability, was granted almost dictatorial powers to deal with national political and economic troubles. Among his major priorities was the need to silence growing demands from the African colonies for total independence. On September 28, 1958, a referendum was held in which Africans were asked to vote on whether or not they wanted to remain a part of the French community. It was felt that most colonies would not accept the challenge and vote yes, and indeed only French Guinea, under the leadership of Sekou Touré, voted for independence. Touré had hoped for the establishment of some form of West African federation of states, but this idea was not popular among other African leaders in French West Africa. As a result of the referendum, France withdrew all of its technical and administrative assistance and left Guinea totally on its own. Guinea, though independent, was faced with economic collapse, and Touré had few alternatives but to turn to the United States and the Eastern Bloc for assistance.

Guinea had set an example, however, and other French colonies soon began to reconsider their decision to remain a part of the French community. In 1959, Senegal and Soudan (Mali) formed the Mali Federation and demanded, and were granted, independence. While the Federation did not last, and the two states separated in 1960, others followed their lead and by 1960 all French colonies in West and Equatorial Africa were independent.

Significantly, the African leaders of France's sub-Saharan colonies had all been trained in the French colonial administration and some even in the French National Assembly. They had participated in local politics before independence and were much influenced by the French brand of politics and government. There was no apparent need for the constitutional conventions and the building of governmental organizations which characterized British territories.

Belgian Congo had a substantial white settler involvement, and when the "winds of change" began to approach gale force across Black Africa, Belgium only reluctantly began to contemplate the idea of an independent Congo. Like France, Belgium was beset by enormous domestic problems at home in the late 1950s; but, unlike France, Belgium had not begun to train an indigenous leadership class in the colony. Before 1957, Africans became involved in politics only as a result of their association with European political groups which had set up branches in the colony, and through indigenous cultural associations.

Belgium practiced a form of pragmatic paternalism, claiming that the colonial power dominated Africans so that they might be served. The colonial welfare state was supported by a "Platonic Trinity," which included the colonial bureaucracy, large economic concerns, and the Catholic Church, all of which were seen by the Belgians to contribute to the creation of a docile, subservient African population.[1] The state regulated African social behavior; the companies employed Africans in low-paying, low-skilled jobs; and the missions educated and socialized the African people to accept a subordinate role in society.

23. Senegalese schoolgirls celebrate the anniversary of their country's independence.
Photo courtesy United Nations/ CH/ jr.

In the postwar era Belgium began to develop a select African bourgeoisie with the intention of creating an indigenous "buffer" class, educated in Belgian culture and supportive of the system. Yet, at the same time, it was apparent that segregation and discrimination were emerging. As a result, instead of developing the supportive attitudes that the Belgians had hoped for, many Africans began to take note of the contradictions which existed in society. They were inspired by the writings of a young Belgian professor who in 1955 published a proposal for the independence of the Congo by 1985. Following this, African organizations began to emerge and to call for total independence. At first these groups were not political parties but were indigenous cultural organizations such as the *Abako* among the Kongo people, the Lulua Brotherhood, and the Songye Society. Not until late 1957 did these ethnic associations begin to evolve into political parties competing for elective office. Political party activity gradually escalated in 1958, and by 1959, on the eve of independence, party activity was at its peak with more than a hundred separate, predominantly ethnically-based political parties in the urban areas. Only two parties, however, the *Abako* and the African Socialist Party, had any real roots in the countryside. The cities had become centers of African discontent and protest; political and labor union rallies were frequently held and were often accompanied by inflammatory speeches and mass and bloody rioting. A significant number of the rural population were politicized after 1959 when African party activity was temporarily banned following large-scale rioting.

Among the political organizations to develop in this period, only one approached being a national movement, Patrice Lumumba's National Congolese Movement (MNC). The MNC was not ethnically based, as were most other parties, and had branches in all areas of the country. But independence fever spread so quickly that there was little time for the formation of a dominant nationalist movement in the Congo.

Belgian efforts to temper African demands for political participation only led to more violence, and it was clear that nothing short of total independence would suffice. In response to these pressures, a conference to discuss the possibility of immediate independence was held in Brussels in January 1960, and six months later, in spite of the protests of European settlers, Belgian Congo was free and independent.

Multiple factors shaped the course of independence in the Congo: internal pressures from within Belgium itself; the rising economic costs of maintaining the colony; Belgian reluctance to be overly repressive; and there were many other intangibles. Perhaps the most important factor, however, was the perception of the Congolese elite that the time had come when the political system would admit change, and they directed their actions toward that end.

The last major European colonies to achieve independence were the Portuguese possessions of Guinea-Bissau, Mozambique, and Angola. Of all the colonial powers, Portugal had the longest history of an African presence, occupying coastal enclaves as early as the fifteenth century. Until the 1930s Portuguese colonial policy could best be described as exploitative neglect. Africans were either left alone or forced to work as slaves or contract labor, depending upon the economic exigencies of the time. Following World War II, Portugal began more active involvement in its colonies, encouraging European settlement in Angola and Mozambique. However, even where there were few settlers, as in Guinea-Bissau, Africans were kept in a state of near servitude, with little opportunity for education or socioeconomic advancement.

Portugal ruled with the same authoritarian zeal in Africa as at home, but in the colonies ethnic origin as well as class determined the structure of society. Since the colonies were thought to be provinces of Portugal, it was unthinkable

24. A decorated arch marks the attainment of independence by Rwanda.
Photo courtesy United Nations/ BZ/ b.

that they could be set free. It was this rationale that eventually led African liberation movements to begin an armed struggle in Angola in 1961, to be followed by wars of liberation in Guinea-Bissau and in Mozambique, starting in 1962 and 1964 respectively. The factors which determined the nature of the nationalist struggle were not necessarily related to the number of settlers in Portuguese colonies but rather to the manner in which Portugal perceived its possessions. These were all seen as extensions of the metropole, and for this reason Portuguese leaders felt justified in spending well over half of the country's annual revenues for military purposes. They fought almost as hard to hold on to Guinea-Bissau as they did Angola and Mozambique. Public unrest in Portugal over the desirability of continuing counterrevolutionary activities in the colonies was one of the factors which led to the military coup in April 1974, which brought to power a reform-minded military regime. By this time it was apparent that the costs of maintaining the colonies far outweighed the long-term gains, and it was decided precipitously to acknowledge the call for African independence. Guinea-Bissau achieved independence in 1974 and Mozambique and Angola in 1975.

Conclusion

In just over twenty years virtually the entire continent of Africa had thrown off the yoke of imperialism. In most areas the colonial presence had lasted no more than sixty or seventy years and Africans had never ceased to struggle in one form or another. A multiplicity of factors in the post World War II era combined to make the drive for decolonization and independence an irresistible force. Local factors often determined the nature of the decolonization process as well as the tenor of the independence movement. Dynamic African leadership and organization and the extent of European settler interests were key variables. Where Europeans were able to entrench themselves, nothing short of armed rebellion or revolution would dislodge them. History has shown that the more established the Europeans are in Africa, the more difficult they are to move—for example, in South Africa, Rhodesia, and Namibia, the last strongholds of white minority rule in Black Africa. It seems reasonable to suggest that these redoubts will eventually suffer the same fate as did the Portuguese colonies. Much depends upon the ability of African liberation movements in those areas to attract outside military support for their efforts.

Although most of Black Africa has secured political independence, it has not been able to achieve total economic independence. As brief as the colonial period was, it was of sufficient duration to intertwine the economies of Africa with those of Europe. Africa remains not only underdeveloped but also dependent upon the former imperial powers and the capitalist West in general. African states today continue to attempt to consolidate their political independence through the twin goals of economic independence and broadly based social development. The challenge to future African generations will be to overcome the ill effects of dependency and underdevelopment, the legacy of colonialism.

NOTE

1. Crawford Young, *Politics in the Congo* (Princeton: Princeton University Press, 1965), p. 10.

SUGGESTIONS FOR FURTHER READING

Apter, David. *The Gold Coast in Transition.* Princeton, New Jersey: Princeton University Press, 1955.
Carter, Gwendolen M., ed. *African One-Party States.* Ithaca, New York: Cornell University Press, 1962.
Coleman, James S., and Carl J. Rosberg. *Political Parties and National Integration in Tropical Africa.* Berkeley, California: University of California Press, 1964.
Fanon, Frantz. *A Dying Colonialism.* New York: Grove Press, 1965.

Gibson, Richard. *African Liberation Movements*. London: Oxford University Press, 1972.

Hodgkin, Thomas. *Nationalism in Colonial Africa*. New York: New York University Press, 1957.

Wallerstein, Immanuel. *The Politics of Independence*. New York: Vintage, 1961.

Young, Crawford. *Politics in the Congo*. Princeton, New Jersey: Princeton University Press, 1965.

Zolberg, Aristide. *Creating Political Order*. Chicago, Illinois: Rand McNally, 1966.

THE TRADITIONAL IN CONTEMPORARY AFRICA

III

James H. Vaughan
Social and Political Organization in Traditional Societies

11 Philosophers have long noted that man is a social animal, and social scientists have confirmed this, observing that it is usually through cooperative behavior that mankind survives and surmounts the problems encountered in particular settings. However, groups can be organized according to many different principles. For example, they may be related by reason of shared residence, or through genealogy, regardless of where they live, and they may, of course, be organized according to both of these principles with each organization having a kind of precedence in certain spheres of life. These observations are neither more nor less true for Africans than they are for any other peoples of the world, but Africans are organized sometimes in ways which are unfamiliar to others. This chapter will explore some of those ways and describe the characteristics and functions of African organizations.

From time to time in the following discussion approximate percentages are suggested for the occurrence of certain institutions. These figures are derived from material in the "Ethnographic Atlas,"[1] which presents characteristics on 862 societies of the world. Of this number, 277 may be said to be from sub-Saharan Africa. This, however, represents only a fraction of the total number of African societies, and it may reflect a greater accuracy of reporting for some areas and societies than for others. Therefore, the assertions of frequencies are to be taken as suggestions rather than as precise representations.

Marriage and the Family

In all societies the family is of major importance, though its forms and functions may vary. There are two functions of the family that are widespread in African societies. First, the family is the social unit primarily responsible for the early development and socialization of the young, and second, very frequently it is a primary economic unit of the society and is organized in ways which facilitate production.

There are several characteristics of African marriage which differ significantly from what is commonly thought of as being typical of marriage in European or American societies. African marriage is best seen as a formal relationship between two groups of people rather than between two individuals. The marriage of course focuses upon individuals, but each individual represents a larger group. In a loose sense African marriage is an alliance between two families through the conjugal union of a female from one with a male from the other. Both as a symbol of the marriage and as a tangible tie between the two groups, there is a transfer of wealth from the family of the groom to the family of the bride. This is called *bridewealth* and usually consists of money, livestock, or some other socially recognized valuable. Bridewealth occurs in about 80 percent of African societies, and in another 10 percent there are variations such as small token payments or services performed for the bride's family.

Bridewealth is a complex institution with many functions and motivations. In societies such as those of traditional Africa, where every individual's labor is important regardless of sex, bridewealth compensates a family for the loss of one of its members. (This assumes that the bride will go to live with her husband.) Perhaps more importantly, but more indirectly, the transfer of wealth gives both families a vested interest in the survival of the marriage; one group has invested its resources in it and the other has received benefits which might have to be forfeited should the marriage fail. Finally, in most African societies the formal action of paying bridewealth is a major symbol of the legitimacy of the union, and, as such, bridewealth in Africa is as important as is a marriage certificate in other societies.

Another very common characteristic of African marriage is *polygyny*, the custom which permits a man to have two or more wives. Polygyny is preferred in approximately 98 percent of African societies. Two questions invariably arise concerning this custom: How can polygyny operate in a society with a relatively equal number of males and females, and why should such a custom be preferred in a society? The first is very much easier to answer than the second.

Permitting or preferring polygyny does not mean that all or even most marriages must take this form. Polygyny rates of 25 to 30 percent might be regarded as typical, and a rate of 50 percent as high. But even if this is taken into consideration, there is still the problem of the ratio of sexes. This difficulty may be overcome by the custom of having men marry at significantly older ages than women. As we saw in chapter 2, the distribution of ages in traditional societies is such that generally there are more individuals at any given younger age than there are at an older age. For example, there will be more individuals over the age of 15 than there will be over the age of 25 (see figure 9). Consequently, if men delay marriage until age 25 while women marry at age 15, there will be more women of marriageable age than there will be men of marriageable age. Under such conditions, polygyny becomes much more practicable. Actual census figures confirm these observations. In the Guinean census of 1954–55, the singulate mean age at marriage (SMAM) of women was 15.8 while for men it was 26.7, and the ratio of married women to married men was 168:100. In contrast, in Burundi, where the SMAM for women and men was 22.1 and 22.9 respectively, the ratio of married women to married men was only 104:100.

Why polygyny exists, or when and why it began, cannot be answered. The available information on this institution comes from societies that are fully functioning, and there is no evidence on its beginnings or why it was adopted. Furthermore, an explanation as to why an individual practices polygyny would likely be suspect on the grounds that he or she would be conditioned by the prior presence of the custom in the society. However, it is possible to note the way in which the custom interacts with various circumstances that prevail in African societies, and thus we may at least approach an understanding of its

POPULATION PYRAMID

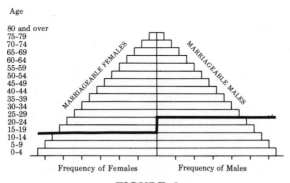

FIGURE 9

persistence. For example, it has been concluded that polygyny has the effect of lowering fertility.[2] This leads to improved maternal health and decreases infant mortality, since having too many children is bad for both mother and child. Also, through polygyny the population base of a family may be broadened and thus made more secure. In agricultural societies, which characterize most of traditional Africa, labor is critical and a polygynous family is a more productive, stable, and secure group.

Polygynous families necessitate special arrangements that lead to a complexity of structure not found in monogamous families. Westerners think of the family as an indivisible unit, but in a polygynous family there are internal subdivisions which are frequently recognized by its members and which become the basis for differentiation of activities and feelings. For example, each wife and her children may have mutual cooperative and emotional ties which are stronger than those they have with the other wives and their children. Although this provides a smaller, more intimate reference group within the larger group, it also raises organizational problems and has the potential for engendering competition between subsets. It is therefore common that in polygynous families there are fairly formal rules which will minimize destructive competition. For example, among the Hausa of Nigeria a system of seniority among wives establishes an order which is not based upon favoritism, and sexual relations between husband and wife are on a strictly rotational basis; this reduces the probability of jealousy, although the term for co-wife is still "the jealous one."[3] Co-wives tend to conform in their behavior toward their husband lest they be accused of seeking favors, and cooperation among wives in relation to their husband often elicits favors and advantages not typical of monogamous marriages. A successful husband in a polygynous household must be a careful manager of his time, his resources, and even his affections; and a successful wife must balance possessiveness with cooperation and learn to share both resources and affection. In 1960, I knew two wives of the same man who voluntarily saw less of him so that he might spend more time with a new wife; in 1974, the three wives were cooperating to make the newest co-wife happy.

Just as polygynous families have certain advantages, larger familial groupings may also prove beneficial. These compound units, consisting of linked "stem families," are called extended families. The linkage is usually through ties of kinship. For example, there might be a man, his wives (in a polygynous family), his unmarried children, married sons, daughters-in-law, grandchildren, and possibly the wives of his grandsons. Such an extended polygynous family is depicted in figure 10. Obviously, such families are complex units with greater potential for cooperation in economic and social matters than smaller units,

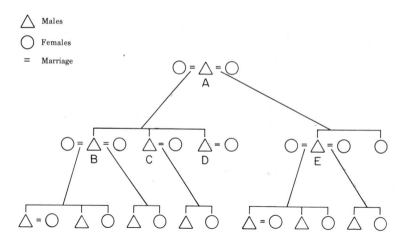

EXTENDED FAMILY

FIGURE 10

though of course they too may have organizational problems. Some of the dynamics of a polygynous society with extended families may be suggested by noting in figure 10 that the death of A could very possibly lead to a split, with E and his stem family, together with his unmarried sister, forming the nucleus of a new extended family, while B, C, and D would remain together, though with obvious potential to separate as their families expand. Extended families occur in about 43 percent of African societies, with a marked concentration in West Africa, as, for example, among the Ashanti.

Marital residence patterns, that is, the location of the households of married couples, are of major importance in African societies and differ greatly from those of Europe and America. The most common residence pattern found in Africa is that wherein a woman leaves her family and goes to live with her husband. This pattern is technically called *virilocal residence.* Approximately 94 percent of African societies prefer or require that a woman ultimately live with her husband and his kinsmen. However, since a person may reckon kinsmen in several ways, there are two major distinctions within virilocal residence. In approximately 84 percent of the societies, a wife lives with her husband and his patrilineal kinsmen, a pattern called *patrilocal residence.* When the wife lives with her husband and he is living with matrilineal kinsmen it is called *avunculocal residence.* This occurs in 8 percent of African societies. (The remaining 2 percent have the option of either patrilocal or avunculocal residence). Patrilocal residence is the custom in so many societies that naming one seems arbitrary, but it is particularly characteristic of pastoral societies like the Maasai. Avunculocal residence has a slight concentration in West Central Africa among societies like the Kongo. In less than 2 percent of the societies a husband is expected to live with his wife and her matrilineal kinsmen, a custom known as *matrilocal residence* and illustrated by the Bemba of Zambia. Under 3 percent prefer that the couple establish an independent residence, which is called *neolocal residence*.

Kinship and Descent

The African family, intricate and complex though it may be, is an elementary unit of society. It is an individual's first milieu, and frequently it is the society's fundamental subsistence unit. But it is still a relatively small and vulnerable unit, even allowing for its extended forms and for alliances formed through marriages. It simply does not constitute an extensive group of adults intrinsically pledged to mutual support and security. Further, there is a need for just such a larger group, particularly in societies with relatively low levels of technology in environments which are conducive to disease and high mortality rates. One of the most effective of such larger social units and one which is perpetuated by a simple set of rules is the *descent group*. A descent group is a subgroup of kinsmen with extensive yet exclusive membership which exists in perpetuity or so long as its members reproduce.

In most societies individuals recognize kinsmen bilaterally, that is on both paternal and maternal sides. However, such a group does not exist permanently, for it is necessarily ego-centered. One's own kinsmen are different from one's cousin's, and furthermore everyone is a kinsman of very many people who in turn may not be related to each other. However, when descent is reckoned through a single ancestral line, these problems are eliminated. When the rule of *unilineal descent* is applied, two major types of descent groups are generated: *patrilineal descent* and *matrilineal descent*. In patrilineal descent, relation is reckoned through males only, and in matrilineal, through females only. (Caution: Do not view this unilineal descent as "father's side" or "mother's side." Descent is reckoned through males only or through females only. For example, in a patrilineal system, although your father's sister's children are "on your father's side," they are *not* in your patrilineage, since they are related to you through a female. To take an electrical analogy, it is as though males are conductors and females nonconductors in a patrilineal system, while in a matri-

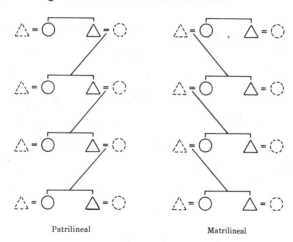

Patrilineal   Matrilineal

UNILINEAL DESCENT SYSTEMS

FIGURE 11

lineal system it is the women who are the conductors and the men who are not.) Figure 11 illustrates two groups of individuals, one related patrilineally and one matrilineally.

Persons of Euramerican ancestry do not reckon their descent unilineally. They consider themselves descended equally through males and females, a system called *bilateral*. (Most Americans do acquire their surnames by the patrilineal principle, however.)

Approximately 88 percent of African societies reckon descent unilineally, with a marked preference (74 percent) for patrilineal descent, as among the Nuer. Matrilineal descent occurs in only about 14 percent, most of which, like the Suku, the Tonga, and the Bemba, live along a belt running across South Central Africa. Of the remaining societies approximately 7 percent reckon their descent bilaterally, and 5 percent combine both forms of unilineal descent into a form called *double unilineal descent*. Each of these latter types has a very spotty distribution, though it might be noted that most of the hunting societies, such as the San and the Pygmies, tend to have bilateral descent.

Groups generated by the rules of unilineal descent are usually called *clans*, and subdivisions of clans are called *lineages*. Occasionally these terms are used interchangeably, and more rarely the term *sib* is used as a synonym of clan. Clans are probably the most important and widespread social groups in African societies. In many parts of Africa clans constitute corporate groups in that they are considered to be legal entities, and land is ultimately owned by these bodies rather than by individuals. Although individuals usually have full use of land, they are restricted in their right to transfer it to any person not a member of the clan. Clan legends may be the society's main source of history, and clan ancestors may constitute a pantheon of spirits intimately concerned with the daily activities of living members. The existence of clan ancestors assures the living that they will have an importance and "existence" after death. Clan members are also ready and willing to assist one another in times of crisis or ceremonial need. Finally, the clan is an individual's ultimate reference group; it is his identity, his reputation, his pride. One African expressed his feelings about his clan in the following way: "If I have walked for a very long way and I am tired and can walk no farther, I will collapse with exhaustion. But if someone says the name of my clan, I will get up and walk on." In simple terms, he was saying that his clan is more important than his tiredness, more important than his problems, that its very memory supports him. Such a view is not unusual, for a clan often supports its members psychologically as well as materially.

A final point might be made about kinship and the support it provides an individual. Anthropologists often note that societies have different kinship terminologies, and particular emphasis is placed upon what is called *cousin terminology*, the terms which a society applies to kinsmen of one's own generation—persons whom English-speakers call brother, sister, or cousin. This is a highly specialized and complicated topic and only a few observations need be made about such terminology in Africa. First, the pattern that English-speakers use and which we might think "natural" is very rare in Africa, occurring in only 3 percent of African societies. Secondly, and more importantly, the two systems used in about 60 percent of African societies have the effect of "generating" siblings (brothers and sisters in our terminology). Although in our society the terms brother and sister have very narrow definitions, there is no reason why our cousins should not be called by these same terms—and that is precisely what approximately one-fourth of African societies do. Of course, individuals know the difference between a "brother" who is a true sibling and one who is, say, the son of a father's brother. Nonetheless, the system means that no one is without siblings and the mutual support and responsibility which is characteristic of relationships between siblings. Naive Europeans or Americans have sometimes thought that Africans could not understand such terms as uncle, mother, or son because they seemingly used the terms so loosely, when in fact it was the non-Africans who failed to understand the African system. That system is noteworthy since it provides every individual with a group of "primary" kinsmen, and that has many advantages in societies which rely upon close cooperation, as opposed to our isolating type of terminology in a society which emphasizes individuality.

Frequently, kinship terms may be used between nonkinsmen to indicate relative status or intensity of relationship. An older person might be called by a term equivalent to the English word grandparent, or a companion might be called by a sibling term, though neither person is related to the speaker.

Social Stratification

Class

Stratification by *class* is another way of generating social groupings. It is usually based upon the unequal distribution of some socially valued item. In industrial societies class is primarily based upon wealth and the power, influence, and reputation it engenders. In traditional African society this process is somewhat more complex. Wealth is important, that cannot be denied, and in some societies it is the principal basis of power. In others, however, the reverse is often true; that is, a person may have wealth *because* he is regarded as a person of power, influence, and reputation. These latter qualities, furthermore, are often based, at least in part, as much upon a person's hereditary position in society as upon his individual achievement. This may be epitomized in the concept of nobility, by which is meant a class of people, usually clans, who have access to power and influence solely or largely on the basis of their membership in that group. Typically it is manifest in terms of a ruling clan or clans who constitute a society's nobility and thereby occupy positions of privilege as compared to the rest of the populace. However, in traditional societies the differences may be quite minor and of little material importance except for the few nobles who actually hold offices and wield effective power. About one-third of African societies, exemplified by the Nyoro of Uganda, have clearly demarcated class systems, although slightly more than one-half recognize distinctions between those who possess valuables and those who do not.

Caste

Grouping by occupation is another basis for social differentiation which is found in many societies throughout the world. Along the Guinea coast of West Africa, this takes the form of craft guilds. These guilds are able to operate as truly professional groups, setting standards, running systems of apprenticeship, and regulating prices. But a more widespread form of craft organization is the *craft caste*, which occurs particularly in the western Sudan, the Upper Nile, and in Ethiopia and the Horn.

A caste is an endogamous hereditary social grouping: that is, members must marry within the caste into which they are born. It is, therefore, a closed system, the only recruitment being by birth. Most Euramericans are familiar with the term caste from its manifestation in India. However, this is but a particular form of caste, and an unusually complex version at that. Many of the Indian characteristics are not typical of African castes. For example, the notion that certain castes are despised, which apparently is characteristic of India, is not present in all African systems. The strong hierarchical nature of the Indian system, while not totally lacking in Africa, is nonetheless often secondary to the tasks which each caste performs for the mutual benefit of its members.

In Africa, castes are therefore associated with one or more occupational specialties, the most common being ironsmithing. The effect is to produce a group of persons who by birth will be craft specialists. This system thus affords a long period for apprenticeship, and since recruitment is by birth there is little danger that the craft will die out for lack of interested professionals. In at least some African societies, such as the Margi of northeastern Nigeria,[4] each caste does something that another does not, yet needs. Thus, they are in a symbiotic relationship, for their mutual benefit. About one-fifth of African societies have such craft castes and another 5 percent have castes which are additionally based upon ethnicity. For example, the pygmoid Twa live as a hunting and craft caste among the Nilotic and Bantu peoples of Rwanda.

Limbry

Another form of social stratification which must be discussed is usually termed slavery but may best be called *limbry*. This is an unusually difficult topic to discuss. First, the institution has been illegal for many years; descriptions of it are therefore frequently incomplete, inaccurate, or otherwise faulty. Second, the imposition of European and, to a lesser extent, Arab slaving and conceptions of slavery significantly altered the indigenous institution; it became necessary for Africans in contact with slavers to have persons to trade or else they might have been enslaved themselves. This distorted the indigenous institution, making it both more extensive and more inhumane. Furthermore, the African institution in such areas of contact became very much like European commercial slavery. Third, there is some evidence that the indigenous African

25. An ironsmith at work in M'Baiki, Central African Republic.
Photo courtesy United Nations/ Gararcciolo/ b.

institution was markedly unlike what is commonly understood by the term slavery.

It recently has been suggested[5] that the outstanding characteristic of the African institution was its tendency to make its members marginal to the society, neither a part of the society nor apart from it—suspended, as it were, in a social limbo. Members of limbic institutions were not freemen, and they may have had masters for whom they worked, but in traditional African societies they were not treated as though they were inanimate, nor were they unduly exploited. Their limbry consisted less in what they did than in what they were in their societies: that is, they were marginal people. Among the frequent conditions which could lead to this state were capture in warfare and punishment for serious crime. Once established, the position tended to be hereditary, though there was some variation in this. The existing data, albeit tenuous, suggest that about 80 percent of African societies had limbry.

The institution was observed in operation among the Margi,[6] and there it was found to be surprisingly benign. One member of the limbry class was a man of some wealth and considerable prestige. Furthermore, among the Margi one major political office was reserved for members of this class. In many other African societies members were treated with consideration and kindness, much as though they were part of their masters' extended families. In sum, African limbry, as opposed to slavery, was a form of institutional marginality in which individuals were restricted in their participation in the society but were not on the whole mistreated, dehumanized, or exploited.

Age Grades

Stratification by age generates yet another form of social grouping in Africa. Although the institution can become quite complex, the fundamental principle is simple. All persons within given ages constitute an *age set*. They occupy a status which is called an *age grade*. At an interval usually equal to the age span within the set, that age set moves, in an appropriate ceremony, to the next age grade. In this fashion the society is divided into a number of age grades through which its members pass. The several age grades have distinctive responsibilities and privileges associated with them. Thus, in addition to providing for individuals reference groups composed roughly of their peers, the age-grade system constitutes an organization charged with the implementation of social goals.

Figure 12 illustrates a very simple and idealized system in which the society has four grades of fifteen years duration, though the last includes all older persons. Each individual is born into the Red grade. At fifteen-year intervals, all of the members of Red—whose ages may differ by as much as fifteen years—

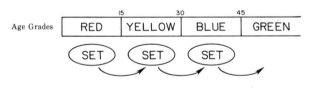

AGE—GRADE SYSTEM

FIGURE 12

become members of Yellow, while the members of Yellow move to Blue, and so on.

Variations on the age-grade system include several sets within a grade, an open period for entering a set followed by a closed period during which individuals must wait for the next open period, an age-grade system which covers only a portion of the life span, and, among some peoples of northeastern Africa, a cycling age-grade system in which the names of grades are limited and are repeated at intervals. The cycling systems may produce a situation in which a society's older members are in a grade with the same name as that to which younger members belong, which, in turn, may lead to a useful alliance between them. Age grades are very important in East Africa, and are found as well in parts of West and Central Africa.

Political Organization

An organization which focuses upon the public affairs of an autonomous territorial group is referred to as a political organization. Political organization has been defined as "that aspect of the total organization which is concerned with the establishment and maintenance of internal cooperation and external independence."[7] Such a definition, however, gives no hint of the variety or complexity of ways in which these ends may be accomplished. Within sub-Saharan Africa there exist some of the world's most simple political systems, as well as some of the most complex; within a radius of about five hundred miles one can find a full range of complexity of political organization, from nomadic bands, through intermediate forms, to complex kingdoms.

There is so much diversity in the structures and complexities of African political systems that a fundamental underlying principle may be overlooked. That is, virtually all of these diverse political organizations are based upon the validity of public means of resolving disputes and conflicts, that is, upon the *rule of law*. This is not to say that traditional societies have statutes which in and of themselves regulate behavior—rarely is there anything so conscious or formal; rather, members of societies accept that there is a moral basis to public order and that publicly sanctioned resolutions of disputes and conflicts are necessary for the continuance of social life beyond the family or clan.

In more complex societies the administration of justice was relatively formal and specialized. Lower courts with the right of appeal to higher courts existed in societies as widespread as the Nupe, the Nyoro, and the Lozi, among others. However, in other societies, such as the Ndendehule, the Kpelle, and the Tiv, and sometimes within complex societies like the Nyoro, there were more informal means of arriving at a publicly acceptable settlement to disputes. But in all these societies there is a respect for the rule of law, whether formal or informal, which promotes order and cooperation. Of course, this does not mean that disputes do not arise; it speaks only for the perceived need to resolve such conflict. So long as each political unit regarded itself as autonomous, disputes between units were often not resolvable in a peaceful manner—indeed, warfare might occur with some frequency. Although African societies seem to have had a strong basis in internal law, they seem not to have been much concerned with "intersocietal" law. Finally, although there were efforts to codify and formalize traditional law in many parts of Africa, most Africans today live under national legal systems which, though reflecting much that is traditional, have largely modified or eliminated traditional courts.

A pioneering work on African political systems noted that there were three types of systems: "a group of people all of whom are united to one another by ties of kinship, so that political relations are coterminous with kinship relations . . . societies in which a lineage structure is the framework of the political system . . . [and] societies in which an administrative organization is the framework of the political structure."[8] These three do not exhaust the political types found in traditional African societies. For example, in some societies the age-grade system may constitute the structure of political organization. Furthermore, as knowledge of African societies has increased it has become clear that each political type is capable of subdivision or reformulation. Nonetheless, these three types are illustrative and this discussion will be limited to them.

The societies of Africa in which political relations and kinship are coterminous are few, but the San are illustrative of the type. The !Kung, a San subgroup who live in the Kalahari Desert of Namibia, live in nomadic bands, hunting and foraging over many hundreds of square miles, rarely seeing a member of another band. A typical band numbers from twenty-five to thirty individuals, and the members are related either by ties of kinship or by marriage. Bands are mutually autonomous, though they are not hostile to one another, and intermarriage creates ties of support and friendship between neighboring bands. The area in which a band hunts and gathers wild foods, together with its water holes, is the property of the band as a whole and constitutes its only resource. Each band has a headman who leads it in its migration and represents it in dealings with other bands. It is an office with few specific duties, no privileges, but grave responsibilities. The headman is much like the head of a large extended family (though a band in fact is a collection of nuclear families) and must co-ordinate the activities of the familial units as they eke out a living in this inhospitable environment. Most decisions are reached by consensus and the head-

man does not need to arbitrate disputes. In the final analysis, cooperative behavior and consensual agreement upon norms and values hold the band together
with the headman acting largely as their "presiding officer."

In many African societies, such as the Tiv of Nigeria, a more subtle relationship exists between kinship and politics. In such societies, all of which have unilineal descent and clans with lineage subdivisions, two principles from the
descent system have far-reaching political consequences. The first might be
referred to as the structural regulation of internal affairs (see figure 13). Here a

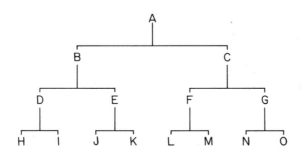

SEGMENTARY LINEAGE PRINCIPLE

FIGURE 13

quarrel between two members of H is entirely a matter for H to settle. Should
a member of H have need to deal with a member of I, however, that would be
the concern of D; similarly, members of H and M relate as members of B and C.
This principle tends to limit the arena of concern to the smallest relevant unit.
However, despite the efficiency with which this limits relations, it tends to work
against unified leadership. A leader of lineage A will also be a member of one
of the smaller units, for example H, and each of the intervening ones, D and B.
Thus he is likely to be suspected of favoritism by all units of which he is not a
member.

The second principle from the descent system to influence political organization concerns membership in *political* groups in addition to membership
in descent groups. Suppose the descent groups of a society are represented,
though highly stylized and simplified, in figure 14. G through M represent
deceased ancestors, the heads of various sublineages. Thus there are two households in G, which, together with the households of H and I, constitute the
larger sublineage, D. Note that the members of F and C are the same because
no other lineages were founded by descendants of C.

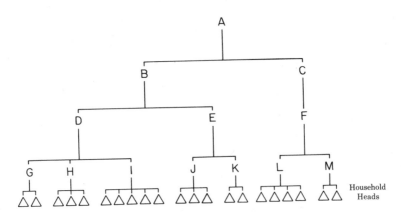

SPECIMEN SEGMENTARY LINEAGE

FIGURE 14

To this point, the diagrams have indicated descent only. However, politics is more than descent, and political units must be viable in ways that lineages need not. For example, a political unit must defend itself, which implies a minimum size, and it must have internal cohesion, which implies a maximum size. In figure 14, units of two households are too small politically, and those of seven are too large (these sizes are unrealistic but must be used for illustrative purposes). Now, using these limitations and the descent principle illustrated in figure 14, it is possible to generate a political organization which is at once like the descent system and different from it (see figure 15).

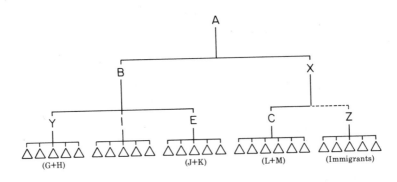

POLITICAL SEGMENTARY LINEAGE

FIGURE 15

Thus Y (G plus H, unified for political purposes), I, E, and C become equivalent as political units though not as descent units. Also, it might be assumed that a migrant group of households, Z, has settled near and has become allied with C. Together they constitute a new group, X, which, because of C's descent relationship, is structurally the equivalent of B.

Figure 15 depicts a hypothetical situation and does not reflect the complications that size, alliances, intermarriage, and migration can bring. The important thing is to see that the organization of the political units is *as though* they were units of the lineage system, yet, at the same time, different.

The African kingdom, with its relatively complex structures, has received a great deal of attention. There are two reasons for this interest. First, sub-Saharan Africa has an unusually high percentage of state or state-like political structures. Secondly, many of these states have functioned well into the contemporary period, unlike those in many other parts of the world (aboriginal America, for example), and this has meant that most of our knowledge about the actual operation of so-called rudimentary states has come from Africa.

African kingdoms have been characterized as "divine kingships," and al-

26. The installation of a Ghanaian chief.
Photo courtesy United Nations/ PR/ mh.

though this has been challenged, my own field research indicates that this is a valid characterization. The concept of divine kingship is based upon the assumption that the king is the actual embodiment of the kingdom, that there is a mystical union between the two. This belief is manifest in two major characteristics. In the first, the king is regarded always as a symbol of his kingdom and, in particular, a fertility symbol. Among the Margi there is a summer ceremony in which the future growth of the year's crops is foretold by actions of the king; if he performs well, the crops will prosper. In another ceremony, when the first fruits are brought from the fields, the king's senior wife, dressed like a bride, is led from the fields and presented to him. In a third ceremony, at the end of the harvest, the king himself is led from the fields as though he were the life-sustaining harvest.[9]

The second major characteristic of divine kingship, regicide, is much more exotic, and since it has been outlawed, reports of it are less reliable. In its classic form, divine kingship sanctioned killing the king when he became infirm or when things were going badly in the kingdom. The custom stems directly from the belief in the unity of king and the kingdom, for that means that the prosperity or failure of either may be regarded as that of both. A king can thus be held responsible for conditions in the kingdom: should he be ill or weak, the kingdom will be in danger; or should conditions in the kingdom be bad, there must also be something wrong with the king. Furthermore, a change in the person of the king will change conditions in the kingdom. To be sure, matters were seldom simple and regicide frequently became tinged with political overtones. But societies like the Margi accepted this relationship between kingdom and king, and regicide continued well into this century.

However, African kingdoms have political dimensions that should not be overshadowed by the more exotic aspects of divine kingship. The kings frequently have complex governmental structures, courts, multiple residences, retinues, and a number of bureaucratic assistants. Officials are often specialized as to function (for example, Minister of War, Master of Ceremonies) and clientele (Representative of Blacksmiths, Representative of Commoners). Systems of taxation and censusing are reported in the traditional kingdom of Dahomey.

It may be suspected that divine kings and such panoply of government might tend to authoritarianism, but several institutions militate against this in African states. In some kingdoms, such as the Ashanti, village and regional divisions are sufficiently organized so as to decentralize the secular authority of the king. In many instances, the dependence upon the rule of law and a respect for law seems to have inhibited ambitious rulers. Nor should it be forgotten that regicide itself was an ultimate check upon the excesses of a king.

One institution which serves as a restraining force upon many African rulers deserves special attention, both for its subtlety and for the emphasis it places upon the importance of the family in African society. In many African kingdoms an individual may be designated as close kinsman of the king, though he or she may not in fact bear that genealogical relationship to him. The "kinsman" will behave toward the king in a familial rather than a political manner. The most frequent positions are "mother," as among the Swazi, and "sister," as among the Lozi. These individuals relate to the king in that familiar way that mothers or sisters relate to sons or brothers. As such, they are in the unique position of being able to criticize or deflate him in public in a particularly humiliating way. Furthermore, the "kinsman" may usually give sanctuary to anyone believed to be unjustly abused by the king. Among the Margi, no man may become king if his father is living, yet a "father of the king" is designated as a part of the king's council. The "father" treats the monarch with all of the indifference and disapproval so often shown by fathers toward their adolescent sons. Since such displays in extreme form would be particularly humiliating to the king, he is very careful not to merit criticism or censure.

Not only are African political systems interesting because of their internal structure, they also relate to other aspects of society. For example, there is a clear relationship between population and political complexity; in general it may be said that the higher the population density of the political unit the greater its tendency to have a relatively complex form of government. In addition, a statistically significant relationship may also be noted between political complexity and the size of the average local community. In addition there is a statistically significant relationship between political organization and the presence of social classes in the society; that is, societies with class systems are much more likely to have complex political systems than those without classes.[10] These relationships suggest that political organization is in many ways a reflection of other factors within the society, and it may be concluded that the relatively large variety of traditional states in Africa is evidence of the general complexity of African society.

NOTES

1. George P. Murdock, "Ethnographic Atlas: A Summary," *Ethnology*, VI (April 1967). See also chapter 2 above.
2. Vernon R. Dorjahn, "The Factor of Polygyny in African Demography," in William R. Bascom and Melville J. Herskovits, eds., *Continuity and Change in African Cultures* (Chicago: The University of Chicago Press, 1959), pp.109–12.
3. M. G. Smith, "The Hausa of Northern Nigeria," in James L. Gibbs, Jr., ed.,

Peoples of Africa (New York: Holt, Rinehart and Winston, 1965).

4. James H. Vaughan, Jr., "Caste Systems in the Western Sudan," in Arthur Tuden and Leonard Plotnicov, eds., *Social Stratification in Africa* (New York: The Free Press, 1970).

5. Igor Kopytoff and Suzanne Miers, eds., *Slavery in Africa: Historical and Anthropological Perspectives* (Madison: University of Wisconsin Press, 1976), Introduction.

6. James H. Vaughan, Jr., "Makafur, a limbic institution of the Marghi," in Kopytoff and Miers, eds., *ibid.*

7. I. Schapera, *Government and Politics in Tribal Societies* (London: Watts, 1956), p.218.

8. Meyer Fortes and E. E. Evans-Pritchard, *African Political Systems* (London: Oxford University Press, 1940), pp.6–7.

9. James H. Vaughan, Jr., "The Religion and World View of the Marghi," *Ethnology* 3 (1964), 380–397.

10. The statistical relationships between size of local community and political complexity and between social classes and political complexity are derived from data in George P. Murdock, "Ethnographic Atlas" (*op. cit.*).

SUGGESTIONS FOR FURTHER READING

Fortes, Meyer. *The Dynamics of Clanship Among the Tallensi* and *The Web of Kinship Among the Tallensi*. London: Oxford University Press, 1945 and 1949.

———, and E. E. Evans-Pritchard. *African Political Systems*. London: Oxford University Press, 1940.

Gluckman, Max. *Order and Rebellion in Tribal Africa*. New York: The Free Press, 1963.

Mair, Lucy. *Primitive Government*. Baltimore: Penguin Books, 1962.

Maquet, Jacques. *Power and Society in Africa*. New York: McGraw-Hill, 1971.

Radcliffe-Brown, A. R., and Daryll Forde. *African Systems of Kinship and Marriage*. London: Oxford University Press, 1950.

Schapera, I. *Government and Politics in Tribal Societies*. London: Watts, 1956.

Tuden, Arthur, and Leonard Plotnicov, eds., *Social Stratification in Africa*. New York: The Free Press, 1970.

Harold K. Schneider
Economic Man in Africa

12 For more than a decade students of traditional African societies have debated with one another about the economies of traditional Africa.[1] To one group the economies were (and are, when they survive) unlike the market economies familiar to Westerners in that production, distribution, and consumption of goods were thought to be determined by feelings of responsibility and obligation rather than by profit incentives or the demands of the market. Thus, from this point of view, when a pastoral Pokot in Kenya slaughtered a steer for a feast, he did so out of a sense of etiquette rather than to gain something for himself. He was not concerned with obtaining the meat of the animal for its own sake, or with building obligations against the future from his neighbors with whom he shared the beef.

In recent years, however, this interpretation has come into question. It has been seen that while Africans often conducted their economic affairs in ways not comparable to those of Europeans and Americans, their behavior can still be considered commensurate with a market process. Thus scholars are increasingly inclined to believe that Africans were not as altruistic and non-market-oriented in their relations with one another as previously thought.

What is meant by the market process? It does not necessarily mean taking goods to a marketplace, although traditional African societies, especially in West Africa, had highly developed marketplace systems. It does mean that people engage in producing things in order to obtain other goods in exchange. In America this is represented by the worker selling his labor for wages, or by the manufacturer producing goods for profit and then using that profit to obtain other desired items. In a society where the market process operates, goods are produced to one degree or another for exchange and not for direct consumption only.

The significance of this point can be illustrated by reference to the concept of "subsistence economy." Traditional Africans are often characterized as having subsistence economies,[2] which usually means that individual households produce the necessities of life—food, clothing, and housing—exclusively for their own consumption. There are no markets and therefore no market economies. However, some scholars are now beginning to realize that Africans did not have subsistence economies in the full sense of the word even though individual households usually produced much of what they consumed.

Traditional Modes of Production

Traditional Africans produced food in many ways, of which three were especially important: raising animals, especially cattle, sheep, goats, and camels; horticulture (a term which here means tilling the land by use of the hoe rather than the plow), including cultivation of tropical crops such as palm oil, bananas, and sweet potatoes, and grassland (savanna) crops such as sorghum, bulrush millet, and maize; hunting and gathering, which is today the mainstay of only a few people, such as the San of the Kalahari Desert.

Different production techniques or combinations of production techniques tended to be predominantly associated with distinctive habitats. The northern section of the Sahara Desert, Zone 1a on map 26, was inhabited by camel nomads, and the southern part of the Kalahari Desert (Zone 1b) by San hunters and gatherers. The tropical rain forest, Zone 2, was inhabited by horticulturalists, and the savanna grasslands, Zone 3, by people who combined horticulture with the raising of cattle, sheep, and goats, although a few peoples in this savanna area, like the Maasai, the Samburu, the Somalis, and the Turkana, were almost exclusively raisers of livestock. Zone 4 was also savanna, but the people were primarily horticulturalists because the presence of the tse-tse fly, a carrier of sleeping sickness, prohibited the raising of cattle, which are vulnerable to this disease.

The close association between production modes and types of habitat has sometimes led to the unwarranted conclusion that habitat forces a people into a certain kind of production. A better way of thinking about this is in terms of environmental constraints combined with opportunity. The kind of production practiced is that best suited to attain the highest return given the type of habi-

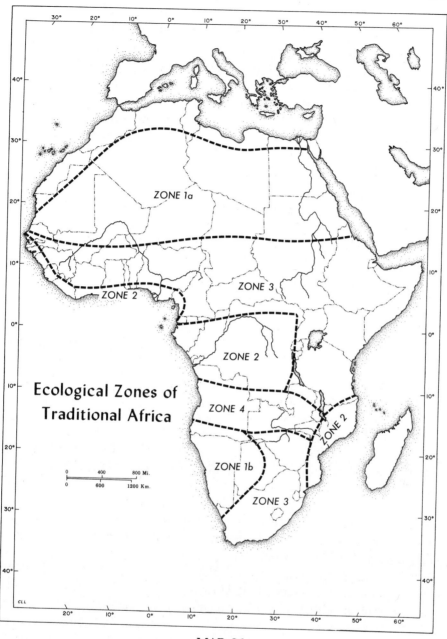

ZONE 1a

ZONE 3

ZONE 2

ZONE 2

Ecological Zones of
Traditional Africa

ZONE 4

ZONE 2

ZONE 1b

ZONE 3

MAP 26

tat and technology available. Thus every part of the African savanna that is suitable for raising cattle has been subjected to pastoralism because cattle and camels are so much more valuable in the eyes of almost all Africans than are the crops that might also be grown on most grazing land. In other words, Africans do not raise cattle in the savanna because they are forced to do so by the habitat. Rather, they raise cattle in the savanna because the animals are highly prized and because cattle do best in the parts of the savanna where there is no tse-tse fly. People in the tse-tse fly area of Zone 4 are unable to raise cattle, however, so they select from available technology and horticulture. They could as well have resorted to hunting and gathering, but that is, for them, a less rewarding method of production.

Many aspects of African life, particularly the social system, are related to what is produced. However, the conclusion should not be drawn that the production system *determines* the social system. While this seems to be a view favored by some scholars, notably Marxists, the way people organize their social life is also a matter of choice, and some forms of organization achieve better results in terms of a people's aspirations than do others. For example, in horticulturalist Central Africa (Zone 4) there was a high incidence of state systems of government, and families arranged themselves matrilineally (that is, they reckoned descent through the mother's side of the family). The hunting and gathering San of southern Africa favored roving bands. Some societies rich in cattle, particularly in northeast Africa, leaned toward segmentary lineage systems, that is, social systems without centralized government; their principle of organization depended on large, localized family-like groups which dealt with each other almost as foreign nations except that they were unified by the belief that they all descended from a common ancestor. In West Africa, the complex production of rainforest crops, combined with iron production, ironworking, brass casting, weaving, carving, and so forth, may relate in important ways to the rise of large-scale states, slavery, and the kinds of kinship systems peculiar to that area. How variations in production systems interact with social and ideological forms is not yet altogether clear, but there seems little doubt that some kind of fit will be found.

Classifying African economies by reference to food production is liable to give the misleading impression that Africans, unlike ourselves, existed at a subsistence level, interested only in food production for their own needs. No one, on reflection, strives to earn a living just to eat. Everyone has aspirations in life in addition to this. Some people may even reduce consumption of food in order to consume other things. Money is spent on radios to satisfy a burning desire for music and news, on gifts to make friends or to bring joy to others, on flowers to satisfy aesthetic cravings. Africans do the same, which is only another way of saying that they engage in production for reasons other than simple subsistence. And since it is seldom possible for persons to produce by themselves all that they desire, Africans produce what they can and exchange some of their possessions for things that they desire more.

Some observers have concluded that Africans, because they do not always value the things valued by non-Africans, are not "economizers." To such observers, Africans appear to be wasteful and irrational because they do not consume a food like pork but do eat termites, which Americans consider undesirable as food. It is therefore important to remember that when people engage in systems of production and exchange they do so within a framework of values which limits choice. Some people do not consume pork because it is too expensive; others refuse to eat it because they believe it is filthy. Western refusal to eat horsemeat or dogmeat—or termites—is equivalent to the general northeast African rejection of pork, but that does not mean that Westerners—or Africans —are not economic men.

To summarize, students of traditional African life are recognizing that Africans are indeed economic men, that they produce goods for a variety of reasons, and not merely for subsistence. Africans arrange social life to facilitate production; they exchange products in order to try to get the best combination of goods, given their resources; and they utilize some commodities as money. They are constrained in these economic activities, however, by certain values which make some kinds of economizing unacceptable.

Subsistence Farmers or Market-oriented Producers?

A general theory of African traditional economics, equivalent to a theory of capitalism or socialism, is not yet available. As a substitute, various elements of African economics are characterized in this chapter, beginning with a study of the Hausa economy, which has often—though erroneously—been characterized as "subsistence."[3] This is followed by a discussion of aspects of production, exchange, consumption, and the relation of economy and society.

With a population estimated at about 15 million people, the Hausa of northern Nigeria are among the largest of the ethnic groups to be found in Africa. The ethnic uniformity of rural Hausa can be seen in their use of a common language, in their houses constructed of mud and wattle with grass roofs, and in homesteads that are surrounded by fences and to which access is gained through a gatehouse. The Hausa grow some things—tobacco, peanuts, cassava, sweet potatoes, and henna (a red cosmetic leaf)—which are primarily for sale.

The things they produce for their own consumption—the staple crops of sorghum and bulrush millet, as well as cowpeas—are often also sold. And, most important, it cannot be said that they sell only the surpluses of the crops produced for their own consumption. Farmers often find themselves in a position where they can sell these subsistence crops for a profit. The proceeds from the sale may then be used at another time and place to purchase the same food, or the same type of food, at a cheaper price. In other words, the Hausa have a real cash or market economy. They acquire their wants not merely by raising for themselves what they need and desire, but also by utilizing the forces of the market to get the best quantity for the best price relative to cost. In this respect they are no different from an American farmer who sells all his milk to the dairy and then purchases some for family consumption at the local supermarket. The myth of the independent, self-contained Hausa homestead can thus be laid to rest. The subsistence sector of the market cannot be separated from the cash or market sector, and the Hausa economy is thus a unified system binding the people together.

It is clear that the Hausa are not unusual in this respect. It has been suggested that all West African rural communities are also market systems, and my own work among East African cattle-raising people has led me to the same conclusion concerning their economic system. Consider, for example, the Turu of central Tanzania: their success at raising bulrush millet and cattle is so great that they find it unprofitable to spend any time producing pots, baskets, and iron goods, which they import from surrounding peoples instead.

An essential ingredient of a market economy is that producers calculate what to grow, and how much of their resources to spend on land, labor, or capital in terms of the price of these things relative to the value of what will be produced by each. In order for Hausa farmers to decide rationally whether to engage in market exchange, they must know prices and be able to relate them to exact quantities. Goods are measured by a standard measuring bowl (*tiya*) and information about prices is disseminated daily by word of mouth, especially by children. Of course this is not to say that different African societies are not oriented to the market in different degrees. Some rural Hausa communities seem unusually market oriented, even to the extent that most farmers do not save seed grain but prefer, like American farmers, to buy or borrow seed each year.

The essential thing about market orientation, however, is not the degree to which Africans exchange, but whether they are prepared to exchange if the opportunity presents itself and the act is profitable in some general sense. To understand the significance of this distinction, consider the problem of the "development" of so-called underdeveloped economies. If the assumption is that traditional African economies are subsistence economies, then bringing about change is mostly a matter of altering people's values and getting them to try something new. But if Africans are seen as economic men, change is brought about by offering new, more profitable opportunities.

One important result of the operation of African rural market economies is the production of wealth differentials. And here another myth, the myth of social equality among Africans, is demolished. Wealth differentials are indexed among the Hausa by the fact that some *gandu*, a production unit composed of a father and his married sons, are much larger than and contain many more sub-units than do others. Furthermore, these large *gandu* have more manured land in crops, more bushfields (unmanured fields), and more marshland. In this society, therefore, a good deal of effort is being expended by people to increase the size of their holdings and the scale of their production in order to increase their wealth—and obviously some people are more successful at this than are others.

Those who do not believe that traditional African societies had market systems suggest that evidence of such systems is a reflection of colonial and Western contact, especially in the last hundred years. It has been clearly shown, however, that this is not the case with the Hausa; traditional aspects of Hausa economy which persist today include local manufacture of iron tools, use of donkeys to transport produce, and continued construction of houses and granaries in the traditional manner. Also, though people like the Hausa have adopted new types of currency (in this case a monetary system derived from the British), there were indigenous currencies consisting of cowrie shells, livestock, copper bars, and iron goods which made indigenous markets possible.

Africans as Planners

Africans, as do people everywhere, have to make hard choices about what to produce and how to produce based on their desire to do the best for themselves. Africa south of the Sahara may be characterized as utilizing a technology based on the hoe (rather than the plow), combined with extensive (rather than intensive) agriculture of the "slash-and-burn" (swidden) variety. In this type of agriculture, a plot is cleared of tree branches but not of trunks or stumps, which are burned to produce ash for fertilizer, and the field is then used for a couple of years until the fertility built up through years of being fallow is gone, after which it is abandoned to lie fallow again and a new plot is cleared.

Anthropologists have usually explained the difference in agricultural methods between Black Africa and Europe on the grounds that Africans did not use plows and intensive methods of agriculture because knowledge of this technology had not diffused to Africa. In recent years scholars have begun to ask whether this explanation is sufficient. They wonder whether Africans did not *choose* extensive agriculture, rather than that this method of production was forced upon them by circumstances. They point out that under conditions such as those which characterize much of traditional Africa, where labor is in short supply and therefore relatively more expensive than land, it made sense to utilize an agricultural technique like swidden which economizes on labor at the expense of land. Also, plows require draft animals, and such animals were nonexistent in the rainforest areas (Zone 2) as well as in the tse-tse infested savanna (Zone 4), while in the other savanna areas (Zone 3) the value of the animals as repositories of wealth worked against their use for pulling plows until recent times.

The Hausa, on the other hand, are intensive agriculturalists, retaining and using the same land year after year. This underscores the fact that not all Africans depended on extensive agricultural techniques, although this option was used more frequently in Africa than in Europe. It may be that many of the technological characteristics of traditional African life will in the end prove to have been strongly influenced or partly determined by basic economic considerations about how best to utilize available resources.

Another pervasive myth about African economic life has been that Africans did not need to make plans or decisions about what to produce since they merely followed tradition. People such as the Hausa were described as growers of sorghum and bulrush millet, as if they were too bound by tradition to change to new crops and as if at the beginning of the agricultural season they went, robot-like, to the fields to plant their cereal crops and then went later, robot-like, to harvest them. This interpretation has also been challenged by recent studies that show that Africans, like farmers all over the world, are in fact faced with complicated decisions about what to produce. The Kamba, who live in Kenya's savanna, raise more cattle than do the Hausa. Nevertheless, like most African cattle-raising people, they also rely heavily on agriculture. The number of possible ways a Kamba farmer can combine his resources (land and seeds of various types, labor, etc.) to achieve different end results was investigated using a method of analysis of decision making called linear programming.[4] It was noted that if, as is true of the Kamba, various mixes of maize and beans, peas, millet, sorghum, and finger millet can be planted, if the various combinations are affected in different ways by different patterns of rain during that season, if the amount of land available to each farmer varies, if the time of weeding varies with the crop and the pattern of growth of that year, and if the amount of labor that can be used varies with each farmer, then, in order to get the best return from whatever opportunities are available to him, the farmer must select among 243 possible combinations. There is no way for him to act "traditionally." He must make a choice, even if a bad one. If he is a rich man, with many wives, much land, and plenty of seed, he would be wise to use one combination of crops, land, and labor; if he is a poor man, with little land, only one wife, and few friends, he would be wise to choose a different combination.

Similar conclusions have been drawn concerning economies in the Congo basin.[5] Contrary to what had been believed in the past, agriculture there is both complex and diverse. It is not uncommon for a farmer to grow thirty or more different crops (as many as sixty are recorded) and to have several varieties of many of them. In addition to main fields, a number of special fields in varying micro-environments suited to particular crops are often cultivated. And rather than being a simple technique, swidden agriculture turns out to have at least twelve varieties. Even methods of manuring are complex, including the use of ash, compost, and manure.

A further interesting detail may be added to this emerging picture of the unexpected complexity of African agricultural production. Among the Gwembe Tongo of Zambia,[6] hunting and gathering is not merely an old-fashioned method of food production but continues in varying degrees to be important for agriculturalists and pastoralists, particularly during hard times. When there are serious crop failures, the people of Africa often turn to hunting and gathering. Even in good times wild foods may be a regular part of the diet; among the Turu of central Tanzania, for example, the usual evening meal consists of bulrush millet mush (*ughai*) dipped in a vegetable dish made from a kind of wild grass growing around the village.

The environmental determinism which takes the close association of habitats and types of production as proof that production is determined by the habitat has been called into question in this chapter. One way to support this challenge is to locate a kind of production that is uncharacteristic of its environment. Such an example can be found in the savanna area to the southwest of Lake Victoria where the Haya grow bananas.[7] Ordinarily bananas are raised on soils of extremely high fertility where there is plenty of moisture and warmth. This would seem to confine them to places such as the north shore of Lake Victoria, to narrow belts of volcanic land on the south sides of such mountains as Meru or Kilimanjaro in northern Tanzania, or to the Congo basin and the West African rainforests. The Haya live in an area that has the warmth and moisture, but the savanna soils are unsuitable for bananas. Nevertheless, the enterprising Haya have overcome this obstacle by constructing compact villages into which they pour mulch, mainly cattle manure but also the leaves of dead banana trees, whereby they have built up the soil to the texture and fertility necessary for growing bananas. Rather than being determined by the habitat, the Haya have overcome a constraint to achieve their goal. But why did they do it? It is certainly far more costly for a people to create the soil necessary to raise bananas and to build it up continually than it is to grow in the soil a less costly crop like sorghum. The answer surely must be that for reasons peculiar to the Haya situation it was worth the cost in terms of the "profit" to enrich the soil. Hence in Africa, as elsewhere, incentive can overcome some restraints.

Methods of Exchange

It has already been noted that an important feature of market economies is exchange of goods between people. Exchange can be accomplished in a variety of ways, from the simple act of barter between two people to the use of money and sophisticated credit techniques such as credit cards. Most African societies had money of some sort, although they also used credit extensively, especially among close friends and relatives. A characteristic essential to the definition of money is that, in comparison to other goods, it is the thing most continually in demand yet also inexpensive to keep. In Africa grain was not money because demand for it varied so greatly; just before the harvest it was very much desired, but after the harvest it was not saleable. Things which were used as money included cowrie shells, copper and brass bars, iron goods such as hoe or ax-heads, pieces of cloth made of raffia palm, and, surprisingly, livestock. Not all of these things served as money everywhere, and frequently a combination of them composed a currency system, as in East Africa where cattle, sheep and goats, iron goods, and beads and cowries, in that order of value, made up the system. Cattle, and sometimes camels, were, of course, the big bills of the system.

When goods like iron, copper, salt, or livestock become important as a medium of exchange, the value which originally propelled the good to the status loses significance. In some places in the Congo iron knives acted as currency and eventually became so important in that role that they could no longer serve as knives because they were manufactured in such a way that they could not cut and did not have proper handles. Cattle, when they assume this role, are no longer judged primarily for their beef- or milk-producing abilities, but rather for their durability. Hence African cattle tend to be small, tough, and low in milk production. Another effect of the predominance of their monetary

27. The cattle and camel market at Kassala, Sudan.
Photo courtesy United Nations/ TW/ gf.

function was a noticeable reluctance on the part of Africans to eat their cattle even though beef was a very desirable food.

These currencies, as well as other valued goods, were especially useful for exchanging rights in women. If the most important purchase made in the lifetime of an American is a house or a car, to the African man the most important purchase was rights in a woman's reproductive capacity and horticultural labor, as well as her less valuable talents such as cooking and beer-, pottery-, and basket-making. Westerners are so accustomed to the idea that marriage is an act of love that they find it hard to grasp that it could be an economic act, but ultimately this should be no less understandable than that a factory worker sells the use of his labor to a manufacturer for so many dollars per day. An almost universal rule in African societies is that a man may not marry a woman of his own clan. This rule forced the establishment of wide-ranging exchange processes as men of one clan moved money and other forms of wealth to other clans in return for rights in women. At times this kind of trade even crossed ethnic lines, as in Kenya where pastoral Maasai acquired Kikuyu wives, and vice versa,

28. General view of Akpapa Market, Cotonou, Dahomey.
Photo courtesy United Nations/ PL/ db.

or in central Tanzania where Turu exchanged cattle with the Sandawe for women. For the Sandawe, who were until very recently hunters, indigenously motivated "development" was fueled by the export of women in return for cattle, the most valuable traditional produce in East Africa.

Another misconception about traditional Africa has to do with what may be called foreign trade, trade between different societies. Even those who recognize that exchange was important *within* African societies sometimes fail to see that it was also often very important *between* societies. One of the most interesting examples of such trade early in this century involved the Acholi, Didinga, Dodoth, Kokir, and Tirangori of northeast Uganda.[8] The basis of this trade system was that each of these societies was trying to obtain a certain balance of grain, livestock, and metal goods, but each was differently successful in producing one or the other. So they traded with each other, directly and indirectly, to balance their wants. Occasionally this required importing some things which were not themselves desired or needed from another society in order to trade these acquired goods to yet another society for more desirable things. For example (see figure 16), the Kokir bought goats from the Tirangori

29. An East African cattle herder.
Photo courtesy United Nations/ BZ/ b.

in return for cattle. The Kokir then traded the goats to the Didinga to their south for cattle. The Didinga, in turn, shipped grain to their south to get goats. And the Didinga traded goats to the Acholi to their west to get grain and iron goods. A little reflection makes it plain that what must be happening is this: the Kokir are buying cattle from the Didinga in order to resell to the Tirangori for profit in goats, and they are buying goats from the Tirangori to sell to the Didinga for profit in cattle. That is to say, they are middlemen in the livestock trade. Similarly, the Didinga are selling goats to the Acholi for grain in order to resell the grain to the Dodoth for a profit. Looked at in its entirety, this is an elaborate, interlocked, international system in which goats, cattle, grain, and iron goods are being redistributed to achieve a maximized balance of preferences, and the redistribution is being accomplished by a profit system.

It is now becoming apparent that this sort of commerce was extensive in traditional Africa. Similarly, the wide range of international trade in West Africa is now quite well understood. One indication that it was important in the savanna (Zone 3) is that the value of cattle was strangely comparable over the whole area, suggesting that as different peoples traded livestock back and

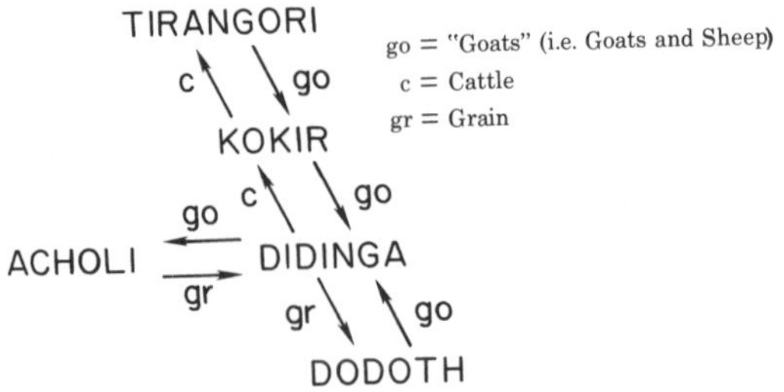

TIRANGORI
go = "Goats" (i.e. Goats and Sheep)
c = Cattle
gr = Grain

c / \ go
KOKIR
go c / \ go
ACHOLI — DIDINGA
gr
gr / \ go
DODOTH

INTER—SOCIETAL EXCHANGE
FIGURE 16

forth, prices tended to stabilize due to the integration of the international market.

Africans as Consumers

Consumption, like other economic activities, must be seen in the context of the general market system. The amount that people desire to eat is affected by the cost of eating in relation to other uses to which food can be put. For example, the use of cattle as money reduces the level of meat production, since a cow as money does not have to be fat. A dramatic example of variation in consumption has to do with seasonal hunger. Among the Pokot of Kenya where I observed this phenomenon, the surprising thing was that the people were not upset by what was happening to them. They saw their hunger as a necessary consequence of the fact that they chose not to sell any of their livestock to obtain grain. In other words, the eventual profit to them of retaining their capital was more important than the momentary discomfort of going hungry.

Consumption, then, is affected by the market. Freshly harvested bulrush millet is tastier than the old, stored grain, but grain producers are inclined to eat the old grain because the new has a longer storage life. Most East Africans like to eat meat, but they will seldom kill livestock—goats, sheep, and even chickens—to obtain meat; the animals, alive, have greater value for exchange.

Enough is now understood about African economies to be able to say with a good deal of assurance that consumption of material things, and therefore also the production of these things, was constrained by the fact that Africans seem to have preferred to invest their resources in personal relations. That is to say, most African societies were not consumption-oriented. A man with wealth obtained more satisfaction out of loaning or giving it to others in return for personal support and obeisance than in using it to buy goods. This did not make their actions any less economic, if one defines economics more generally, attributing value to *all* things, including prestige. However, it is true that if only the economizing of goods is labeled as economics, Africans did not have economies as extensive as those of the Western world.

Economy and Society

Traditionally, African social systems have been discussed with little reference to their relationships to the economy, particularly to production. Today more is known about how social structures and methods of production relate to each other. For example, as was noted in chapter 11, a large number of African societies are organized on the basis of lineage. A distinctive feature of lineage is that the members are born into reciprocal obligations; that is to say, they feel strongly obligated to extend credit to each other in the form of labor or goods. Lineage organization, in turn, seems to be a concomitant of hoe/swidden agriculture in that this method of production appears in a situation of relative labor shortage. Lineage reciprocity is a way of insuring that labor will be available during critical periods in the production process, such as when weeding or threshing is to be done. Interestingly, those societies in which production becomes capital intensive, such as where livestock raising is central, seem to move away from emphasis on lineage to age organization as if the decreased need for labor makes lineages unnecessary. A study of the So in Uganda makes the interesting suggestion that the degree to which reciprocity is followed within a lineage expands and contracts with the prosperity of the group, declining as resources decline and expanding as affluence sets in.[9]

The practice of slavery in traditional Africa is also related to the relative shortage of labor. That is to say, where the best returns to be made come from greater inputs of labor rather than from land or capital, and where such labor is unavailable, there is pressure to institute various forms of voluntary and involuntary servitude. The Central African area (Zone 4) was particularly noted for this, as might be expected given the great dependence on swidden agriculture, but forced labor also occurred in a variety of forms in West Africa as well. Slavery seems to occur less frequently where livestock production is central and a large labor force is unnecessary.

The rise of states also seems related to production and to the general economic system. It has been maintained that in Central Africa the *citemene* (cutting) system of swidden was unusually productive of surplus grain, and that powerful groups or persons were able to get control of this grain and to dispense it in order to acquire obligations that were converted into political relations.[10] The king's power rested on his control of grain. This is arguable if only because there is some question about the truth of the claim that *citemene* swidden is more productive than other techniques. Another possible explanation for the high number of states in this area is that a state-type organization is well-suited for mobilizing labor, which was especially short relative to the type of production depended upon in Central Africa. In order to increase production, economies of scale may have been introduced by means of state organization; when labor is organized on a large scale, the amount of food that can be produced is greater than the sum of what individuals working alone could produce. This illustrates the point that major features of social and political organization may be intimately related to the economy.

Since the 1930s, when social anthropologists began intensively to study African social organization, there has been great interest in certain basic elements in these systems: the descent systems, patrilineal, matrilineal, and cognatic (reckoning kinship through both parents); marriage systems; divorce, including the disposition of the bridewealth; and the features of levirate (the custom by which a wife marries her dead husband's brother) and sororate (where a man marries his wife's sister or kinswoman). Some of these features have already been discussed in chapter 11. Recent studies seem to support the conclusion that African societies display a tendency to assume a patrilineal, cognatic, or matrilineal descent structure, with accompanying correlated features such as levirate and sororate, on the basis of the value of the wealth paid for a bride. Where the bridewealth has a low value, the husband does not control his bride, descent is matrilineal, and control of the wife continues to reside, for the most part, in the hands of her brother or father. As the value of the bridewealth rises, control shifts to the husband in greater and greater degrees and the system shifts to patrilineal descent and to the practice of levirate and sororate.

In Europe and Asia the decline of unilineal descent is related to the appearance of the plow, a device which allows the productivity of an individual to rise so greatly that the production system shifts to a capital-intensive operation.[11] Furthermore, since the men now become the chief agricultural operators because they do the plowing, whereas in Africa the women are the chief operators because they wield the hoes, bridewealth fades, to be replaced by dowry, a payment made by a father to his intended son-in-law to compensate the son-in-law for taking the daughter off his hands.

Africans as Economic Men

Traditional Africans were not men who produced, exchanged, and consumed by rote. They were economic men, continually faced with the need to make decisions about what and how to produce, what and when to exchange, and what and when to consume. The economic stability which they often displayed is better thought of as due to the continuing rationality of traditional economic activities than to inflexibility or an inability to innovate. While it may be true that increasingly extensive contacts with Europeans were often responsible for new opportunities that led to revolutionary changes in African economic life, Africans did not need outsiders to prod them into changing—if the changes made sense.

An early example of this flexibility is the gradual increase in production of tobacco by farmers in Malawi. Tobacco as a crop was introduced into Africa in the sixteenth century by the Portuguese, who brought it from the Americas. As external markets for tobacco appeared, Malawian farmers responded—in economic terms and quite predictably—by increasing their production of the crop. The amount of labor and land devoted to tobacco was increased as the return on tobacco sales increased to exceed the return for other crops. The crop spread over much of Africa, and in this century tobacco is often thought of as a "traditional" African crop.

Other examples of economic change can be found throughout Africa. In Uganda, the Iteso, one of the peoples who put strong emphasis on raising cattle, shifted a significant proportion of their resources into growing cotton when the returns on that began to equal the value of resources put into raising cattle. The Chaga around Mount Kilimanjaro, following a pattern reminiscent of the Ashanti, shifted their activities from growing sorghum and bananas to growing coffee when good markets for coffee appeared during the period of British colonial rule.

It is not surprising, therefore, that in modern times Africans have shown entrepreneurship as new opportunities to better their lives have opened to them. For example, in Ghana in the latter part of the last century, Ashanti farmers, on their own, began large-scale production of cocoa. The interesting thing about cocoa production is that cocoa was a crop introduced from the outside and Africans themselves did not consume it. When the Ashanti farmers saw a market for cocoa that would produce income which would exceed the value of the production of indigenous crops, they began to grow cocoa. Today cocoa is still the major source of income for Ghana.

Conclusion

Examples such as this could be multiplied but would merely further under-score the point that Africans seem quite ready and willing to change their eco-nomic systems, and, correspondingly, their social systems, in response to new economic opportunities which promise a better life. But this should come as no surprise. Many economic revolutions have taken place as Africans changed from hunters and gatherers to agriculturalists, as they added cattle to their eco-nomic activities somewhat later, and as they incorporated bananas into some economies after their introduction from Southeast Asia, and corn (maize), to-bacco, and cocoa into still other economies after they were introduced from the Americas. It can be expected that similar revolutionary production shifts will continue to occur.

NOTES

1. Studies that represent the differing approaches to traditional economic sys-tems are listed in the bibliography at the end of this book.

2. Paul Bohannan and George Dalton, *Markets in Africa* (New York: Double-day, 1965), p.32.

3. Polly Hill, *Rural Hausa, A Village and a Setting* (Cambridge: Cambridge University Press, 1972).

4. Judith Heyer, "Preliminary Results of a Linear Programming Analysis of Peasant Farms in Machokos District, Kenya," *Proceedings of East African Institute of Social Research Conference* (Kampala, January 1965).

5. Marvin Miracle, *Agriculture in the Congo Basin* (Madison: University of Wisconsin Press, 1967).

6. Thayer Scudder, *Gathering Among African Savannah Cultivators—A Case Study: The Gwembe Tonga* (Zambian Papers No. 5, Manchester University Press for Institute for African Studies, University of Zambia, 1971).

7. William Allan, *The African Husbandman* (New York: Barnes and Noble, 1965), p.171.

8. J. H. Driberg, *The Savage as He Really Is* (London: G. Routledge & Sons, 1929), pp.25–29.

9. Charles D. Laughlin, Jr., "Deprivation and Reciprocity," *Man* (September 1974), pp.380–96.

10. Jacques Maquet, *Civilizations of Black Africa* (New York: Oxford Univer-sity Press, 1972), pp.91–93.

11. Jack Goody, *Technology, Tradition and the State of Africa* (London: In-ternational African Institute, 1971).

12. Polly Hill, *The Migrant Cocoa-Farmers of Southern Ghana* (Cambridge: Cambridge University Press, 1963).

13. Edwin R. Dean, "Economic Analysis and African Responses to Price," *Journal of Farm Economics* (1965), pp.402–409.

SUGGESTIONS FOR FURTHER READING

Barth, Fredrick. "On the Study of Social Change." *American Anthropologist*, Vol. 69 (1967), 661–69.

Douglas, Mary. "The Lele—Resistance to Change," in Paul Bohannan and George Dalton, *Markets in Africa*. New York: Doubleday, 1965.

Goldschmidt, Walter. "The Brideprice of the Sebei." *Scientific American*, July 1973, 74–85.

Goody, Jack. *Technology, Tradition and the State in Africa*. London: International African Institute, 1971.

Hill, Polly. *Studies in Rural Capitalism in West Africa*. Cambridge: Cambridge University Press, 1970.

Hopkins, Anthony. *An Economic History of West Africa*. London: Longmans, 1973.

Lee, Richard. "!Kung Bushman Subsistence: An Input-Output Analysis," in D. Damas, ed., *Contributions to Anthropology: Ecological Essays*. Ottawa: Queen's Printer, 1969.

Maquet, Jacques. *Civilizations of Black Africa*. London: Oxford University Press, 1972.

Schneider, Harold K. *The Wahi Wanyaturu, Economics in an African Society*. Chicago: Aldine, 1970.

Hasan El-Shamy
African World View and Religion

13 Man lives in two worlds: the natural-physical and the social-cultural. He tries to comprehend the nature of his total environment and in so doing forms an integrated image of both worlds in relation to himself. This image is commonly called a world view and influences an individual's actions. No matter how strange or irrational the behavior of a person, an ethnic group, or a nation may seem to the outsider, it makes sense in terms of the world view of that person, ethnic group, or nation. One way to better understand a culture or society is to perceive it from the intellectual and emotional standpoint of the individual participant, to examine what members of a community know, feel, and do and what motivates their actions.

African World View

The diversity of the social and cultural environments under which various African groups live and the variety of geographic conditions found in Africa make it impossible to speak of *one* inclusive world view characteristic of *the* African. However, the uniform social and cultural conditions shared by some groups, particularly those living in what is called a "culture area," give rise to strong similarities in the way in which members of these groups will view their world.

How a person views his world is determined by several factors: the social and cultural conditions under which he lives (family, economy, power structure, religion); the physical environment (semidesert, rainforest, animals and plants); his past experiences; his wants and goals; and his physiological structure and condition (weak, strong; healthy, sick). The more stable these determinants are in a community, the more alike will be the world views of its members.

The influence of social and cultural factors on the development of the world view of an individual is crucial. A child is born with the potential to participate fully in the life of the community in which he or she is being raised. During the early stages of life, and particularly prior to the effective acquisition of language, many of a child's cognitions develop through direct experience and observation of both the physical and social environment. However, a great deal of what a person knows, particularly in traditional cultures, is acquired from other members of the community, either directly through instruction or indirectly through his imitation of the actions of others.

A young person among the !Kung, for example, grows up within the family, the only social unit larger than the family is an autonomous band composed of several families and led by a headman. The child becomes aware of the physical features of the people and the roles each member must play within the group. The hot, semiarid physical environment, with its seasonal rainfall, its thunderstorms, and its drought-resistant vegetations, and a country covered with grass, brush, and scant small trees are all perceived. The young person recognizes a variety of wild plants, berries, and roots as edible and a certain type of plant gum as a delicacy. A number of dangerous animals—lions, leopards, hyenas—are also identified, as are a variety of big antelopes found in the region: wildebeest, springbok, eland, and so forth. One animal, the gemsbok, a gray antelope with spectacular black markings, is particularly admired, and is taken as a model according to which young girls are scarified on the legs, thighs, and buttocks for beauty.[1]

The San live under open skies; the sun and the moon are a constant part of their existence and figure importantly in their world view. They are well adapted to the harsh environment and view the world as a mixture of good and evil forces which must be attracted or driven off. The cognitions of the San differ from those of the Mbuti pygmies, who inhabit the Ituri Forest in Central Africa. Although both groups live by hunting and gathering, a techno-economic system which gives rise to similar social organization in the two societies, the difference in their respective physical environments results in different world views.

The Mbuti child learns about the physical environment: the forest, with its dense vegetation and towering trees, the abundance of game and other forest products—mushrooms, nuts, roots, fruits, and wild honey. The young boy learns about the limits of the hunting grounds for his band and about his family's trading partners among neighboring village-dwellers, with whom the Mbuti exchange forest products, especially meat and hut-building materials, for produce of the village. The Mbuti are well adapted, both physically and socially, to living in the dark, sunless forest, for it is their source of livelihood, well-being, and protection. The forest is benevolent; it is the life-giver. Exposure to the sun, or moving away to a nearby village, causes a deterioration in health. Heavenly phenomenon are little known to the pygmy; the forest is dark, and therefore darkness is good.

Cultural adaptations determine the extent to which a group can cope with its physical environment. The Mbuti view of the forest differs radically from that of village-dwelling neighbors who live by "slash-and-burn" horticulture. In contrast to the pygmy, the villager views the dark forest as the abode of evil forces which reluctantly refuse to surrender any agricultural land while supporting other dense vegetation. The villagers attribute misfortunes to a variety of hostile agents, which they confront with magic, witchcraft, and sorcery. The pygmies, on the other hand, in accordance with their overall view of a benevolent world, never apply any of the villagers' techniques to coerce the forces around them. For the pygmies, there is no evil spirit to confront or countervail.[2]

A single cognition does not occur independently. The separate cognitions of the individual develop into clusters which, in turn, are interconnected and joined into larger systems of knowledge. These add meaning to single cognitions and form parts of the image of the world that members of the social group perceive. Cognitive systems (for example, religious, familial, political) interconnect with one another and form an integrated view of the world.

When a person encounters a strange element which is not a part of the known system, the entire cognitive process is seriously impaired. New elements are seen in terms of what is already known; this is a universal characteristic of human thinking. The relating of the Shakespearean drama of Hamlet to the Tiv of central Nigeria is an interesting example of this phenomenon. The story begins with the ghost of a murdered king appearing to some friends, then to his son Hamlet and informing him about the murderer. The world view of the Tiv does not include the concept of the *ghost* of a dead person. The Tiv do not believe in the survival of any part of a person after his death. They believe, however, that witches can raise a corpse and send omens to warn of coming events. Thus, a Westerner reports the following episode, which began with a question from an old man in the audience:

"What is a 'ghost'? An Omen?"

"No, a 'ghost' is someone who is dead but who walks around; people can hear him and see him, but not touch him."

They objected. "One can touch zombies."

"No, no! It was not a dead body the witches had animated to sacrifice and eat. No one else made Hamlet's dead father walk. He did it himself."

"Dead men can't walk," protested my audience.

I compromised: "A 'ghost' is a dead man's shadow."

But again they objected. "Dead men cast no shadows."

"They do in my country," I snapped![3]

As pointed out earlier, the world view of an individual is composed not only of intellectual, cognitive knowledge but of emotional, affective components as well. When these emotional components are added to cognitions or knowledge, a tendency to act or behave in a certain way arises. These three components, cognition, emotion, and action tendency, make up what is called an attitude. The acquisition of knowledge, and how this knowledge develops into an attitude through social interaction, is illustrated by Camara Laye, a Malinke writer from Guinea, in describing his first encounter with a snake.[4] As a child of only six or seven exploring the environment immediately outside his home, he encountered a snake. He toyed with it and observed its characteristics, especially its fangs. An adult snatched him away and the event aroused a great commotion. Camara Laye observed that his mother was shouting hardest of all and she gave him "a few sharp slaps." Later she warned him solemnly never to play with snakes again. The reaction of adults to a child's encounter with a dangerous object generates a tense emotional atmosphere readily perceived by the child; the tension is reinforced by the physical punishment. The mother's warning never to play with snakes again designates the direction for future action. Thus, a negative attitude toward snakes is instilled in the child.

Attitudes develop around specific objects in each person's world. They can concern the physical environment, family, economy, education, politics, religion, or art. The entire concept of kinship, for example, which is the central factor for social organization in African societies, revolves around institutionalized sets of characteristic attitudes toward the members of the kinship group. In an Ashanti family, a distinctive set of attitudes govern the relationship between a son and his father, his mother, and his mother's brother (that is, the boy's maternal uncle). This set of attitudes is congruent with another set, the relationship among a man, his sister, and his wife. "To his sister a man entrusts weighty matters, not to his wife. He will give his valuables in her care; not into his wife's . . . [The sister is often] a watchdog of a wife's fidelity."[5]

Attitudes group together into clusters and systems which characterize the behavior of an individual. Since most attitudes are learned within the context of living within a specific community, members of that community exhibit the same attitudinal systems. Thus, the cognitions and attitudes of the members of the same kinship group will tend to have internal uniformity, these will differ from those of neighboring kinship groups, and, comparatively speaking, there will be even greater variation from those of a group which lives under different physical and social conditions.

The Supernatural

Belief in the supernatural is not based on direct observation but rather on cognitive experiences that transcend the immediate, observable world. Experiences in this sphere depend mainly on emotions rather than logic and can be divided into sacred beliefs, which are associated with a deity, and nonsacred beliefs. A good illustration of nonsacred supernatural beliefs can again be found in Camara Laye's writings about his childhood learning experiences in regard to snakes.

In Camara Laye's village there were different types of snakes; all except one were killed. "One type in particular . . . a little snake, black with a strikingly marked body" evoked awe, respect, and reverence in both men and women. The boy's mother forbade him to "ever interfere with it," while his father had to deliberate whether the time was "a little too soon to confide such a secret [about the nature of the snake] to a twelve year old boy." The father spoke to his son about the snake for "the first and last time." He told his young son how he had first encountered the snake, how the snake visited him in a dream and revealed its role as the guardian of their people, and how his success as a goldsmith was due to the snake's "guiding spirit."

The solemnity of the occasion and the reverence and endearment with which the father and mother treated the matter generated an emotion which was completely different from that associated with other types of snakes. The truth about that snake was to be divulged only to mature, trustworthy persons. The impact of the situation led Camara Laye to total and unquestioning acceptance of the qualities of the snake and of its significance for the Malinke.

Yet, a number of years later he writes, "But what exactly *was* a 'guiding spirit'? What were these guiding spirits that I encountered almost everywhere, forbidding one thing, commanding another? I could not understand it at all, though their presence surrounded me as I grew to manhood." Under these conditions the child not only learned about a specific type of snake, he also became cognizant of either its danger or its supernatural qualities. Each situation was charged with emotions expressed in the reactions of adults, how they felt, what they did and said. In the first case it was clearly a situation of fear and defensive action, while in the second it was one of reverence and protection.

Similarly, with reference to "souls and ancestors," the Tiv believe that every man has a *jijingi* that is manifest in his shadow and in his reflection in water or a mirror. As noted earlier, however, the Tiv believe that dead men cast no shadows: the *jijingi* departs at death. If the shadow of a corpse is pointed out to them, they say solemnly that this is not a *jijingi* any longer, it is merely his *mure*, which is the word for the shadow of a tree or an inanimate object. For the Tiv, this belief is not a subject for proof or disproof through verifiable evidence; it is accepted as a matter of unquestionable faith. Thus, when they were told that a ghost was a dead man's shadow, they readily dismissed the claim and considered it similar to the "fancies of the young."[8]

When a number of beliefs and associated practices cohere around an object that is considered to be supernatural, they form what is usually referred to as a cult. A cult institution may be defined as a set of rituals all revolving around a common cognitive element, all justified by a set of interconnected beliefs and attitudes, and all supported by the same social group. These include rituals in honor of beings and forces which are not worshipped. Cults are thus associated with the supernatural but are not necessarily directly derived from the sacred.

Cults also develop around animals, plants, or other natural objects. Among the Malinke, the belief and practices associated with the snake, the guiding spirit, may be viewed as a snake cult, but this cult does not stem from institutionalized religious dogma. Formal Islam, the religion of Camara Laye's family, does not recognize the snake as a guiding spirit or as a supernatural being.

Associated with this concept of cults are African attitudes toward the dead. These practices and beliefs have often been called ancestor worship by outsiders. In many cases, however, this is a misnomer. Although dead ancestors are feared, placated through food offerings and rituals, or simply revered, they are normally not deified or worshipped. These practices and attitudes simply constitute a cult.

The Nature of African Religion

Studies on African traditional religions have largely been undertaken by scholars whose orientations were guided either by their own religious perspectives—Judaism, Christianity, Islam—or by evolutionary theories presupposing the "primitiveness" of African religious systems. A Nigerian scholar at the University of Ibadan points out that a great many non-African scholars who write about African traditional religion have failed to comprehend its nature. They mistook "the appearance for reality," "confused religion with other aspects of culture," and reflected "the ever-menacing habit of biased comparisons" between African religions and their own. African religions should be studied with "openness," "sympathy," and "reverence."[9] The latter, reverence, is perhaps the most difficult for outsiders to achieve, for it necessitates the presence of the same emotional foundation that the believer experiences within the context of his own religion. These emotions are mostly acquired only through the long process of acculturation, the development over a period of time of the world view associated with an individual's culture.

In its most basic form, a religion is a system of socially shared beliefs and attitudes toward sacred, supernatural entities and forces. Deities and associated concepts are at the center of religious belief systems. A number of universal categories of religious behavior may be identified: belief in supernatural beings and forces; belief in the existence of one or more deities; prayer which addresses the supernatural; physiological exercises; reciting the sacred code; *mana*, or touching things for their desirable qualities; *taboo*, or not touching things to avoid an automatic penalty; feasts; sacrifices; and congregations.[10] All religions, including those of Africa, manifest most of these categories.

African Conceptions of God

A belief system which does not recognize a deity may not be considered a religion. The characteristics of a deity are central in a religious belief system. Religions are readily perceived as either monotheistic or polytheistic. In monotheism only one god is recognized, whereas in polytheism two or more deities share the power of the universe.

It is sometimes argued that the historical development of the concept of monotheism began in the northeastern corner of the African continent in Egypt as a religious revolution against the worship of numerous gods. This monotheistic dogma was preached by Ikhnaton (Amenhotep IV) but collapsed, at least as the formal religion of the state, shortly after it had been instituted. It was the Hebrew form of monotheism that developed into the three major monotheistic religions—Judaism, Christianity, and Islam.

Many students of African belief systems differentiate between "God" and deities and see African religions as essentially monotheistic. For example, the term "God" has been limited by one scholar to the supreme creating and supernatural entity. This distinction is made in a number of African languages which differentiate between the Supreme Deity and lesser entities. The Supreme Deity in African belief systems may be viewed as paralleling "Elohim," "Jehovah," and "Allah," whereas "deities" may be compared to lesser or minor supernatural entities such as angels, and the devil and saints in monotheistic religions. For Africans, it is argued, the Supreme Deity is "real, unique, the absolute controller of the universe," and "God is one, the only God of the whole universe."[11] Although each of these attributes of the Supreme Being appears in a number of African religions they may not all be present together. However, African religions need not share the same image of God as do Christians in order for them to experience the same type of emotions in relation to God. For example, a great many African religions have what theologians call an *otiose* God. According to this concept, God created the world and everything in it, then withdrew and left men to run their own affairs. The Tiv of Nigeria, the Mende of Sierra Leone, and the Nuba of Sudan are among the several African groups who share this belief.

In actual practice, monotheism in its strictest sense is an ideal. Although all three Semitic religions attribute creation and control of the universe to a single god, all, as practiced by their adherents, assign supernatural functions to other spiritual entities.

Traditional African religions recognize a number of major deities who control nature and other significant aspects of human existence. The !Kung, for example, seem to have believed in a protagonist who had supernatural powers but who looked and acted like men on earth. "The !Kung claim that this old protagonist and the great god of their present belief are one and the same. . . ."[12] Currently, however, they believe in the existence of two gods: a great god who lives in the eastern sky where the sun rises and a lesser god who lives in the western sky where the sun sets. The Mbuti pygmies recognize the forest or a forest deity as the main force which shapes their world. The Kalenjin of East Africa have a limited number of gods: the god of rain, who inhabits the clouds; the god of destruction, who inhabits the dark places; the god of beauty, who inhabits the plains; the god of the underworld and good fortune; and the god of kindness, who inhabits the sky.[13]

Other African groups acknowledge many deities. The Yoruba of southern Nigeria are reported to have a pantheon of several hundred deities, which are called *orishas*. The individual Yoruba does not necessarily know all of them.

Each *orisha* has his or her own special power and domain and reflects some aspect of the diversity of the Yoruba physical environment, of technological abilities, or of economic institutions. For example, Olorun, whose name means Owner of the Sky, the Supreme Deity who rules over both heavens and earth, is the Creator and the Lord. Orunmila, the eldest son of Olorun, is the all-knowing *orisha*; he has the authority to speak to humans, particularly diviners, and to reveal the plans of Olorun. Other examples of lesser deities are Ogun, the deity of iron and protector of hunters, blacksmiths, warriors, and, more recently, truck drivers and even surgeons—all those to whom iron is of particular importance; Eshu, deity of confusion and chance, who confuses and misleads people (under Christian influence he has become equated with the Devil), is responsible for carrying messages and sacrifices from humans to the sky deity; Shango is the deity of thunder and lightning; Oshun, a female deity, is one of Shango's wives and is herself the deity of the Oshun River; Orisha-Oko is the deity of agriculture and the patron of farmers; and Sonponno is the deity of smallpox and other diseases.[14]

The nature of the deity as perceived by believers guides their actions toward it. In the ancient Middle East, female deities shared supernatural powers with male deities. However, since the introduction of Semitic monotheism, a single masculine god replaced all other deities in formal religious dogma. In a broader context, some deified humans, commonly referred to as saints, are females. African traditional religions seem to manifest the same dominance of a supreme masculine deity as do Semitic monotheistic religions. This is particularly true with reference to the Creator. "Whereas in most of Africa, God is conceived in masculine terms, there are localities where the deity is thought of and spoken of in feminine terms."[15]

Religion is often identified by its functions. Answering perplexing questions, justifying existing social institutions, and reinforcing social and cultural values are among the most important. The crucial issues of creation, the nature of the world, the origin of social practices, the reason for their existence, and the necessity for their preservation are addressed and answered by a religion. Such issues are beyond immediate and empirically verifiable observation.

Religious dogma provides answers that are *non*-rationally accepted as a matter of faith. For example, it is the Creator who made all things the way they are. Semitic monotheism instructs its followers that God created the world in six days and rested on the seventh. He created Adam and, out of his rib, Eve. Through Eve's suggestions these first humans disobeyed God and were cast out of Paradise. African traditional religions also attribute creation to a Creator who is differentiated from other deities. For the !Kung:

> The great god is the creator of all things. He created himself and named himself. He then created the lesser gods and a wife for each of them. The wives bore them children. The great god gave names to all these beings. . . . From the beginning he created men and women to be mortal. When mortals die he takes their spirits to the place where he lives in the eastern sky. . . .
>
> The great god gave men bows and arrows and poison and digging sticks and taught them to shoot animals and dig for food. Everything men know he taught them.[16]

The interconnection between beliefs and practices is evident in *all* religions. For the Mbuti pygmies, when a crisis such as sickness or lack of success in hunting arises, it is seen to be caused by a lack of benevolence, rather than by evil forces. After secular (nonreligious) solutions are exhausted, the Mbuti resort to an elaborate ritual, the *molimo*. Through songs and dances, the *molimo* is addressed to the forest, soliciting the aid of "a benevolent forest deity." The purpose of the ritual is simply to attract the attention of the deity (the forest), who is benevolent. Similarly, initiation rituals, *elima*, require close contact with the forest. In the initiation of a young boy into manhood, scarification of the forehead and the use of a healing remedy made from forest plants are required. This is viewed as "visible physical evidence of the presence of the forest in the body of man."[17]

The account of creation of the Dogon of Upper Volta illustrates how a practice such as female excision is inseparable from the Dogon concept of God and creation. The god, Amma, created the sun, moon, stars, and earth. He was lonely and drew near to the female earth to unite himself with it. His passage was barred by a red termite hill, but he cut it down and the union was completed. This obstacle made the union defective, however, and a jackal was born. Further union, though, resulted in the birth of twins called Nummo.

The Nummo twins were disturbed by the nakedness of their mother, Earth, and clothed her with plants. The deceitful jackal then seized his mother's skirt and defiled her. Because of this, Amma decided to create live beings without Earth, and the Nummo twins, fearing that twin births might disappear, drew a male and female outline on the ground, one on top of the other. "And so it was, and has been ever since, that every human being has two souls at first; man is bi-sexual. But a man's female soul is removed at circumcision, when he becomes a true man, and the corresponding event happens to a woman at excision."[18]

As in any religious system, the Dogon account, among other things, explains and validates social and cultural beliefs and institutions: the act of creation, the role of the jackal as the anti-God, and the necessity of male circumcision and female excision. Each one of these aspects is interconnected with all the others. Attempts to change one aspect of the belief system are resisted by other components, which will also indirectly come under attack. Generally speaking, the systemic qualities of a religion make the introduction of new information or the alteration of one aspect of the system extremely difficult without undermining the whole. To suggest to a Dogon that female excision is an inadvisable practice is to put the very concept of God and creation under attack.

Symbolic Representation

Symbolism is of great significance in the practice of religious belief. It is not the idea, the act, the place, or the time in itself that is significant, but its symbolic association within the system as a whole and the emotions that it may evoke.

Attitudes of reverence develop toward all elements of the religious cognitive system. These include the *verbal* medium of communicating with God, the prayer or hymn, whether it is the Christian Lord's Prayer or the Yoruba Hymn to Eshu; *bodily movements* symbolizing religious functions, whether the making of the sign of the cross, the way Muslims kneel in prayer, or an African ritual dance; *insignias*, whether the Star of David for the Jews, the Crescent for the Muslims, or the Golden Stool for the Ashanti; *places*, whether it is Jerusalem for the three Semitic religions, or Kere-Nyage (Mount Kenya, the abode of Mogai, the Lord of Nature and the Divider of the Universe) for the Kikuyu; *time*, whether it is the Sabbath for Jews and Christians or the fifth day (the day of worship after the four days of creation and hence a week of four days) for the Yoruba. All these elements are among the significant components of a religious belief system and help to reinforce the devotion of its adherents.

Conclusion

Although religions may seem different, and indeed do differ in details, they address the same basic issues, perform the same functions for individuals and for the group, and have their roots in human emotions. Thus, even though there are different religions, there is only one type of religious experience. Religion is an important and central component of the world view of individuals and of groups. It can be understood only in the context of specific emotional and environmental systems.

NOTES

1. See Lorna Marshall, "The !Kung Bushmen of the Kalahari Desert," in *Peoples of Africa.* ed. James L. Gibbs, Jr. (New York: Holt, Rinehart and Winston, 1965), pp.243–278.

2. Colin M. Turnbull, *The Forest People* (New York: Clarion, 1962), esp. pp.92, 228; see also Turnbull, "The Mbuti Pygmies of the Congo," in *Peoples of Africa*, pp.281–317, p.308.

3. Laura Bohannan, "Hamlet and the Tiv," *Psychology Today*, vol. 9, no. 2 (July 1975), pp.62–66, p.63.

4. Camara Laye, *The Dark Child* (New York: Farrar, Straus and Giroux, 1971), p.18.

5. Meyer Fortes, "Kinship and Marriage Among the Ashanti," in *African Systems of Kinship and Marriage*, ed. A. R. Radcliffe-Brown, and D. Forde (London: Oxford University Press, 1950), pp.252–284, p. 275.

6. Laye, *The Dark Child*, pp.22–23.

7. Paul Bohannan, "The Tiv of Nigeria," in *Peoples of Africa*, pp.515–546, p.538.

8. Laura Bohannan, "Hamlet and the Tiv," p.63.

9. E. Bolaji Idowu, *African Traditional Religion* (Maryknoll: Orbis Books, 1975), pp.16–21.

10. See Anthony F. C. Wallace, *Religion: An Anthropological View* (New York: Random House, 1966), esp. pp.52–74.

11. Idowu, *African Traditional Religion*, pp.149–165.

12. Marshall, "The !Kung Bushmen . . . ," pp.269–270.

13. Tabanlo Liyong, ed., *Popular Culture of East Africa* (Nairobi: Longman, 1972), pp.31–32.

14. See Harold Courlander, *Tales of Yoruba Gods and Heroes* (Greenwich, Conn.: Fawcett, 1973).

15. Idowu, *African Traditional Religion*, p.149.

16. Marshall, "The !Kung Bushmen . . . ," p.269; see also her "'!Kung Bushman Religious Beliefs," *Africa*, vol. 32, no. 3 (1962), pp. 221–252, esp. p.223.

17. Turnbull, "The Mbuti . . . ," p.307.

18. Geoffrey Parrinder, *African Mythology* (London: Hamlyn, 1967), pp.23–24.

SUGGESTIONS FOR FURTHER READING

Armstrong, Robert P. "The Affecting Presence," an essay in *Humanistic Anthropology*. Urbana, Illinois: University of Illinois Press, 1971.

Beier, Uli. *The Origins of Life and Death: African Creation Myths*. London: Heinemann, 1966.

Evans-Pritchard, E. E. *Theories of Primitive Religion*. London: Oxford University Press, 1965.

Guerrier, Eric. *Essai sur la cosmogonie des Dogon: l'arche du Nommo*. Paris: R. Laffant, 1975.

Hammond-Tooke, W. D. "African World-view and its Relevance to Psychiatry," *Psychologia Africana*, Vol. 16, No. 1 (June 1975), pp.25–32.

Mbiti, John S. *African Religions and Philosophy*. New York: Praeger, 1969.

Meyerowitz, E. L. R. *The Akan of Ghana: Their Ancient Beliefs*. London: Faber and Faber, 1958.

King, Noel Q. *Religions of Africa, A Pilgrimage into Traditional Religions.* New York: Harper, 1970.

———. *Christian and Muslim in Africa.* New York: Harper, 1971.

Williams, Denis. *Icon and Image: A Study of Sacred and Secular Forms of African Classical Art.* New York: New York University Press, 1974.

Roy Sieber
Traditional Arts of Black Africa

14

To understand the traditional arts of Africa south of the Sahara it is necessary to set aside several popularly held assumptions. First, African arts are not primitive, if by primitive is meant simple, crude, or original in the sense of being without a history. The arts of Africa are, in fact, sophisticated and possess a long history. Second, African art is not produced solely for aesthetic ends—that is, it is not art for art's sake, as is so much of recent Western art; rather, it is deeply embedded in the belief patterns of the society. Third, and this refers to more than the arts, Africa's history, although difficult to reconstruct at times, is certainly as long and as rich in texture and fabric as is that of any other world area.

In this chapter these points are further explored. A section on style and form is followed by a section on history, which in turn leads to an examination of the arts associated with leadership. Next, the arts of less centralized groups with less easily retrievable history, either in terms of surviving art objects or in terms of oral traditions, will be touched upon, especially with reference to the use of the arts in securing human survival and in social control. Finally, there is a brief description of the range of arts, from masks and figures to body arts and crafts.

Style and Form

African art may be characterized as conservative, for it lay at the core of commonly held traditional belief patterns and strongly reflected those shared values, at the same time reinforcing and symbolizing them. It was radical in the sense that it was at the root of all beliefs and values. It was symbolic or representative rather than abstract or representational. Viewed from Western traditions of realism or naturalism, African sculpture seems not to be "correct." The human body is presented most frequently in a 1:3 or 1:4 proportion of head to body, whereas accurate measurement would be approximately 1:5 and Hellenistic and Mannerist proportions edged past 1:6. Thus, to Western eyes, African figure carvings tend to appear head-heavy, and this tendency is combined with an emphasis on balance and symmetry (plates 30–34 and 42). There is no easy explanation for the style characteristics of African art, or indeed for the arts of any other culture. The proportions appear and become accepted; once accepted they become required and expected. The result for Africa is a norm that is frontal and symmetrical and that gives an impression of fixed austerity, which is reinforced by the absence of transitory facial expression. Masks and figures, for the most part, present expressionless, cool countenances; facial twitches of rage, pleasure, or horror are absent. Bodies exhibit long torsos and short legs, bent at hip and knee; arms, often bent at the elbow, are usually placed calmly against the belly or side and only rarely indulge in emphatic gestures. Stance, gesture, and expression combine to lend a strong sense of calm and austere power to most African figurative sculpture.

Despite these abstract and often simplified forms, details are accurate: characteristic hair styles, body ornaments, or scarification patterns will be depicted with clarity and correctness, probably because they describe lineage affiliation or social condition as well as local fashion.

This "basic" style is combined with a limited number of figure and mask types. Like the basic style, the types appear broadly in sub-Saharan Africa. Essentially, figure types are limited to standing, seated, occasionally equestrian, and, more rarely, kneeling postures. Women with children are frequently depicted, expressing the great emphasis on continuity of the family and of the group. Mask types fall into four divisions: face masks, crest masks, bucket or casque masks, and horizontal masks (plates 35–38).

To survey African figure carving across West and Central Africa, the area where figurative art appeared most frequently, is to experience more than a single style and a limited number of types, however. Rather, a rich and amazing diversity of area, tribal, and subtribal styles can be discerned.

This complex body of styles and types amazed Western artists and critics early in this century and aroused their often extravagant admiration, but it also proved a snare and an illusion. Artists, seeking to break with the conventionalities of Western art, classicism and idealism, naturalism and materialism, assumed, quite inaccurately, that African art was highly inventive and innovative, whereas it was in fact extremely conservative in style as well as in meaning. An example of this conservatism is the continuity of the "basic" style over centuries: over-size head, short legs, detailed coiffure, expressionless and calm balance describe equally well the art of the Nok culture of two thousand years ago (plate 30) or that of the Dogon of a few centuries ago (plate 33), as it does Luluwa (plate 31) or Yoruba (plate 32) figures made in the past century.

Recent scholarship has tended to emphasize the differences of styles and forms and the multiplicity of uses of African art; in short, it has tended to dwell on a rich variety of trees while ignoring the forest. In the broadest sense there does seem to be an African figure style, quite possibly developed in perishable materials, usually wood. Grafted on this general style is the particular style of an area. For example, figure carving from the western Sudan tends to be tall, vertical, spare, and austere (see plate 33). The body and arms become vertical cylinders. At the same time, the surfaces are carefully, often delicately worked with reference to scar patterns and bangles. Other variations of the basic African style can be found in other geographical areas. The forms of the sculptures of the Yoruba of the rain forest of southwestern Nigeria, for example (see plate 32), tend to be rounder and fuller than the more spare forms of the arid western Sudan. Such large geographic area styles are discernible not only for the western Sudan and the Guinea coast, but also for the Equatorial rain forest and for the northern and southern Congo River basins.

Within these larger geographic areas, "tribal" styles have also developed. The term *tribe* in African art studies refers to an ethnic and cultural base for a discrete style. In a sense, these tribal styles are the most visible because they are the most easily identifiable, and indeed, most survey books of African sculpture emphasize the styles of "tribal" groups.

In addition to the larger style areas and the tribal styles, still smaller units may be found. In fact, if one examines African sculptural forms closely, it is possible to determine "subtribal" styles, village styles, and even the styles of individual carvers. Thus the style of the Dogon or the Yoruba reflects both the larger style area and the increasingly smaller, specific style areas to which it belongs, and ultimately it is possible to identify the "hand" of the particular sculptor. Unfortunately the names of these artists are too often lost. At times they have been forgotten by the owners and users of the carvings, but more frequently the scholars who collected the pieces neglected to establish the identity of the artists, for they assumed, often incorrectly, that the sculptors were anonymous. The opposite of this assumption is far more often true. Where we do have evidence, it becomes clear that the individual sculptors were known, their works were admired, and their genius was celebrated.

History

There are no written records for the greater part of the past of sub-Saharan Africa. As noted in chapter 4, African history is often reconstructed from a variety of sources. Writing was usually the province of outsiders, such as travelers, merchants, and missionaries. Their descriptions of the arts, when they do exist, are often flawed by prejudgments based on religious faith, monetary goals, or cultural bias. Very few art objects were taken out of Africa before the late nineteenth century; indeed, few objects of any sort survive from the early years of European contact (plate 39). Since the prime reason for the European presence on the African coast was trade in pepper, ivory, gold, and slaves, scant attention was paid to objects such as sculpture. However, there was some interest in crafts, particularly woven cloths, which were used as mediums of exchange in the mercantile trade on the West African coast. Benin cloth was exchanged for gold at Elmina; and the Portuguese imported cloth from North Africa and quickly established factories in the Cape Verde Islands where cloth used as currency was manufactured. However, almost the only art objects carried to Europe were apparently produced for Europeans: the so-called Afro-Portuguese ivories (plate 40). These examples of late fifteenth and sixteenth century ivory carving were exported from the areas of Sherbro (present-day Sierra Leone), Benin, and the kingdom of Kongo. Although for the most part they took European forms such as saltcellars and spoons, they were nevertheless African in style and workmanship.

For clues to the early history of African art, it is necessary to depend on archaeology, the scientific study of objects that survive underground. Most art objects produced in recent times are of perishable materials such as wood and vegetable fibers, and there is no reason to suppose that this has not always been the case. Arts in less characteristic materials such as fired clay, bronze, and brass are very nearly the only ones to survive underground. Of necessity knowledge of earlier arts is limited to such objects and as a result the view of earlier arts and cultures is warped. Yet art historians must depend on these survivals for some idea of the character, form, and style of early African art forms.

The terra-cotta figures of Nok in Nigeria are, thus far, the earliest sculptural tradition that has been discerned south of the Sahara. Dating from the late first millennium B.C., it seems to spring from an early iron-using society that may have practiced settled agriculture. There is no clear evidence to explain the

30. Figure of a kneeling man. Nok culture. Northern Nigeria. Late first
millennium B.C. Terra-cotta. H. 4⅛".
Collection: Jos Museum. Photo courtesy Bernard Fagg.

32. Twin figures (*ibeji*). Yoruba. Abeokuta, Nigeria. Wood, beads. H. 9⅜".

Private collection. Photo by Ken Strothman.

31. Standing figure. Lulua. Zaire. Wood. H. 17".

Collection: Indiana University Art Museum. Ex. Wielgus Collection. Photo courtesy Indiana University Art Museum.

3. Standing male ancestor figure with upraised arms. Dogon. Mali. Wood. H. 44".
Wielgus Collection. Photo courtesy Raymond Wielgus.

34. Personal protective figure (*ikenga*). Igbo. Southeastern Nigeria. Wood. H. 24".
Collection: Indiana University Art Museum. Photo courtesy Indiana University Art Museum.

35. Face mask in the form of a hornbill. Men's society.
Dan style. Liberia. Wood. H. 12½".
Collection: Indiana University Art Museum. Photo courtesy
Indiana University Art Museum.

37. Casque mask for Bundu women's society. Mende. Sierra Leone. Wood. H. 15".
Private collection. Photo by Ken Strothman.

36. Crest mask in the form of an antelope. Bambara. Mali.
Wood. H. 35⅝".
Collection: Indiana University Art Museum. Gift of F.
Stafford. Photo courtesy Indiana University Art Museum.

38. Komo horizontal mask. Bambara. Mali. Wood. L. 27".
Collection: Indiana University Art Museum. Photo courtesy
Indiana University Art Museum.

39. Divination tray collected at Ardra (Porto Nuovo) before 1650.
This may be the earliest surviving example of African sculpture
brought to Europe. Clearly Yoruba in style, it closely resembles
examples collected in the twentieth century. Wood.
Collection: City Museum, Ulm, Germany. Photo courtesy Ulmer
Museum.

40. Afro-Portuguese saltcellar. Sherbro. Sierra Le-
one. Sixteenth century. Ivory. H. 12".
Collection: Katherine White. Photo courtesy
Cleveland Museum of Art.

41. Fragmentary head. Ife. Southwestern Nigeria. The classic phase at
    Ife has been dated as early as the ninth century and is certainly before
    the thirteenth century. Terra-cotta. H. 6″.
    Collection: The Brooklyn Museum, lent by the Guennol Collection. Photo
    courtesy Brooklyn Museum.

42. Figure of an *oni* (king) of Ife. Southwestern Nigeria. Classic phase.
Bronze. H. 18⅜".
Collection: Oni of Ife. Photo courtesy of Museum of African Art, Eliot
Elisofon Archives, Washington, D.C.

43. Head of an *oba* (king) from an ancestral altar. Benin. Southwestern
Nigeria. Middle period. Possibly sixteenth century. Bronze. H. 11¼".
Collection: Indiana University Art Museum. Photo courtesy Indiana Univer-
sity Art Museum.

44. Plaque from palace facade depicting an *oba* with attendants. Benin.
Southwestern Nigeria. Middle period. Sixteenth to seventeenth century. Bronze. H. 19½".

Collection: The Metropolitan Museum of Art, The Michael C. Rockefeller
Memorial Collection of Primitive Art. Photo courtesy Metropolitan Museum
of Art, New York.

45. The Golden Stool of the Ashanti. Ghana.
Cast gold.
Archives: Museum der Basler Mission, Basel,
Switzerland.

46. Portrait of head used in royal funerals. He-
man, Ghana. Sixteenth to seventeenth century. Terra-cotta. H. 9".
Collection: The Grunwald Collection. Photo courtesy Ken Strothman.

47. Chief sword-bearer to the Asantehene
ing two state swords.
Photo courtesy Martha Ehrlich.

48. Fertility doll (*akuaba*). To insure the health, beauty, and successful delivery of an unborn child. Ashanti. Ghana. Wood. H. 13¾".
Collection: Indiana University Art Museum. Photo courtesy Indiana University Art Museum.

49. Mask worn by young initiates of the Mukanda initiation camp at public dances. Yaka. Zaire. Wood. H. 14".
Collection: Indiana University Art Museum. Photo courtesy Indiana University Art Museum.

50. Bedu mask. A major responsibility of Bedu is to protect a village by warding off misfortune: disease, witchcraft, evil, drought. Bondoukou area, Ivory Coast and Ghana. Wood. H. 83⅜".
Collection: Indiana University Art Museum. Photo courtesy Indiana University Art Museum.

51. Men's looms.
Archives: Museum der Basler Mission, Basel, Switzerland.

53. Women's loom. Okene, Nigeria.
Photo courtesy R. Sieber.

52. A young Senegalese girl with a finely plaited coiffure.
Photo courtesy United Nations/ CH/ jr.

54. Maasai girl with an accumulation of jew
Photo courtesy C. Zagourski.

meaning or use of the terra-cotta figures. It might be inferred from later instances, however, that they were commemorative or ancestral and that the persons honored were of high status, priests or rulers or priest-rulers. One small figure shows a bearded man heavily bedecked with ornaments, particularly ropes of beads (plate 30). An accumulation of ornaments is often related closely to prestige, expressing status and displaying wealth.

One of the excavations at Igbo-Ukwo, also in Nigeria, dating from the late first millennium A.D., revealed the burial of an important person. The arts associated with the burial and with a nearby shrine reveal an impressive command of lost-wax metal-casting for the first time in West Africa. The lost-wax technique consists of encasing a wax model in clay; after the wax is melted and poured off, the hollow thus created is filled with molten bronze or brass. Although figurative elements are rare, the majority of the objects seem designed to celebrate the leader, possibly a priest-king.

The terra-cottas and bronzes of Ife (plates 41 and 42), cast by the lost-wax method, were in use before the thirteenth century A.D. and clearly celebrated leadership. The present *Oni*, or king, and his elders recognized at once the costume and attributes on the sculptures to be those of an *Oni*. However, an interruption of some sort must have intervened to separate the objects from living memory, for the specific meaning and use of the figures and heads are not recalled. There is some evidence that seems to indicate that the sculptures were displayed on altars, just as later commemorative bronze heads of deceased *Obas* (kings) were placed on altars at Benin. In fact, there is at Benin an oral tradition that the leadership and the brass-casting tradition originated at Ife.

Benin, unlike Ife, was visited by early European travelers, and references to bronze heads from the *Obas'* altars (plate 43) and plaques from the palace facade (plate 44) occur in European accounts of the mid-seventeenth and early eighteenth centuries, although the tradition was then several centuries old. Many of the traditions were lost and the sense of continuity was broken when, late in the nineteenth century, an unfortunate misunderstanding led to an ambush of a visiting group of Europeans and their attendants by a Benin war party. This so-called massacre resulted in the "Punitive Expedition" of 1897, when the city was sacked by British troops and the *Oba* was sent into exile. Because only the *Oba* could commission the brass-casters, their workshop ceased until the early 1930s when an *Oba* was again allowed to rule. Since then the workshop has produced mostly tourist pieces that copy earlier types.

After the fall of Benin, as earlier in Ethiopia and at Kumasi (the Ashanti capital in the Gold Coast), objects of intrinsic, aesthetic, or curiosity value were taken as loot to be auctioned in Europe. The proceeds went to establish a fund for the widows and orphans of British soldiers killed in the engagement. This prize-taking, as it was politely called, resulted at Benin in the stripping of the altars of bronze heads and other relics, and the removal of a great number of plaques. Taken without any record of placement or meaning, these items nevertheless have found their way into many museums and collections, where they are among the most prized examples of African art.

Unlike the "interruptions" at Ife and Benin, traditional leadership and the arts associated with it have continued more or less unbroken among the Akan peoples of modern-day Ghana despite the British-Ashanti wars of the last quarter of the nineteenth century. Symbols of leadership that remain in use range from the Golden Stool of the Ashanti (plate 45) to terra-cotta heads used at royal funerals (plate 46).

Although Western aesthetic preferences clearly fall upon the magnificent figurative sculptures in bronze and terra-cotta, other types of leadership arts reveal the fascinating growth of symbolic forms. Among the Akan, stools and swords were, and are, utilitarian objects. It is easy to understand how a sword can become a symbol of power and how its form may change to reflect the transformed meaning, until, in the end, it becomes useless as a sword. Akan royal swords, with gold handles, lace-like openwork blades, and ornately decorated scabbards, are symbolically useful as important tokens of royal authority, although they are functionally useless as swords (plate 47).

The change of stool from furniture to symbol is also traceable. Among the Akan, stools, which are personal household furniture, are believed to house the soul of the owner. If the owner is a chief the stool becomes far more important than that of a commoner because the Akan believe that the leader is divine and that the well-being of the kingdom is allied to the well-being of the king's soul. Thus the stool of a living leader becomes tied to the kingdom, and the stool of a dead leader becomes both the repository of his soul and a part of the dynastic heritage. To cap this system, which existed in many Akan kingdoms, the founder of the Ashanti state invented the Golden Stool (plate 45), which is believed to house the collective soul of the Ashanti people. It has become the ultimate symbol of the solidarity and cohesion of the nation. Because of its importance it is carefully guarded, has a throne for itself, and is exhibited publicly only on the most important state occasions.

Arts of Security and Social Control

In all societies the arts serve a multiplicity of functions. In Africa, in addition to exalting leadership, a major focus of the arts is religion. Masks may honor the dead, implore rain, cleanse a village of disease or witchcraft, or celebrate a deity. Other carvings may depict ancestors or symbolize nature spirits, aid a diviner or protect a shrine or household from evil forces.

Each person occupies a particular place in his world. The attainment of that place, indeed the entire flow of a person's life, may be carefully controlled by the culture. All members are born and die; many attain adulthood, are married, and become parents. Some are special, such as twins (plate 32) or those believed to have been born under supernatural guidance. For these and many other conditions, art forms often become part of the system to insure success in achieving goals. For example, birth may need the supernatural aid that is symbolized by a wooden figure such as the *Akuaba* of the Akan of Ghana (plate 48).

The transition from childhood to adulthood is a time for instruction in the ways of the group: accepted behavior patterns are defined, and the responsibilities of marriage and parenthood are delineated. Further, the history of the group and the "secrets" of either the men's or the women's organizations are taught, often along with a craft. An individual enters the period of instruction as a child and emerges as an adult. Masks used by the adult initiators or by the initiates in the rituals that surround the coming-of-age ceremonies often become the symbols of the society and its secrets. Examples range from the men's Poro and the women's Bundu societies of Liberia and Sierra Leone (see plates 35 and 37) to the Mukanda initiation camps of central Zaire (plate 49).

In cultures that have noncentralized political systems, control of activities is often accomplished through group decisions or social pressures. In such cultures works of art may serve as agents of social control. Masks such as the Igala *orumamu* mask may supervise the discovery and punishment of murderers; among the Bambara, certain masks symbolize and reinforce the authority of men's groups to seek out and destroy antisocial behavior, adulterers, poisoners, and witches (plate 38). Much of the misfortune that may settle upon a village in the form of illness, sterility, or crop failures is felt to be of supernatural origin and the result of evil forces. These evils can be eradicated and the village cleansed by sanitizing acts, ritually and regularly performed by masked dancers. One instance of this is the Bedu masking tradition of western Ghana and the eastern Ivory Coast (plate 50).

At times masks can be the symbols of governance as well. For example, some Poro society masks are badges of authority; the masked figure may serve as a judge, settling quarrels between individuals, families, or larger groups (plate 35). Thus masks which act as protectors, as peacekeepers, or as agents of social control all contribute to a larger sense of group solidarity and security.

In addition, the future and its uncertainties can be faced more confidently if some of its possibilities or pitfalls are anticipated through divination. Many

African societies have complex systems of divination in which decorated objects aid in the casting of the future (plate 39). Also an individual's security may be enhanced by cult membership or through the use of a personal shrine, such as the *Ikenga* of the Ibo of Nigeria (plate 34).

It is not possible here to specify all the uses of African sculptures. It must suffice to state that the range and the variations of uses are great but that ultimately each seeks in a specific fashion to make more secure the way of life of its users. Art becomes more than the symbol of a better life, it serves as an active agent in the attainment of that goal.

At the same time that the motivation for African art seems to lie in utilitarian concerns, there is both explicit and inferential evidence for aesthetic guidelines and preferences. Beauty and skill were used to enhance the power and effectiveness of objects. At times aesthetic preferences must be inferred from the careful craftsmanship and the brilliant command of forms and materials; at times there is direct evidence of attitudes that exercised control over the artisans. One noteworthy criterion of Yoruba aesthetics that seems to be widespread in Africa is an emphasis on youthful form in figure carvings. Many ancestral or commemorative figures depict young adulthood whatever the real age of the subject. Thus, for example, twins or kings (plates 32 and 42) are shown as young adults even though the twins probably died in infancy and the kings may have lived to old age. From such evidence it is possible to suggest that the concept or awareness of an ideal is one aspect of African aesthetic preference. Thus it is clear that although African art served both practical and spiritual purposes, the objects reflected a well-developed sense of aesthetic discrimination.

The Range of Arts

Among the Yoruba it was held that each village should be self-sufficient. Just as each family was responsible for its own food, each village unit was responsible for its own tools and utensils, its political and religious experts and its craftsmen and craftswomen. For the most part this ideal of self-sufficiency seems to have existed in much of traditional Africa. These seemingly self-sufficient groups, however, were in fact often in contact with other cultures. Thus works of art and the artisans served a far greater audience than is usually assumed.

The men were blacksmiths and sculptors, workers in wood, iron, and brass, and the women were potters. In many parts of West Africa male weavers, working on narrow horizontal looms, produced cloth as a family industry (plate 51). Women weavers, using wide vertical looms, worked more to meet family needs, although some ritual and some trade weaving existed (plate 53). The famous Benin cloths used in early trade may have been made by women. Men produced the fine raffia cloths of western and central Zaire, and women embroidered the famous cut pile designs of the Kuba. Artists were rarely self-taught. Often a skill was learned because the specialty was a family affair, as with blacksmiths and weavers. In the western Sudan blacksmiths constituted a group apart, endogamous and ritually independent of the groups they serviced. An artisan could also learn a skill by becoming apprenticed to a master. Despite their special skills, few artists earned a living at their trade and nearly all were part-time specialists who were also agriculturists like the majority of the population. The products served the basic needs of the community, and for the most part practical needs were simply met. Hoes, knives, adzes, pottery, cooking vessels, or baskets and calabashes for storage were utilitarian and most often undecorated. Yet rich and ornate decoration did exist, and nearly all aspects of life were open to aesthetic elaboration. No surface was unavailable or inappropriate for ornamentation. Thus the human skin could be painted, tatooed, or scarified, hair could be coiffed (plate 52), cloth painted, dyed or stamped, or woven with simple stripes or rich overlay designs, doors carved, the body hung with jewelry or cloths (plate 54), the house painted, the shrine decorated, the stool engraved, the pottery bowl incised, or the calabash pyrograved.

In brief, no aspect of material life was immune from decoration, and that decoration, often expressive of prestige, was at times symbolic as well as handsome. Stamped textile designs might have historical connotations, or designs might be named for the rulers for whom they were invented, as with the *adinkra* and *kente* cloths of Ghana. Other patterns could bear names that were simply, like the pattern itself, to delight. An *adire* cloth of the Yoruba was called "Amerika" apparently because the name was synonymous with wealth and the exotic.

Conclusion

Thus the arts of sub-Saharan Africa range across the entire fabric of life. They are rich in associations that reflect the basic belief patterns of the cultures that produced them. Ranging from cosmetics to sculpture, from basketry to bronze-casting, from the decorative to the deeply symbolic, they indicate the inventive richness of traditional African life patterns.

SUGGESTIONS FOR FURTHER READING

d'Azevedo, W., ed. *The Traditional Artist in African Society*. Bloomington: Indiana University Press, 1973.

Bascom, William. *African Art in Cultural Perspective*. New York: W. W. Norton & Co., Inc., 1973.

Cornet, Joseph. *Art of Africa*. London: Phaidon, 1971. (Zaire)

Delange, Jacqueline. *The Art and Peoples of Black Africa*. New York: Dutton Paperback, 1974.

Sieber, Roy. *African Textiles and Decorative Arts*. New York: The Museum of Modern Art, 1972. (survey of crafts of weaving and jewelry and body ornamentation)

Sieber, Roy and Arnold Rubin. *Sculpture of Black Africa*. The Paul Tishman Collection. Los Angeles County Museum of Art, 1968. (discusses style areas)

Thompson, R. F. *Black Gods and Kings*. Museum and Laboratories of Ethnic Arts and Technology, Los Angeles, 1971; Bloomington: Indiana University Press, 1976. (Yoruba)

Willett, Frank. *Ife in the History of West African Sculpture*. New York: McGraw-Hill Book Company, 1967.

Alan P. Merriam
Traditional Music
of Black Africa

15 For most Westerners "traditional" conjures up visions of the old, and of the continuity of the old into the present. In applying the concept to societies outside the Western world, the tendency is to insert the idea of the static as well. For Westerners, traditional societies are rural societies which are not modern, which cling to old ways, and which have not kept up with the times. As noted in the introductory chapters, this view is not an accurate one, particularly when applied to Africa, a continent of rapid changes which reach deeply into many aspects of life. The term traditional describes the handing down of knowledge, belief, and custom from generation to generation, and is usually thought of as being accomplished by word of mouth; in this sense, all societies and their knowledge are at least partly traditional. Furthermore, what is and is not traditional depends both upon the individual's perspective and upon the time at which the judgment is made.

Music is perhaps particularly susceptible to misjudgment in this matter, for Westerners seem especially prone to look upon the music of other peoples as old, static, and representative of past ages. Certainly less information is available for African music than for many other aspects of African life. Music leaves tangible residue only in the form of some instruments and occasional pictorial evidence; the sound of music, the succession of music intervals, the ideals sought in vocal expression, the role of the musician, the uses and functions of music— these are almost impossible to recover. Thus, with a few exceptions, knowledge of African music is of recent origin.

Music Areas of Africa

While in some ways Africa may be viewed as a whole when discussing music, closer examination shows that generalizations on this broad level are not particularly fruitful, except as they permit problems of description and analysis to be broken into manageable units. It is useful here to divide Africa into two parts: one, the Sahara Desert region and the entire area of North Africa, and the other the southern fringes of the desert and all Black Africa to the south. The music of these two areas differs markedly. The music of the northern region is Arabic in origin, style, and tradition, a situation that seems to have begun at an early date. With the establishment of Islam in the seventh century A.D., the Arab world was relatively unified, and Egypt was soon taken into its orbit. In 1056, the Berber Almoravids became a political force in North Africa, and from this period at the latest, Arabic music style was firmly established in Africa north of the Sahara. This Arabic tradition is best studied within its own framework and will not be considered here except to point out that desert and North African styles do show influences from Africa south of the Sahara and that the Arabic style has had a definite impact on the south.

The focus of this chapter, then, is Africa south of the Sahara, a vast area within which substantial diversity occurs. Stretching across its middle portion, however, in West, Central, and East Africa, is a great belt of peoples who form the heart of Black Africa and whose music systems come to mind when Westerners think about African music. While some legitimate controversy exists as to whether East Africa, for example, should be split off musically from the remainder of the area because of some of the peculiarities of music style found there, in the grand view this is not a pertinent debate.

This central music area is bounded on the north by the area of Arabic influence; less generally recognized is that marked variations in the basic Black African music style are also found to the east, to the south, and even within the central core. To the east is the Cushitic tradition of Ethiopia and the Horn area in general. This includes the music of the Coptic Church, which has been separated from both Western and Orthodox Christianity for more than fifteen hundred years; its music tends to be slow, restrained, ametric, antiphonal, heterophonic, and somewhat melismatic, and the influence of the Arabic tradition is evident. Other music of the East Horn shows Black African characteristics, but these are less well known and less studied than are the Coptic and Arabic traditions.

To the south, two musics exist which to the Western ear stand as variants from the central style rather than as markedly different forms such as the Arabic and Coptic. The first of these, the music of the San of the southwestern part

of Africa, is characterized by the use of falsetto, yodeling, hocketing (a technique in which the melodic line is distributed among several voices), disjunct
melody (wide skips in the melodic line), and dense texture represented by polyphony, various vocal timbres in hocket, and solo voices which sometimes emerge
as leading melodic indicators. One of the mysteries of African music is that this
style is duplicated to a remarkable degree by the music of the African Pygmies,
who are scattered about in small groups, primarily in Zaire, Congo, Central
African Republic, and Gabon. A number of possible explanations for this phenomenon have been suggested, such as diffusion, independent invention, psy-
chic unity, and others, but none seems to be at all satisfactory.

The most elaborate explanation[1] for the situation suggests that the music
of the African Hunters (the San and the Pygmies) represents an aboriginal,
even primeval basis for Black African music. The assumption is that these
peoples are Africa's oldest extant population and that they once inhabited a
much larger portion of the continent than they do at present. Their music style
was then borrowed by other, non-Pygmy or non-San peoples, and even today
the groups whose music style is most akin to that of the African Hunter are
those who are their closest neighbors, and their songs are usually the most conservative. According to this interpretation, the African Hunter style fades out
and disappears among the Berbers, Arabs, Cushites, and other peoples to the
north and east: "the common stylistic thread which unites all Africa is repeti-
tious, cohesive, overlapping or interlocked, multi-leveled, and hot," and these
are characteristics of African Hunter music.

In order to accept this view, it is necessary to make a number of highly
problematic assumptions. The explanation depends upon the notion that the
African Hunter peoples have sustained a single music style for thousands of
years. Yet during this time they have experienced dispersal across the continent,
a sharp decline in number, and a mode of life which emphasizes tiny groups of
people. While continuity of a single style is conceivable, nothing confirms it in
such extraordinary detail. And if the African Hunters began as a cohesive group
and then spread all over Africa, so many factors would come to bear upon a
music style in such a migratory situation that it seems inconceivable to suppose
the style would remain the same in all places. Thus the mystery remains, for San
and Pygmy styles *are* highly similar, and the same style occurs sporadically in
many parts of Africa among both Pygmy and non-Pygmy peoples.

The second group to the south is made up of Nguni peoples, including,
among others, the Zulu, Swazi, and Xhosa. While those who have studied their
traditional music hear it as more or less characteristically Black African, its variant status is indicated by its usual lack of a steady tempo, its slow movement,
the presence of spoken recitative, strong portamento (sliding from one note to

the next), its large but flaccid sound, and its extremely dense texture. Much remains to be learned about this music, but, on the basis of recorded samples, it seems to diverge from the central stream of Black African music.

The broad musical picture of Africa south of the Sahara, then, shows a large central musical core in which a substantial number of stylistic characteristics are shared, bordered by strongly different styles in the north and northeast and by variant forms in the south. Two further points must be added to complete this discussion of music areas. The first is that no consideration is given here to the music of settlers in Africa, such as white South Africans, or East African Asians, since these music styles do not fall within the purview of traditional Black African music. Second, the generalizations apply specifically to elements of music stylistics or structures. If the distribution of music instruments, mental concepts about music, or the role of the musician were examined, for example, it is almost certain that some very different groupings would emerge.[2]

Music in African Society

Many comparisons have been made between music in Africa and music in the Western world in terms of what is usually called functionality. It is asserted that more importance is placed upon music in Africa than in the West, that no distinction is drawn between the artist and the craftsman or the artist and the audience, and that music is an all-pervasive and continual aspect of African society. These generalizations have not proved to be significantly true. It is sufficient to think of the enormous proportion of the population of the United States involved in music making to realize that the first assertion is exaggerated. In respect to the second, while it is true that in African societies many persons participate in music, some do so infrequently, some half-heartedly, and some not at all, the last sometimes claiming, incidentally, to have what Westerners may describe as a "tin ear." Furthermore, outstanding performers receive special recognition, while lesser lights are dismissed as journeymen; and celebrated bards gather large, expectant, and knowledgeable audiences who listen to their performances with care and discrimination.

The old cliché which holds that African societies are marked by a constant ongoing round of music making also deserves to be laid quietly to rest. Some communities clearly mark a daily cycle of events with more music than do others. West African societies may be particularly strong in this respect, and it often seemed to me, while living with a group of Pygmies in the Ituri forest region of what was then the Belgian Congo, that someone was singing or playing a music instrument at every hour of the day and night. On the other hand, among the Songye people of Zaire, days can go by without any music at all, and the only periodic celebration which *required* music occurred at the beginning of each lunar cycle. On specific occasions, of course, such as the "coming out" of twins, or a funeral, the village was filled with music of many kinds.

This leads to an important series of generalizations about how music and its role are conceived by Africans, and here a clear contrast with Western conceptions is to be noted. In Africa, music tends to be tied tightly to the sociocultural events for which it is created; without the events, the music is not produced. Furthermore, this connection extends to the conceptualization of music entities: songs are not thought of as independent and separable units with distinctive titles but rather as sound entities which are identified as a part of the interrelated set of activities that constitute an occasion. While Westerners tend to stress composer and song title, Africans stress the type of song and the situation of which it is a part; African songs often have no titles at all.

The kinds of events with which music in Africa is associated are legion, and examples can be cited from every aspect of society. Social songs, for example, include all those for the various points in the life cycle, as well as for a myriad of social events. Music often plays a strong part in politics, both as the citizens sing of political events and as the ruling hierarchies employ musicians for their own purposes, at court, in legal disputes, to sing praise, and on many other occasions. The connections between religion and music are especially strong, for song and instrumental forms are used to celebrate man's relationship to the cosmos and its beings. Music and dance are inseparably related, and song can form a substantial portion of individual folktales. Music is used everywhere in Africa for purposes of entertainment, and it often serves to educate children and to help keep track of historic events. Its use as a means of social control is widespread: everywhere in the world, and certainly in Africa, people can speak in song as they are not allowed to speak in ordinary discourse, and songs of derision, as well as of advice to erring members of society and to political leaders, are frequent.

Texts form an extremely important part of the music event; indeed, one African scholar regards the close text-music relationship as perhaps the most significant characteristic of African song.[3] This relationship derives in considerable part from the fact that most African languages are tonal; that is, tone itself carries meaning. Thus, the meaning of a two-syllable word with a high tone and a low tone can be completely different from the meaning of the "same" word pronounced with a low tone and a high tone. The importance of phonemic tone for song texts is immediately evident, for if a melody is altered, so is the meaning of the text. Much discussion of this phenomenon has taken place, and some authors have taken the extreme view that all African melody is "in a straightjacket." It is clear, however, that compromises are easily reached;

while music melody must definitely pay strong attention to phonemic tone and to speech melody in general, the rules can be violated and the text meaning retained through the understanding provided by context. It is phonemic tone which makes the phenomenon of linguistic drum-signaling possible; the signaling devices are made in such a way that they can produce more than one tone, and through telescoping and stereotyping based on tone and understood through context, messages can be sent within any language unit. But the important elements in a music event are the messages communicated in song, the close relationship between linguistic and musical tone, and the expressive quality of language through music.

Performers on the African scene range from amateurs to professionals, from casual to fervent practitioners, and from individual to group participants. A person may join a singing group, for example, when moved to do so by a particular series of events on a particular occasion, but on the next such occasion he may choose not to participate at all. Professionals, on the other hand, take part consistently in those music events for which they are qualified, and by the nature of their professionalism they are most often the leaders. In the Western world a "professional" is a person who earns his living from his special skill. This definition, however, is not applicable on a worldwide basis; many persons of the highest musical skill are paid in ways other than monetarily, and some are not paid at all. A professional can better be defined as a person who is accorded recognition by the members of his society as an outstanding performer in his special area of expertise. Viewed in this way, music professionals in Africa range from performers in Pygmy groups, who are seldom, if ever, paid for their performances except by social approval, to highly involved specialists such as the *griots* of the western Sudan, who are professional in every sense of the word, including the economic. If these examples are at the opposite ends of the scale, many others range between, such as the musicians in Songye society, who are ranked according to a hierarchical set of criteria but none of whom, even those at the top of the scale, make their living entirely from music.

Both professionals and amateurs are trained in a number of ways, ranging from almost complete informality to direct schooling. Most members of African societies, and some persons who become professionals as well, learn music through imitation. Especially in West Africa, the institution of the bush school, a protracted training period in which both boys and girls (usually separately) are taught the important aspects of their way of life, provides a special opportunity to learn music. Some persons are tapped by various processes of social selection for special training as musicians, and this is often achieved through a formal apprenticeship which can be highly rigorous and of long duration.

As the range of musicianship and that of instruction vary, so does the role behavior of African musicians. The musician in Songye society, for example, illustrates a pattern which appears in several parts of the world, including other parts of Africa. In this case, both the musician and the members of society at large view professionals as persons of low status who exhibit patterns of behavior which deviate from the usual and which are considered excessive, distasteful, or both. At the same time, the service performed by the musician for the community is felt to be of such signal importance that life without him is almost inconceivable. This ambivalent attitude allows the Songye musician to indulge in behavior which would not be tolerated from other persons, and it is clear that he takes advantage of the situation to flaunt his independence of conventional norms. Some evidence from the Songye, from the island of Madagascar, and from other parts of Africa also associates the deviant pattern of musicianly behavior with transvestism (but not with homosexuality), but such a correlation is by no means clear. At the other end of this particular continuum lie the Dan of the Ivory Coast, whose musicians show no special actions, clothing, or any other identifying role behavior, although professionals are a part of the society.[4] Once again, the diversity of African practices is underlined.

Professional bards are very much a part of the African scene, often making a living at their profession; they are highly skilled not only as musicians, but as dancers and raconteurs as well. Music groups are sometimes organized along sex lines and are sometimes mixed; they may come together spontaneously and briefly, or they may be highly organized on a permanent basis, with leaders and officers. Children are musically active, and game playing frequently involves the singing of songs.

It should be clear at this point that it is not easy to generalize about the relationships between African society and African music. For each generalization, an opposite generalization almost always seems possible. This is due in part to the great diversity in African music and in part to the lack of knowledge concerning the social aspects of music in Africa. It may be that further study will indicate that even the assumptions of diversity have simply been the result of a lack of understanding of African music.

Music Instruments

African music instruments show an extraordinary variety of forms and musical uses—and here the evidence is complete enough to confirm this diversity. Both orchestras and instrumental soloists are found in Africa. The soloists play on almost every imaginable type of instrument: harps, lutes, lyres, zithers, drums, horns, reed pipes, and flutes, among others. Orchestras vary from the traditional three-drum choir of West Africa, through groups made up of several xylophones plus drums and rattles in Central Africa, to huge ensembles involving perhaps twenty xylophones and similar numbers of dancers and singers among the Chopi of Mozambique, or the twenty-drum choirs of parts of East Africa. African instrumental efforts are often directed toward the accompaniment of song, and the instrumentalist is sometimes also the singer and sometimes simply the accompanist. In the latter case, a singer or group of singers may be accompanied by a single instrument or by an orchestral ensemble.

Perhaps, the most pervasive instruments in Africa are those which fall into the class known as idiophones ("any instrument that yields a sound by its own substance, being stiff and elastic enough to vibrate without requiring a stretched membrane or strings."[5]). Among these are xylophones, which are distributed over most of Africa south of the Sahara; their form ranges from a simple slab or two laid across the knees, as among some Pygmy groups, to at least twenty-five keys, as among the Pende of Zaire. A second major idiophone is an instrument which most believe to be of African invention; often called *sansa* or a related term in West Africa, *mbira* in East and southern Africa, and *likembe* or *kasayi* in Central Africa, its distribution is again almost ubiquitous south of the Sahara, although it is perhaps least frequently found in West Africa. The instrument consists of eight to thirty keys which are fastened at one end, run across a bridge, and are left free at the other end: the free end is plucked with the thumbs and/or the fingers. Among other important idiophones are rattles of many types, as well as bells, gongs, and slit drums; it has often been said that almost any object which can be plucked, struck, shaken, beaten, or rubbed can, depending upon the context, be absorbed into an African musical performance.

Membranophones ("any instrument in which sound is produced by vibration of a stretched membrane, brought about by striking, friction, or sound waves") are represented in Africa by a wide variety of types, including single- and double-headed, short and tall, with closed or open end. Round, square, tympani- and pot-shaped drums are found, and water drums are by no means uncommon. Drums are played with sticks, with hands, or with a hand and stick combination; drummers often use a complex system of techniques for striking, using different parts on the hand on different points on the drumhead in order to produce a variety of sounds. Drums may be played singly, in pairs, in groups of three (common in West Africa), and in large ensembles of twenty or more (East Africa). They may be stood upon the ground, carried by a strap, held in the arms or between the legs, or sat upon when played. Although it is often

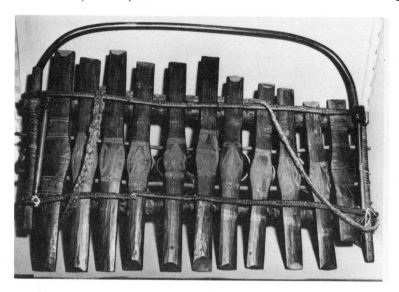

55. A xylophone of the Kuba, Zaire.
Photo by C. Lamote, Congopresse.

56. Musician playing the *notmbe lokombi*, a type of zither, Isange, Zaire.
Photo by C. Lamote, Congopresse.

suggested that drums are the major instrument of Africa, idiophones are more important when the area is viewed as a whole, and some societies in Africa south of the Sahara hardly use drums at all.

Aerophones ("any music instrument in which tone is generated by means of air set in vibration") are represented by horns, flutes, panpipes, and ocarinas. Horns, which are most common in West Africa and the Congo basin, may be constructed of horn, ivory, wood, gourds, and, today, metal. Some are end-blown and others side-blown. Although they are used primarily for signaling and as an addition to other music, they are also played in groups as musical ensembles in their own right. Flutes are widespread in Africa, appearing sometimes with fingerholes and sometimes without (whistles); they, too, may be end- or side-blown. Panpipes are found in much of Africa south of the Sahara, but little is known of their music. Ocarinas (globular flutes) are also widespread, both as signaling and as music-making devices.

Chordophones ("any music instrument having strings as tone-producing elements, the pitch of the instrument being dependent on the strings") are represented by a number of instruments. The musical bow is found almost everywhere, and in a great variety of forms; it is sometimes furnished with gourd resonators, and sometimes the mouth is used as the resonator. The single-stringed bowed lute (western Sudan and East Africa) is probably an instrument adapted from the Arabic *rebec*. Plucked lutes, lyres, harps, and many types of zithers abound, perhaps most especially in East Africa. Special forms include the *kora* of the western Sudan and the *mvet* of Cameroon, both of which are combination instruments—harp-lutes.

This represents only a small sampling of the music instruments of Africa, but it seems reasonable to say that Africans south of the Sahara use a variety of indigenous music instruments perhaps as great as that of any area of the world with the exception of the West.

Structure and Style in African Music

Most characterizations of structure in African music have been arrived at by Western analysts and not by African musicians or scholars, with a few notable exceptions.[6] And although hundreds, possibly thousands, of publications concerning the structure of African music have appeared, scholars are still far from a complete understanding of basic principles. Those who have studied African music generally agree that its most characterizing feature is the all-pervasiveness and complexity of its rhythmic structure. While the principles upon which the rhythm is based are understood differently by various researchers, almost all theories of African musical rhythm assume the presence of four basic rhythmic elements: an equal pulse base; meter, or something like it; a specific organizing principle which holds a diversity of simultaneous rhythmic streams together; and a specific starting point for rhythmic groupings (also implied in meter).

"Equal pulse base" involves a conception of time which is held in most of Western society and which may be basic to mankind as a whole. In this conception, time is organized in a series of equally spaced pulses which extend infinitely both backward and forward from a particular time point. Important here are the equality of the spacing of the beats and their infinite quality—they have always gone on, and they will always continue, so far as is known. This conception of time may be derived from the rhythms of the human body, particularly the steady heartbeat, but it is not known whether this is in fact true, or even whether all people of the world share the Western view. In any case, researchers in African music take it for granted that this conception of time is also held by Africans, and, indeed, judging from the nature of the rhythms used, this assumption, although as yet unverified, is not unreasonable.

Given an equal pulse base, the presence of a steady musical beat, which indeed occurs in most African music, may also be assumed. The presence of a steady beat in turn suggests that some underlying structure must be present. Thus most researchers do not think of African music as a simple progression of single beats (1 1 1 1 1 1 1 1 1) throughout the duration of a song; instead, theorists have in the past ascribed the Western notion of meter (the regular recurrence of stressed and unstressed beats in time) to African music and have thus been able to speak of 3/4 or 2/4 or 4/4 time. This, in its turn, implies the presence of measures and bar lines, of accent, and of an initial accent or downbeat. A further outgrowth of these assumptions is the principle of multiple meter, or the simultaneous use of two or more meters, a tenet accepted in some form by most researchers. Many of these conclusions have been challenged, and they are certainly difficult to prove; those who hold them point to their logicality, given the music as Westerners hear it.

Since African musical rhythm is undeniably complex, scholars have searched for a basic organizing principle which would hold the various rhythmic streams together and centralize them into a single, pulsating, driving unit. This principle is explained by various experts in terms of the beat of "the big drum" in the West African ensemble, which is played in duple meter and never alters its beat;[7] it can also be explained in terms of African motor behavior,[8] or by postulating a "metronome sense" whereby Africans learn to supply a central equal pulse beat no matter what the particular rhythmic circumstances of the music to which they are listening.[9] Yet another explanation [10] is the presence of an inexorable handclap pattern, also based on the equal pulse principle, which continues through a song regardless of whatever else may be happening. In West African music especially, the iron gong, or a similar instrument, sets a steady pulse in a fixed pattern of beats.

To be truly explanatory, these approaches all demand a specific starting point for rhythmic groupings. Recently the concept of "pattern" has been suggested, and this is the most reasonable unifying suggestion thus far; furthermore, it is borne out by the assertions of African musicians themselves. Here "pattern" means a repeated sequence of pulses, arranged in some particular rhythmic organization which either does not vary or which varies minimally, which has defined starting and ending points, and which serves as a centralizing factor for the rhythms of a piece of African music. That pattern exists has been suggested in a number of ways. For example, one scholar[11] uses the concept but not the word in his idea of "crossing the beat" and emphasizes further that the "inexorable handclapping," to which reference has already been made, always starts on a common beat, no matter how many persons are clapping or what the extent of variations in beat patterns might be. In my own experience, the Songye conceptualize xylophone melodies in terms of patterns, and it was not until I could "feel" the beginning and ending points of the patterns that I could make even minimal progress in understanding how to play their xylophone music. The idea of pattern solves a number of the problems raised here: it points directly to an equal pulse base; it implies the presence of meter, measures, accents (less so), and downbeats; and it is itself the organizing principle. Pattern is the most useful concept of African musical rhythm presently available.[12]

However brief this discussion of rhythm, both the idea and the music itself are of a substantial degree of complexity, so much so that it has been suggested that Western notation is inadequate for its representation. Thus a number of ingenious suggestions for different kinds of notation have been made, based either upon graph or upon tablature systems,[13] but none has as yet been generally accepted.

Far less information is available concerning the melodic aspects of African music, and far fewer generalizations have been made, quite probably because scholars have been especially intrigued by the complex problems of rhythm and thus have concentrated their attention upon it.

The pitch system in African music is felt by most researchers to be much like that of Western music, but only one explanation for this apparent similarity has been suggested: that in prehistoric time the Old World landmass, including Africa, was one, and that a widespread music system which shared many similar characteristics was the result. Thus, the Eurafrican music area has been set off from the Sino-Mongolian, the Indo-Arabic, and so forth. Whether or not this is true, few today regard the African pitch system as microtonic, as was once supposed to be the case, although most refer to it as a "natural" (as opposed to a "tempered") scale such as that of the West. Flexibility of pitch also seems to characterize the African system; that is, a given "note" allows for wider ranges of variation than in the West. Indeed, African music does not usually include a central pitch which is always fixed at a certain number of vibrations per second. Instead, a central pitch is chosen, and an instrument like the xylophone is tuned in relation to that pitch. African music, then, can be referred to as based upon a relative rather than a fixed pitch system.

Within the present understanding of this system, very few generalizations are possible concerning scales and modes. However, four types of scales have been distinguished, one based partly upon tuning, one partly on types of intervals used, and two on combinations of both.[14] Whether these are specifically African in form and whether they have identifiable distribution in Africa south of the Sahara remain to be demonstrated. Suffice it to say that African scales consist of two, three, four, five, six, and seven notes, and that chromatic scales are not lacking.

No special internal form of African melody seems to take precedence over others, although some distinctive characteristics are present. Melodic level from beginning to ending tone is either even or slightly descending: sharp descents are found where Arabic influence has been strong. African melody has also been characterized as having rather sharp internal rises, followed by slow descents, so arranged that a given single melody still shows an overall descent from beginning to end. African melody is also frequently considered to be binary in form, with the two parts built about different tones (often spoken of as "dominant" and "tonic") in the scale. African melody has also been characterized as utilizing "off-beat phrasing of melodic accents," by which it is meant that the melodic pulses often fall between the rhythmic pulses instead of coinciding with them.

In terms of overall form, strophic (or "verse") organization, as in the Western ballad, is often present, particularly in the work of solo singers, and some songs are through-composed. The most frequent form, however, is litany, which consists of short phrases repeated over and over, with or without variation. This is manifested in the call-and-response pattern, in which a leader(s) sings a phrase to which a chorus then sings a response; an almost infinite number of variations on this basic form is practiced.[15] The leader and chorus lines also often overlap, leading, some suggest, to forms of canon. Of substantial importance is another litanic form, the melodic-rhythmic ostinato, a repeated rhythmic pattern which forms the basis for a simultaneously played or sung melody. In some parts of Africa, the song cycle acts as an organizing formal principle. Such cycles usually begin and end with specified selections, and are marked by songs which have special meanings and which must be sung at particular times and in particular sequence.

This discussion of melody has applied primarily to vocal forms, but instrumental music shows many of the same characteristics: descending melody, binary form, off-beat phrasing, litany, call and response, and ostinato patterns. Some forms, however, are longer than usual, and the example most frequently cited is the *ngodo*, an orchestral-song-dance form of the Chopi which consists of nine to eleven well-integrated movements and which may last as long as forty-five minutes.

The texture of much of African music can be characterized as dense, although the variety of the music must again be cited, since shepherds, for example, play unaccompanied flute melodies. Even when a single instrument is being played, however, it is most often accompanying a singer, and thus melodic voices are expressed simultaneously.

This leads to the observation that polyphony is common in African music; some authors hold, as well, that harmony is present. Suffice it to say that African music is marked by the simultaneous sounding of two or more pitches. This may take the form of the interplay between a voice and a music instrument, between a chorus and an orchestra, or between music instruments in an orchestral ensemble. Its specific form may be in heterophony (relatively infrequently); in true polyphony, in which two or more independent but complementary melodic lines are sung or played simultaneously; in the use of a melodic ostinato in which one person plays or sings a short, repeated melodic line while a second plays or sings a different line, the phrases of which are often longer than those of the first (this also commonly occurs in xylophone playing); in polyphony created by the use of hocketing; in music instruments, such as the musical bow, which sound overtones clearly; in the singing of parallel intervals, most commonly thirds in West Africa, and frequently fourths and fifths in East Africa; and in various other ways. Whether polyphony or harmony, the simultaneous use of two or more pitches, and thus a dense texture, is a commonplace in African music.

Few studies of vocal style have been made in connection with African music, but it can be said that while singers use an open, resonant voice production, a wide variety of tonal qualities is employed by any single singer. This variation in timbre is most often expressed in different kinds of "burred" tones; that is, both singers and instrumentalists strive not so much for a clear as for a fuzzy or buzzing tone. This shows clearly in music instruments such as the *sanza*, which is often capable of producing a clear, bell-like tone parallel to that of an exceptionally good Western music box, but which is almost invariably fitted with attachments, such as tiny metal collars or bottle caps, which give the tone a buzzing quality. The same is true of xylophones, the resonators of which are often fitted with a particularly heavy spider web which results in the same sort of buzzing quality as that produced by the Western kazoo. This search for a non-clear tone is a characteristic of the African musical sound.

Ornamental devices used by African singers include various forms of the vocal bend and dip, as well as the glissando. Rising attack and falling release are also characteristic, and some songs are shouted, spoken, or whispered.

Conclusion

What is known best about African music is its structural form; much remains to be discovered about music as social and cultural behavior. This chapter began with a discussion of the meaning of the term traditional, and it must be reemphasized that most African music today is traditional, and that much of it is likely to remain so for some time. This is not to say that change has not occurred, that it is not presently occurring, or that it will not occur in the future. Indeed, change is going on today at a faster rate than ever before in African music history, as is shown in chapter 22. However, enough is known about the impact of African music in other parts of the world to show that in many ways it retains its "Africanness" almost no matter what the circumstances. In its simplest dimensions, and assuming by the word "traditional" what sounds African to Africans, traditional African music seems certain to persist for a long time to come.

NOTES

1. Alan Lomax, "The Homogeneity of African–Afro-American Musical Style," in Norman E. Whitten, Jr., and John F. Szwed, (eds.), *Afro-American Anthropology: Contemporary Perspectives* (New York: Free Press, 1970), pp.181–201.

2. Details of music areas in Africa can be found in Lomax, *op cit.*, and in Alan P. Merriam, "African Music," in William R. Bascom and Melville J. Herskovits (eds.), *Continuity and Change in African Cultures* (Chicago: University of Chicago Press, 1959), pp.49–86.

3. Francis Bebey, *African Music: A People's Art* (New York: Lawrence Hill, 1975).

4. Hugo Zemp, *Musique Dan* (Paris: Cahiers de l'Homme, 1971), pp.242–57.

5. Definitions of the great classes of music instruments are taken from Sibyl

Marcuse, *Musical Instruments: A Comprehensive Dictionary* (Garden City, New York: Doubleday, 1964), *passim.*

6. For example, Bebey, "African Music"; J. H. Kwabena Nketia, *The Music of Africa* (New York: W. W. Norton, 1974).

7. W. E. Ward, "Music in the Gold Coast," *Gold Coast Review*, III (July-Dec. 1927), 214, 217, 218, 219, 220.

8. Erich M. von Hornbostel, "African Negro Music," *Africa*, I (Jan. 1928), 25–28.

9. Richard A. Waterman, "African Influence on the Music of the Americas," in *Acculturation in the Americas*, ed. Sol Tax, Proceedings of the Twenty-Nineth International Congress of Americanists, Vol. II (Chicago: Chicago University Press, 1952), pp.211–212.

10. A. M. Jones, "African Rythm," *Africa*, XXIV (Jan. 1954), 26, 27, 28, 39.

11. Ibid.

12. Many of the ideas presented in this section concerning rhythm have been discussed in detail in Merriam, "African Music."

13. See A. M. Jones, *African Music in Northern Rhodesia and Some Other Places* (Livingstone: Occasional Papers of the Rhodes-Livingstone Museum, Number Four, 1949); Moses Serwadda and Hewitt Pantaleoni, "A Possible Notation for African Dance Drumming," *African Music* Vol. IV, No. 2 (1968), 47–52; James Koetting, "Analysis and Notation of West African Drum Ensemble Music," *Selected Reports* Vol. I, No. 3 (1970), 116–46.

14. Nketia, "The Music of Africa," Chapter 11.

15. Ibid.

SUGGESTIONS FOR FURTHER READING

The reader should consult those books and articles cited in the notes to this chapter; in addition, the following will be useful.

Blacking, John. *Venda Children's Songs*. Johannesburg: Witwatersrand University Press, 1967.

Carrington, John F. *Talking Drums of Africa*. London: Carey Kingsgate Press, 1949.

Jones, A. M. *Studies in African Music* (London: Oxford University Press, 1959), 2 vols.

Merriam, Alan P. *African Music on LP: An Annotated Discography*. Evanston: Northwestern University Press, 1970.

Nketia, J. H. Kwabena. *Drumming in Akan Communities of Ghana*. Legon: Thomas Nelson for the University of Ghana, 1963.

Tracey, Hugh. *Chopi Musicians: Their Music, Poetry and Instruments*. London: Oxford University Press for the International African Institute, 1948. Revised edition, 1971.

Wachsmann, Klaus P., ed. *Essays on Music and History in Africa*. Evanston: Northwestern University Press, 1971.

Waterman, Richard A. "African Influence on the Music of the Americas," in Sol Tax, ed. *Acculturation in the Americas*. Chicago: Proceedings of the 29th International Congress of Americanists, Vol. II, pp.207–18.

THE FORCES OF MODERNIZATION

IV

Sara S. Berry
Economic Change
in Contemporary Africa

16 In many African nations independence was expected to usher in a new era of prosperity; as Africans gained control of their own economic resources, it was anticipated that they would use them for the benefit of their compatriots rather than that of their former colonial masters. Those who held these expectations have frequently been disappointed. Although Africa has achieved substantial increases in production since independence, the benefits of this growth have been concentrated in a few countries and are enjoyed by a minority of the people. For the majority, independence has brought little improvement in diet, health, housing, or prospects for steady productive employment—and, for some, conditions have actually worsened.

Economic growth in Africa has entailed increasing involvement in the world economy. Such involvement need not have adverse effects, however; countries such as Britain and the United States have prospered greatly from their international trade and investments. In Africa, on the other hand, economic growth since World War II has often been achieved by increased use of imported capital equipment and supplies without a corresponding expansion of export earnings, and this has resulted in rising external debts. The pace of economic expansion and the kinds of goods produced continue to be heavily influenced by world market conditions and the interests of foreign investors, rather than by the needs of Africans. The extent to which this situation has been a continuation of the disadvantaged position which Africa had in the world economy during the colonial period and the extent to which it has resulted from the policies of African governments or producers since independence are major concerns in this chapter.

Economic development in Africa is not a new phenomenon; African economies have been expanding and absorbing new products and productive techniques for centuries. What distinguishes economic change in contemporary Africa from that of earlier periods is the beginning of industrialization and the widespread practice by governments of economic planning to achieve growth and a more diversified economic structure. These two developments are not unrelated. Planners and politicians frequently regard industrialization as a major if not the most important component of development, and they believe, justifiably, that rapid industrialization will not occur in Africa without massive government action. Thus development planning has usually focused on devising a strategy to bring about industrialization, and the pattern of industrial growth in recent years has been strongly influenced by government policies.

As of the mid-1970s, few African economies could be described as highly industrialized. Compared with other productive activities such as agriculture, raising livestock, or commerce, industry still accounts for only a small proportion of total output in most of Africa (see figure 17).

FIGURE 17

Proportion of Gross Domestic Product Originating in Mining,
Manufacturing, Construction, and Electricity Combined

	1960	1970
North Africa	24.6%	35.9%
West Africa	13.1	25.6
Central Africa	21.4	26.9
East Africa	21.2	22.9
All Africa*	19.9	29.6

Source: UN Economic Commission for Africa, Survey of Economic Conditions, 1970, Part I.
*Excludes South Africa and nonindependent territories.

Manufacturing alone accounted for less than 12 percent of gross domestic product (GDP) in 1970, even though production of manufactured goods expanded very rapidly during the 1950s and absorbed a considerable share of public and foreign resources available for investment.[1] Moreover, industrial growth itself, and policies designed to promote it, have had important (though not always intended) effects on other economic sectors as well. To see why planned industrial development began when it did, what form it has taken, and how it has affected African economies in general, it is necessary to examine some major economic developments in Africa before the Second World War, and then to consider the process of industrialization after the war in its economic and political context.

Economic Change Before World War II

From the sixteenth to the nineteenth centuries, as has been noted in chapter 8, millions of Africans were "exported" from the continent, shipped as slaves to the Americas, the Mediterranean, and the Middle East. As the trade in slaves gradually declined, especially in the second half of the nineteenth century, agricultural and mineral products became Africa's principal exports to the international economy. By the 1840s, West Africans had begun to produce palm oil and peanuts for export to the growing European market for vegetable oils and oilseeds, and by the end of the nineteenth century they were beginning to export cotton, coffee, cocoa, and rubber. Production of export crops expanded rapidly in the twentieth century: two especially notable cases were the Gold Coast's exports of cocoa, which rose from a few hundred tons per annum in the 1890s to 305,000 tons in 1936-37, and peanut exports from Senegal, which increased fourteen-fold in the same period.[2] For sub-Saharan Africa as a whole, nonmineral exports grew at an annual average rate of 7.2 percent between 1907 and 1935.[3] At the same time, the Industrial Revolution in Europe generated a growing demand for minerals, and European firms began to invest in African mines, especially in the southern part of the continent.

The growth of African exports of foodstuffs and raw materials began in response to changing world market conditions well before the imposition of direct European rule at the end of the nineteenth century. In chapter 9 it was noted that European powers established colonial rule in Africa partly to protect an already expanding volume of trade and investment. Although in some areas colonial administrations sought actively to induce or coerce Africans to produce more crops and minerals for European markets, on balance their effect on African economic growth was limited. In terms of economic policy, for example, colonial governments sought to secure a favorable environment for the operation of private enterprise but left it to the companies themselves to determine where and how to exploit Africa's productive potential. In eastern and southern Africa, Europeans acquired direct control of arable land and of forest and mineral resources, and most of the primary products exported from these areas were produced by European-owned concerns. Nearly three-fourths of private European capital invested in sub-Saharan Africa went to the major mineral exporting regions: Union of South Africa, South-West Africa, Northern and Southern

57. A West African woman picking cocoa.
Photo courtesy United Nations/ BZ/ me.

Rhodesia, and Belgian Congo.[4] Colonial administrations permitted white farmers in East and Central Africa to occupy some of the best agricultural land.
They facilitated a steady supply of cheap labor to these farms by, for example,
limiting opportunities for Africans to sell their own agricultural produce on the
world market, or raising taxes in order to force them to seek wage employment.
Where so-called economic incentives proved inadequate, colonial governments
resorted to forced labor and mandatory resettlement of Africans in "reserved
areas" in order to clear additional land for European cultivation. Under these
forced circumstances, neither European nor African farmers were likely to de-

vote much energy to increasing yields or labor productivity on their farms. The exploitation of forest reserves was carried out without regard for conservation and, in some cases, literally at the point of a gun, as on the rubber and palm concessions granted by the colonial governments to private firms in French and Belgian Congo.[5]

In West Africa, on the other hand, Europeans invested primarily in trade rather than in the actual production of export goods. Apart from occasional ventures into mining, especially in the Gold Coast and Sierra Leone, Europeans left the cultivation and extraction of export commodities to Africans and concentrated instead on monopolizing the export-import trade. Thus, the growth of agricultural production for export, which began well before the colonial period, was largely due to African initiative and enterprise. The establishment of colonial rule facilitated the growth of export production by bringing to an end the state of war which had existed among a number of West African peoples for much of the nineteenth century, and by constructing railways into the interior. For example, the construction of railways to northern Nigeria from the coast stimulated peanut and cotton production for the world market. The railways, however, did not serve as the basis of an expanding internal transportation network since they were built only between areas of cash crop production and major ports (see map 9). Moreover, every effort was made to finance railways and other public works out of colonial revenues rather than from the imperial treasury. Indeed, most British colonies actually benefited Britain by exporting more to it annually than they bought there in return.

Colonial officials made occasional efforts to establish plantations or to raise agricultural production by decree in West Africa, but such attempts were usually unsuccessful. In 1908, the governor of the Ivory Coast recorded an incident in which Anyi farmers sabotaged an official effort to establish communal cocoa plots in their villages by pouring hot water on the young plants at night. The Anyi reasoned, with understandable logic, that if Frenchmen were so anxious to have them grow cocoa it must be the French and not themselves who would benefit from the crop, and they wanted no part of it.[6] By contrast, in the Gold Coast and Nigeria, African farmers discovered the commercial advantages of cocoa, coffee, and other crops before British officials were aware of their posibilities, and they developed production entirely on their own.

Whatever the means used, particular colonial peoples were induced to expand export production, and the basic economic result was the same throughout Africa. Colonial economies devoted an increasing proportion of their land, labor, and capital to producing foodstuffs and raw materials for the world market. The consequences of this increasing specialization in agricultural and mineral production for export have been debated extensively by both scholars and statesmen. Some have emphasized the enterprise and ingenuity displayed by African producers in adapting to changing world market opportunities and in expanding production for export. Others have painted a gloomy picture of Africa's growing dependence on foreign capital and uncertain world markets; and they have further argued that this pattern of specialization has contributed to a long-run process of underdevelopment, in which Africa has fallen further and further behind the wealthy, capitalist economies in productive capacity and material well-being. Actually, these two views are not necessarily inconsistent. Individual Africans have adopted new methods of production and invested in the means to increase productive capacity in a variety of circumstances. Many West African farmers took advantage of relatively favorable market opportunities to open up extensive areas for cultivation and to accumulate productive capital in the form of coffee, cocoa, and rubber trees. As their incomes from the sale of export crops increased, so did their expenditures on a variety of domestically produced goods, ranging from foodstuffs to furniture, which in turn created new opportunities for expanded production and commerce within West Africa. Tree crop farmers also invested part of their earnings in other forms of capital, including trade, transport, and housing, and in such public facilities as schools, clinics, and market stalls. They also often paid school fees for their children and other young relatives, thus contributing to the growth of an educated labor force. Although the gains from agricultural growth were more modest, farmers in other parts of Africa proved equally enterprising. For example, even under the decidedly adverse conditions in pre–World War II Northern Rhodesia, where Africans were excluded from the best arable land, denied ready access to the railway, and forced to sell their crops at prices well below those available to European farmers, African farmers adopted ploughs, expanded the size of their farms, and produced a growing supply of maize for sale during the 1920s and 1930s.[7]

The nature of international markets for foodstuffs and raw materials tends to reduce the likelihood that a region which specializes in producing one or a few primary commodities for export will experience sustained economic growth and diversification. Prices for primary commodities, especially agricultural goods, tend to fluctuate widely from one year to the next. This is because the amount available for sale may fluctuate drastically with changes in weather, and because consumers are often unwilling or unable to obtain acceptable short-run substitutes for a particular crop or mineral. Hence, even small variations in supply lead to relatively large changes in price, as buyers try to maintain a fairly steady volume of purchases. This created a serious problem for African countries which came to depend on a single export crop during the colonial period and it continues to do so today. For example, Ghana, Senegal, and Zambia each earns between two-thirds and four-fifths of its annual foreign exchange from the sale of a single item—cocoa, peanuts, and copper respectively. Poor harvests or a sudden drop in the world price can force these governments to incur costly foreign loans or painful reductions in import spending, and domestic programs of investment or public services may be disrupted or permanently cut back to release resources for future interest payments on the growing foreign debt. Instability of world prices is not such a problem, however, for countries producing several different primary goods for export and domestic consumption.

In addition to short-term instability, the long-run prospects for many agricultural and even mineral commodities are not especially favorable. Economic growth in the wealthy, industrialized countries does not generate a corresponding increase in their purchases of agricultural goods, since their need for foodstuffs tends to grow more slowly than does their income. In addition, the growth in income of any primary producing country may be reduced by competition, as additional suppliers enter the market, or by the development of synthetic substitutes. Although there is no evidence that the prices of all foodstuffs and raw materials have fallen relative to prices of manufactured goods, this has certainly happened for some commodities. In short, a country specializing in one or two agricultural or mineral commodities for export, as many African economies have come to do over the last hundred years, faces an uncertain international market.

Futhermore, although increased export production has often raised domestic income and demand for locally produced goods, it has generated few direct linkages with other sectors of the domestic economy. Traditional African methods of cultivation require relatively few produced inputs, such as tools, machines, chemical fertilizers, or pesticides, so that in many cases the growth of agriculture has not generated much demand for increased output from other sectors of the domestic economy. Also, since most African raw materials are exported in unprocessed form, there has been little development of processing industries associated with expanded production for export. Finally, foreign enterprise has received a substantial part of the income generated by increased raw material exports, both through their ownership of mines and plantations and, especially in West Africa, in the form of commercial profits, and little of this income has been reinvested in Africa itself.

Africa's emergence during the nineteenth and twentieth centuries as an important supplier of raw materials on the world markets represented a major achievement on the part of African farmers and workers and, in some areas, generated increases in local income and demand; yet, in overall terms, the potential for sustained development based on specialization in primary production for export has proved limited. African economies entered the post–World War II period with low per capita output and incomes, a relatively undiversified system of production, and extensive foreign control over both productive resources and the income arising from production for international exchange. Despite substantial progress in recent years, Africa remains one of the poorest regions of the world (see figure 18).

FIGURE 18

Per Capita Gross Domestic Product

(in current $US)

	1960	1970	1973
North America	2,750	4,760	6,180
Europe	1,060	2,480	4,140
Latin America	330	590	680***
East & Southeast Asia (excluding Japan)	80	120	—
Africa	130	216	300
North Africa	166	258	359
West Africa	93	154	224
Central Africa	89	116	168
East Africa*	69	121	155
Other Africa**	310	550	765

Sources: UN, Economic Commission for Africa, Statistical and Economic Information Bulletin for Africa, no. 7, 1975.
UN, Yearbook of National Accounts Statistics, 1974.
*According to UN definitions, East Africa includes Zambia, Malawi, Botswana, Lesotho, and Swaziland.
**Other Africa includes South Africa and nonindependent territories. As of August 1975, this included Angola, Mozambique, Rhodesia, Namibia, and a number of islands.
***Figure refers to 1972.

Planned Economic Development After 1945

Just as the growth of African primary production for export began long before the advent of formal colonial rule in most of sub-Saharan Africa, so the beginnings of planned industrialization preceded independence. Both European governments and African nationalists emerged from the Great Depression and the war with a new interest in promoting economic development in Africa and with an enthusiastic faith in the ability of governments to initiate and control this process. In addition, as the wartime savings of Americans and the resources of the United States government were applied to the tasks of rebuilding shattered European economies and recovering or surpassing pre-1929 standards of living, the rapid growth of demand in industrialized countries led to rising world prices for foodstuffs and raw materials. European firms at the same time developed a renewed interest in exploiting markets for manufactured goods in Africa and in other parts of the Third World. During the late 1940s and early 1950s, colonial treasuries bulged with grants and loans from the imperial powers and with profits of the revived export trade. Between 1947 and 1958, the French government invested twice as much in French West Africa, mostly for public construction, as it had from 1903 through 1946, and this inflow of capital was accompanied by a substantial migration of skilled Frenchmen seeking employment in Africa.[8] Similarly, the British Colonial Development Corporation made public funds available to construct roads, power plants, and schools in the British colonies. Expanding educational facilities proved especially popular and on the eve of independence some anglophone African countries were spending over 40 percent of their recurrent budgets on education alone.[9]

Both Britain and France also undertook various schemes to raise levels of agricultural production and the income of African farmers. Frequently these projects attempted to introduce European style large-scale mechanized farming to African economies. Unfortunately, they did so without taking into account ecological differences between the tropical and temperate zones, let alone differences in the economic circumstances of African and European farmers. Even if African farmers had been able to afford tractors and other expensive types of equipment, the farming methods they were advised to use would not have produced significant increases in output. In the most notorious cases, such as the Tanganyika groundnut scheme or the Niger Agricultural Project in Nigeria, crop yields per acre were actually lower on the project than on neighboring African farms, and the schemes were abandoned after a few years.[10]

The pace of industrialization, which had been limited before the war, also accelerated after 1945. In such countries as Nigeria and the Gold Coast established European trading firms began to experiment with local production of goods previously imported, and in East Africa Asian traders took advantage of postwar prosperity to establish new, import-substituting industries.[11] Although African governments began to draw up development plans even before independence, these were usually little more than shopping lists of investment projects which colonial administrators and their African counterparts wanted to initiate. On the whole, government participation in the economy was still confined to providing basic facilities and services, such as transport, power, and communications.

58. A sewing room at a fiber manufacturing corporation in Kumasi, Ghana.

Photo courtesy United Nations/ PJ/ bb.

Planning and Development in the Independence Period

Both planning and industrial development became more systematic in the late 1950s and the 1960s. The prices of many primary products reached a peak in the early '50s, then declined for a decade or more, forcing Africans to exchange their exports for imported manufactured goods on increasingly unfavorable terms. This led to shortages of foreign exchange, lower tax revenues to finance government projects and services, and a higher cost of living. Food prices, especially, increased with the rising cost of foreign exchange, since domestic agricultural resources were oriented toward production for export and many countries had come to depend on imported foodstuffs to a significant extent.

In the face of these mounting problems, newly independent African governments sought to reduce their dependence on world markets and foreign entrepreneurs, in an effort to relieve short-run imbalances and to increase their capacity for self-sustained growth in the long run. Industrialization was seen as the primary means of achieving these goals. To promote industrial growth,

African governments followed the lead of private investors and concentrated on developing industries which would produce local substitutes for imported products. This basic strategy was implemented by a variety of tax concessions and trade restrictions, such as tariffs, quotas, import and foreign exchange licenses, designed to increase profits and reduce the risks of investing in domestic manufacturing by protecting local industries from foreign competition. At the same time, comprehensive planning was undertaken to coordinate developments throughout the economic system in an effort to control prices and costs and to reduce the risks of industrial investment. The cost of these programs was borne primarily by the agricultural sector. Farm products—especially export crops— were often taxed to provide revenue for industrial investment. In many countries, for example, farmers were required by law to sell their crops to state marketing boards, which paid them prices well below world market prices and used the difference as a form of public revenue. In addition, farmers had to pay higher prices for the tools and other products which they purchased from domestic industries and for locally manufactured consumer goods. Thus the purchasing power of farmers fell while the profits of domestic manufacturers rose.

The adoption of these policies was accompanied by a rapid increase in industrial growth in the 1960s. According to the Economic Commision for Africa, manufacturing output grew at an average annual rate of more than 6 percent in 25 African countries (excluding South Africa) and 9 percent in 17 African countries. As a result, the combined share of mining, manufacturing, construction, and electricity in gross domestic product rose from 20 percent to 30 percent during the decade (see figure 17). However, contrary to the expectations of planners, the industrial growth of the 1960s failed to relieve shortages of food and foreign exchange or to reduce the role of foreign capital in African economies. Moreover, it probably helped to aggravate the shortage of productive, well-paying jobs and the unequal distribution of income and resources.

Many of the adverse effects of recent industrial growth in Africa can be attributed to the particular policies which governments have used to promote import-substituting industrial development. Typically, domestic manufacturers are protected from foreign competition by tariffs or quotas on imported manufactured goods, which permits them to charge higher prices in the domestic market than those on the world market. At the same time, they are permitted to import machinery, raw materials, or semifinished goods duty-free and to purchase foreign currency for importing equipment and materials at less than the official rate of exchange. These measures not only increase manufacturers' receipts and decrease their costs, thus ensuring them a substantial profit even if they are not very efficient, but also encourage them to import large amounts of

59. Miners returning from their shift at Rhodawa copper mine in
Rhodesia.
Photo courtesy United Nations/ lb.

equipment and materials. Indeed, the liberality of government in making foreign exchange available to manufacturers has also fostered practices such as
over-invoicing, whereby a foreign supplier agrees to overcharge an African firm
for imported equipment or materials and deposits the difference in a foreign
bank where it becomes the personal property of one or more of the firm's managers. Thus, African consumers often pay as much for domestically produced
items as for imported ones and little or no foreign exchange is saved. Instead of
substituting domestic for foreign goods, imported semifinished goods are substituted for imported final goods. In Zambia, for example, the value added in the

domestic manufacturing sector rose from 48 million kwachas to 164 million between 1965 and 1972, but the cost of imports used in domestic manufacturing increased from кw24 million to кw110 million or from one-half to two-thirds of total value added.[12] In other cases more firms have been established than are actually needed to supply the domestic market. It is not uncommon to find fully equipped canning or textile factories which—because of the absence of necessary supplies, adequate skilled personnel, marketing outlets, or even transportation to move materials into and finished products out of the factory—have never produced a can of tomato paste or a yard of cloth. Such white elephants are partly the result of inexperience and poor planning, but policies which encourage wasteful spending on expensive equipment do little to educate planners or producers in the ways of better management.

The combination of trade restrictions, tax concessions, and foreign exchange licenses to promote domestic manufacturing also tends to encourage use of highly capital-intensive techniques of prodution, requiring large amounts of imported machinery and spare parts but relatively few workers. In Kenya, for example, nonagricultural output grew 9.8 percent per annum from 1964 to 1969, while nonagricultural employment rose by only 2 percent per annum.[13] Zambia's synthetic textile mills will have to rely entirely on imported materials and equipment until the country develops its own heavy machinery and petrochemical industries, a remote possibility at best. Capital-intensive techniques of production also do little to alleviate unemployment or to provide better-paying jobs for African workers. Data on industrial employment and urban growth suggest that, while migration to African cities has been occurring at a rapid rate since 1950, the supply of industrial jobs has grown slowly or not at all. Thus even as industrialization has helped to stimulate migration, it may also have increased the rate of urban unemployment.

The income generated by industrial growth has not been widely distributed within African societies. A substantial part of it is transferred abroad by foreign investors or personnel who often supply a good part of the capital and skilled manpower employed by African industries. The rest remains and is received by Africans who supply capital, labor, or intermediate goods and services to the manufacturing sector. Although reliable data on income distribution are almost nonexistent for most African economies, it is unlikely that the domestic income from industry reaches more than a small number of people. The chief domestic supplier of capital for industrial ventures is usually the government, which sometimes enters into partnership with foreign private companies and sometimes sets up parastatal corporations, especially in transport, power, and communications, which negotiate foreign loans and take direct responsibility for managing production and investment. Thus the government receives that part of the profits of industrial establishments which is not distributed to foreign creditors or shareholders or to the very small group of domestic private investors who may have purchased shares in a firm. However, it is by no means clear that these profits represent a net addition to public revenues, since the government usually provides a variety of subsidies to domestic industry through tariffs, favorable rates for foreign exchange, tax concessions, and so on.

Similarly, the number of African workers who are employed by industrial establishments is relatively small. The tendency to employ capital-intensive techniques of production in African manufacturing means that the rapid growth of industrial output since the late 1950s has not been accompanied by a corresponding growth in industrial employment. In some cases, the total number of people employed in government and industry has actually declined. Africans who hold skilled managerial and technical positions in manufacturing industries do receive substantial incomes, but they are relatively few. Together with the bureaucrats who are employed in parastatal or joint public-private firms or who administer industrial loans or regulations, and whose incomes derive largely from the industrial sector (either as salary payments or as kickbacks), skilled industrial employees constitute a kind of privileged elite, to which few of their less fortunate compatriots are likely to gain access under present patterns of economic expansion. Moreover, there is little evidence that the concentration of income in the hands of a small group of African capitalists and skilled personnel is contributing to the future growth of the economy through a higher rate of saving and investment. On the contrary, well-to-do Africans often spend a substantial part of their incomes on such luxury imports as automobiles or television sets, or invest in low-risk but relatively unproductive forms of capital such as real estate.

The rest of the industrial labor force, Africans with few skills who hold relatively low-paying positions in the manufacturing sector, has also not grown in proportion to the growth of industrial output. Because of the limited job openings and relatively high wages which frequently obtain for the industrial worker, some observers have argued that they too constitute a kind of middle-level elite—a "labor aristocracy" in contemporary African society, whose interests tend to conflict with those of the rural masses and the thousands of urban Africans who eke out a precarious living as petty traders, artisans, or casual laborers.[14] While there is clearly some basis for this view, the line between industrial employees and other African working people is not altogether distinct. In terms of money, their wages are usually higher than, say, the average net receipts of farmers or other rural producers, but the cost of living in the city is also considerably higher than in the countryside, so that in terms of purchasing power the gap between rural and urban incomes is often not very great. Indeed, many industrial employees also engage in petty trade or craft production in their spare time to make ends meet. Industrial workers do often enjoy a greater measure of economic security than other low-income Africans, since their wages are paid regularly, and they may belong to a union, which can to some extent protect them against arbitrary dismissal. However, workers with steady jobs are often expected to support friends and kinsmen without such means, so that their standard of living is not appreciably higher than that of most other urban residents. The argument that the industrial work force is a privileged elite compared to the rest of the working population ignores both the wide range of income transfers and remittances between industrial employees and their kinsmen and other associates in both rural and urban areas, which certainly has the *potential* for considerable redistribution of income. At the present time, not enough information has been collected on these aspects of African economic life to warrant conclusions about the actual pattern of income distribution outside the public and large-scale industrial sector.

It is also not yet clear to what extent industrial growth in Africa has occurred at the expense of the rural sector. Insofar as African governments have imposed heavy taxes on agricultural exports while according favored tax treatment to the manufacturing sector *and* concentrating public expenditures in urban areas, they have in effect subsidized urban and industrial growth out of agricultural incomes. On the other hand, it is by no means obvious that the slow growth of agricultural output and the high rates of migration into the cities observed in many African countries since the mid-1950s are simply due to high taxes and low prices for agricultural products. Agricultural growth requires a variety of new inputs and services—seeds, fertilizers, pesticides, water control–and the technical knowledge to employ them to good effect or to rearrange cropping patterns and cultivation practices to raise the level and reduce the variability of agricultural output. To provide the necessary inputs and information and coordinate their use requires careful planning and administration.

In recognition of the need for a more balanced development strategy, many African governments have in recent years expanded efforts to promote agricultural as well as industrial expansion. Agricultural development schemes range from extension and credit programs designed to increase production of individual crops to regional rural development projects, which seek to expand the range of opportunities for rural people to earn higher incomes by providing roads, water supply, credit, new techniques, and even changes in such basic institutions as land tenure or settlement patterns. Costs of the schemes vary

60. Oil exploration at Port Gentil, Gabon.
Photo courtesy United Nations/ BZ/ me.

widely. In Kenya, for instance, the Tea Development Authority spent $15.6 million between 1960 and 1971 to increase tea production on small farms and, by 1972, had 66,500 farmers participating. By contrast, the Kenya Livestock Development Project spent $11.3 million between 1970 and 1974 to provide loans and other services to less than 3,000 "ranchers and pastoralists."[15]

Although rural development projects have multiplied in recent years and, in some cases, have effected significant increases in output of particular crops, overall their impact on agricultural prodution and farmers' incomes has been extremely modest. There are a number of reasons for the continued relative stagnation of African agriculture. For one thing, as the failure of the Tanganyika Groundnut Scheme and other early postwar projects demonstrated, agricultural technology cannot be readily transferred from one environmental region to another, and often basic research has not been adaquate to identify the particular combination of seeds, pesticides, and cultivation methods which will raise output in a given area of Africa. Thus, agricultural extension agents often have nothing to tell farmers. But there is also a pervasive problem of communication. In the same village one may meet farmers who demand the means to improve their farms and raise their incomes, and extension agents who complain that the farmers ignore their advice. This apparent anomaly seems in turn to reflect a state of mutual distrust based on an underlying conflict of interest. Bureaucrats whose salaries and pensions ultimately have nothing to do with whether or not they succeed in raising agricultural output in a village have little incentive to undertake the long, difficult task of ascertaining farmers' needs and identifying and working with those local institutions which have the capacity to organize development efforts at the community level. At the same time, farmers are justifiably suspicious of instructions issued by government agents who demonstrate no long-term commitment to making things work on the local level and who offer no method of insurance against hunger or loss of limited resources should a particular experiment fail. As far as the farmers are concerned, the government can be as unpredictable as the market. Planned development, therefore, has not yet provided much incentive for farmers to abandon crops or cultivation methods which may not be very productive but which assure them at least a minimal income, whatever the vagaries of the weather, the market price, or the tax collector.

Conclusion

In the worldwide economic recovery which followed the Second World War, African economies expanded their export of primary commodities to unprecedented levels and began to develop domestic manufacturing sectors. As primary product prices declined after the mid-1950s, African governments took an increasingly active role in maintaining or accelerating the pace of industrial growth, which they saw as a crucial means of achieving both economic development and economic independence. Many of the policies they use, however, have tended to promote a pattern of industrial growth which is ill-suited to the needs of African economies and which has done little to promote development or to reduce African dependence on foreign capital and world markets for individual crops. In recent years, planners and politicians have become increasingly aware of the need for a more balanced approach. Clearly, greater emphasis is needed on agricultural growth and diversification to meet a growing demand for foodstuffs and fibers, to provide employment opportunities for the large majority of Africans who have not found well-paying jobs in the city and who are not likely to do so in the near future, and to generate a continuing source of foreign exchange earnings. A dynamic, prosperous agricultural sector would, if properly organized, also serve to widen domestic markets for nonagricultural goods and to achieve a more even distribution of the gains from economic growth within African societies. These aims would also be served by greater emphasis on industrial ventures which employ relatively labor-intensive techniques.

Recognition of the need for changes in development strategy is one thing; realizing them, however, is another. In this respect, many African nations face something of a dilemma. To design and implement a more balanced and equitable strategy for economic development requires a significant shift in government policies, not only to devote more resources to nonindustrial sectors but also to enlist the participation of the great majority of African farmers and workers in the identification of local needs and the realization of increased production. The politicians and bureaucrats who make these decisions, however, are also some of those who have gained most from past patterns of growth and who therefore have little incentive to undertake a major restructuring of government policy. Even if present policies are maintained and bureaucrats remain relatively unresponsive to interests other than those of domestic and foreign elites, economic growth may still continue—especially in countries with high-priced resources such as petroleum—but in an uneven manner which is likely to involve increasing social and political conflict. Economic change and political change in contemporary Africa are thus likely to be closely interrelated, a problem that is examined further in chapter 18.

NOTES

1. UN, Economic Commission for Africa, *Survey of Economic Conditions, 1971* (Part I).

2. A. G. Hopkins, *An Economic History of West Africa* (London: Longman, 1973), p.174.

3. This figure and information in the following paragraph are taken from S. H. Frankel, *Capital Investment in Africa* (London: Oxford University Press, 1938), pp.172, 211–12, Table 28 and Chart E.

4. Ibid., p.214.

5. C. Coquery-Vidrovitch, *Le Congo au temps des grandes compagnies concessionaires, 1898–1930* (Paris: Mouton, 1972), pp.180–83; R. Harms, "The End of Red Rubber: A Reassessment," *Journal of African History*, XVI, 1 (1975). On colonial agricultural policy in East and Central Africa, see, e.g., T. O. Ranger, *The Agricultural History of Zambia* (Lusaka: National Educational Co. of Zambia, 1971) and J. Iliffe, *Agricultural Change in Modern Tanganyika* (Nairobi: East African Publishing House, 1971).

6. The Ivory Coast incident is described in A. J. F. Köbben, "Le Planteur Noir," *Etudes Eburnéennes*, V, 1954, p.18. On Ghana, Nigeria, and other African colonies, see P. Hill, *The Migrant Cocoa-Farmers of Southern Ghana* (Cambridge: Cam-

bridge University Press, 1963); S. S. Berry, *Cocoa, Custom and Socio-economic Change in Rural Western Nigeria* (Oxford: Clarendon Press, 1975); and J. S. Hogendorn, "Economic Initiative and African Cash Farming," in P. Duignan and L. H. Gann, *Colonialism in Africa, 1870–1960*, vol. 4 (London: Cambridge University Press, 1975).

7. R. E. Baldwin, *Economic Development and Export Growth: A Study of Northern Rhodesia, 1920–1960* (Berkeley: University of California Press, 1966), pp.163–64.

8. E. J. Berg, "The Economic Basis of Political Choice in French West Africa," *American Political Science Review*, LIV, 2 (June 1960), 394–95.

9. G. K. Helleiner, *Peasant Agriculture, Government and Economic Growth in Nigeria* (Homewood, Illinois: R. D. Irwin, 1966), p.307

10. K. D. S. Baldwin, *The Niger Agricultural Project: An Experiment in African Development* (Oxford: Blackwell, 1957); Alan Wood, *The Groundnut Affair* (London: The Bodley Head, 1950); R. Dumont, *False Start in Africa*, 2d ed. (New York: Praeger 1969).

11. P. Kilby, *Industrialization in an Open Economy: Nigeria, 1946–66* (Cambridge: Cambridge University Press, 1969), and "Manufacturing in Colonial Africa," in Gann and Duignan, *op. cit.* See also C. Leys, *Underdevelopment in Kenya: The Political Economy of Neo-colonialism* (Berkeley: University of California Press, 1974), and J. Rweyemamu, *Underdevelopment and Industrialization in Tanzania* (London: Oxford University Press, 1974).

12. A. Seidman, "Import Substitution Industry in Zambia," *Journal of Modern African Studies*, 12, 4 (December 1974). "Value added" means the total value of a firm's output minus the cost of goods purchased from other firms.

13. Leys, *Underdevelopment in Kenya*, p.139.

14. G. Arrighi, "International Corporations, Labor Aristocracies and Economic Development in Tropical Africa," in R. I. Rhodes, ed., *Imperialism and Underdevelopment* (New York: Monthly Review Press, 1970).

15. Uma J. Lele, *The Design of Rural Development: Lessons from Africa* (Baltimore, Maryland: Johns Hopkins University Press, 1975), pp.8–9.

SUGGESTIONS FOR FURTHER READING

Amin, Samir. *Neo-colonialism in West Africa*. Harmondsworth: Penguin, 1973.
Arrighi, G., and J. S. Saul. *Essays on the Political Economy of Africa*. New York: Monthly Review Press. 1973.
Baldwin, R. E. *Economic Development and Export Growth: A Study of Northern Rhodesia*. Berkeley: University of California Press, 1966.
Ghai, D., ed. *Concepts and Strategies of Economic Independence in Africa*. Nairobi: Institute of Development Studies, University of Nairobi, 1972.
Kilby, P. *Industrialization in an Open Economy: Nigeria, 1946–66*. London: Cambridge University Press, 1969.
Leys, C. *Underdevelopment in Kenya: The Political Economy of Neo-colonialism*. Berkeley: University of California Press, 1974.
Seidman, A. *Planning for Development in sub-Saharan Africa*. New York: Praeger, 1974.
Uppal, J. S., and L. R. Salkever, eds. *Africa: Problems in Economic Development*. New York: Free Press, 1972.
de Wilde, J., et al. *Experiences with Agricultural Development in Tropical Africa*. Baltimore: Johns Hopkins University Press, 1967.

Michael Armer and Marian Gewirtz
Sociocultural Change in Contemporary Africa

17 As with economic and political developments, changes in social and cultural patterns have also transformed African societies during the past century. Kinship relations, educational and stratification systems, residential patterns, and life-styles and values were all affected both in themselves and through interaction with political and economic forces. In all instances, the major cause of change has been cross-cultural contact.

Although cross-cultural contact has increased and intensified during the past century, it is not a new phenomenon for African societies. For thousands of years African societies have migrated, fought, traded, and mixed with one another and with non-Africans. Since the seventh century, one of the most important forces causing change has been the spread of the religion, technology, and sociopolitical patterns of Islam. During the past century, European colonialism also became a most profound and pervasive force causing sociocultural change. Among the most significant cultural changes has been the spread of the doctrine of economic development and modernization. This doctrine promotes, as goals for all societies, the standards of wealth, political and economic independence, and social welfare of the industrially advanced nations of the world. Aspirations for societal modernization and improvements in human socioeconomic conditions have been successfully inculcated in virtually all societies of the contemporary world. Ironically, though, these aspirations ultimately played a major role in mobilizing African and other colonized peoples to force an end to formal colonial domination, which itself was gradually seen as a major obstacle to achievement of these goals. Nevertheless, the legacy of European domination remains, even in independent African nations, and must be included in an examination of contemporary sociocultural change in Africa.

Like all societies, African societies have responded to cultural contact by selectively incorporating, reinterpreting, or adapting alien elements into their existing life styles. The degree and content of acculturation vary greatly from society to society, depending on differences in traditional cultures, geographic variations, and historical circumstances. Since the African continent is characterized by heterogeneity, statements about Africa as a whole must, of necessity, be broad generalizations that may not necessarily be applicable to a given society or region at a particular point in time. Sociocultural change is a generic concept that encompasses all aspects of social and cultural life. This chapter concentrates on four of the most important areas of change, especially in the past fifty years: kinship, education, stratification, and urban development. The discussion also deals indirectly with religious trends, migration patterns, and value changes.

Family and Kinship

The descent group, typically consisting of a man's parents and grandparents, brothers and sisters, uncles, aunts, and cousins, has been the most basic institution of traditional African society. It exerts a pervasive influence on virtually every aspect of life.

An important characteristic of descent groups is their corporate nature. Members tend to be wholeheartedly loyal to their lineages, meeting the standards of conduct established by the head of the descent group and following his directives. In return, the lineage provides security, protection, and companionship for the individual. In accordance with the tenets of corporate responsibility and liability, a crime committed by a member of a lineage may be avenged against his kin. Similarly, if a fine is levied against an individual, all the members of his descent group will contribute toward its payment.

The concept of corporate responsibility is often inconsistent, however, with the emphasis on individualism increasingly demanded in the modern sector of the economy. Jobs, for example, are given to individuals, not families. Legal codes imposed by the colonial forces and retained by new African nations require individual responsibility for conduct and punish individuals when their behavior is not in accordance with the laws. Thus there has been a decline in communalism in many African societies. Individual responsibility and independence have become more highly valued and have replaced the emphasis on cor-

61. A young boy riding a homemade wooden scooter.
Photo courtesy United Nations/ BZ/ me.

porate responsibility and mutual dependence among members of one's descent group. Cooperation and mutual aid, which once applied particularly to relationships within a descent group, are now shifted to clubs and associations comprised of schoolmates, workmates, or agemates.

It has been suggested that African family patterns are becoming Westernized and are approaching the nuclear model consisting of parents and their children, and that as a result the descent group will no longer be important in African social life. While this is not entirely accurate, many aspects of traditional family life have indeed been touched by urban migration. The households of urban migrants are, almost by definition, separated from those of their descent-group kin who remain in the rural areas. An individual may be isolated from all or most of his kin. Of necessity, then, many traditional family relationships cannot operate as they do when an entire lineage shares a common residence. Interestingly, while a typical urban residential unit contains fewer persons than do units housing a descent group, most urban households shelter at least one person who is not a member of the nuclear family. There is evidence that the size of an urban household is related to its income; for example, wealthier towndwellers tend to house a proportionately larger number of kin. Some urban residents retain close contact with members of their descent groups who remain in the rural communities. They tend to visit regularly, they often send gifts and money to their kin, they maintain families in their original rural communities, and many plan to return to their rural farms. On the other hand, some of the more financially secure view their kinship obligations as distasteful responsibilities, and those who fulfill these obligations often do so with increasing reluctance. Kinship relationships seem no longer reciprocal for those who are economically secure in the towns.

Although polygyny has been accepted and positively sanctioned in traditional African society, only a small portion of Africans engage in it. As noted in chapter 11, for agricultural regions in which women performed much of the farm labor and infant mortality was extremely high, plural marriage, with its concomitant increase in family size, was a definite asset. However, usually only the wealthier men could afford the bridewealth and other costs involved in acquiring and supporting additional wives. Polygyny is even less common among urban populations than in rural African communities, but this does not necessarily show an increasing preference for nuclear family units. Instead, the low incidence of plural marriage in urban areas may be partly the result of other demographic characteristics of the urban migrants. They tend to be better educated than their rural counterparts, and Western education has been found to be negatively correlated with polygyny. They are also more likely to have attended missionary schools and undergone conversion to Christianity, which explicitly prohibits plural marriage. The predominantly male population in urban centers is another possible explanation for the low incedence of urban polygyny, as is the lack of economic factors that make additional wives an asset. The urban male cannot afford to feed, clothe, shelter, and educate more than one nonproductive family. However, there is some evidence of compensating institutions and practices: wealthier towndwellers who can afford modern divorce sometimes engage in serial monogamy; also, prostitution and cohabitation have become established urban phenomena.

Individuals migrating to a town or city seek out their closest kin and, in fact, try to migrate to those urban areas in which a member of their descent group has already settled. If that is impossible, migrants rely upon members of other descent groups that originate from the same rural community. In many cities, particularly in West Africa, these arrangements have been institutionalized through the establishment of ethnic associations. These groups vary in size and in criteria for membership but typically include migrants from a specific region who share a common language and culture. They facilitate the adjustment of migrants to the urban milieu, helping them to find employment and housing. Later, they serve as mutual aid societies and provide a variety of social services. Thus, functionally, in the absence of the descent group, ethnic associations have emerged to take their place.

Urban migration has also altered some mating patterns. Many town dwellers, particularly the well-educated, meet their future spouses during their schooling or elsewhere in the urban environment. These marriages often do not receive unanimous approval from members of predominantly rural descent groups. In accordance with traditional values, rural residents tend to prefer marital partners selected from their own villages and consider all other persons as "strangers." However, in the urban environment new loyalties develop on the basis of common interests, levels of education, and economic status. A mate chosen by a rural descent group is likely to be poorly educated and this often exacerbates the conflict, since the spouse may be deemed unsuitable by urban associates. However conflicts are resolved, urban residents still pay a bridewealth to the prospective bride's family. As in the past, the payment and the acceptance of bridewealth does not represent "purchase" of a wife but rather an assurance of the participating parties' good faith and an insurance against the instability of the marriage. If the dissolution of a marriage is deemed the wife's responsibility, the bridewealth reverts to the husband's descent group; if the husband is at fault, the wife's family retains it. However, in the urban context payments are more likely to be made in cash than in kind, and the prospective urban bride sometimes contributes to the bridewealth to hasten the date of her marriage.

Education

Traditional African education consisted primarily of informal socialization and training for future specialized family and community responsibilities. Many societies also maintained highly structured arrangements for apprenticeships in trades and crafts, and Islamic schools operated throughout Muslim regions. Except for Islamic education, traditional forms of education stressed the transference of skills and knowledge in the local culture, primarily through oral communication. In contrast, schooling provided by Christian missions and colonial administrations stressed literacy in local and European languages and, in addition, formal education following European curricula and methods. In Islamic schools, there was instruction in Arabic literacy and the Koran.

The educational systems established by the colonial powers generally were not designed to produce scholarship, political skills, or industrial and entrepreneurial acumen among the Africans. Rather, the colonial intent was largely to produce trained manpower to fill clerical and low-level administrative and management positions in the government and in commercial enterprises. The missionaries operated schools to promote Christianity among the students and to train indigenous clergy who could translate and teach the Bible. Only a small proportion of the school-age population was able to go to school and even fewer went beyond primary education. Curricula were effectively identical to those offered European children; only since independence have governments tried to adapt curricula to the African experience and to African needs.

The first literate Africans obtained comparatively prestigious and lucrative jobs as clerks, lay preachers, and teachers. Although initially suspicious of European education, Africans quickly realized that literacy and schooling provided distinct economic benefits, and they eagerly took advantage of educational opportunities for themselves and for their children. Moreover, many Africans attributed European domination and apparent superiority to literacy and education and to the attendant skills and technologies. As a result, families and communities often pooled their resources to build a primary school or to send one or more of their members, especially males, to secondary schools or universities. Education came to be widely viewed as a prerequisite to future success, at least for the masses, and the quest for education became a firmly entrenched value in most African societies.

The varying literacy rates among African nations today partly reflect variations in colonial educational policies and length of colonial influence, as well as differences in the degree of indigenous resistance. In some countries, such as Chad, Niger, and Upper Volta (formerly outlying areas of French West Africa), less than 10 percent of the population is literate. In other areas, such as Kenya, Uganda, and southern regions of Nigeria and Ghana, the figure is now approximately 50 percent. Nationalist leaders, most of whom were educated at Christian missionary schools, strongly protested the limited access to education afforded by the colonial powers. When these men became leaders of newly independent African nations, popular demand for education remained high and the expansion of educational facilities became a goal of high priority. Since that time, large proportions of national budgets have been spent on educational expansion.

Following a trend set during the colonial period, the expansion has pro-

62. A literate Liberian woman teaching her friend how to read.
Photo courtesy United Nations/ DAVIS/ ga.

gressed most rapidly in urban areas and in countries with a comparatively sound economic base. Primary schools are increasingly being located in rural communities; however, only a small portion of the African population ever attends secondary school or obtains a university degree. Those who do have emerged as an elite of high-status civil servants, technicians, professionals, and politicians.

For the majority of Africans who do not receive secondary or university-level schooling, educational development may shape aspirations and values in ways that are largely dysfunctional for the society. Although most of the African nations have rural-agrarian economies, educated Africans often consider agricultural labor unattractive and move to urban areas in search of employment which they feel more in keeping with their educational status and desired life style. The initial waves of these educated migrants (usually referred to as "school leavers") obtained relatively prestigious jobs. However, as competition for these openings increased, governments and businesses began to require additional educational certification. The African who completed primary school, for example, was once confident of securing a clerical post, but this level of edu-

63. Adult literacy campaign in Liberia.
Photo courtesy United Nations.

cation may now qualify him only for semiskilled manual labor. Similarly, in several African nations, especially immediately following independence when government services were expanded, Africans with some university training were virtually guaranteed high-status positions, as administrative and commercial structures underwent "Africanization." However, the increasing numbers of well-educated Africans and the limited number of jobs has now fostered competition for white-collar positions. In general, African nations are not experiencing sufficiently rapid economic development to absorb the graduates of their educational institutions and to provide employment commensurate with their training and aspirations.

These same nations often lack technically trained manpower because African secondary schools and universities are still primarily oriented toward teaching professional and adminstrative skills rather than technical skills needed for industrial development and economic self-sufficiency. One serious consequence of this imbalance is that many university-educated Africans move to European and other industrial countries to obtain employment.

Social Stratification

African patterns of social stratification have undergone major transformations during the colonial period. In traditional societies status differentiation was based primarily on ascribed criteria of age and sex. Age sets, which cut across descent groups, provided a way to assign rights and duties within the communities. Members of the oldest age set governed the village and were accorded respect for their experience and wisdom. In some communities an elder member of each descent group represented his lineage on a village council, which then selected a chief. Membership in these age sets was restricted to males, although in some societies the females participated in their own, less formal, age groupings. An individual might gain added prestige by exhibiting exceptional valor in warfare or by acquiring wealth from his agricultural or trading endeavors. In most communities, however, acquired status did not translate into higher status for one's offspring. Even in regions in which material goods could be inherited, rich men tended to have more wives and more children among whom their wealth was redistributed. Also, membership in the traditional ruling elite did not provide a markedly different life-style from that of the wider community. Thus, apart from differences in status deriving from age and sex, members of these societies tended to share relatively similar standing.

Many traditional African societies appear to have operated in this somewhat egalitarian fashion within age and sex categories. However, far more complex systems of stratification evolved in the larger states. The administrative organizations of these states varied widely, but the ruler of the kingdom was typically chosen from among the members of one or more noble lineages. Where states were based on military conquest, the lowest strata usually consisted of the most recently conquered peoples, who often served as slaves. Intergenerational mobility could result from outstanding individual merit, and in some societies even slaves could become wealthy, powerful, and important.

The imposition of European colonial rule on the African continent held serious consequences for indigenous patterns of social stratification. Most apparent was the racist nature of European domination. The white colonial forces everywhere represented an elite ruling caste that was far less permeable than any preexisting African elite. This situation undermined respect for traditional African authorities, because they no longer held ultimate power. Religious authority was undermined by the Christian missionaries' activity and subsequent African conversions. Those Africans who had previously been responsible for adjudicating community disputes largely had their powers revoked as the Europeans imposed foreign legal codes. More significantly, the introduction of literacy and European forms of education set the stage for the emergence of new criteria to determine social status within the indigenous African population. Africans educated in either mission or government schools attained prestigious positions and similarly impressive financial remunerations. They became both wealthier and more highly respected than the traditional African elite. The only exceptions were in the few countries in which colonial rule was administered through traditional authorities. Here the traditional elite often maintained their relative status and sent their sons and daughters to school to prepare them for subsequent elite roles.

The attainment of political independence by African nations essentially eliminated whites from stratification systems. As educated Africans assumed positions that the colonizers vacated, a new elite began to emerge that consisted of the wealthiest and most highly educated Africans. This new elite cuts across ethnic distinctions and is based on achieved rather than on ascribed criteria for social status. Since many of its members come from humble backgrounds, the elite status appears open to all who can attain sufficient education, and it serves as a reference group for the aspiring members of a wider population.

In many nations the elite now appear to constitute an established social class characterized by a distinctive neocolonial life-style. Their numbers have somewhat stabilized, and they appear increasingly closed to new membership. Since they are predominantly urban based and financially affluent, they have been able to give their children the best education, thus ensuring that they will likely become future members of the African elite. These professionals, military and political leaders, and high-level managers and civil servants constitute the upper echelon of the contemporary African social structure. Below them is a small middle class of urban clerks, technicians, and semiprofessionals, but also persons who work as shopkeepers, craftsmen, and traders. The African "working class," primarily composed of factory and mine workers, manual laborers, and domestic servants, is predominantly urban with little education and few skills. Over 80 percent of the African population remains rural, agrarian, and largely illiterate, and constitutes the lowest social and economic category.

Urban Development

African urbanization is a study in contrasts. Especially in the northern and western areas, large cities have flourished for centuries. Many cities—Accra (Ghana), Abidjan (Ivory Coast), Nairobi (Kenya), Dakar (Senegal), Kano (Nigeria), Kinshasa (Zaire), Lagos (Nigeria)[1]—that had fewer than 100,000 inhabitants prior to World War II now have 500,000 or more. Indeed, the rate of growth of African cities, 5 to 6 percent per year, is the world's highest, and towns over 100,000 inhabitants have a growth rate of 8 percent. Yet Africa is the least urbanized of the world's major regions. Only 13 percent of Africans live in communities of over 20,000, as compared with almost 30 percent of the world's population, and there are relatively few African towns of intermediate size. As a result, most urbanized Africans live in areas of over 100,000 inhabitants.

Since Africa's overall growth rate is only 2.5 to 3 percent per year and fertility rates are even lower in urban areas, migration is responsible for much of the urban growth rate. Migration is not a new phenomenon in Africa, nor is the concomitant use of cash as a medium of exchange. However, both became more common because most colonial powers imposed an annual tax that had to be paid in cash. As a result, large numbers of men, including even subsistence farmers, migrated to mining areas and other urban centers in search of short-term employment. Their families stayed in the villages to tend their farms, and the men returned home to the village when they had met their monetary objectives. As this type of migration became more common, men also began to seek temporary employment to earn money for such large purchases as bicycles, radios, licenses, and household goods, or for marriage expenses. While in the city, these migrants tended to have low living standards because their wages were low and they wanted to save money for a specific purpose. Because they often left their jobs once the financial goal was reached, they have been called "target workers."

Short-term migration has become less typical in recent years. Increased urban employment, rural underdevelopment, and competition for scarce jobs have gradually encouraged the target worker to become a permanent, or at least semipermanent, urban dweller rather than risk abandoning his source of income to return to his village. Families have been reuniting and settling in the burgeoning towns. Although the sex ratio remains disproportionate, the trend seems to be shifting toward eventual equalization.

Another large group of migrants to urban communities are Africans who have completed their primary or secondary school education. Reluctant to farm, they seek better jobs than are available in their rural villages. These migrants

64. A typical "shantytown."
Photo courtesy United Nations/ BZ/ ara.

are usually males between fifteen and twenty-five years of age. There is a direct relationship between the educational level an individual has attained and both the likelihood and the distance that he or she will migrate. The more highly educated African is more likely to move to an urban area, particularly to the capital cities, where there are reputed to be more opportunities for satisfactory employment.

African cities, like urban areas around the world, also draw migrants because they offer a higher caliber of education and better social services than do rural villages, more cultural and recreational facilities ranging from movies and theaters to museums and athletic clubs, and a variety of consumer goods. Also, cities are thought to be exciting and stimulating in contrast to a rural agricultural existence, and they are the seats of political power and of national development.

For most urban dwellers, the facts of urban life do not match their popular image. Urban populations are expanding far more rapidly than are employment opportunities, and unemployment and poverty are growing urban dilemmas. In 1967 it was estimated that in most African towns, between 12 and 22 percent of the urban population was unemployed. This trend will probably continue among the unskilled and the uneducated even if increased rates of economic expansion are achieved, because such expansion is likely to be dependent on machines rather than labor. Many urban migrants have lowered their inflated aspirations and have begun to learn traditional or modern crafts or trades in order to support themselves and their families. Nevertheless, up to one-third of all able-bodied males between the ages of fifteen and fifty-five living in Africa's major urban centers today would be classified as unemployed.[2] Urban population growth has overcrowded housing facilities and produced slums or "shantytowns" in almost every major city. Public utilities and other social services have not expanded rapidly enough to match the phenomenal rate of African urbanization.

Researchers have not given systematic attention to the implications of rapid urbanization for rural communities. Nevertheless, these are the areas that are experiencing this heavy out-migration of comparatively well-educated, working-age males. There is also a high rate of return migration after age forty-five, largely for retirement. Rural areas consequently tend to be disproportionately inhabited by the less educated and by women, children, and the elderly. The self-selection processes involved in migration to urban centers may leave the rural areas increasingly resistant to change. However, it is also possible that, especially as community development programs and agricultural development schemes expand, rural-urban ties will serve a change-inducing role.

Prospects for Further Change

Perhaps the most significant changes affecting the peoples of Africa over the last century have been concerned with economic growth and societal modernization. Everywhere there is a desire to increase national resources and human welfare in ways enjoyed by economically advantaged nations of the world, notably the urban industrial powers. The major differences in this desire are in the conception of appropriate political strategies and developmental priorities. Some nations or groups prefer a socialist strategy; others, a liberal or *laissez-faire* approach. In some, educational expansion is given top priority, while others stress the development of small-scale industries, transportation, civil service, or modern agricultural systems. Each society is full of hope and determination for a socially and economically bright tomorrow; the hope is brightest in the newly independent nations, which attribute much of their present underdevelopment to colonialism. What, in fact, was the general effect of colonialism, and what are the prospects for industrial development in future African societies?

There have been two common views. The procolonialist view of change is that European powers were instrumental in bringing African societies into contact with the modern world and in establishing the infrastructure for eventual development as full-fledged, economically advanced members of the international community. Without the investment of the colonial powers, according to this argument, it might have been decades or centuries before African nations could emerge and join in world affairs. According to this view, the continent might still be populated by scattered bands or despotic empires engaged in internecine warfare and suffering the scourge of malnutrition, poverty, and primitive life styles. With independence, these societies no longer have the benefit of colonial expertise, guidance, and assistance as in the past, and, it is felt, they will develop more slowly or not at all.

The alternative, anticolonialist view is that great civilizations already existed in Africa at the time of the European penetration and that the colonial influence served primarily to impede and divert developments on the continent. The colonies became increasingly weak, consolidated, and dependent upon the powerful industrial nations and developed in ways that primarily benefited these nations rather than the colonies themselves. Now that the shackles of colonialism have been thrown off, according to this argument, these societies can assume their rightful place in the world system as strong, independent, economically viable nations. The two perspectives are similar only in their assumption of a normal evolution of societies toward urban, industrial development and improved living conditions.

Increasingly, students of social change and economic development have recognized the importance of the international context in determining the nature, degree, and probability of socioeconomic development. The direction of change dictated by the international environment may be quite different from the urban, industrial model exemplified by European societies. The prospect of many African nations, or of other developing societies, becoming strong, industrial powers is very limited under existing world economic conditions. Becoming a wealthy industrial power requires, among other things, that other societies become dependent on what the developing country can produce. The combination of valuable resources or products and a ready market to buy them is rare. There is little realistic likelihood of economic takeoff and large-scale industrial development for most African nations, no matter what strategies and priorities they use, except for those few nations that have exceptional natural resource bases of vital minerals, such as Nigeria with its oil supply. Moreover, if such nations succeed in rising to a position of power in the world economic system, it will probably be partly with the aid and at the expense of other African nations, which will depend upon them for goods and materials they produce.

During the next decade the social and cultural trends of the recent past may continue but societies will probably remain largely agrarian, relatively poor, and dependent. Social changes in kinship, education, stratification, and urbanization will continue to affect a proportion of the population, but for most people economic conditions and general social welfare may not be greatly altered. Instead, work activities and life styles will continue to change in ways consistent with the development of societies in dependent, nonindustrial nations. Some of these changes may involve further improvements in transportation, communication services, and other institutions, which will in turn improve living conditions in various ways, perhaps facilitating some traditional practices, such as visiting relatives, and fostering some new ones, such as traveling to other areas. Standards of living may improve in an absolute sense, but probably not to the level currently enjoyed by economically advanced societies. As long as present world economic patterns continue, there will be some powerful, highly industrial societies and many less powerful, less industrial, dependent societies. The latter will share or adapt some of the sociocultural changes and products of the world powers to the extent that these are consistent with local patterns and needs, but always later in time and lesser in degree.

NOTES

1. For individual city estimates, see U.N. Demographic Yearbook 1970 and Africa South of the Sahara (London: Europa Publications Ltd., 1975).

2. See Peter C. Gutkind, "The Energy of Despair: Social Organization of the Unemployed in Two African Cities, Lagos and Nairobi," Civilizations, Vol. 17, Nos. 3 and 4 (1967), and Gunilla Bjeren, Some Theoretical and Methodological Aspects of the Study of African Urbanization (Uppsala, Scandinavian Institute of African Studies, Research Publication No. 9, 1971).

SUGGESTIONS FOR FURTHER READING

Armer, Michael, ed. African Social Psychology: A Review and Annotated Bibliography. New York: Africana Publishing Corporation, 1974.

Berghe, Pierre L. van den, Africa: Social Problems of Change and Conflict. San Francisco, California: Chandler Publishing Co., 1965.

Herskovits, Melville J. The Human Factor in Changing Africa. New York: Alfred A. Knopf, 1965.

Lloyd, P. C. Africa in Social Change. New York: Praeger, 1967.

Paden, John N., and Edward W. Soja, eds. The African Experience: Volume I: Essays. Evanston, Illinois: Northwestern University Press, 1970, pp.252–399.

Ruth Berins Collier
Political Change and Authoritarian Rule

18 The kaleidoscopic pattern of events in Africa in recent years has given some observers the impression of political chaos. Parties are banned, governments are overthrown, and political leaders rise and fall with some frequency. Through all of this, however, African politics are not chaotic. Many of the changes that are taking place can be seen as a process of political jockeying and institutional experimentation as leaders seek to establish effective rule over the newly independent states. This process has been more difficult and tortuous in some countries than in others, and these differences have in turn led to different types of national political regimes. This chapter suggests that this process of experimenting with new forms of political rule has gone through certain well-defined stages and has followed certain orderly patterns. Understanding what has happened at each stage provides important insights regarding what happens at the next stage. The discussion focuses on ex-colonial Black Africa, that is, on the twenty-six countries of Tropical Africa which were the former colonies of Britain, France, and Belgium.

Elimination of Competitive Party Politics

A useful starting point for exploring the origins of contemporary regimes in Africa is the period of nationalism or decolonization which spanned the approximately fifteen-year period from the end of World War II to roughly 1960 (see chapter 10). This period saw the introduction in the African colonies of many of the democratic institutions of the European colonial powers. Elections were introduced, the right to vote was extended until it became universal, political parties appeared on the scene to contest these elections, and the powers of government increasingly resided in an elected parliament and prime minister rather than with the colonial rulers. The culmination of this process of decolonization was, of course, formal political independence.

The introduction of new political institutions was an interesting experiment in the transfer or "export" of democracy. These democratic institutions had originated and flourished in the very different historical context of Europe. Generally speaking, they evolved there rather gradually and in a context of somewhat higher levels of economic and social modernization. Would these democratic institutions take hold in Africa, where they were being introduced rapidly and in a very different social, cultural, historical, and economic setting?

Soon after independence it became clear that the Western democratic model would not be followed. Leaders of the newly independent nations moved rapidly and deliberately to eliminate competitive party politics and the popular election of political leaders, two crucial features of competitive democracy. This process occurred in two interrelated phases.

The first phase involved the attempt to form one-party regimes, that is, regimes in which effective political power is held by only one political party. The appearance of one-party regimes actually occurred in some countries before independence, during the period of decolonization. In most of these earlier cases, the overwhelming electoral victory of a single party or the merger of two parties into one made it possible for that party to eliminate effectively all competition. By 1960, the year in which most of colonial tropical Africa became independent, nine countries had one-party regimes. Amid statements by both political leaders and social scientists justifying or rationalizing the one-party development as a potentially "democratic" form of government suitable to the multi-ethnic societies of Africa, there followed in the next half decade the formation of seven additional one-party regimes. In most of these later cases, however, the one-party status did not result from electoral victory or merger, but rather from the straightforward banning of all opposition parties or from the outright rigging of elections. Even in the one-party states which achieved that status by more legitimate means, the supremacy of the single party was maintained by repressing the opposition and was sometimes ratified in law or in new constitutions proclaiming that only one party could legally exist. As civil liberties began to disappear throughout tropical Africa, it became increasingly clear that the attempt to transplant democracy from Europe to the African colonies had not been successful. Rather, authoritarian regimes were being established on the African continent.

A number of reasons have been advanced to explain the abandonment of democratic practices and the impetus for the formation of one-party regimes. First, Western democratic institutions had been only very recently introduced.

As foreign transplants they did not correspond to the needs or interests of those wielding political power, and the democratic values they embodied were neither deeply seated nor widely held. There were thus relatively few institutional and cultural constraints on authoritarian tendencies, on the desire of political elites to restrict or eliminate opposition in order to have greater control of political affairs, whether it be for reasons of personal power and aggrandizement or to facilitate decision-making and pursue national goals of one type or another.

A related reason for the formation of one-party regimes and the elimination of competitive party politics was the changing interests of the political leaders. The introduction of competitive democracy was initially supported and even demanded by the nationalist elite in the preindependence period because it aided them in the struggle for self-government and independence. Elections formed a basis for appeals to popular sovereignty and were an international symbol of readiness for independence. Once independence was achieved, however, the political game changed substantially. What was important for coming to power was not necessarily viewed as appropriate for maintaining power or for achieving policy goals. During the nationalist period, the African masses had been mobilized and politicized as part of the campaign to press for independence, and had been promised an improvement in the conditions of life. With this background of rising mass expectations and with the inability of the new independent governments to deliver, the one-party regime, with its elimination of competitive party politics, served to control one channel of mass demands, which the government either could not or chose not to fulfill. One-party systems also served to deny rival elites the important political resource of mass popularity and backing.

It has further been argued that one-party regimes are more compatible with planning and with "objective," technocratic solutions to economic and social problems. They have been said to depend less on the delicate balancing of political groups and to facilitate consensus. They can thus, it is argued, more easily take decisive policy positions, which may be viewed as necessary for achieving development goals, particularly those that may meet with opposition either from the masses or from certain entrenched interests. This belief in the greater effectiveness of the one-party regime was another factor stimulating its formation in Africa. The other side of this, of course, is that such regimes are less responsive to groups and interests in the society, and can also provide an effective mechanism for the perpetuation and self-enrichment of a privileged political class.

Another reason for the formation of one-party regimes may be that distinct problems are associated with party competition in the African context of multi-ethnic societies. In such a situation, political competition tends to coincide with ethnic divisions, since different parties tend to represent different ethnic groups. Political conflict that has an ethnic basis often has no easy solution. There may be no outcome that reduces the conflict, no compromise that is satisfactory to both sides, as any benefit offered to one side is seen as a cost or disadvantage to the other. The formation of a one-party regime, in which all groups in the country would be embraced in the single political party, was seen as a way of promoting national integration and avoiding the politicization of ethnic ties and secessionist movements based on ethnic-regional parties.

The second phase of the attempt to eliminate competitive party politics took the form of the military coup, in which the civilian governments in some of the new independent states were overthrown by the armed forces. This phase became dominant in 1966. The first military coup in tropical Africa actually occurred in 1960 in Congo-Leopoldville (Zaire), following closely on the heels of independence. In 1963 three more coups occurred, in Congo-Brazzaville, Dahomey (Benin), and Togo. In all four cases, the military did not stay in power but simply intervened to bring about a change in the civilian government. In the next two years there were four more coups, but three of these were in countries where coups had already occurred and the other, in Gabon, was reversed by the intervention of French troops, which restored the former civilian government. The military coup was definitely a fact of political life on the African continent, but it did not yet seem that is was a pervasive phenomenon.

The events of 1966 changed this assessment. There were coups in five additional countries (indeed there were two coups in two of them) and the list, for the first time, included ex-British as well as ex-French and ex-Belgian colonies. By the end of the decade there were eight additional coups, bringing the total up to twenty-two in twelve countries. In the 1970s this trend has continued. Between 1970 and 1975 there were eight more coups, four of them in countries that had not previously had any. This brought the total up to thirty in sixteen countries. The army has clearly become one of the most important sources of political change in Africa.

The year 1966 signaled as well a change in the role of the military after coups. Coups no longer involved a short-term intervention for the purpose of installing a new civilian government. Rather, the role of the military was expanded, and the military not only seized power to oust the civilian regime, but retained power, setting up military regimes. In 1976, fourteen Black African countries were ruled by military governments (see figure 19).

The causes of military coups and the establishment of military governments are many and are wide-ranging in nature: some are underlying and some are

FIGURE 19

Contemporary Regimes in Tropical Africa, 1976

One-party Plebiscitary	One-party Competitive	Military		Other
Cameroon	Kenya	Benin	Niger	The Gambia
Gabon	Tanzania	Burundi	Nigeria	Malawi
Guinea	Zambia	Central African	Rwanda	Sierra Leone
Ivory Coast		Republic	Togo	
Mauritania		Congo	Uganda	
Senegal*		Chad	Upper Volta	
		Ghana	Zaire	
		Mali		

*Senegal has recently allowed the formation of two additional official parties, one to the right and one to the left of the ruling party. The role these parties might be allowed to play is still unclear.

immediate sparks for the coup. One salient cause is often a sense of threat to the armed forces itself. For instance, officers may feel threatened by a cut in the military budget or by what they view as insufficient military appropriations (in fact, coups are usually followed by increases in the military budget); by the fear or perception that they are losing power to other institutions concerned with security matters, such as the police or special security forces; or by other kinds of policies affecting the military as an institution. Key groups of officers may be antagonized by a lack of opportunity for promotion within the ranks, or may be motivated by personal rivalries and factional in-fighting. Other causes are less related to the specific needs of the military and refer more generally to the inadequate performance of the overthrown regime. They include economic mismanagement; unpopular policy decisions, such as devaluation of the currency or austerity measures; corruption, nepotism, and inefficiency; the inability to control mass demonstrations or unrest; and inter-elite strife and the political stalemate that may result from it.

The most general and underlying cause of military coups is the weakness of the civilian regimes that are ousted: their lack of support, power, prestige, and legitimacy. This weakness is the outcome of the experience that the countries had with competitive party politics during the period of decolonization and with the subsequent pattern of dismantling democratic institutions. Though there have been many coups across the African continent in the decade and a half since independence, not all countries have had coups, and their occurrence has not been random. Where they have occurred depends to a great degree on previous patterns of political change.

Types of One-party Regime Formation and Military Coups

In order to understand why some countries have had coups while others have not, it is necessary to go back and take a closer look at what happened earlier, in the first phase of the establishment of authoritarian rule in independent Africa, that is, with the attempt (or lack of it) to form one-party regimes. Different patterns of one-party regime formation, in turn, reflect the prior experience that each country had with competitive party politics during the period of decolonization. In the following discussion, one-party regimes will be defined as those in which one party holds all national elected posts, including parliamentary seats and the office of president or prime minister.

As indicated above, one-party regimes have been established in three ways: by the electoral success of one of the parties, by a merger of parties, or by the repression of all but one party. In addition to the countries which followed one of these patterns, there are those in which a one-party regime was never formed.

Whether and how a one-party regime was established depended on the power and popularity of the dominant party in each country. Where a one-party regime was formed by election, as in Ivory Coast and Tanzania, the dominant party had the least opposition and was able to fill all the elected legislative seats on its own. The cases of one-party regime formation by merger, as in Guinea, also represent a situation where one party became clearly dominant but faced some opposition from a much weaker party which it could not eliminate electorally. It was nonetheless sufficiently dominant that the opposition party finally decided it would fare better inside the dominant party than in opposition to it. One-party regimes formed by electoral victory or by merger, then, were based on clearly dominant parties. They emerged relatively well-consolidated with a relatively large amount of power and little opposition in the immediate postindependence period.

Where a one-party regime was not established by election or merger, the dominant parties had been relatively weak in the preindependence period and had never been able to establish as broad an electoral base. These parties were thus unable either to eliminate the opposition in a legitimate election or to absorb it through merger. In these cases the most dominant party had relatively less support and legitimacy and more opposition, and, with a few exceptions, did not have the same capacity to institute a successful one-party regime. Many of these countries attempted to set up a one-party regime through coercive means by simply outlawing opposition parties, as in Upper Volta, or by effectively prohibiting the opposition from contesting elections, as in Togo. Other regimes, as in Nigeria, did not attempt to institute a one-party regime by such measures, but tried to work within the framework of a multiparty system.

The ex-French and ex-British colonies which had not formed one-party regimes by election or merger tended to choose differently between the remaining alternatives. The former French colonies employed a variety of methods, including repression, harassment, and the rigging of elections, to institute a one-party regime. In no former French colony was a multiparty system retained. Among the former British colonies, however, there was much greater hesitancy to employ these methods and a greater tendency to retain a multiparty system.

The type of one-party regime formation that occurred around the time of independence had important consequences for the kinds of regimes that have appeared in the first decade and a half of independence in Africa. In countries such as Ivory Coast and Tanzania, where a one-party regime was formed by election or merger, these regimes were based on parties that had fared well under the competitive elections introduced during the period of decolonization. Furthermore, this method of achieving one-party status was more or less within the rules of the political game then being played. Consequently, these regimes had relatively little opposition and greater legitimacy. They have not been susceptible to military overthrow—the major exception being Mali—but rather have experienced substantial political continuity since independence.

In countries such as Togo where one-party regimes were established by coercive means or Nigeria where mutiparty systems continued to exist, no party had fared as well under the competitive elections in the period of decolonization. The postindependence regimes in these countries had less legitimacy and more opposition. In such a situation an attempt to form a one-party regime involved the elimination of rivals who were viable power contenders. This more coercive method of forming a one-party regime was rarely successful, and instead of producing a more unified political system, it tended to intensify rivalries and increase opposition. Almost all of these regimes have been overthrown in military coups. In Congo-Brazzaville the announcement of the intention to form a one-party regime provided the spark for mass rioting and demonstrations and one of the few popular coups that have taken place on the continent. In most other cases the effect was not so immediate, though the military tended to oust these governments within a year or two.

The 1961 elections in Togo illustrate the coercive means often employed to form a one-party state. The election rules were changed to make it mandatory that any party participating in the election put up candidates for every assembly seat. All voters would then vote for the entire party list of candidates, thus assuring that only one party would have seats in the assembly. In addition to this, however, the candidates running on the opposition ticket were disqualified for filing too late. The opposition claimed they had been prevented by the government from doing so on time. The formation of a one-party regime in Togo, then, was not based on relative consensus and neither reflected nor created a politically united country. In the year that followed, opposition became more active and was met with greater repression. The government became increasingly unpopular and was left with little support when the military decided to intervene in 1963.

Those countries which did not establish a one-party regime initially continued to have multiparty elections. Most of these regimes have also been overthrown, and in fact one of the direct and immediate causes for military coups in these countries has been the unworkability of those elections. For instance, Nigeria and Sierra Leone in ex-British Africa, as well as Burundi and Zaire in ex-Belgian Africa, all maintained multiparty regimes in the immediate post-independence period and eventually held a multiparty competitive election. In each case, however, the outcome of that election was disputed by some of the parties or was unacceptable to some group. In the power struggle which followed, no acceptable solution could be reached and no one party was able to predominate. In each case, the military intervened. Of the countries that did not try to establish a one-party regime in the postindependence period but rather continued to operate multiparty systems, only Gambia has not had a coup—and it must be mentioned that Gambia, with less than half a million people, does not have an army.

The tendencies to retain or to abolish competitive elections in the newly independent countries correspond to a more general difference in the way in which the transferred democratic institutions were dismantled in the two ex-colonial groupings. Among the ex-British colonies, there was a widespread tendency to retain some form of electoral competition. Electoral competition was eliminated completely only in Malawi, Ghana, and Uganda. Elsewhere it was maintained either in its original form as a multiparty elective system, or in modified form as a one-party competitive system which allowed voters to choose among candidates who were all members of the single party. Among the ex-French colonies, in contrast to the British African experience, there was a universal move to abolish political competition through the elimination both of opposition political parties and of electoral competition within the dominant party. This occurred in those countries with a dominant party which had been able to form a one-party regime by election or merger and also in those with weaker parties which had used coercion to establish a one-party regime.

These patterns of political change may be summarized as follows. In those countries with parties which fared well in the multiparty competitive elections introduced in the period of decolonization, the dominant parties managed to eliminate the opposition and form one-party regimes in the course of these elections—either through complete electoral victory or through the merger of a weaker party into a clearly dominant one. There were two different kinds of one-party regimes that were formed, however, and this difference was associated with former colonial rulers; in the first kind, primarily found in former French Africa, all electoral competition was eliminated, while in the second, primarily found in former British Africa, electoral competition was retained within the framework of a one-party system. In those countries where the majority party had not fared as well in the multiparty elections of the preindependence period, the final result has been military rule, though it is possible to distinguish two alternative intermediate steps. In the former French African countries that followed this pattern, coercive means were used to establish a one-party regime; in the ex-British and ex-Belgian colonies, a multiparty regime was initially retained. Neither of these subpatterns produced a viable solution to the problem of a lack of consolidation of power, however, and in both cases the regimes tended to be overthrown and military rule ultimately established.

Mass Participation and Authoritarian Rule

From the foregoing, it is possible to distinguish three types of authoritarian rule in contemporary Africa: the plebiscitary one-party regimes of former French Africa, the competitive one-party regimes of former British Africa, and the military regimes (see figure 19). One possible starting point for distinguishing among types of authoritarian rule in Africa is the presence or absence of political parties and, where they exist, the institutional framework within which they carry out what appears to be their principal function of holding elections.[1] These factors imply somewhat different distributions of power, different roles of the party, different degrees or types of popular participation, and different bases for the legitimacy of the regime.

As noted above, the ex-French colonies which formed a one-party regime by election or merger have tended to have plebiscitary one-party regimes in the postindependence period. By holding plebiscitary elections in which the voter can vote only for or against the one official candidate for each office, the government seeks to generate support for the regime. In Ivory Coast, for instance, these elections have been held on schedule every five years since independence, and are plebiscites quite literally. There is no opposition and no choice among candidates. The fundamental feature of these elections, however, is that they appear to involve a substantial amount of popular mobilization. Close to half the total population is generally reported as voting. Official returns in most of these countries also show at least 90 percent of those registered actually voting, and nearly 100 percent of the voters giving their support to the official candidates. Even allowing for substantial over-reporting in the official figures, it seems clear that sizable numbers of people are mobilized in a ritual act of voting on election day. This is a fairly impressive feat for countries in which systems of communication are not highly developed. For comparative purposes it may be noted that in the United States about 60 percent of the electorate has voted in recent presidential elections. The mobilization in Africa and the seriousness with which these elections are taken are also reflected in a tremendous amount of campaign and election coverage in the local media.

The fact that these elections are taken seriously indicates that they are more than mere drama, a charade, or a sham. They do, or have the potential for doing, at least three things: in their extensive mobilization, they elicit support for the regime, its officeholders, and its policies; they provide an opportunity for communication with the masses; and they give the political leaders a regularized and ritual opportunity for changing or rotating certain personnel and playing a kind of patronage game.

In plebiscitary elections, there is only an appearance of the possibility of rejecting official candidates; the real function is to legitimate them. In making a show of the mass support that can be mobilized behind a regime, its candidates, and its policies, these elections serve as legitimating mechanisms. The plebiscite, a political device often used by an authoritarian state, has the main purpose of unifying the people behind the party and ratifying the decisions of the state.[2]

By eliciting support, plebiscites may also serve to integrate the citizen into the political system by providing the occasion for the affirmation or reaffirmation of his sense of identity with it. In the campaigns, which form an important part of plebiscites, people are encouraged to attend rallies and meetings. In getting people out in this manner, the campaigns make the citizens more aware of the government and raise national consciousness. Campaigning is based on a national, rather than an ethnic, appeal and an effort is made to impart a feeling of being a participant in a single nationwide event and to build a sense of identification with the nation.

In addition to functioning as a support mechanism, plebiscitary elections and the election campaigns are also useful devices through which the leadership can communicate with the people, publicizing the goals and programs of the regime. They provide opportunities to explain and to propagandize. They also provide opportunities to get a feeling of grass roots sentiments—to sound out opinion at the local level and get some feedback on the impact of government policies.

Finally, plebiscitary elections serve as an occasion for personnel change among legislative deputies. The elections provide a periodic, legitimate, and institutionalized opportunity for removing and replacing a substantial portion of the members of national legislatures. In plebiscitary elections, of course, these personnel choices are made not through the vote but through the nominating process, and nomination is similar to appointment. Nevertheless, this gives the regimes a source of political patronage that may be important regardless of the power—or lack of power—of the legislature. Nomination to the legislature or removal from it is an important way of rewarding political friends and paying political debts, of co-opting potential opposition leaders, and of punishing—or threatening to punish and thereby keeping in line—those who stray from the path of political loyalty.

A somewhat different pattern has emerged in the ex-British colonies that formed one-party regimes. Rather than plebiscitary, these regimes can be characterized as one-party competitive. Such regimes have been instituted in Tanzania, Kenya, and Zambia. Here some degree of political competition exists, but within the context of a one-party system. In Tanzania the party selects two competing candidates to stand in each constituency, and the voters select one of the two in the general election. In Kenya there is a competitive primary in which voters select the one official candidate who will stand unopposed and be declared the winner on election day. In Zambia voters select three candidates in a competitive primary and then elect one of them in the general election. In these situations, electoral choice is not eliminated, but it is restricted to candidates within the single party who are running on the overall program of the party.

One-party competitive and plebiscitary elections both provide a focus for the task of national integration. In both types, the national government, through the campaign, is brought to the people, and citizens are encouraged to attend rallies and meetings. Yet there are differences in the functions of the two types of elections. Turnout in one-party competitive elections is considerably lower than the reported turnout in plebiscitary elections. For instance, the percentage of the population reported voting in the plebiscitary elections in Ivory Coast in 1965 was more than twice as great as that in the competitive one-party elections in Tanzania in the same year. This contrast would appear to reflect a major difference in actual turnout as well as a difference in the desire of the governments to give the appearance of massive participation by inflating the figures. In one-party competitive regimes the government does not seem to consider it so symbolically important to claim universal participation and support. Legitimacy in these regimes may derive more from popular choice, however limited or controlled it may be, than from apparent or elicited mass support and ratification. Though there is obviously, to varying degrees, central control over the nominations in one-party competitive regimes, the system is more open than plebiscitary regimes, since the preferred candidates must stand in a competitive primary or election and incumbents can be held more accountable to the people by the threat of non-reelection. In Tanzania close to half (45 percent) of the former members of Parliament who ran in the 1965 elections lost their seats by vote of the electorate. It is interesting to compare this to the United States, where in the 1972 election only 7 percent of the U.S. Representatives who ran for reelection were voted out of office in either the primary or the general election. The presence of electoral competition also means that the patronage function is diluted, since there is less control over the final outcome. It may also mean that the communications function is different, since in the one-party competitive regimes there is more room for the expression of grass-roots sentiment. Studies have shown that in both Tanzania and Kenya electoral campaigns are oriented around *local* issues and do not serve to promote the broader goals of the national regimes. It appears that one-party competitive elections are less well suited to mass mobilization for national goals.[3]

The final type of authoritarian regime in Africa is the military regime. Military regimes actually represent a wide range of styles of rule, from very personalistic, such as Idi Amin's Uganda, to quite bureaucratic, such as Acheampong's Ghana. Relative to the two types of one-party rule, however, military regimes have certain characteristics in common which set them off as a group. These regimes are dominated by coalitions of bureaucrats and army officers, and the usual pattern is for all parties to be banned, though a single party is occasionally allowed. Although there have been some cases in which the military has held either competitive or controlled elections, the more general policy of the military has been to stay in power and to rule without holding elections. An interesting exception to this is found in Zaire, where the military rulers have set up and legalized a single party, which they control and which they apparently would attempt to use to move toward a more plebiscitary pattern of rule. Generally, however, military regimes do not make any use of controlled or manipulated electoral mobilization present in the other two types of authoritarian rule. Here, of course, the decline in popular participation is the greatest, since there are no electoral and often no party channels left at all. Patterns of recruitment into public office are different, coming more predominantly from the military instead of from the party. Given the more provincial background and traditional orientation of members of the armed forces, it would appear that the types of individuals placed in high government positions may therefore be different.[4] Finally, there is a difference in the basis of legitimacy of a military regime, since there is no use of elections of either type to provide apparent support, ratification, or representation. As a result, military regimes must put greater reliance on force as well as on the popularity of their policies in order to maintain themselves in power.

Conclusion

It is clear from this discussion that the experiment in the transfer of Western democracy to contemporary Africa has not worked. Competitive democracy has not been sustained, and the countries of tropical Africa are ruled by authoritarian regimes. However, these regimes tend to be relatively weak, with limited financial, personnel, and political resources at their disposal. They operate in a context of extreme underdevelopment, political and economic dependency on the advanced industrialized world, and internal strains and conflicts among different ideological, political, economic, and ethnic groups. Furthermore, the scope of central political authority is quite limited, being generally restricted to the relatively small modern sector.[5]

This description of African regimes as weak is applicable to one-party and military regimes alike. One aspect of the weakness of one-party regimes may be seen in the declining role of the party.[6] In the immediate postindependence period, these parties grew in strength as an attempt was made to incorporate into them all the elements of society. Mass mobilization was encouraged and to varying degrees was achieved through participation in the activities of local party units. Separate party auxiliaries were formed to mobilize and incorporate youth, labor, women, and farmers. A major goal of the party was to elicit widespread allegiance to the new state. This phase of party evolution did not last long, however. Party officials were recruited into government posts, and as the activities of the party declined, mass involvement declined with it. Party auxiliaries increasingly became an outlet for criticism rather than support for the government. As a result, their leaders were purged and the auxiliaries were brought under the control of the appropriate governmental ministries and deactivated. The parallel structures of party and government proved inefficient and produced rivalries. Given the increased demand for technical expertise and the more dependable loyalty of the civil servants, the governmental structure became dominant. Accompanying this decline of the party was a great reduction in its mobilization activities and a corresponding restriction of one important channel for the expression of popular demands.

Thus, while it was once thought that the African one-party regimes could be compared to Communist one-party regimes, implying a strong, highly organized, hierarchical party eliciting overwhelming popular support and with considerable capacity to mobilize the citizenry and pursue social and economic goals, it has since been recognized that this model does not apply. Rather, the parties, which were never very strong, have been reduced in importance and perform fewer and fewer activities as the government bureaucracy and the civil service have become more dominant in political life.

Similarly, it has been recognized that the military regimes which have come to power in Africa are not necessarily more successful than the civilian regimes they replaced. Some analysts had thought that the military was an advanced, Westernized, well-disciplined, "de-tribalized," and technically oriented institution, which upon assuming control of the state could reduce corruption, avoid the bickering and politicking of different political parties or factions, overcome ethnic rivalries, and address itself more directly and efficiently to the problems of administration and economic development. This also was a false impression. In fact, "many African armies are a coterie of distinct armed camps owing primary clientelist allegiance to a handful of mutually competitive officers of different ranks seething with a variety of corporate, ethnic, and personal grievances. One direct corollary is that when the military assumes political power it is frequently not able to provide an efficient, nationally oriented, and stable administration," but rather is subject to all the same strains, tensions, rivalries, abuses, and weakness as the civilian government it replaces.[7]

The conclusions about the weakness of all types of authoritarian rule in contemporary Africa can be overstated, however. Along with important similarities among these regimes, there are differences. All African regimes may be weak, but some are clearly weaker than others. The countries with military regimes tend to be more unstable than those with one-party systems. This can be seen not in the obvious fact that the first independent civilian governments in the former category were overthrown, but rather in the fact that the military governments that replaced them have themselves tended to be overthrown. Furthermore, though all African regimes may be authoritarian, it is possible to identify different patterns through which these authoritarian governments emerged, as well as different types of authoritarian regimes, which are the contemporary outcomes of these different patterns. Throughout Africa, elitist bureaucratic institutions have become dominant over the participatory institutions that were initially introduced in the period of decolonization. Yet in some countries a controlled electoral arena continues to exist. It is the presence or absence of this arena and the kind of electoral participation permitted which allow us to distinguish different types of authoritarian regimes.

It would be interesting to take these differences one step further and consider the relationship between the various types of regimes and the adoption and successful pursuit of development goals (see chapter 19). This topic has not yet been carefully analyzed by scholars concerned with Africa, but certain preliminary observations may be made. Though it does not appear that one kind of regime tends to be more radical or more conservative than another, it may be that the capacity of different governments to pursue development goals successfully, whether capitalist or socialist, depends in part on the type of regime involved. It would be interesting to explore the different kinds of organizational, symbolic, and coercive resources that military regimes and the two types of one-party regimes bring to the task of building long-term development policies. One-party regimes may have certain resources available to them that are not available to military rulers: the continuity of political institutions that may be provided even by a weak one-party system; somewhat greater use of political symbols and ideology that may play a critical role in contexts in which material resources are in short supply; and the possibly greater political flexibility of party structure in responding to opposition and crisis. In light of the apparent importance of such resources, it is noteworthy that several Black African countries often identified as having particularly well worked out development policies—such as Ivory Coast, Tanzania, and Kenya—are one-party regimes. There may thus be an important relationship between the differing structural characteristics and political resources of these regimes and their effectiveness in important areas of public policy.

NOTES

1. This corresponds to criteria for distinguishing types of authoritarian rule proposed by Juan J. Linz. See his "Notes toward a Typology of Authoritarian Regimes," paper delivered at the 1972 annual meeting of the American Political Science Association, Washington, D.C., especially pp.31 and 49; and "Totalitarian and Authoritarian Regimes," in Fred Greenstein and Nelson W. Polsby, eds., *Handbook of Political Science*, Vol. 3 (Reading, Mass.: Addison-Wesley Publishing Co., 1975).

2. A. J. Milnor, *Elections and Political Stability* (Boston: Little, Brown, and Company, 1969), p.115.

3. Goran Hyden and Colin Leys, "Elections and Politics in Single-Party Systems: The Case of Kenya and Tanzania," *British Journal of Political Science*, Vol. 2 (1972), pp.389–420.

4. Ali A. Mazrui, "Soldiers as Traditionalizers: Military Rule and the Re-

Africanization of Africa," *World Politics*, Vol. 28, No. 2 (January 1976), pp.246–272.

    5. Aristide R. Zolberg, *Creating Political Order* (Chicago: Rand McNally and Company, 1966), pp.131–134.

    6. Immanuel Wallerstein, "The Decline of the Party in Single-Party African States," in J. LaPalombara and M. Weiner, *Political Parties and Political Development* (Princeton: Princeton University Press, 1966).

    7. Samuel Decalo, *Coups and Army Rule in Africa: Studies in Military Style* (New Haven: Yale University Press, 1976), pp.14–15.

SUGGESTIONS FOR FURTHER READING

Bienen, Henry. "One-Party Systems in Africa," in S. P. Huntington and C. H. Moore, *Authoritarian Politics in Modern Society*. New York: Basic Books, Inc., 1970.

First, Ruth. *Power in Africa*. Middlesex, Eng.: Penguin Books, Ltd., 1972.

Lofchie, Michael F. "Political Constraints on African Development," in M. F. Lofchie, *The State of the Nations*. Berkeley and Los Angeles: University of California Press, 1971.

Mazrui, Ali A. "Soldiers as Traditionalizers: Military Rule and the Re-Africanization of Africa." *World Politics*, Vol. 28, No. 2 (January 1976), 246–272.

Post, Ken. *The New States of West Africa*. Baltimore: Penguin Books, 1968.

Wallerstein, Immanuel. "The Decline of the Party in Single-Party African States," in J. LaPalombara and M. Weiner, *Political Parties and Political Development*. Princeton: Princeton University Press, 1966.

————. "The Range of Choice: Constraints on the Policies of Governments of Contemporary African States," in M. L. Lofchie, *The State of the Nations: Constraints on Development in Independent Africa*. Berkeley and Los Angeles: University of California Press, 1971.

Zolberg, Aristide R. *Creating Political Order*. Chicago: Rand McNally and Company, 1966.

Richard Stryker
Development Strategies

19 Development is not the same as change. As the preceding three chapters make clear, social, political, and economic change is pervasive in contemporary Africa. But change can be, and in Africa often has been, regressive and destructive, limiting rather than fulfilling individual and collective aspirations for a better life. Africans have not achieved concensus on what constitutes progress toward a better life any more than have most other people. Discussions of development, therefore, are efforts at persuasion in an ongoing struggle over the direction of change.

The goals of development involve nothing less than the progressive, evolutionary or revolutionary transformation of human conditions throughout the world today. As one thoughtful writer has stressed, development is not just a matter of "rational actions in the economic, political, and social spheres. It is also, and very deeply, the focus of redemptive hopes and expectations. In an important sense, development is a religious category."[1] Developed and underdeveloped should be seen as relative not absolute concepts, and comparisons are called for not only between nations but also between achievements and aspirations in particular countries. There is probably no definition of development, and certainly no ranking of development goals, that would satisfy everyone. There is agreement, however, that Africa, characterized by poverty, inequalities, dependency, conflict, and powerlessness, remains relatively underdeveloped by almost any standard. The purpose of development strategies is to alter those conditions.

For some, who may be termed liberals, development is largely a matter of *economic growth and modernization,* a process of acquiring the technological, organizational, and other resources deemed necessary to attain standards of living comparable to those in Western societies. Radicals, on the other hand, regard development more in terms of goals such as equality and self-reliance, a process of *liberation* for Africa and Africans from exploitative domination and dependence upon the West. The liberal vision of "plenty" (and privilege?) and the radical vision of "equality" (and coercion?) cannot be easily reconciled. They provide the bases for the two major conflicting development strategies of our time, capitalist and socialist. It should be noted that not all value conflicts in Africa or elsewhere are adequately expressed by this overriding controversy. Ethnic, religious, and regional differences, for example, cannot be reduced to a single ideological dimension. Nevertheless, the issues between capitalism and socialism encompass much of critical importance in the process of African development.

Liberal Optimism and Capitalist Strategies

During the 1950s and the early 60s, when African nationalist movements were at their peak and most of the continent achieved political independence from European colonial rule, there was considerable optimism about development prospects, whether defined as modernization or as liberation. African nationalism was perceived as an awakening on *all* fronts. There were new social and economic dynamics (commercialization, urbanization, Western education, some industrialization), new political orientations (the decline of traditional authorities and the rise of new leaders and organizations committed to self-rule at a territorial or even pan-African level), and movements to stimulate a cultural revival (asserting an *African* identity). The political liberation of Ghana, Guinea, and other new states was to be merely the opening wedge for the political liberation of all Africa, which would, in turn, lead to the continent's social, economic, and cultural transformation.

The most widely read book of the 1960s on African politics, *Africa: The Politics of Independence,* exulted that "Independence, as the nationalists had always insisted, makes a lot of difference." The author believed that the "modernizing elite, which is in control of most of the newly independent African nations," would be successful in the tasks of development if they could integrate the new political order around a strong nationalist party and a symbolic national hero. Growing national integration would "make possible economic development and increase the ultimate prospects for a flexible democracy."

65. Women building a road in Lesotho.
Photo courtesy United Nations/ Muldoon/ jr.

Furthermore, pan-Africanism could be viewed as the logical culmination of both liberation and modernization: "The strength of the pan-African drive can be attributed precisely to the fact that it is the weapon of the modernizers—those throughout Africa who are most radical in their nationalism. . . ." Finally, the trend of development in Africa appeared to be "modern without being Western. . . . having emerged from colonial rule, Africa is determined to be subject to no one but itself. . . . This desire for autonomy is not unique, but it is found in Africa in a very concentrated form."[2]

This optimism combined elements of both the radical and the liberal traditions in Western social thought about development. But liberal theory and ideology clearly predominated among students of Africa and the other under-developed areas. The conventional view presumed that all societies passed through certain predictable, universal stages of development. The initial stage was invariably "traditional," characterized by ascriptive values, parochial social and political orders, low productivity, and other not always accurate stereotypes. Next was a "transitional" stage or stages, characterized by dramatic changes as tradition was forced to give way to new, "modern" values, types of organization, and technologies. The best-known portrayal of the transition was the notion of the "preconditions for take-off." These were essentially seen as the economic and political changes associated with the rise of capitalism and the industrial revolution in Western Europe from the seventeenth to the nineteenth century. Supposedly parallel changes are occurring in twentieth-century Africa, Asia, and Latin America. The take-off itself was described as "the great water-shed in the life of modern societies," when the "forces making for economic progress . . . expand and come to dominate the society. Growth becomes its normal condition."[3] Thus, for many liberals, economic growth, rather than political liberation, was the key "engine" of development. The developed or modern society, the final stage in the theory, was indistinguishable, as might be expected, from contemporary Western society—the capitalist, industrial nation-state.

Optimism about economic growth and modernization pervaded the writings of the 1960s, officially declared the First Development Decade by the United Nations. After reviewing the economic distance between Africa and the industrial countries, for example, an official of the U.N. Economic Commission for Africa wrote in 1964 that

> The aim is to raise the current low level of economic well-being in the continent to that in the industrial countries—and this to be attained in half a century, or an adult's lifetime. . . . The growth rate needed is neither forbiddingly high, nor the period unbearably long. There is thus little basis for the pessimist's pathetic patience to postpone the possible—the very rapid elimination of want and poverty.[4]

The equation of underdevelopment with poverty is a touchstone of the liberal outlook, as is the tracing of poverty to internal causes. Precolonial Africa, for example, perhaps even more than other underdeveloped areas, was perceived in terms of a natural and virtually unchanging vicious circle—composed of "tradition," tropical and debilitating climate, inadequacies of technology and organization, and the rest—which generated and reinforced primordial poverty. The Western impact, including colonialism, may have had many faults in the eyes of liberal observers, but it became the historic vehicle for transmitting modernity to Africa and, thereby, for breaking out of the vicious circle of underdevelopment. As a prominent African liberal insisted recently, colonialism did bring "a certain number of benefits, beginning with the shock which pulled underdeveloped countries out of their isolation and their millenary stagnation."[5] A leading American political scientist concurs: "colonialism at its best has been one very useful mechanism for modernizing."[6]

The vast majority of African leaders adopted an essentially capitalist strategy following political independence and sought continuity with what they regarded as enlightened colonial policies for modernization. They gave top priority to international cooperation, that is, foreign aid, investment, and trade ties with the Western capitalist world. This might also be called a strategy of *external infusion*. The country is opened up to the presumed stimulating effects of foreign capital, technology, manpower, and consumer goods in order to promote rapid economic growth and modernization. If a country chooses to develop along these lines, there are well-established international networks for that purpose, dominated by Western capitalism. A multitude of public and private institutions—from the World Bank and the American Agency for International Development to the Chase Manhattan Bank, Unilever, Gulf Oil, and Union Carbide—are eager to become "partners in development."[7] Some African countries, it must be noted, are too poor and have too few resources to make very interesting partners for Western capitalism. Moreover, the costs of external infusion can be very high, permitting foreign control over the most dynamic parts of the local economy and creating powerful dependencies upon decisions made by foreign institutions and upon the ebb and flow of the American and European economies. But whenever African governments have had a choice, most have openly pursued increased cooperation with the West, the source for the most modern and familiar infusions. Liberals argue that some dependency is an unavoidable cost for poor countries seeking rapid economic growth.

Economic growth is not the only goal of African capitalist strategies, but it is clearly the first. Long-term development goals may also include greater national independence and social equality, but a capitalist strategy rejects the possibility of doing everything at once in a poor country. Rather, development goals must be achieved in sequence—in short, first things first—and the first concern should be sustained economic growth to lay the foundations and provide the dynamics for long-term development. Meaningful independence, for example, is seen as possible only after the expansion and strengthening of the national economic base; that requires rapid growth, which, in turn, requires dependency at present. Premature concern with self-reliance can only frustrate growth and postpone greater independence in the long run.

Much the same argument is made by liberals in considering growth and equality. In a poor country, the total size of the "pie" is very small. Even if everyone had an equal share, nobody would have very much. Therefore, a capitalist strategy insists upon enlargement of the pie without much concern for fair shares. At a later stage, when the size of the pie is much more substantial and its continuing growth is reasonably assured, then issues of distribution make more sense.

During the process of economic growth, inequalities tend to increase dramatically. Disparities of wealth, power, and other resources exist in all societies, but they are least pronounced in those which have experienced little or no growth. They are greatest in those societies which are still relatively poor but are undergoing rapid growth. Once societies as a whole become wealthier, the extent of inequality tends to decline, though all industrially advanced countries today still exhibit very important gaps between rich and poor. This sequence is an article of faith among liberals and reflects the assumption of stages of development: low growth and high equality in the traditional stage; high growth and high inequality in the transitional stage; then continued high growth and lower inequality in the modern stage.

A major reason why inequalities increase so greatly is that the only way to obtain rapid growth, at least following a capitalist strategy, is to "build on the best."[8] In other words, start with those individuals, groups, cities, regions, and resources that are already the most developed or that already possess advantages such as education, skills, wealth, power, good location, easy availability, and so on. The purpose of starting with "the best" is to get the quickest return for each investment, the most output for the least input, the fastest growth along the lines of least resistance. The result is rapid growth *and* accentuation of all possible inequalities—between people, increasingly defined as productive or unproductive; between dynamic and backward regions; between great, booming cities and stagnant rural areas. To build on the best is the very essence of the capitalist development strategy. It promotes a systematic bias in favor of efficiency rather than equity.

In time, the strategy promises to reconcile growth and equality. The process by which this comes about is not a sudden redistribution of resources, but a continued growth that spreads or "trickles down" to poor people and poor areas. A good deal of Western economic theory is devoted to explaining or predicting that "trickling down" of the benefits of capitalist growth. As the economy expands, agriculture and industry should produce increasing numbers and kinds of goods (diversification) and stimulate more interactions between producers and outlying regions, as well as with the outside world. Consequently, employment opportunities should increase and wages should rise; public services, from health and education to social security and rural roads, should multiply. So long as growth continues, its benefits should spread more widely and deeply, not equally, but bringing absolute improvements to nearly all.

Radicalization and Socialist Strategies

From the vantage point of the middle and later 1970s, it is difficult to share or even fully recapture the mood of optimism sketched above. That mood has given way, among most serious students of Africa, to deep pessimism and considerable radicalization. *False Start in Africa*, originally published in French in 1962, was an insightful precursor of the new radicalism and a caustic indictment of colonialism and the persistance of colonial policies after independence. *Wretched of the Earth*, also originally published in French in 1961, was more uncompromisingly radical and even more influential. Prominent book titles in recent years, indicative of the current temper, include *The Pillage of the Third World, Can Africa Survive?*, and several deploring neocolonialism.[9] Liberal theory and ideology are more and more on the defensive, while Marxist interpretations are becoming increasingly popular. As one disillusioned liberal, an eminent Pakistani economist with the World Bank, put it, "liberalism cannot survive in an illiberal world. The developing countries are passing through a very dark and ugly mood. They are questioning all the assumptions on which they based their early development strategy."[10]

There can be little doubt that the pessimism and the turn toward more radical strategies reflect important realities in contemporary Africa. Neither political independence nor economic growth has lived up to its promise. The political liberation of Africa is not only incomplete, Rhodesia and South Africa remaining as formidable obstacles, but political independence elsewhere on the continent has rarely resulted in any of the goals of political development. Stability, order, civil liberties, popular participation, organizational effectiveness, national integration, and pan-African solidarities all seem more remote than they did in the euphoric glow cast by the parties and heroes of independence. Most of the heroes are gone now, and few of those who are still in place lead regimes of progressive character. Political parties, the key institutional creations of African nationalism, have declined almost everywhere, or vanished with scarcely a trace following military coups. Soldiers are as numerous as are civilians

in heading African governments today, and faith in the efficiency or incorrupti-
bility of the former would be even more misplaced than faith in the popular
bases of the latter. In the best of cases the modest accomplishments of political
independence underscore the weakness of the new states in their efforts to cope
with the internal and external problems of underdevelopment.

A seeming trend toward political decay is complemented by doubts as to
the possibility of widespread or continuous economic growth in contemporary
Africa and, especially, by doubts about the likelihood that whatever growth
there is will trickle down to the impoverished majority. A good number of
countries, from Senegal, Mali, Guinea, and Ghana, to Chad, Sudan, Uganda,
and Somalia, have faced stagnation or decline over the past decade. Many
rural areas within every African country have regressed. Growth has been more
uneven and has generated starker inequalities than predicted by either liberal
theory or Western experience. The lot of the poorest—peasant farmers, unskilled rural and urban workers, the unemployed—may be deteriorating not only
relatively but often absolutely as well. The numbers of rural emigrants and urban unemployed multiply daily. In the best of cases there may be a kind of
"growth without development." The growth is precarious, the trickling down
constricted, and the dependency deepening. A privileged class is strengthening
its political and economic position, and there are no forces on the horizon to reduce the widening inequalities. The benefits of external infusion invite skepti-
cism, as the direct costs show up in trade deficits, balance of payments problems,
and debt crises. The indirect costs of dependency may be even higher: an export-
oriented agriculture which monopolizes resources increasingly needed for food
crops, an imported technology which emphasizes efficiency at the expense of
employment, and social distortions of all kinds due to the introduction of every
conceivable luxury for the few in the midst of the most severe poverty for the
many.

Radicals argue that African underdevelopment is not simply a matter of poverty, that its causes are not primarily internal, and that the current difficulties
are not a transitional stage on the road to modernity. Poverty is no more than
a symptom of underdevelopment. In Africa and the other areas of Western
colonization, underdevelopment is part of the same historical process by which
capitalism developed in the "mother countries." That process, stretching from
the sixteenth to the twentieth centuries, resulted in slavery, brute exploitation,
and loss of control over her own destiny for Africa; it resulted in unparalleled
wealth, industrial and military power, and domination of an expanding world
capitalist system for Europe. This is not to say that in the absence of European
domination Africa would have become industrially developed, wealthy, and

powerful on her own, though this can never be known. But there is a great deal of evidence (contrary to the popular stereotypes of precolonial Africa) to indicate that the continent was not unchanging, not nearly so "traditional" and lacking in innovation as often supposed, and not without progressive political and economic forces of its own. These forces were crushed or subordinated by the European intrusion, so that any *indigenous* development was blocked. Africa was relatively *un*developed but became *under*developed through exploitation for purposes of European development.

The exploitation of Africa and the other colonial areas was not, it should be added, necessary or sufficient to explain the capitalist and industrial revolutions of the West. European development was primarily generated internally, but the transformation was enormously facilitated by the provision of massive quantities of cheap resources, cheap labor to extract or produce them, and protected markets in the colonies. An "unequal partnership" was imposed which enhanced the power, the technological superiority, and the profits of the industrial-commercial partner but which restricted the subordinate partner to a narrow specialization in mining and export agriculture, to political and technological stagnation, and to no more than incidental or accidental benefits from the relationship. In the absence of Western capitalist domination of the southern hemisphere, it *can* reasonably be presumed that the world would now exhibit far greater diversity of political, economic and cultural types of development, that Africa, with other areas, would have evolved a far more autonomous pattern of development, and that there would be far less extreme international inequalities between the very rich of the North Atlantic region and the very poor of the tropical regions.

Given this perspective, colonialism is hardly regarded as a progressive, modernizing force by radicals. Even at its most enlightened, colonialism sought to develop Africa as an extension of Europe, as a respectable but junior partner in the capitalist firm. Political independence did not change this relationship; it merely removed the most embarrassing and expensive burdens from the senior partner. Political manipulation, economic control, and cultural imperialism remained under the typical postindependence conditions of *neocolonialism*. International cooperation is regarded as a euphemism for keeping the ex-colonial countries open to capitalist penetration, which needs both the natural resources and the consumer markets of the entire world at its potential disposal. Foreign aid is no more than a modest inducement to the ex-colonies to keep them in the game; when all the accounts are balanced, the aid costs the capitalist countries little or nothing. The total of all transactions (capital, goods, and services) between the producers of raw materials, who are also the borrowers, and the producers of manufactures, who are also the lenders, works out to the clear advantage of the senior partner. The results of cooperation for the junior partner are a distorted, dependent economy and a distorted, inegalitarian society.

Radicals insist on reversing the conventional terminology. Economic growth and modernization *within* the established capitalist system signify not development but the increasing underdevelopment of Africa. Real development can only mean liberation *from* that system. Political independence was a first step, but it is a fraud until the break with colonialism and neocolonialism is complete. The struggle of the new states, of Africa, and of the Third World has just begun.

The leading goal is not economic growth, a destructive force unless harnessed to political and social goals like independence and equality. A capitalist strategy enshrines growth, but radicals demand a socialist strategy which combines independence, equality, and growth simultaneously. The capitalist sequence is regarded by many as a myth, especially for the Third World. Dependency and inequality on a world scale are not transitional but structural, that is, they are intrinsic to the dual process of capitalist development and underdevelopment. The stages of development no longer apply (if they ever did), because external forces determine the character of change in African and other dependent countries. The West is rejected as a model for development and in its place are models based on revolutionary liberation from Western domination—occasionally the Soviet Union, but especially the People's Republic of China, Cuba, or Vietnam.

In order to achieve independence, equality, and growth, a socialist strategy must lay the groundwork by attacking inequalities at all levels. Within the nation, this means eliminating privileges and seeking to "build on the worst"— the poor, the disadvantaged, the backward rural areas, the peasants and workers. This is a Maoist strategy "to involve everyone in the development process, to pursue development without leaving a single person behind, to achieve a balanced growth rather than a lopsided one." In the long run, it is believed, this kind of development will lead to a society of new men and women who neither exploit nor are exploited, who are more productive because exploitation and inequality have been ended.[11]

On an international level, a socialist strategy is committed to self-reliance for the nation, the African continent, and the Third World. Autonomy from external capitalist forces is a prerequisite for social development. This means controlling, if not forbidding, the infusion of foreign capital, at least private capital, consumer goods, especially luxuries, and so on. The door to the outside must be guarded, even closed to the extent that this is possible. Agriculture must be redirected to feeding the nation, industry to providing necessary consumer goods, and services to serving the masses. At the same time, the ex-colonial countries should organize their own "poor power" to confront the rich countries on issues of international inequality and dependency. Cooperation with the capitalist powers is not rejected, but it must become a form of collective bargaining between equals rather than the discredited partnership of the past. Only then can a new, more just world order begin to emerge.

Development Choices in Africa

The previous sections of this chapter represent an effort to summarize the opposing views of the dominant positions concerning African development and underdevelopment. The roots of African underdevelopment are, on any honest and thorough appraisal, both internal and external, as are the obstacles to African development, however defined. The consequences of Western colonialism and capitalist expansion have been generally destructive and distorting for Africa, but the balance between modernization and exploitation is more ambiguous than either side will usually admit. Nevertheless, the two perspectives and the alternative strategies cannot be easily reconciled. Difficult choices have to be made, by Africans, by the student of Africa.

In making such choices, the specific circumstances of the country in question must be taken into account. Different strategies, or at least different priorities, will probably be required in different countries and situations. All African countries face fairly severe obstacles and none has a very wide range of options by comparison to, say, Britain, Sweden, or Japan, much less the United States or Soviet Union, during the early stages of their development. Still, the options available to Nigeria are clearly greater and more attractive than those available to Mali. Among the factors which are particularly important in charting a country's development strategy are size (population, territory, and income), available natural resources, economic organization and capacity (in agriculture, industry, transportation, energy, etc.), the character of the ruling elite (stability, ideology, capability), the extent of popular participation and support, relationships with neighboring countries, and relationships with foreign capitalism and with the major powers.

It was pointed out above that in the years following independence most African governments followed a strategy of development that could be labeled capitalist. Capitalist development remains predominant, but two qualifications should be made here. First, all African governments intervene actively in economic and social affairs within their countries; none pursues a "hands off" or *laissez-faire* policy. Second, some African governments have adopted a self-conscious ideology of capitalist development and fairly consistent policies to support that ideology. A number of other governments, however, are capitalist only in that they seem to follow the path of least resistance, allowing private enterprise (foreign and domestic) an open field out of weakness and corruption rather than pursuing any kind of coherent strategy at all. African countries which have attempted to promote a generally consistent capitalist strategy, and which have been most successful on their own terms, include Ivory Coast and Kenya. African countries which have attempted to devise socialist strategies of special interest, even more varied in ideology and in policies, include Algeria and Tanzania. In order to provide the reader with a somewhat more concrete appreciation of alternative strategies, these four cases will be briefly compared.

Ivory Coast and Kenya

Ivory Coast, a former French colony in West Africa, and Kenya, a former British colony in East Africa, are probably the outstanding success stories achieved by the capitalist option in contemporary Africa. They are both highly controversial cases because they illustrate so clearly both the positive and the negative aspects of this choice. Their leaders, Félix Houphouet-Boigny and Jomo Kenyatta, are among the grand old men of African politics, survivors from the era of heroes. Houphouet-Boigny was one of the founders and the leading figure in the nationalist movement of Ivory Coast and that of French West Africa as a whole after World War II. By the early 1950s, he had cast aside his radical anticolonialism and decided that a better deal could be obtained, at least for Ivory Coast, through a cooperative relationship with France. Shortly after assuming the presidency of an independent Ivory Coast in 1960, Houphouet-Boigny declared,

> In the envisaged task of economic development, the place of private foreign initiatives is to remain large and, in order to encourage them, my government will continue to assure them liberal facilities and guarantees.[12]

Similarly, Kenyatta was notable on the international pan-Africanist scene as well as becoming the acknowledged leader of Kenyan nationalism by the later 1940s. Following his detention by the colonial regime for allegedly directing the Mau Mau Rebellion of the 1950s, Kenyatta became an advocate of partnership with Britain and the West. As president, he pledged that

> The Government of an independent Kenya [in 1963] will not be a gangster Government . . . and will not deprive foreigners of their property or

rights of ownership. We will encourage investors . . . to come to Kenya and carry on their business peacefully, in order to bring prosperity to this country.[13]

Both Ivory Coast and Kenya *have* achieved considerable prosperity through cooperation with Western capitalism. From 1960 to 1972, Kenya's economy grew at an impressive rate of nearly 7 percent per year, and the Ivory Coast record was even better, just over 7.5 percent per year, compared to an average below 5 percent for Africa as a whole. Only a handful of African countries had comparable performances, and most of these had large petroleum or mineral resources. Ivory Coast and Kenya have based their growth on rapid expansion of commercial agriculture for export (primarily coffee and tea in Kenya; coffee, cocoa, fruit crops, palm oil, and also timber in Ivory Coast) and light manufacturing industries (for consumer goods and the processing of primary commodities). Both have sought and received large infusions of external capital and manpower to develop their modern sectors, including substantial improvements in transportation, education, and, especially in Kenya, tourist facilities. Abidjan and Nairobi, the capitals, rank among the most modern cities on the continent, serving as regional centers for, respectively, former French West and former British East Africa. The two countries have been consistently hailed as models of political stability, with the founding fathers and their parties still in command. Kenya has been marked by growing violence and blatant corruption in recent years, however, and both countries face uncertain successions to their aging leaders.

There are more immediate and serious problems also, resulting from the very prosperity brought by capitalist-style development. These can be summarized as increasing internal inequalities and increasing external dependencies. Reliance upon external infusion for modernization requires maintaining a liberal atmosphere of hospitality for Westerners, that multitude of experts, managers, salesmen, officials, and tourists who always accompany or follow important foreign investments. There are roughly 50,000 white residents in each country, who continue to dominate the upper levels of the private sector and who receive a significant share of the total private income. They, along with the hordes of affluent tourists, flaunt a standard of living which is unattainable for any but a small minority of Africans. The foreigners are highly visible, at least in the cities, and their style of life is emulated by the African elite. This elite, based on commerce, small industry, urban and sometimes rural property, but especially on politics and the bureaucracy, represents "the best," the privileged class whose advantages depend upon external infusion. The rhetoric of the Ivorian and Kenyan elites is increasingly nationalistic, but their policies do not recognize any strategy for development other than growth and "cooperation."

There are also new inequalities between wealthy farmers, often absentee landlords from the political elite, whose holdings are expanding and whose productivity is increasing, and peasants with little land, credit, or modern technology. Despite redistribution of considerable land from white settlers to Africans, many of them landless peasants, over the past fifteen years in Kenya, there is more and more land hunger and displacement of those who cannot compete successfully. Ivory Coast, with a higher proportion of arable land, imports masses of seasonal agricultural laborers from poorer surrounding countries, and they constitute a sizable rural poverty class. Inequalities have increased greatly not only within the rural areas but also between town and countryside, and, as a result, migration to the cities has increased. Rapid economic growth has not, unfortunately, meant equally rapid growth of urban employment, housing, or services. Abidjan, Nairobi, and other centers have been overwhelmed by spiraling unemployment, vast slums, and an inability to meet basic urban needs. The poorest 10 percent of the total population receives less than 2 percent of the income in each country; the poorest 40 percent receives only around 10 percent (even less in Kenya). The richest 5 percent, on the other hand, obtain over 45 percent of Kenyan income and nearly 30 percent of Ivorian income. The enrichment of a few and the impoverishment of the many has accelerated since independence; all the gaps have widened. This poses acute political dangers in Kenya, where inequalities are compounded by severe ethnic hostilities, and in Ivory Coast as well, though to a much lesser extent. Stability is likely to require mounting repression, especially once the great leaders depart.

If inequalities are somewhat greater in Kenya, dependency is somewhat more concentrated in Ivory Coast, though the two problems are closely interrelated. Trade, aid, and investment ties remain more intensive between Ivory Coast and France than between Kenya and Britain. The number of expatriates living in the two countries is similar today, but Kenya's total population is well over two times that of Ivory Coast, so the European presence is even more striking and Africanization even less advanced in Ivory Coast. The state plays a larger and larger role in both economies, but banking, import-export trade, insurance, manufacturing, and other modern activities are still mostly in foreign hands. A rapidly rising public debt, over $1 billion now in Ivory Coast and approaching that sum in Kenya, and the appearance of balance of payments difficulties are part of the price of dependency too. The capitalist strategy has stimulated impressive growth in Ivory Coast and Kenya, but some other goals of development seem to be receding.[14]

Algeria and Tanzania

Algeria, long a French possession in North Africa, and Tanzania, the former Tanganyika mainland of British East Africa, are probably the most prominent examples of African efforts to develop along socialist lines. The conception of socialism and the strategy chosen are fundamentally different in the two cases, however. Algeria seeks "economic liberation" to become an independent industrial power and a leading force both in North Africa and in the wider Arab world. Tanzania is pursuing a much more modest "self-reliance," based on peasant agriculture. Measures to promote greater equality have high priority in Tanzania but have been subordinated to rapid industrialization in Algeria. It can be said that, allowing for the much smaller scale and the far less extensive coercion in each African case, Algeria takes the Soviet Union for a model, while Tanzania favors the People's Republic of China.

The political and economic backgrounds of the two countries have little in common. Algeria was administered for over a century as an integral part of France, but citizenship rights were extended only to the numerous French settlers and to a few "assimilated" Arabs. The nationalist movement which began in the 1930s sought French citizenship, not a separate Algerian nation. France's failure to grant meaningful reforms led to more radical demands and, beginning in 1954, an armed struggle for independence. Not until 1962, after nearly eight years of protracted warfare, the most brutal and extended in modern African history, did a negotiated settlement give self-rule to Algeria. The new rulers proclaimed a popular, democratic, and socialist state. Of the million French settlers, no more than 150,000 remained after 1962, and all foreign-owned farm land was confiscated in 1963, followed by nationalization of many foreign industrial and mining companies over the past decade. Under the Ben Bella government from 1962 to 1965, popular participation and equality were also priority goals, and self-management of agricultural estates by the new worker-owners seemed a revolutionary innovation. Since then, President Boumediene, the former army commander who seized power in 1965, has subordinated all goals to the building of a strong, state-controlled industrial economy. Despite a number of serious economic problems, especially in agriculture, Algeria's growth rate over the period 1960–72 was nearly 6.5 percent per year. The country is rich in petroleum and natural gas reserves, which are being counted upon to finance the massive industrialization effort. As a leading member of OPEC (Organization of Petroleum Exporting Countries), Algeria profited richly from the oil price rise imposed in 1974, and the ambitions of the development planners are to transform the country's economy into an independent industrial one before the end of the century.

Tanzania, by contrast, achieved independence from Britain in 1961 via peaceful transfer rather than armed struggle, and the leadership's commitment to socialism emerged only gradually in succeeding years. The Arusha Declaration of 1967 set forth this commitment to a socialism based on democratic participation, equality, priority to agriculture, and self-reliance—a clearly conceived strategy of "building on the worst." The president of Tanzania since independence, Julius Nyerere, has explained the meaning of the Arusha Declaration as follows:

> Inherent in the Arusha Declaration . . . is a rejection of the concept of national grandeur as distinct from the well-being of its citizens, and a rejection too of material wealth for its own sake. It is a commitment to the belief that there are more important things in life than the amassing of riches, and that if the pursuit of wealth clashes with things like human dignity and social equality, then the latter will be given priority.[15]

This contrasts the Tanzanian path with the Algerian as much as with the Kenyan or Ivorian paths. Even after Arusha, Tanzanian socialism proceeded moderately and did not, for example, treat foreigners, either Europeans or Asians, much differently than they were treated in Kenya. Nationalizations extended government control systematically over the commanding heights of the economy, but confiscation has not been practiced. Similarly, the effort to reorganize the countryside into *ujamaa* ("socialist") villages and to discourage the emergence of rural capitalism was essentially voluntary until recently. If the progress of socialism was gradual but steady (income inequalities *have* been reduced), so was the progress of the economy, which grew at just over 5 percent per year during 1960–1972, only slightly above the African average. Export agriculture (coffee, cotton, sisal) remains important, there is little mineral wealth, and industrialization is very limited. The record is not spectacular, but Tanzania was not doing badly on several fronts, and its leadership inspired widespread admiration.

A number of severe problems have resulted from the socialist options of Algeria and Tanzania, some of which have been exacerbated in the past few years. In Tanzania, the fairly balanced and moderate approach gave way in 1974–75 to increasing radicalization and impatience with the slowness of the effort to achieve socialism, especially in the rural areas. President Nyerere announced that the entire rural population would be organized into *ujamaa* villages by the end of 1976, and, while that was unlikely, the proportion of such villages jumped from about 20 percent in late 1973 to a reported, probably exaggerated, 75 percent in mid-1976. This was brought about by abandoning the voluntary character of the program and resorting to official force against resistant peasants, including the use of soldiers to put selected villages and fields to the torch. Drought has exacerbated the problems of Tanzanian agriculture, but the productive dislocation and food shortages of the past few years may result less from nature than from man-made decisions. Socialism has generated other problems in Tanzania, such as the loss of private investments needed to fulfill planning objectives. Finally, it should be noted that socialism here has not been much more successful than has capitalism elsewhere in Africa in coping with a number of endemic problems—growing regional inequalities, reliance on export agriculture, unemployment, crises in public finances, and so on—though of course the history of the Tanzanian socialist effort is still a very brief one.

Algeria's problems have less to do with socialism than with the ambitious nature of its industrialization. Yet that is what socialism is mostly about in contemporary Algeria, especially since the end of the "romantic" experiments under Ben Bella. The traditional agricultural sector has been ignored and the collective farms, former French estates, have never achieved more than a fraction of their earlier productivity, proving inefficient under both decentralized and centralized management. The total resources devoted to agriculture are very limited since thorough industrialization is to precede the modernization of agriculture. Similar imbalances exist within the cities, since the industries being developed are all based on advanced technology rather than being adapted to a large and unskilled labor force. The urban unemployment problem in Algeria may, in fact, be the most severe on the entire continent. Despite its oil bonanza since 1974, Algeria shows signs at present of running up against growth and debt difficulties not unlike those of less well-endowed countries. This is largely a consequence of the grandiose ambitions of the leadership. The oil may be gone long before Algeria crosses the threshold of becoming an independent industrial power.[16]

Conclusions

In evaluating these and other development strategies, it is important, first of all, to "get the facts straight," to the extent that this is possible. That means seeking out a wide range of available sources, none of which should be regarded as presenting the whole, unbiased picture. In the final analysis, personal values are probably decisive in judging development issues. But values are not simply matters of taste, and they require continuing reflection and clarification. Values can be based on adequate or inadequate information, short- or long-term perspectives, probable consequences or pure fantasy. A few considerations that might assist in clarifying values about development are noted here in conclusion.

Both the capitalist and the socialist strategies are based on myths. The capitalist myth is that growth is an unmixed blessing, that prosperity for some is the best recipe to attain plenty for all, and that strictly economic dynamics can build harmonious societies of happy people. The myth is, of course, often mere propaganda to gain the acquiescence of the many to the exaggerated privileges of the few and to justify economic coercion. Faith in the myth is still widespread, though declining, and the fallacies of the myth should be exposed. That cannot be undertaken here, but the environmental, social, and ethical consequences of unbridled growth are the subject of proper and increasing concern in the world today.

The socialist myth is that revolutions are truly revolutionary. That is, an unswerving faith persists that socialist revolutions can eliminate "the old order," whether tradition or capitalism, can wipe the slate clean, end all oppression and privileges, liberate the masses, and create new kinds of people through the guidance of an enlightened political elite. This myth is also mere propaganda in many cases, to gain the acquiescence of the many to the decisions of the "vanguard" and to justify political coercion. The fallacies of this myth should be exposed as well, though that is more difficult because socialist systems are typically closed to critical inquiry.

Both myths are based on the assumption that if the correct strategy is followed, if the leaders will only persevere in their commitment to all-out growth or all-out revolutionary transformation, then all things sought are possible. The good society can then be realized, and development goals can all be reconciled. In contrast it might be suggested that *trade-offs* are a permanent necessity in an imperfect world. Hard choices between competing goods and between competing evils never end. The multiple goals of development—plenty, equality, liberty, security, dignity, and the rest—can never be finally reconciled. Conflicts, tensions, and dilemmas are inherent in every stage or type of development, though their character varies and changes over time.

These considerations point to a need for more modest expectations, perhaps especially in Africa, where waves of optimism and pessimism run to extremes but where neither the opportunities nor the constraints are so great as elsewhere in the Third World. A more *human* perspective on development is needed. Proponents of all strategies tend to lose sight of fundamentals–human dignity and choice *today*–in their pursuit of "development" tomorrow.

NOTES

1. Peter Berger, *Pyramids of Sacrifice* (Garden City, New York: Anchor Books, 1976), p.17.

2. Immanuel Wallerstein, *Africa: The Politics of Independence* (New York: Vintage, 1961), pp.85, 93, 101, 119, 134, 137, 151.

3. W. W. Rostow, *The Stages of Economic Growth* (New York: Cambridge University Press, 1960), pp.6–7.

4. Surendra Patel, "Economic Transition in Africa," in Irving Markovitz, ed., *African Politics and Society* (New York: Free Press, 1970), pp.330, 320.

5. Mohamed T. Diawara, speech to the United Nations Conference on Trade and Development, May 1972.

6. David Apter, *The Politics of Modernization* (Chicago: University of Chicago Press, 1965), p.52.

7. See the report by the prestigious Commission on International Development, *Partners in Development* (New York: Praeger, 1969).

8. See John Gurley, "Maoist Economic Development," in Charles Wilber, ed., *The Political Economy of Development and Underdevelopment* (New York: Random House, 1973), pp.308–09.

9. René Dumont, *False Start in Africa* (New York: Praeger, 1969); Frantz Fanon, *Wretched of the Earth* (New York: Grove, 1968); Pierre Jalée, *The Pillage of the Third World* (New York: Monthly Review, 1968); Basil Davidson, *Can Africa Survive?* (Boston: Little, Brown, 1974); Samir Amin, *Neo-Colonialism in West Africa* (New York: Monthly Review, 1973); and others.

10. Mahbub ul Haq, "The Crisis in Development Strategies," in Wilber, *Political Economy*, p.372.

11. Gurley, "Maoist Development," pp.312–13.

12. President Houphouet-Boigny, speech in *Fraternité*, January 6, 1961.

13. Cited in Colin Leys, *Underdevelopment in Kenya* (University of California Press, 1974), p.62.

14. Information in this section on Ivory Coast and Kenya is derived from numerous sources, the most comprehensive of which are Leys, *Underdevelopment in Kenya*, and Richard E. Stryker, *Neo-Colonialism as a Development Strategy* (forthcoming).

15. Julius Nyerere, *Ujamaa: Essays on Socialism* (New York: Oxford University Press), p. 92.

16. Information in this section on Algeria and Tanzania is derived from numerous sources. A useful overview is provided in Paul Alpert, *Partnership or Confrontation? Poor Lands and Rich* (New York: Free Press, 1973), pp.151–83.

SUGGESTIONS FOR FURTHER READING

Alpert, Paul. *Partnership or Confrontation? Poor Lands and Rich.* New York: Free Press, 1973.

Berger, Peter. *Pyramids of Sacrifice: Political Ethics and Social Change.* New York: Anchor Books, 1976.*

Erb, Guy, and Valeriana Kallab, eds. *Beyond Dependency: The Developing World Speaks Out.* Washington, D.C.: Overseas Development Council, 1975.*

Leys, Colin. *Underdevelopment in Kenya: The Political Economy of Neo-Colonialism.* Berkeley: University of California Press, 1974.*

Lofchie, Michael, ed. *The State of the Nations: Constraints on Development in Independent Africa.* Berkeley: University of California Press, 1971.*

Markovitz, Irving, ed. *African Politics and Society: Basic Issues and Problems of Government and Development.* New York: Free Press, 1970.*

Stavenhagen, Rodolfo. *Social Classes in Agrarian Societies.* New York: Anchor Books, 1975.*

Stryker, Richard E. *Neo-Colonialism as a Development Strategy: The Political Economy of Ivory Coast.* Forthcoming.

Wilber, Charles, ed. *The Political Economy of Development and Underdevelopment.* New York: Random House, 1973.*

*paperback edition available

Emile Snyder
Modern Africa in Literature

20 African literature written in a Western language, such as French, English, or Portuguese, is a relatively modern phenomenon. That is not to say that African literature is recent. It is as old as the continent itself, in the various vernaculars, in the form of praise poems, genealogies of chiefs, old and mythical tales told at night vigils, songs for work, or songs for special social and religious events, oral literature, recited and sung by the *griots*. In this discussion a literature written in Western languages during the last fifty years will be considered. This reflects the life experience and education of writers who suffered the experience of colonialism. And, because they had been partly assimilated to Western culture while they retained many of the values of their traditional culture, they felt the necessity, in the first half of this century, to analyze their cultural ambiguity and to take steps to recover a sense of their true identity.

French African Literature

In the French colonial system, political and economic subjugation was reinforced by a cultural policy which attempted, through the school system, to make Frenchmen out of Africans. This resulted, after many years, in the progressive alienation of the African from his cultural past, his traditional roots, indeed even from his vernacular, the use of which was prohibited in many mission schools.

The *Négritude* movement initiated by the Senegalese poet Léopold Sédar

Senghor was an attempt to combat this denigration of traditional African culture. Senghor defined the concept of *Négritude* as the need to recover the cultural heritage of Africa, its values and its spirituality. Aimé Césaire, the militant poet from Martinique who coined the term "Négritude" in his long poem *Cahier d'un retour au pays natal* (*Return to My Native Land*, 1956),[1] saw in *Négritude* the black man's willingness to accept himself and to commit himself to social and political action on behalf of all blacks.

The significance of the *Négritude* movement and its ideology was that it created a total cultural revolution. It involved the intellectual in all domains of human knowledge. From this moment on, the black scholar felt morally compelled to work for the rehabilitation of a black past, whether it was in the area of literature, history, politics, religion, linguistics, or aesthetics. For example, anthropologists and historians set out to rehabilitate African history and culture, to show that the continent of Africa had seen great moments of civilization and strong, cohesive empires, thus refuting the earlier racist theory of Count de Gobineau that the only history worth speaking of was "white history." Cheik Anta Diop's book *Nations nègres et culture* (*Black Nations and Culture*, 1954) was one such attempt. Others, such as Paul Hazoumé of Dahomey, in *L'Ame du Dahoméen révélée par sa religion* (1957), attempted to show that the European notion of African fetishism—pejorative in its application—was inadequate to explain African religions. Thus it was not only in the arts, and particularly in literature, that the ideology of *Négritude* expressed itself, but in all domains of human activity lived and experienced by black people on the continent of Africa. The cultural climate was set, and it became the task of poets and novelists to dramatize it in their works.

From the first, black poets took a militant stance against colonialism. They denounced an exploitation which enabled Frenchmen to enrich themselves at the expense of African labor and resources. They exhorted young Africans to rise against this exploitation:

> You who bend you who weep
> You who die one day just like that not knowing why
> You who struggle and stay awake for the Other's rest
> You with no more laughter in your look
> You my brother with face of fear and anguish
> Rise and shout: NO!
>> (David Diop: "Challenge to Force")[2]

The angry voice of David Diop echoed an earlier denunciation of Aimé Césaire, who, in his poems, recalled nightmarish visions of slavery: "My memory is circled with blood. My memory is girdled with corpses." The poetry of *Négritude* was a condemnation not only of colonialism but also of certain African intellectuals who had been attracted to the French language and culture to the extent that they had come to look upon their own culture with a measure of ambiguity and guilt:

> I feel like an awful fool
> accomplice among them
> panderer among them
> cut-throat among them
> my hands hideously red
> with the blood of their ci-vi-li-za-tion

> (Leon Damas: "Bargain")[3]

Thus stated, the problem of young Africans at the beginning of this century was the recognition that through their French education they had been, in part, severed from their African roots. History was not reversible, and so it became impossible for these "modern" Africans to return completely to the world and values of their ancestors. Yet it became just as impossible for them to deny the persistence and viability of old values lest they would betray them. Many poets felt compelled to turn to the theme of Africa as a means to root themselves once more in the land of their elders. They sang of the unity of African life, of its warm communality, of the propriety of its customs and traditions (respect for lineage, a sense of hospitality, a deep feeling for the land), and of its people. And as in the Afro-American poetry of the Harlem Renaissance, the African woman became the symbol of Mother Africa, a symbol of strength, fecundity, and spirituality:

> Negress my hot uproar of Africa
> My land of riddle and my fruit of reason
> You are dance by the naked joy of your smile
> By the offering of your breasts and your secret powers
> You are dance by golden legends of bridal nights
> By new times and ancestral rhythms
> Negress multiple triumph of dreams and stars
> Mistress obedient to the embrace of Koras
> You are dance by dizziness
> By the magic of loins beginning the world anew
> You are dance
> And around me the myths burn
> Around me the wings of learning

In great fires of joy in the sky of your steps
You are dance
And the false gods burn beneath your vertical flame
You are the face of the initiate
Sacrificing madness beside the guardian tree
You are the idea of All and the voice of the Ancient.
Gravely launched to attack chimeras
You are the Word that explodes
In miraculous spray on the shores of oblivion.

(David Diop: "To a Black Dancer")[4]

The image of the African mother is central to an understanding of Camara Laye's novel *L'Enfant Noir* (*Dark Child*, 1953). In this fictionalized autobiography of a young Guinean, the narrator's mother appears as the permanent focus for all the events in the novel. It is she who keeps the family traditions together because she respects them, while dispensing them. It is she who raises her son along the path of the ancestor's ways, so that even later, while a student in Paris, the son sees in the recalled image of his mother a reflection of the dignity of African life:

> However, I am sure she walked away, as she always did, with great dignity. She had always held herself very erect, and that made her appear taller than she was. I visualized her walking along the dusty road, her dress falling in noble folds, her waistband neatly tied, and her hair carefully plaited and drawn back at the nape of her neck.[5]

Not all African writers were pleased with this symbolic portrayal of Mother Africa. Some saw in it a dangerous measure of self-complacency. For after all, if the traditional values of Africa were still viable, they were also in danger under the impact of the colonial system. With time, *Négritude* came to be regarded as only a preliminary step: the step of self-awareness, of a regained pride in oneself. What was now required, beginning with the 1950s, was a more frontal attack upon the structures of colonialism, a paving of the way for future independence.

The struggle against colonialism was the driving force behind the creativity of two writers from Cameroon, Mongo Beti and Ferdinand Oyono, and of a Senegalese novelist and film maker, Ousmane Sembene. In his novels, Mongo Beti denounced not only the blatant injustices of the colonial system, but also the co-option of certain African cadres under the impact of that system. He attacked everything he felt harmful to the future welfare of the African peasantry; the superimposed Christianity, the African sorcerers who exploited the credulity of the masses, and some overbearing and venial chiefs whose sole purpose in life seemed to have been the consolidation of their power and the growth of their material wealth. In his major work *Mission Terminée* (*Mission to Kala*, 1957), Mongo Beti vilified a local chief:

> This local Chief of ours was an ancient lecher with remarkable staying powers. Despite his age, he had got hold of the six prettiest girls in the district and was always on the lookout for more. Like most Chiefs, he occupied an influential position in the community, with all the usual perquisites. He was a rich man by our standards and lived in an imposing villa; his general way of life was luxurious in the extreme. The Colonial Administration (who had nominated him in the first place) buttered him up. In return, he obeyed their commands like a robot and knew they would never throw him out. In the days of the forced labour gangs he had been feared by everyone because he betrayed fugitives to the authorities and acted as an informer.[6]

In Mongo Beti's works, the African peasantry is seen as the only moral force in Africa. Moreover, he places the future of Africa in the hands of the young generation who refuse to bow under the yoke of the oppressors. In *Ville Cruelle* (1954) a mother correctly assesses the psychological distance which separates her generation from the generation of her son:

> In our times, if a White man said to you "get on your knees" you didn't find anything better to do than to get on your knees . . . today, with our sons, it is no longer the same thing. They have grown: they scorn us because we have bent our backs in front of the Whites.[7]

Ferdinand Oyono, in his first two novels, *Une Vie de boy* (*Boy!*, 1956) and *Le Vieux négre et la médaille* (*The Old Negro Chief and the Medal*, 1956), manifested the same political commitment as Mongo Beti. In *Boy!* the decadent lives of the resident colonials in a small Cameroonian village are seen and exposed through the eyes of Toundi, the houseboy who naively recorded his impressions in a notebook. Against a cast of Europeans who make a composite picture of cruelty, indifference, and immorality, the African villagers are drawn with humor, dignity, and affection.

Finally, in this survey of the independence literature of francophone Africa, there are the works of Ousmane Sembene. The author of many novels and short stories, Sembene is also a renowned film maker. His *Borom Sarett* won a prize for short subjects at the film festival of Tours in 1961. Since then, such other films as *Manda bi* (*The Money Order*, 1968) and *Xala* (1975), both bitter satires on present-day African bureaucracy, have been universally acclaimed. Ousmane Sembene discovered his literary vocation while working as a dockworker on the waterfront of Marseilles. His early novel, *Le Docker Noir* (1956), partly retraced his experience not only as a worker but as the leader of the African dockworkers' union. Sembene has always sympathized with the cause of exploited people everywhere. For him, as for Frantz Fanon, the roots of the problem, colonialism or neocolonialism, are not primarily racial but economic. Political ideology fused with literary excellence in his major work, *Les Bouts de bois de Dieu* (*God's Bits of Wood*, 1960), an epic novel retracing in bold strokes the strike of the workers on the Dakar-Bamako railway in 1947–48. A broad historical vision enabled Sembene to involve not only the African workers who struggled against the French company bosses, but people from all levels of African society: the peasants in the villages, the elite in Dakar, the union leaders, and the priest of Islam. Through these characters Sembene showed how the revolutionary potential of the workers, once they had been politicized, could be put into motion, and, just as important, he showed the same revolutionary power of the women. The major contribution of *God's Bits of Wood* is that its dramatizes the mobile power of the dispossessed masses dangerously contained in the *medinas* and *bidonvilles* (ghetto-like conglomerations) of such large urban centers as Dakar and Abidjan.

With the coming of independence in French-speaking Africa (1960), a new literature has emerged. This, like the anticolonial literature, is dialectical in nature, but its opposition is now directed toward the realities of independence. Very few young writers appear willing to rationalize contemporary problems in terms of the aftermath of colonialism. Instead, they seem to prefer ascribing present responsibilities to their own governments and the functioning of their own society. This self-critical literature asks the questions: Now that we are independent, what are we doing with our independence? Who are those, among ourselves, who are perverting our goals?

One of the prevalent themes is that of the family, and in particular of the interaction of the young with their parents and elders. But unlike most of the characters in the early fiction of the *Négritude* period, who narrated the stages of their adolescence, the characters of this new fiction are already grown up. The problems of sex and marriage are central to the concern of today's youth. Thus there are glimpses of courtships, of pre-marital sexual relations, of unwanted pregnancies and growing revolt against parents whose dutiful notions of pre-arranged marriage go against the romantic inclinations of young people in contemporary Africa. The general picture is that of rebellion against traditional customs. The young people attempt to assert their preferences—their conceptions of love and marriage, of sexual relations—although in doing so, they are aware of the sorrows they may be inflicting upon their families. They cannot escape a sense of culpability, yet, at the same time, the pressure of new ideas spurs them on to struggle for their newly found freedom. Proponents of traditional values, usually the older people, ascribe the responsibility for the disintegration of authoritative structures to new ideas being filtered through modern, European-type schools. The concomitant results of this modern education, in the eyes of the traditionalists, are a drive for material goods and the rejection of paternal authority. Thus, generally speaking, the new novels, short stories, and plays (in particular the social comedies of Bernard Dadié of Ivory Coast) represent a plea for the liberalization of customs in the face of changing realities.

A second theme, as important as the family, is that of young men striving to find employment, to launch themselves into careers. Their rightful claims to positions, by virtue of their academic degrees or their skills, are ignored in favor of less qualified but better connected candidates. Nepotism, patronage, bribery, and ethnic ties are the major factors in securing a job. Recent fiction is replete with young men wasting their days seeking employment and being forced to live marginal lives, frequently accepting work outside of their fields of training. Similarly, passing comments are often made upon the waste of talents in modern Africa.

Whether expressed in a grave, melodramatic, or even comical mood, the deep concern for the deteriorating social conditions in independent Africa is an essential element in all of the recent fiction from French-speaking Africa. Does this mean that these writers are primarily political? In a sense, it does, for the new literature is an overt or implicit indictment of the leader and of his *parti unique* (the single party).

After a decade of literary inactivity, Mongo Beti has returned to literature with two aggressive novels, *Remember Ruben* (1974, the original title is in English) and *Perpétué* (1974). They evoke the now almost mythical figure of the Cameroonian labor leader Ruben Um Nyobé, killed by colonial troops on September 13, 1958, and they indict the present head of state of the Republic of Cameroon, Ahmadou Ahidjo, who is converted into the satirical portrait of a drunk and degenerate. To a lesser degree, the indictment of political repression is manifested in Yambo Ouologuem's *Le Devoir de violence* (*Bound to Violence*, 1968), Alioum Fantoure's *Le Cercle des tropiques* (1972), Ahmadou Kourouma's *Les Soleils des indépendances* (1968), and in V. Y. Mudimbe's *Entre les eaux* (1973). Among the less prestigious writers, whose audience is more popular (and who tend to be published by the CLE press in Cameroon instead of by French publishing houses), the critique is more subdued, more implicit than explicit. Political pressure is translated in terms of its secondary effects, the various vexing ways in which, contrary to the expectations of independence, the daily lives of the citizenry are being affected.

The writing of the new generation, beginning in the late 1960s, bodes well for the future of French African literature. Although the quality is uneven and a strong possibility exists that many authors will not go beyond a first novel, these writings represent a prolific activity. They involve writers from countries which produce hardly any fiction. Above all, the worth of this literature, apart from its literary merit, may simply be that it will provide a vibrant and historical documentation of the problems facing independent African countries.

English West African Literature

The primary cause of the *Négritude* movement seems to have been the need, on the part of French-speaking Africans, to recover a sense of identity as Africans. The French colonial experience had been traumatic, not only from a political and economic point of view, but in the ways in which it had attempted to transform the African personality, to uproot it and assimilate it to the francophone world. Generally speaking the young poets and novelists from English-speaking Africa did not experience this degree of uprootedness. While French African intellectuals were sent to universities in France, those from English-speaking Africa were educated primarily at African universities—the University of Ibadan or Lagos in Nigeria, Fourah Bay College in Sierra Leone, the University of Legon in Ghana—and their acquaintance with Britain came much later. From a cultural point of view, the British colonial imposition had not been as devastating as the French. British colonialism did not alienate Africans from their social structures, traditions, and languages as much as did the French system. In short, the British were not intent upon making Englishmen out of Africans. The result was that the English-speaking African poets and novelists wrote in English simply because they had been trained to write in that language; but, in doing so, they did not feel a sense of betrayal of their roots. They were not anguished with a sense of guilt. More important, they did not feel the impossibility of translating African experiences into their newly acquired Western language.

Unlike French African poetry, heavily committed to the "communal" rhetoric of *Négritude*, English African poetry is characterized by its great variety of styles and themes. Most of the poems reflect the poet's concrete and private experiences, set in a context which is purely African. The poetry of J. P. Clark could well illustrate this point: in "For Granny" he recalls his childhood, while in "Night Rain" he conveys the sense of wonder and apprehension that is felt by a young village boy as he listens, at night, to the rain drumming on the tattered roof of his hut. In other poems Clark depicts a young woman bathing in the river, or the colorful sight of the seven hills which surround the city of Ibadan. Similarly, another Nigerian poet, Gabriel Okara, involves us with a scene by a riverside, with the noise of cars passing, people jostling, music blaring while, facing the water and oblivious to these sounds, religious men are praying. Wole Soyinka, also from Nigeria, ranges from the ironic "Telephone Conversation," which retraces the frustration of an African student trying to rent a room in an English boardinghouse, to a gloomy view of the Biafran war and the climate of violence and intolerance it had imposed upon his country.

Although the range of themes in English African poetry is extremely wide, one topic is shared with French African writers: disappointment with the fruits of independence. In "Homecoming," Lenri Peters recorded the bitterness about the aborted promises:

> Our sapless roots have fed
> > The wind-swept seedlings of another age.
>
> . . .
>
> That is all that is left
> > To greet us on the home-coming
> After we have paced the world
> > And longed for returning[8]

Kofi Awoonor has expressed a similar picture of the disintegration of the past. In "Song of Sorrow" he symbolized this through the fall of a great family.

> And Kpeti's great household is no more,
> Only the broken fence stands;
> And those who dared not look in his face
> Have come out as men.[9]

The destruction of old values has not paved the way for viable new values. Unlike the *Négritude* poets, English African poets find no comfort in the past, or in escapes to an idyllic "up-country" Africa. Where is the *real* Africa? asked Aboiseh Nicol, in "The Meaning of Africa?" For "up-country" has changed, too. The bush has been invaded by a technology which the peasants do not yet know how to handle; the problematic future is symbolized by a cyclist pedaling on the wrong side of the road, "as if uncertain of this new emancipation."

The lucidity toward the past, and the awareness of the ambiguity of the present, force the African poet into what the South African writer and critic Ezekiel Mphahlele has called "the dialogue with the two selves." But if the major themes of modern English African poetry confess to a sense of disappointment with the present, a loss of spiritual values, and anguish at a difficult reconciliation with the future, it should not be assumed that they are evidence of a complete lack of faith in the unity of African life. For in spite of the uprootedness which the poet has experienced through colonialism, his own Westernization, and the changing physical shape of Africa largely due to urbanization, for English African poets there still remains a strong sense of *oneness* of their history and culture. The African experience is indivisible, and Kofi Awoonor feels confident that

> There shall still linger the communication we forged
> the feast of oneness whose ritual we partook of.[10]

But the indivisibility of the African experience has been obscured or distorted as a result of the colonial presence. The first notable novelists of English-speaking Africa, and in particular the Nigerian Chinua Achebe, addressed themselves to the task of rehabilitating the African experience in its authenticity. They, like the French African intellectuals, reacted against the European vision of the African past. In Achebe's words, the writer's duty was to demonstrate "that the African people did not hear of culture for the first time from Europeans; that the societies were not mindless but frequently had a philosophy of great depth and value and beauty."[11]

However, unlike most of the French African writers of the *Négritude* period, they did not consider their task to be the idealization of precolonial Africa. In writing *Things Fall Apart* (1958), Chinua Achebe was intent on repairing the foundations of Ibo culture, yet he was not blind to the shortcomings of that culture: "We cannot pretend that our past was one long technicolor idyll. We have to admit that like other people's past ours had its good and its bad sides."[12] *Things Fall Apart* and *Arrow of God* (1964) analyzed the effect of "the wind of change" blowing on the old customs. Although Achebe seemingly centered his novels upon the plight of exemplary heroes (Okonkwo in *Things Fall Apart* and Ezeulu in *Arrow of God*), they were primarily concerned with the collective tragedy of traditional African societies caught in the conflict of cultures.

The restitution of the past was but a minor concern for most English African novelists. They preferred to face the present, postindependence reality. The focus was most often on urban centers (Lagos, Accra, Freetown) and difficulties generated by large population shifts. Hence the preponderant themes of this literature are housing, unemployment, politics, and the inadequacy of traditional values to provide a moral code of behavior for the city dwellers. Cyprian Ekwensi, in *People of the City* (1954) and in *Jagua Nana* (1961), captured the pulse of Lagos life: the frantic pace of living, and the turmoil of the citizens trying to cope with economic pressures.

The protagonists of Ekwensi's novels are all victims of the power which the city (Lagos) seems to hold over its inhabitants. Yet most of the time, they cannot deal with the demands the city makes upon them. Without the necessary education, skills, or political connections, they are forced to live marginal lives, solely involved with the problem of survival. The search for wealth, for security, drives the most enterprising of them toward politics, but they find themselves no match for the scheming politicians already in power. Pathetic figures, haunted by a dream for "High Life," traverse Ekwensi's fiction: Beatrice, in *People of the City*,

> came to the city from the Eastern Greens, from the city of coal. She made no secret of what brought her to the city: "high life." Cars, servants, high-class foods, decent clothes, luxurious living. Since she could not earn the high life herself, she must obtain it by attachment to someone who could.[13]

The novels of Ekwensi generalize a particular dilemma in modern independent Africa: the migratory shifts from rural communities to urban centers. They point to the inability of these urban centers to assimilate waves of rural migrants. Some end up debilitated, some are crushed beyond repair, and some—the fortunate ones—barely manage to limp back to the village to regain a sense of peace and unity.

However, not all of the characters in this modern Nigerian fiction are drawn from the displaced rural people or the frantic city dwellers. Another type of hero in English African literature has emerged: the graduate, the semiliterate or the intellectual, the "been-to," as Nigerians called him. Wole Soyinka's extremely sophisticated novel, *The Interpreters* (1965), deals with Nigerians returning to Lagos after studies in England (hence the meaning of "been-to"). They are idealistic and intent upon helping to shape the future destiny of their country. However, their idealism, their probity, and their skills are ineffective against the stagnant structures and the rampant corruption of the politicians in control.

Similarly, Achebe's two "urban" novels, *No Longer at Ease* (1960) and *A Man of the People* (1966), underscore the drama of independence: the perversion of an ideal. This pessimistic view of modern African social history has been the foundation of the works of Ayi Kwei Armah, the angry young man of African letters. In *The Beautyful Ones Are Not Yet Born* (1968), the hero's struggle to survive in Accra is translated into a vision of a decaying world in which the human creature appears caught like an impotent rat in a maze. With flaming anger, and often with scatological language, Armah denounces politics, which he calls the "national game of Ghana." In Armah's outcry against African leaders, whom he characterizes as a curse upon the people ("how long will Africa be cursed with its leaders?"), in his outcry against African socialism as it is presently being practised, there is the reflection of an unrequited idealism. The same tendency is to be found in Kofi Awoonor's poetic novel *This Earth My Brother* (1971), where the author presents the dilemma of those African intellectuals who refuse to be satisfied with their newly gained status and the material possessions that accompany it, and who ask themselves the purpose of statehood if colonial injustices are replaced by political opportunism and social inequities. In short, all of the recent English African fiction has raised this unanswered question.

The Literature of East Africa[14]

While it was dominated in the 1960s by the works of James Ngugi (now calling himself Ngugi Thiong'o), the literature of East Africa is vibrant but less prolific than that of West Africa. It appears as a homogeneous, broader-based, modern reflection of the cultural complexity of the three countries that make up the geopolitical unit of East Africa: Kenya, Uganda, and Tanzania.

In Kenya, Ngugi Thiong'o has almost stopped writing altogether; yet his three novels, *Weep Not Child* (1964), *The River Between* (1965), and *A Grain of Wheat* (1967), are now, more than ever, regarded as classics and have earned him a place, perhaps next to Achebe and Oyono, as an outstanding anti-colonial novelist. All three of his novels show various generations of the Kikuyu (to which Thiong'o himself belongs), struggling to prevent the loss of their traditions, their sense of identity, while painfully trying to assimilate some aspects of European modernity. Thiong'o's protagonists inevitably find that this assimilation, as it evolves with Njoroge in *Weep Not Child*, or with Waiyaki in a religious sense in *The River Between*, is a self-defeating process, for the more knowledge they acquire, the closer they get to this foreign culture, the farther they move from their own. Hence they become alienated figures drifting back and forth between the two traditions, African and European. His third novel, *A Grain of Wheat*, is also set in the central province of Kenya and blends

Kikuyu legends into a complex narrative. Thiong'o in this novel creates suspense in the relationships between several different characters who represent opposing views in their struggle for independence.

The Ugandan poet Okot p'Bitek, writer of *The Song of Lawino* (1966), is preoccupied, like Thiong'o, with the modern African's struggle with his past and the threat Western culture represents. This lengthy poem, written in Acholi and translated by the author, was originally titled "Stick to the Old Ways"; hence its obvious affinities with many of the anticolonialist writers in both East and West Africa. Superficially this is a poem that strikes out against foreign influence in African life, but more profoundly it is the story of a man who finds himself divided, much like Thiong'o's Njoroge or Waiyaki. He is drawn both to his cultural heritage and to essentially Western-oriented modernity. In Okot p'Bitek's next poem, *Song of Ocul* (1970), Ocul wants to completely obliterate Africa's past; he wants to hang all the professors of anthropology, destroy all the anthologies of African literature, blow up Kilimanjaro, and fill in the Great Rift Valley. The promise of *uhuru* (independence) has been violated. Then, in the final sections of the poem, he feels guilty that he is one of those who has profited from *uhuru*. In his last poems, *Song of a Prisoner* and *Song of Malaya* (1971), he writes of *uhuru* wrecked; with the promise of independence shattered, the poet's only dream now, reminiscent of *Song of Lawino*, is to return to the past, to the old Acholi customs.

Although Tanzania's Sheikh Shaaban Robert's works have yet to be translated from the Swahili, they include some of the greatest achievements in East African literature. A Muslim conscious of the Arabic roots of Swahili literature, Shaaban often used traditional forms and themes in slightly altered ways, and his style can be seen as a combination of the traditional and the modern. His views, although primarily conservative, occasionally struck a prophetic note. In his biography written in the 1920s of the Zanzibar singer Siti Binti Saad, he champions women's rights for self-development. Although she was revolutionary, in that she left her family for a career, Shaaban uses her as a model for Muslim behavior. He holds her life up as a moral lesson for the community. Stressing the importance of self-development, he likened the man who failed to use his gifts, failed to act, to the man who "came into the world poor, lives in darkness, and then leaves without a sign."[15] Shaaban used Swahili whenever he could and hoped that it would become the major language of East Africa; he was convinced that European languages should not be used in African education. Like Thiong'o and Okot p'Bitek, Shaaban was an anticolonialist in the sense that he asked Africans to look to their heritage for their values.

South African Literature in the Context of Apartheid

South African literature in English has been written and is being written in an exceptional context. The case of Dennis Brutus serves to illustrate this point as well as that of any other black South African writer who has striven to express himself within the repressive climate of *apartheid*. From the beginnings of his intellectual life as a student at Fort Hare University College (where he became an important figure in the National Union of South African Students), and also in his professional life as a teacher in Port Elizabeth, Brutus clashed with the forces of *apartheid*. Moreover, as a sportsman he has worked for many years to have the color bar removed from sports in South Africa. He tried—and succeeded at last—to influence international groups, including the Olympic Committee, to stop South Africa from playing international competitions unless it removed the color bar. A constant target of the secret police, Brutus was finally sent to prison on Robben Island. His recollections of life on the Island were agonizingly set down in two volumes of poetry, *Sirens Knuckles Boots*, and *Letters to Martha*, collected in the recent editions of *A Simple Lust* (1973). The themes of Brutus's poetry are oppression, violence, deprivation, and human debilitation. The lyrical texture of the poems is purposefully jarred by concrete reminescences of the sounds of boots of the Afrikaner police smashing in the doors of shacks, of the searchlights scanning the island prison, of sexual assaults, and of desolation. But when everything is said about the political component of Brutus's poetry, the most recurrent theme in it is that of love, of a stubborn desire to retain the ability to feel and to love within this dehumanizing climate of terror. That theme is best expressed in the moving opening lines of one poem:

> Somehow we survive
> and tenderness, frustrated, does not wither.
> > (from *Sirens Knuckles Boots*)[16]

The poetry of Brutus, formal, even classical in structure, speaks of his love for his country (the "Flying into Kimberley"), of his love for a woman, and of the love of life in a time and within a political system that makes these ways of loving illegal for the black man.

Most of the recent young South African poets do not know the poetry of Brutus because the government has banned it. Yet the works of these poets echo similar cries of anguish. The tone is either ironic, metaphorical (censorship compels many poets to disguise their meaning), or at times frankly shrill. This poetry evokes the daily vexations and privations which the black man must endure in South Africa. At the same time, these young poets, victims of hatred, have learned to fight back with words of hatred. Mongabe Wally Serote manipulates the word *shit* as if it were a weapon to be flung back at the face of *apartheid*.

> I'm learning to pronounce this "shit" well,
> Since the other day
> at the pass office
> when I went to get employment,
> the officer there endorsed me to Middleburg
> So I said, hard and with all my might, "Shit!"
> I felt a little better;
> But what's good is, I said it in his face,
> A thing my father wouldn't dare do.
> That's what's in this black "shit".[17]

While looking at this bitter corpus of South African poetry, it must be kept in mind that this poetry, as well as the fiction, is nurtured in a climate of violence. Its voice, its only possible voice, is one of courageous protest against the gag of oppression.

The development of South African fiction in English (novels and short stories) coincided with the escalation of *apartheid's* repressive policies. Prior to the 1950s the works of Olive Shreiner, John Dube, Sarah Gertrude Millin, and others presented Africans as resigned sufferers, finding a comfort in religion. The most classic example of patience is to be seen in *Cry the Beloved Country* (1948), by white liberal writer Alan Paton. The characterization of the black Reverand Stephen Kumalo invites black readers to seek rewards in Christian virtues. Even the early fiction of Peter Abrahams partly eschews the racist dynamics in South Africa. In *Mine Boy* (1946), a dramatization of the life of Africans in the mines of Johannesburg, Abrahams seeks to reduce the dimensions of the problem purely to existing economic conditions. He sees the ideal solution in the unification of the workers, both black and white, against the exploitive company bosses. But in 1948 the Nationalist Party came to power, and, with it, the *apartheid* policies grew more stringent.

The fiction of the mid-1950s began to extol the struggle for independence and revolutionary change. The fight was translated to the level of everyday living. The leaders in this new fiction came from all walks of life: a trade unionist, a mechanic, or a political leader such as Udomo in Peter Abrahams's *A Wreath for Udomo* (1956). Most of the novels conclude with the defeat of the protagonists, yet there remains for the reader a sense of hope in the struggle itself, a possible vision of a future liberation.

The vision, symbolized by the Defiance Campaign and the ringing slogan embodied in the popular tune *"Unzima Lomtvalo"* ("Awake black hearts, win Africa back"), receded in the 1960s with the further escalation of *apartheid* laws, such as the "gag" law. Since then dialogue with well-meaning white liberals has become almost impossible as a result of the extreme polarization. Interracial contacts are avoided or they involve a painful experience. A simple matter of the sharing of a glass of wine between a white man and a black girl in a public café can generate embarrassement or fear. Although the two youngsters in La Guma's story *A Glass of Wine* feel innocently attracted toward each other, they know that within the racist context of present-day South African politics they are forbidden from envisaging a further blossoming of their relationship.

South African short stories, often reduced to journalistic vignettes of daily events which every South African knows, capture the countless frustrations and indignities which the black man must encounter and suffer. The reader is given fleeting visions of police raids upon illegal beer shanty bars, the frantic search of a black man for his pass, a pass which he must carry at all times and present upon the arbitrary command of a strolling policeman. The reader is asked to understand the sudden and irrational revolt of an old man, who by mistake sat upon a bench reserved for whites only ("Blankes Alleen, Whites Only") and refuses to get up. The reader enters the world of the dispossessed: a black child yearning to play on the swings in a park reserved for whites only, until one night, out of frustration, he surreptitiously jumps over the fence in order to enjoy this simple pleasure forbidden to him.

Thus the struggle dramatized in the novels, short stories, and plays of South African writers becomes a total struggle. It puts marginal heroes on the scene, fighting to stay alive in this atmosphere of violence and in the context of laws which, of themselves, are immoral. Alex La Guma's characters in his powerful novella *A Walk in the Night* (1962) are the unemployed, the vagabonds, juvenile delinquents, beggars, and prostitutes who strive to stay afloat in the "whirlpool of poverty, petty crime and violence."[18] Contemporary South African writings, inevitably, "bring to literature a view of society as seen from the bottom."

Writers in South Africa today, including some brilliant white authors such as Nadine Gordimer, are politically and psychologically harassed; as such they cannot find a climate conducive to a more reflective literature and to a more multidimensional presentation of problems and characters. South African literature, for the time being, is and cannot but be a literature of confrontation, reflecting the desperate will of oppressed people to speak and to survive.

NOTES

1. Where works in languages other than English have been translated into English, their translated titles are given in parentheses.

2. David Diop, *Hammerblows* (Bloomington: Indiana University Press, 1973), p.47. Reprinted with permission.

3. In Norman R. Shapiro, *Négritude, Black Poetry from Africa and the Caribbean* (New York: October House, 1970), p.43.

4. Diop, *Hammerblows*, p.13. Reprinted with permission.

5. Camara Laye, *The Dark Child* (New York: Farrar, Straus and Giroux, 1954), p.132. Reprint, 1969.

6. Mongo Beti, *Mission to Kala* (London: Heinemann, 1958), p.18.

7. My own translation.

8. In Gerald Moore and Ulli Beier, *Modern Poetry from Africa* (Harmondsworth, Middlesex: Penguin, 1963), p.79.

9. In Moore and Beier, *Modern Poetry . . .*, p.99.

10. Kofi Awoonor, *Rediscovery and Other Poems* (Ibadan: MBARI Publications, 1964), p.18.

11. *Nigeria Magazine*, June 1964.

12. Ibid.

13. Cyprian Ekwensi, *People of the City* (New York: Fawcett, 1969), p.72.

14. The section on East African literature is written by Jack D. Rollins.

15. Shaaban Robert, *Wasifu Wa Siti Binti Saad*, p.49. Translation by Jack D. Rollins.

16. In Dennis Brutus, *A Simple Lust* (New York: Hill and Wang, 1973), p.4.

17. In Nadine Gordimer's excellent essay, "Writers in South Africa: The New Black Poets," *Dalhousie Review*, Winter 1973–74, pp.657–58.

18. Lewis Nkosi, "South Africa Protest," in *Africa Report*, October 1962.

SUGGESTIONS FOR FURTHER READING

Cartey, Wilfred. *Whispers from a Continent*. New York: Random House, 1969.

Dalhousie Review (special issue on African literature), Winter 1973–74.

L'Esprit Créateur (special issue on African literature) Vol. X, No. 3, Fall 1970.

Garrett, Naomi Mills. *The Renaissance of Haitian poetry*. Paris: Presence Africaine, 1963.

Kesteloot, Lilyan. *Intellectual Origins of the African Revolution*. Washington, D.C.: Black Orpheus Press, 1972.

Larson, Charles. *The Emergence of African Fiction*. Bloomington: Indiana University Press, 1972.

Moore, Gerald. *Seven African Writers*. London: Oxford University Press, 1962.

Mphahlele, Ezekiel. *The African Image*. New York: Praeger, 1962–1974.

Wauthier, Claude René. *The Literature and Thought of Modern Africa*. New York: Praeger, 1966.

Anthologies

Beier, Ulli, and Gerald Moore. *Modern Poetry from Africa* (revised). Baltimore: Penguin, 1966.

Collins, Marie. *Black Poets in French*. New York: Scribners, 1972.

René A. Bravmann

Contemporary Dimensions of African Art

21 *Accra, Ghana:* A high-ranking government minister, beset by family and official problems, has left the capital city for the north. His personal secretary has indicated that he will be consulting the high priest and shrine of Tigare.

Ibadan, Nigeria: A young Christian school teacher danced in the lorry park yesterday in honor of her deceased infant twin. She substituted a plastic doll for the traditional Yoruba wooden commemorative figure known as *Ere-ibeji.*

Kinshasa, Zaire: This week has seen many of our Kuba residents leaving the city of Kinshasa for their home district of Kasai. The Kuba traditional initiation school is coming to a close and relatives and friends are returning to greet and fete the young men who will be officially proclaimed adults by the middle of this month.

Defining Contemporary African Art

Each situation in this kaleidoscopic introduction of events and personalities has been abstracted from carefully observed and recorded research, from moments experienced and described by serious interpreters of contemporary Africa. The artists, art forms, and artistic situations are all remarkably real and form a vital part of contemporary African artistic life. These extracts convey the dynamism which currently exists in the field of the visual arts, and serve to counterbalance a prevailing trend which focuses primarily upon recent Western-inspired artistic manifestations at the expense of traditionally conceived forms carried out through wood sculpture, weaving, beadwork, ceramics, and iron-working. In most writing, little credence is given to Africa's artistic past and its many current extensions, for these writers consider that tradition has little relevance for contemporary problems and life. However, contemporary African art can hardly be discussed without acknowledging the existence not only of recent artistic innovations but also of traditional and historic art forms that are still valid and very much alive on the continent. Ignoring one dimension at the expense of the other can only result in distorting present reality.

It is true that Africa's artistic traditions are changing, and in some cases they are being undermined due to new alternatives that now exist; many of the young are not following in the footsteps of their parents or filling roles deemed crucial by tradition. Change, however, has always characterized the arts of Africa, and the reservoir of artistic talent is still very deep. Time-honored artistic patterns still give meaning to life over much of the continent, although in some regions these patterns are being modernized so that they are relevant within the present-day context.

Everywhere in Africa artists are at work, either creating in tried and valid forms or seeking new lines of expression through contemporary materials and styles. Villages and towns still have their blacksmiths and weavers, and artisanal skills practiced by specialists continue assured where marriage within the group is prescribed and where levels of skill are rigorously enforced and maintained with pride. Female potters, fully aware of the threat of imported enamelware or locally produced plastic products, transmit their skills with increased vigor to their daughters. Any market town reveals the importance of artists' products, even if these must now compete with an increasing number of imported items.

Contemporary life, challenging the imaginations of both the artisan and the consumer, results in new and vibrant artistic icons. Among the Ashanti of Ghana, truck drivers now commission local carvers to commemorate their occupation in traditional stools which bear the image of the passenger truck rather than the conventional proverb-carrying columnar motifs (see plate 66). To the north, in the Bono capital town of Techiman, young sign painters enliven the surfaces of public buildings and Western-styled beer parlors with figurative scenes and Twi or English phrases, in a manner reminiscent of the art of the comic book (plate 67). Traditionally oriented artisans, recognizing the challenges of modern life, are banding together into new associations and cooperatives in order to compete within the contemporary environment. Everywhere traditional patterns and change coexist, and these forces are accurately and poignantly expressed in the artistry of the times.

66. Ashanti personal stool. Wood with enamel paints. W. 23".
Collection: Mr. and Mrs. Goldsmith, Los Angeles.

Art and Artistry in Africa's Cities

The assertion that Africa's artistic heritage is still vitally alive cannot be tested from the perspective of the village or town, for many maintain that these areas are removed from the mainstream of modern African life. They exist away from "modernizing" forces, and are only peripherally influenced by the new religions, educational systems, political and legal institutions, and economic patterns that are sweeping the continent in this century. The mushrooming urban centers, the very heart of contemporary life, must be the testing ground for many of the most revolutionary ideas, techniques, and forces affecting African cultures.

These cities, the nerve centers of innovation, are at the forefront of all that is new and different. Many are not even the products of Africa's past, but are the direct offspring of its colonial legacy, organized upon models of urban life that are far removed from traditional modes and principles. They are large and sprawling, ethnically and culturally diverse, and often bewildering, but their appeal is undeniable and they attract large numbers of rural immigrants. Social, political, and economic problems are rampant and are compounded by the recent growth of these cities. Modernity and tradition, wealth and squalor, indeed, all the elements normally found under urban conditions are present.

The artistry and artistic images which radiate from any contemporary African urban center visually attest to these dichotomies. Coca-Cola signs serve as jarring backdrops to the high priestess and sculpture-laden dancers of Oshun,

67. "Though I am old, my money is not as old as I am," by Yeboah Art Works. A mural at the Black Star Bar, Dwomo Ward. Techiman. Ghana.

Photo courtesy M. D. Warren.

the riverine deity of the large city of Oshogbo, Nigeria. The river Oshun is every bit as important to the residents of Oshogbo as are the Christian, Muslim, or modern governmental tenets which guide the city. The dramatic festival in honor of Oshun is the most direct procedure for purifying this urban center. Far to the northwest in the Malian capital of Bamako, Bamana dancers and acrobats perform masked dances held in honor of the Kono association; their choreographed acrobatics are far removed from the sedate steps generally seen at modern Bamako dance halls. In such examples lie some of the truths which exist in the interplay between traditional art forms, their contemporary renderings, and modern Africa. Art and the city reinforce and reinvigorate one another, and in their interaction they suggest levels of human behavior which need to be understood in the context of contemporary Africa.

Three instances of the arts within urban Africa highlight this theme. The first comes from Bobo Dioulasso, a cosmopolitan city in Upper Volta and an urban center whose origins date back to the sixteenth century. A brief description of the great funeral and masks of the Bobo of Bobo Dioulasso will illustrate the importance of traditional funerary practices and new artistic dimensions in such masquerade artistry. The second discussion will center upon Freetown, the capital of Sierra Leone, where bands of young boys create impressive public masquerades during the Christmas season. These young men belong to rival and often hostile youth gangs, associations for those disillusioned by urban life. Once a year they set aside their differences and produce masks with remarkable artistic skill. Finally, among the Yoruba of southwestern Nigeria a new artistic medium, photography, is being employed in the service of traditional notions of respect and death.

Bobo Dioulasso, with a population of approximately 80,000 in 1972, is an important urban center with a rich history. Located at the intersection of a number of trade routes connecting the Saharan fringe and the West African forest, it is an important commercial center. Commercial success was initially due to the presence of Mande trading families, but this was enhanced in the twentieth century by the arrival of the French, who made it the colonial and economic capital of Upper Volta. Even though Ouagadougou was selected as the capital of the country at the time of independence, the colonial legacy and the historical importance of Bobo Dioulasso have enabled it to maintain a strong urban role in contemporary Voltaic life.

Today, Bobo Dioulasso is still a primary commercial and industrial center in this emerging nation. It is also the administrative heart of the country's West Volta region, and here all government departments are represented. It is one of only two cities in the country with educational facilities at all levels (Ouagadougou is the other), and it has both a substantial Muslim and an increasingly significant Christian population. Ethnically represented by approximately twenty different cultures, the social makeup of the city is typical of most in Africa. Bobo Dioulasso is a financial center, it houses all of the nascent communication media of the country, and it has all the trappings of Western popular culture, ranging from an Elks club to cinemas and discotheques. It is a typical African city, representing all the urban forces and ambiguities of contemporary life.

The Bobo, who live primarily in the suburbs of Kounima and Tounouma, are still agriculturalists and traditionalists. They value the land, the labors of the farmer, and continue to follow rituals and acts sanctioned by the past. Some are converting to Christianity, even more to Islam, but the majority remain attached to what they have always known. How is it that the Bobo continue to live in such a manner under these urban circumstances? The elders of Kounima and Tounouma reply simply with the phrase *"Kire-vo kuni foga,"* by "supporting the waist of your chief with firmness." They claim that Bobo culture remains vitally alive because its members support and adhere to traditional secular and religious authority and thus are able to retain the very foundations of cultural existence. These two suburbs are administratively dominated by the mayor's office and ultimately legally responsible to the Voltaic tribunal system, but their day-to-day existence and the most pressing decisions are still in the hands of religious and political figures guided by the principles of the culture. The chiefs of these suburbs, the leaders of initiation where Bobo boys learn to become men, and the priests who control the shrines and ancestral masks form a highly directed and meaningful triad of leadership. It is they who hold in their hands the present and future of the Bobo of Bobo Dioulasso; they are the models and guardians of tradition and wield the powers necessary for this culture's existence within the city.

The effectiveness of this alliance of Bobo leaders is perhaps most forcefully expressed in their direction of the many procedures associated with death, and specifically with the rites and artistry of the great communal funeral (*sakon kwyie*).[1] These funerals consist of numerous public and private acts, part of an expression of an extensive and coherent system of ontological notions and beliefs regarding the nature of man, his physical and spiritual being, and the importance and status of ancestral existence. Bobo artisans, dancers, and ritual experts must dedicate themselves fully to the tasks of the *sakon kwyie*, for through their actions they reaffirm and renew the ties that exist between the living and the dead. Ancestral confirmation that their efforts have been accepted and appreciated is expressed through the return of the ancestors to this world in the guise of masqueraders. Their appearance highlights the communal funeral and assures that the spirits of the deceased will be released from the human community and transported to the paradise of the ancestors. The Bobo say that these spirits must be removed from the city, for if allowed to remain, they will annoy and harass the living members of society. The climax of the four-day communal funeral comes, therefore, at that moment when the masked ancestors, their right hands tightly clenched, gently usher the appeased spirits of the deceased out of Bobo Dioulasso. This poetic act terminates the *sakon kwyie*.

To ensure that the communal funeral is a success, the talents of potters, weavers, dyers, makers of masks, dancers, and the best available musicians are employed. These individuals pool their skills, not only to create the numerous ancestral masks but also to choreograph the appearance of the ancestors and to direct the musical and verbal dimensions of the funeral. Blacksmiths, whose compounds are considered sacred workshops, invite the various artisans to their homes for the creation of cloth and fiber ancestral forms whose manufacture cannot be observed by women or uninitiated boys. Dancers of the ancestors not only must rehearse traditional dance patterns but also must attempt to improvise new and exciting steps for the pleasure of both the living and the dead. Farmers, weavers, clerks, bank tellers, initiated school boys, and others will assist in these tasks.

Within the last ten years, a number of innovations have occurred in certain of the artistic dimensions of the *sakon kwyie*, particularly with respect to the making and painting of the ancestral masks. All of the traditional masking forms are still represented: the *kokoro*, or rooster of domination; the *soghe*, or panther; the *fledalo*, or crested fiber mask (which is said to represent a beautiful woman); the wooden masks of the sparrow hawk *kele*; the *kimi*, or stork; and others. New materials, however, are being substituted for those traditionally used to create these masks. Vivid red and green dyes, imported from France and England, are replacing the more muted natural ochres and grayish blacks used in the past. Cloth faces are more often sewn with imported thread, which is gradually supplanting the local varieties that are considered coarser and harder to use. Lumber ready-cut and plentiful from a French firm in the city may be substituted for traditional woods that are increasingly difficult to find and are protected by government conservation regulations. The crest of the *fledalo* mask, once carefully carved and shaped from the wood of the nere tree, is easily and economically made from plywood quickly cut with a coping saw. Despite such substitutions, the basic configurations and designs of today do not differ significantly from those found in pieces created a generation ago: material substitutions are made and shortcut techniques are used, but the formal essences of the mask are retained.

It is in the designs and phrases painted upon many of the masks that the most surprising transformations have occurred. Literate young artisans, flaunting their knowledge of French and their acquaintance with world events, are inscribing contemporary sayings and phrases upon these forms. Others are even dating them for posterity, despite the fact that Bobo ancestors are not bound by dimensions of time. The words which appear are interesting, for they include such expressions as "Vive Kounima," "Apollo 1973" (plate 68), "La Béauté de la dance," and "Le premier numero de la dance." Hardcore traditionalists regard such additions as deviations, claiming that these masks will ultimately please neither the living nor the dead. Despite all the objections, however, these ancestral masks perform with the vigor and beauty of those conceived in a conventional manner and the young artisans defend such artistic innovations on several grounds. They argue that they are maintaining basic standards of artistry even if deviations in material are made and a literate veneer is added to the masks. They stress that many of their phrases are purely aesthetic

68. A Bobo ancestral mask of the *fledalo* type dignified by the name "Apollo 1973." Bobo Dioulasso. Upper Volta. April 1973.

evocations, lauding the ability and beauty of the dancing ancestors. Others indicate that literacy enhances ancestral beings, for like Apollo 1973, they are all-powerful, moving across space and through time at a superhuman rate. Man's wonder about his own limitations and fraility in the face of ancestral power is thereby confirmed, at another level, through words of praise. The arguments of the young are both logical and powerful, and all of these masks have been allowed to dance and to serve as new representatives of the Bobo ancestral realm. The leaders of Kounima and Tounouma generally regard them as positive and innovative examples of contemporary artistry applied to more traditional ancestral configurations.

Yet another dimension of creativity within urban Africa is revealed in Sierra Leone in the Eri devil associations of Freetown, where groups of boys have formed masquerade organizations within the last generation.[2] These societies of boys and young men must be distinguished from the Eri devil societies composed of older men and patterned upon old hunting associations of the Yoruba and Krio of Freetown. The youthful Eri devils developed rapidly after the Second World War in response to the needs of those who could not join the adult groups. By the mid-1960s there were approximately sixty Eri devil groups in Freetown whose members ranged in age from ten to twenty-five. These groups are multi-ethnic in composition and reflect the mixed cultural nature of neighborhood residential patterns in Freetown. Most of the boys are the children of recent migrants to the city, members of families who have only a minor stake in the economic life of the city. Only a few have had the benefit of elementary education. In essence, they represent the disenfranchised youth of Freetown.

Eri devil groups are very much like voluntary associations in any African city. They are corporate in structure and exist primarily as social organizations. Unlike the vast majority of such groups, membership in the Eri devils is not dependent upon ethnicity or occupation; the only binding element appears to be that the members are the children of the poor. As in other associations, however, there is a hierarchical organization within each group. Spiritual and administrative heads lead the Eri devils while a secretary handles most of the inter- and intragroup affairs. A small fee is required of all members, as is a short period of initiation. For boys unlikely to partake of educational opportunities or to become upwardly mobile by other means, membership inculcates a spirit of belonging and solidarity and helps individuals develop the strength and courage sometimes needed to cope with a static life in an urban setting.

While primarily conceived of as socially oriented groups fostering bonds of friendship and coming together for important events such as weddings of members, singing and dancing performances at various holidays, and for self-help projects, the Eri devils have recently evolved into urban youth gangs. In the last ten years delinquency and intergroup rivalry have been the dominant features of these societies. Police surveillance is constant and many members have been jailed for petty thievery and a host of more serious crimes. Intergroup conflicts have apparently become the norm rather than the exception, with each group jealously guarding its territory while attempting to expand its influence into contiguous neighborhoods. Some of the social dimensions of the associations persist, but they have become, at best, secondary features.

Groups of Eri devils, however, continue to present masked performances for the purpose of displaying their artistic expertise in competition with other associations. Boxing Day (December 26) is one of the major occasions for parading the masks. Considerable time and effort are expended in the creation and beautification of these masks, for they are the visual representations of the power and skill of the groups. The lead mask, known as the Devil (figure 20), is the focal point of any such display and consists of a large wooden deer head and a cos-

ERI DEVIL
With hand axe, cowtail, and mirror worn at the waist
FIGURE 20

tume made from the finest available cloth. The costume is decorated with mirrors, Christmas tinsel or ornaments, aluminum foil, and other reflective materials. Rich and unusual visual effects are highly desired and members of Eri devil associations have been known to resort to any means to obtain particularly coveted materials. To protect the carrier of the Devil mask, other masqueraders accompany him throughout the performance. The Devil himself carries magical medicines in a hamper or on his costume to protect him from spiritual evil, but his attendants serve to shield him from the more earthly evils which might be perpetrated by members of rival groups. The dancing and singing which accompany the movements of the masqueraders present the public face of the organization to the citizens of Freetown. This variant upon the more usual and spiritual purpose of masquerades allows for the exhibition of strongly innovative design and decoration in the masks and costumes and for atypical choreography and aggression in the dances.

The Yoruba country of southwestern Nigeria provides yet another glimpse of artistry in the city. Photography, obviously not an indigenous art form, has been adapted by the Yoruba to a number of traditional concepts, the most important being the honoring of the dead.

While the traditional Igbomina Yoruba commemorate the death of a twin with a carved *ibeji* figure, Muslim and Christian parents today are often substituting a photograph.[3] These photographs are constructed so that a picture of the surviving twin is printed twice in order to represent both children sitting together (plate 69). In the case of twins of different sexes, the surviving child

69. Surviving Yoruba twin with a photograph representing herself
and her deceased sister. Igbomina area, June 1975.
Photo from *African Arts*, Vol. 9, No. 3, 1976, p. 18.

is photographed first in his or her own clothing and then in the clothing of the
deceased sibling (or siblings, in the case of triplets). The efficacy of this practice is guaranteed because the photograph is fed and cared for as would be a
carved *ibeji*.

The obituary columns of the Lagos *Daily Times* provide another example
of the dead being honored through photography. Yoruba families wishing to
honor deceased kin often submit a photograph to the *Times* with the desire that
it be printed along with a personal message to the deceased from the surviving
family. The verbal style of these obituaries is patterned closely upon traditional
elegiac formulas in that they are praise poems rather than the terse formalistic
descriptions found in European death notices. These remembrances recall the
finest qualities of the departed loved one and are contributed by both the immediate and the extended family. Yoruba carvings traditionally depict the hu-

man form in the full bloom of youth, and this stricture applies to photographs as well. A picture accompanying an obituary will rarely show the deceased in old age no matter what his years at the time of death; rather, it will be a photograph taken during young adult years. In order to approximate the ideal of composure and calm valued in Yoruba tradition, the facial expression in a photograph, as in a carving, is passive and devoid of any emotional content. In this way fundamental canons of artistic representation are maintained and confirmed even when the medium of representation is radically altered.

New Dimensions of Creativity

The foregoing examples are indicative of the relationship of traditional art and its contemporary manifestations within urban Africa. A look at the arts of other cities would most likely corroborate these findings. The arts of contemporary Africa, however, also include new and exciting ventures in artistry, forms, and techniques which are being utilized in a variety of art schools, churches, and civic programs and by individuals who work with different visions. These must also be considered an important part of the contemporary situation.

While countless artistic traditions have not been undermined in this century, it is equally true that contemporary forces have led to new dimensions of artistry. Western ideas and technology, the impact of Christianity and education, and new political and social ideologies have all contributed, some to a greater degree than others, to increasing the repertoire of the arts of the continent. New artistic styles, many oriented toward the major currents found in the arts worldwide, have been introduced and quickly absorbed either through the creation of Western-derived art schools or by young African artists trained in Europe or the United States. New materials and techniques such as easel painting, sculpture in plastic and aluminum, and printmaking are being utilized in many ways that expand the range of media available to the artist. A potentially rich mix of ideas and forms deriving from the encounter between tradition and contemporary life is changing the minds of a whole generation of artists, allowing them to express the excitement and problems which they see and sense as inherent in twentieth-century Africa. These artists are expressing visually the same kinds of concerns and thoughts offered so eloquently by a host of well-known creative novelists and poets (see chapter 20).

> There is so much artistic production still going on in Africa, in greater variety than before, that it seems likely that posterity will judge the second half of the 20th century to have been a period of artistic renaissance for Africa as a whole.[4]

Of the several forces behind the emergence of these new artistic traditions, three have been dominant: Christianity, colonial rule, and Western educational principles and practices. These three have been interrelated. Christianity, individual missionaries, and churches profited enormously from the colonial period. As the religion of the colonizers, Christianity was much more successful in the thirty years between 1920 and 1950 than in the three centuries prior to colonial rule. Officially sanctioned, and thus more secure, a number of new attitudes developed within the church. From an earlier posture of contempt for all that was religious and artistic in traditional life, a new generation of missionaries and workers began to contemplate the possibilities of utilizing local elements in Christian worship. In the 1930s and 40s Paul Gebauer, an American Baptist missionary in British Cameroon, was already experimenting with Bamenda architectural and iconic forms in the building of local churches. The White Fathers, missionaries in Upper Volta, at first rigidly orthodox in their views, quickly saw the need for relaxing their standards and eventually were even to admit masked dancers at certain church services. An increasing number of missions began to commission traditional artisans to make objects suitable for use in religious worship, and when such artists were not available, these missions established their own art schools in order to train local individuals.

The arts fostered by the church were utilized principally to promulgate and enhance Christianity, by visually reaffirming the spirit and truths of the faith. Both Protestant and Catholic missions were involved in these developments, but very few Protestant experiments achieved any real degree of success with the notable exception of the Cyrene mission in Rhodesia directed by Reverend Edward Paterson from 1939 to 1953. Catholic efforts, on the other hand, were to produce a number of noteworthy achievements. The most successful of all church workshops was started by Father P. M. Kelly of the African Mission Society in 1947, at Oye-Ekiti among the Yoruba in Nigeria. Directed by Fathers Kevin Carroll and Sean O'Mahoney, the AMS employed many traditional artists, from carvers to bead-workers, to create a vast array of forms that could be adopted to the Catholic service. Some of the finest Yoruba carvers of this century, men such as Bandele, Bamgboye, and Lamidi, enjoyed the mission's patronage, fashioning a memorable series of church doors (plate 70), baptismal fonts, and New Testament figures and scenes inspired by traditional Yoruba style and compositional devices. Not only did these artisans create numerous works for the mission itself, but they also produced a large range of Christian icons for churches and chapels throughout Yorubaland. Add to these individuals artists like Ben Enwonwu and Osagie Osifu, who were not traditionally trained but were products of Western art schools, and the impact of Christianity as a

70. Carved scenes of the Crucifixion by Lamidi Fakeye for the main
doors of the Catholic church in Oke-Padi, Ibadan, Nigeria.
Photo from Marshall Mount's *African Art: The Years Since 1920*, p. 34.

new source of artistic inspiration becomes apparent. Enwonwu and Osifu are both Christian, but Osifu carves within the guidelines of Yoruba and Bini styles, while Enwonwu extrapolates imaginatively from the history of art, selecting from Byzantine sources, Early Christian figurative renderings, and medieval icons to forge religious images of power and conviction.

Numerous educational experiments and institutions devoted to the arts, begun during the latter part of the colonial period and still vital today, have proved to be the primary motivating sources for contemporary artistry in Africa. Art centers, crafts clubs, art schools, museum and gallery workshops, and art programs associated with various technical colleges and universities were established in nearly all colonies, allowing both trained and untutored artists the opportunity to delve into new artistic directions. For a few exceptionally talented students there was—and still is—the possibility of further training and study in France, England, and the United States.

Of the colonial powers, the British were decidedly the most successful in developing a variety of art programs. Teachers and artists resident in the British colonies were generally more flexible and tolerant, allowing local artists a greater degree of individual initiative and expression; in their educational approaches, the British were apparently influenced by some of the underlying principles implicit in the theory and practice of Indirect Rule. By comparison, the artistic achievements in French, Portuguese, and Belgian territories, and in the new nations that have emerged from these colonial experiences, have been far less conspicuous. Greater directional control and the general expectation that students would follow prescribed European standards of beauty and artistry produced a strict and sterile environment rarely suited to successful training and accomplishments in the arts.

The overall range of contemporary artistry is impressive and has been achieved by numerous creative individuals. For example, among the older generation of artists, men now in their forties and fifties, are those who have received very little formal instruction in art but who were encouraged by European teachers within the confines of relatively loosely structured schools. Mwenze, who worked at Desfosse's school in Lubumbashi, and Zigoma and Ondongo, of the Poto-Poto school of painters in Brazzaville, have been among the most productive of this group, and they continue to work today. Others of this generation were either trained formally in Africa (at such places as the Makerere School of Fine Arts in Uganda, or in Ghana at Kumasi College of Science and Technology and at Achimota College) or in Britain and France. These include such celebrated figures as Maloba, Sekoto, Enwonwu, and Ampofo, artists who work with both traditional and Western materials and techniques and whose subject matter may range from the Westernized to intimate compositions based upon local themes and ideas.

Icons of Contemporary Africa

During the 1960s, with the exuberance and ebullience of independence, many young African artists came to the fore. As with those of the older generation, they came from a variety of backgrounds. Some had little formal education and developed their talents in workshops, the most successful example of these being in Nigeria at Ulli Beier's series of summer schools in Ibadan, and at his Mbari Mbayo school at Oshogbo. The whimsical painter Twins Seven-Seven, who works with oils, and Jimoh Buraimoh, who creates with beads on hardboard, signal the success of this approach. Others received training in conventional art schools and university art departments in Africa, and an ever rising number are now able to enhance their education in Europe or the United States. The Nigerian Idehen, the Ghanaian Kofi, and the Sudanese painters Salahi (plate 71) and Shibrain are the most successful representatives of this

71. "Allah and the wall of confrontation," by Ibrahim el-Salahi. Oil on hardboard. London, Transcription Centre.
From Mount's *African Art: The Years Since 1920,* p. 109.

72. "Awakening Africa," by Vincent Kofi. Bronze cast.
Photo from Mount's *African Art: The Years Since 1920*, p. 131.

group. Skunder of Ethiopia and the Senegalese Ibrahim N'diaye learned their lessons solely in Europe, and their works are closely aligned to those of artists in other parts of the world creating in the most contemporary styles. A few artists have emerged with no apparent formal training, like Malangatana of Mozambique, who emblazons his canvases with color and vigor, commenting upon and decrying the social conditions of contemporary Africa. All of these artists, mostly painters and sculptors, see the infinite possibilities of artistry in the twentieth century. They range between the traditional world of Africa and the galleries of New York City. Some are interested in formal abstraction and in the interplay between design and composition while others are satisfied with the possibilities of more descriptive techniques. They are young and gifted, and it is clear that they will produce exciting works in the near future.

Indicative of contemporary artistry in Africa is a work by Vincent Kofi, Ghana's foremost modern sculptor and art teacher, who died in 1975. Entitled "Awakening Africa" (plate 72), it is a bronze cast of a female nude, body relaxed and yet taut, a reclining figure supporting its flexed body upon rigid elbows. "Awakening Africa" is strongly rooted to its base by large feet, and while the figure is composed, the work appears unsettled. The head is poised, but the face is contorted, revealing anger, defiance, and uncertainty. Its creator was very much a product of twentieth-century Africa. Kofi had experience in the Western world, knowing it through direct contact and critical reflection; but he was also a product of Ghana, specifically of Akan civilization. Thus Kofi was aware of several worlds. "Awakening Africa" is an icon of Kofi himself, but even more importantly it is an icon of the times. It speaks of the timelessness of Akan civilization, of the human beauty of the Akan world, captured in the flat face and broad forehead. Kofi took this dimension of Ghana's heritage and placed it upon a nude, reclining female body, thus matching a Western conception of human beauty and truth, the reclining Venus, with that of his own. Yet the severity of the facial features and the mottled skin of this reclining female deny ultimate serenity to the sculpture. How then may Kofi's bronze statement be interpreted? It is perhaps the ultimate statement by an important artist regarding contemporary Africa. "Awakening Africa" is an image of the times, incorporating the old and the new and suggesting not only the possibilities but the anxieties and ambiguities of the future.

NOTES

1. A fuller discussion of Bobo art and the city can be found in my article "An Urban Way of Death," *African Arts*, Vol. 8, No. 3 (Spring 1975), pp.42–47; 62–64; 90.

2. Helga Kreutzinger's in-depth study of the Eri devils of Freetown is the single most important source on this urban masquerade. "The Eri Devils in Freetown, Sierra Leone," *Acta Ethnologica et Linguistica*, No. 9 (1966), pp.6–72. Jeanne Canizzo is currently conducting field research on children's devils masquerades among the Mende of Sierra Leone.

3. Marilyn Hammersley Houlberg, "Collecting the Anthropology of African Art," *African Arts*, Vol. 9, No. 3 (April 1976), pp.15–19. Mary-Claire Shepherd's master's thesis on "Traditional Yoruba Aesthetics and the Photographic Memorial" deals with this subject more fully.

4. Frank Willett, *African Art* (New York: Praeger, 1971), p.239.

SUGGESTIONS FOR FURTHER READING

Beier, Ulli. *Contemporary Art in Africa*. New York: Frederick A. Praeger, 1968.

Bravmann, René A. "An Urban Way of Death." *African Arts*, Vol. 8, No. 3 (Spring 1975), pp.42–47; 62–64; 90.

Carroll, Reverend Kevin. *Yoruba Religious Carving*. London: Geoffrey Chapman, 1967.

Janheinz, Jahn. *Muntu*. London: Faber and Faber, 1961.

Sieber, Roy. "The Arts and their Changing Social Function." *Anthropology and Art*, edited by C. Otten. New York: The Natural History Press, 1971.

Wahlman, Maude. *Contemporary African Arts*. Chicago: Field Museum of Natural History, 1974.

Willett, Frank. *African Art*. New York: Praeger, 1971.

The journal *African Arts*, published by the African Studies Center at UCLA, is an important source of new information on the contemporary arts of Africa.

John E. Kaemmer
Changing Music in Contemporary Africa

22 The changes which have swept over Africa in the last hundred years have brought about extensive modifications in music practices. Sometimes Africans have rejected their ancient music in favor of foreign styles, but more often new influences have caused adaptations in ways of making music. Change in music relates to social life, as is indicated by a ceremony which I witnessed in late 1973 in Rhodesia.

The *kurova guva* (beating the grave) ceremony is usually held a year or so after the death of an important person to assure his spirit that it has not been forgotten, and to indicate that it may now venture forth to find a medium to be its future home. On this occasion the ceremony was not held for an elder, but for the spirit of an adolescent boy, whose lack of descendants would normally be an indication that his spirit would never trouble anyone. However, his family had been told by a diviner that the spirit of the boy was causing illness, and the ceremony was considered necessary. Because the spirit being honored was that of a boy, the young people had a greater part in the ceremony than was customary, including the unusual procedure of singing some African "jazz" pop songs at the graveside.

The event was also different because it was not the customary night-long vigil with graveside ceremonies at sunrise. Since government troops were searching for guerrilla forces in the area, the people preferred to remain home at night. Thus, the events of the ceremony began in midmorning and were finished by sunset. As a result, the recreational dancing performed by the youths before going to the graveside was not the customary drumming and dancing in the moonlight, but consisted of dancing in the shade of a tree to music provided by the latest recorded hits from the city. The older people conformed to custom by spending this time indoors dancing and singing the favorite songs of the ancestors. A ceremony which was once a conservative force in the community had become a vehicle for change.

Change in contemporary African music involves modifications of musical forms, of the place of music in society, and of its meaning to the individual. Musical activity is the result of a great interplay of processes that include the introduction of new attitudes toward traditional African music and toward music in general, social, political, and economic changes, and the introduction of Arabic and European musical stylistic influences.

Changing Attitudes Toward Music

With the beginning of the colonial era, African music was subjected to pervasive new influences as Europeans affected ideas concerning the value of traditional African music, which they frequently regarded with scorn and condescension. Many Africans performed Western-type music in an effort to win acceptance. In other areas, however, where whites or colonial administrations were strongly disliked, Western music was rejected. In South Africa the use of traditional music was resisted in many places because it was encouraged by the government and represented yet another aspect of *apartheid*.

The influence of Europeans upon African musical attitudes was due in part to their lack of understanding of African music itself. As noted in chapter 15, African music has complex rhythms; the Europeans who first heard it were unable to organize it in their minds, and thus they falsely concluded that the performers themselves were drumming and singing without any organization. Because the relationship between language tones and melody was not understood, African changes in European tunes were considered manifestations of stupidity rather than necessary adaptations. Moreover, Europeans had little idea of how boring the rhythm of hymns could be to sensitive African musicians who felt a desire to make creative innovations as they did in their own music.

Western schooling was a significant factor in changing musical attitudes. Children attending mission boarding schools or growing up in towns did not hear much traditional music and were attracted by the new music which was available to them. Consequently, many middle-aged Africans today know very little about their own music. Schooling not only introduced new types of music to the students but, in some instances, also encouraged the application of the concept of formal instruction to African music. In Rhodesia, for example, old Shona musicians are unable to give step-by-step instruction in the *mbira* (often erroneously called "thumb piano"), but younger musicians frequently do so. African music has been a subject of formal instruction for some time at Makerere College in Uganda, at the University of Ghana, at Kwanongoma College in Rhodesia, and other universities have now begun to teach the subject.

Western education in Africa introduced not only a written language but also the idea of writing music. An unfortunate result of this was the belief that written and accumulated music was somehow of better quality than music learned and performed by rote. In the mid-nineteenth century an Englishman named John Curwen invented a type of music notation called tonic sol-fa, which became widely used for teaching in anglophone Africa. Although it was simpler to print and learn than staff notation, it was much less flexible, particularly where rhythm was concerned, since indications of rhythm followed the European measure with its strong and weak beats. Thus, the rhythmic effects which could be incorporated into written music were limited, and the compositions of Africans were often unnecessarily restricted to what could be written down. This problem was particularly noticeable when the ideal was to follow the art music tradition of conservatory graduates of the Western world.

In South Africa an extensive literature of songs developed, mostly in the choral style but with syncopations which indicated their African origins, and these songs are still sung at school contests throughout southern and Central Africa. Although lengthy compositions have been rare, musicals consisting of numerous songs have been a new development. *King Kong*, by Todd Matshikiza of South Africa, tells the story of an African boxer and his eventual downfall, and the Nigerian novel *The Palm-Wine Drinkard*, by Amos Tutuola, was translated into Yoruba and made into a musical by Kola Ogunmola.

Since independence many imported ideas about music have continued to exert an effect; yet at the same time, a rising sense of pride in African culture and accomplishments has helped to revive traditional music styles. Urban composers are now writing music in an African idiom which aims at worldwide audiences; Akin Euba recognizes that such efforts are basically in the tradition of Western music, and one of his compositions, *Olorumbi*, combines African polyrhythm with the twelve-tone technique of Arnold Schoenberg. In Uganda a work by Kyagambiddwa called *The Martyrs of Uganda* was basically conceived as concert music, but it has been recognized as clearly and originally African in style.

Social, Political, and Economic Change

Urbanization, changing social relationships, and the creation of new social classes all indirectly influence music, and, in turn, music can help people adapt to new social conditions. Music and dance clubs with dues and formal organization have developed in cities and provide a sense of identity and unity for individuals who have come from rural areas. The Kalela dancers in a copper mining town in Northern Rhodesia all came from the same rural area and danced their traditional dances together, and yet they wore Western clothing. This has been interpreted as representing their continuing ethnic affiliation, while it also expresses vicarious participation in elite African urban society.[1] Among Christianized Africans the church denominations in the cities often provide links with specific rural areas, and the choirs become a type of club, frequently competing with each other in concerts and contests.

Much traditional African music is related to religious beliefs and practices. Early missionaries failed to distinguish between religious and nonreligious African music and usually condemned it all. This represented a moralistic reaction to the dances associated with the music, and an ethnocentric judgment about the quality of the music itself. The Livingstonia Mission in Malawi was an exception because it encouraged converts to compose Christian hymns based on traditional African tunes.[2] More recently sporadic efforts have been made to increase the use of African music in churches, especially since nationalism has caused a general reappraisal of indigenous culture. However, in many areas Western hymn tunes have become firmly established and their use is still widely considered an important part of being Christian. The decision of the Catholic Church to use local languages rather than Latin has given an impetus to African style church music; for example, a book of hymns using traditional Bemba tunes has recently been published in Zambia. Some music in Nigeria has combined Yoruba drums with the pipe organ, and the well-known *Missa Luba* from Zaire is another example of the use of traditional African music style in contemporary religious services. Separatist African churches are to be found throughout the continent, and the characteristics of the music they use is one way to distinguish the followers of one sect from those of another. The extent to which aspects of African culture are permitted in the church is often reflected in the number of Africanisms retained in the music. Many of these churches use tunes of European hymns but perform them with African instruments, rhythms, and improvisational technique.

Since music in traditional Africa was frequently used to enhance and symbolize the position of a king or chief, its place in contemporary Africa has changed considerably with the rise of modern states. Where chiefs and headmen still remain, traditional music is often played on ceremonial occasions. Music also serves as a modern indication of political power, however. Colonial officials and some modern African rulers have organized police or military bands which use European instruments to perform during ceremonial occasions and official entertainments.

The political aspect of music can also be seen in social comment, which has always been an important factor in traditional music. Much contemporary popular music involves criticism as well as praise of local and national political leaders. Approval is often expressed outright, such as in the song "How Can Banda Be Wrong?"[3] Criticism, on the other hand, is usually hidden in metaphorical expressions, as in the Shona song *Gwindingwi rino shumba inoruma* ("The forest has lions which bite"), which can be understood as criticism of white rule even though it is not specifically stated.

Songs often serve to unite Africans in their struggle for freedom. *Nkosi Sikelel' iAfrika* ("God Bless Africa"), composed in 1897 by a black South African, Enoch Sontonga,[4] was later translated into many languages in Central and southern Africa, was sung at political meetings, and became a symbol of African aspirations. Today it is the national anthem of Zambia and in white-ruled Rhodesia where its performance is banned, it is sung as an act of defiance. Frelimo, the party which led Mozambique to independence, used traditional African songs as a means of mobilizing African self-respect and as a way in which the various peoples could share something of their culture with each other. Many Angolan freedom songs were Christian hymns with new words.

The influence of economic changes upon music has been largely indirect. In the past professional musicians were supported by rulers, but today, largely because of the popularity of the new music, it is possible for some musicians to live on their earnings as performers, through nightclub appearances and record sales. Popular music, which may be defined as music whose appeal is temporary, has always existed in Africa; when this type of music is generated by the music industry, however, it is a relatively new phenomenon.

The music industry has developed in several ways, one of which is the activity of entrepreneurs at the local level. Since modern music is in great demand in urban areas, and the hiring of a band is very expensive, entrepreneurs make profits by renting out equipment for playing records at weddings and other festivities, or by financing bands themselves and sharing the profits. After independence, overseas recording companies became increasingly interested in the African market. In the colonial period records were pressed in Europe, thus making them very expensive in Africa, but more recently they are being pressed in a number of African countries, including Nigeria, Guinea, Rhodesia, and South Africa. The streets of African cities frequently resound with the latest hits blaring from numerous record shops. In general, traditional African music is available on recordings made for the overseas market, and the local market is provided with popular hybrid types of music.

Technological change has had an important impact upon the contemporary situation of music in Africa. Until the invention of the transistor in 1948, the use of radios and record players was difficult and expensive because they required large batteries if they were used in areas without electrical power. Now many rural communities boast numerous radios and record players, all bringing a wide range of musical performances to formerly isolated communities. Music is now an important part of many radio and television commercials, which are usually aimed at the more affluent urban Africans and which blend African and Western styles.

The development of inexpensive tape recorders has made it unnecessary for musicians to concern themselves with musical notation for the preservation of their musical ideas. This has actually encouraged musical creativity, since it requires more ability to hear music and then reproduce it than to see it written down and then transfer it to an instrument such as a piano which produces the correct note without the performer having to conceptualize it in his mind. It also eliminates the restrictions imposed on music making by a system of notation.

Westernized elites have recently become a significant audience for the new popular music. This music is of three types in sub-Saharan Africa: West African highlife, the popular music of black South Africa, and Congolese or Zairean music. These are all characterized by the use of the guitar, although they vary in the way the instrument is used.

The term "highlife" today denotes a wide variety of popular music from West Africa, usually from Ghana and Nigeria. The actual style of the music varies from place to place according to the background of the performers. The beginnings of highlife are obscure, because scholars only took an interest in it after it had become well established. It has been suggested that highlife bands originally played a Ghanaian dance called konkomba, with guitars as the principal innovation. These performances often took the form of street music, but later the bands began to play in the dance halls of the whites or the African elite. Because the high admission prices kept out the majority of Africans, the name highlife was given to the music as a means of expressing both envy and criticism of the lifestyle which it represented.[5] Since many bands are provided with European instruments, the music which they play has been called dance band highlife as contrasted with guitar band highlife, the latter developing among urban Africans who could not afford the expensive brass and woodwind instruments but produced similar sounds with guitars. The recent use of electric guitars, however, has blurred the distinction between the two types.

In South Africa popular music has been heavily influenced by jazz; South Africa's traditional music consists of rhythmically complex singing accompanied by a steady beat, a style which also characterizes jazz. Since complex stringed instruments are not common in southern Africa, there is no tradition of plucked strings to apply to the guitar. Thus guitar music from South Africa is not plucked in the manner of classical guitar, but is strummed. A variety of types of songs have waxed and waned in popularity over the years. In the 1950s the *kwela* was a frequently performed dance and featured a long tin flute called the pennywhistle, which was accompanied by bands producing a sound similar to that of the swing bands of the West popular at that time. More recent types of band music feature electric guitars and produce a sound similar to rock.

The modern music emanating from Zaire, the most popular in Africa, is listened to more often than local music in East Africa, and is broadcast across the continent from Sierra Leone to Malawi. It is essentially an African adaptation of Latin American dance rhythms, which, in turn, were of partially African origin. The basic idiom of the Zairean music is the guitar, but unlike the strummed guitar of Southern Africa, the playing in Zaire involves individually plucked notes, frequently forming several voice parts. In some ways it can be viewed as an adaptation of traditional African string playing.

New Stylistic Influences

The causes of musical change have not been limited to social, economic, and political factors; the novelty of the sounds of non-African music certainly plays an important part in modern developments. For example, the impact of Arabic music is of much greater antiquity than the influence of Western music and is restricted largely to the areas where Islamic culture in general has been significant—primarily North and East Africa and the Sudanic area of West Africa. This influence can be heard in singing styles, but the principal influence is in the adoption of Arabic musical instruments.[6]

Musical instruments have also been an important factor in the impact of

Western music, since European instruments have the advantage of being more durable, more versatile, and louder than many of their African counterparts. The light tone of musical bows or of *mbira* has been one factor preventing their use in a wider context. Some characteristics of modern popular music in Africa are, perhaps, simply the result of the substitution of European for African instruments. Guitars are frequently cited as an example of this; the adaptation of traditional songs or improvisational techniques to rock bands is a similar phenomenon.

The expense of European instruments has been a problem, and Africans have frequently made their own instruments modeled on the overseas types, particularly guitars and banjos. In other cases they have substituted cheaper instruments, such as a pennywhistle for a trumpet, an acoustical guitar for an electric one, or a friction drum for a stringed bass. Because they are less expensive, harmoniums (small portable reed organs) have frequently been used in place of pianos or pipe organs in churches.

Although certain types of harmony are found in some African music, the effect of a simultaneous chord of several voice parts was a "new" sound to Africans, and many found it exciting. Consequently, much contemporary African music uses the basic chords found in European harmony: the tonic, subdominant, and dominant (I, IV, V, respectively). This harmony characterizes many of the Victorian gospel songs introduced by missionaries and the European songs taught in African schools. The appreciation of chords, however, has not led to the appreciation of modulation, or transfer of a tune from one key to another; one reason for this is the difficulty of learning to sing accidentals without a properly tuned Western instrument. Also, the appreciation of something new is limited to its simpler forms; when the social group does not appreciate the complex forms, the musician finds it unrewarding to master them. The same phenomenon is to be found when non-Africans limit their appreciation of African rhythms to the simpler ones.

Although traditional forms of African music provide for the importance of language tones, many contemporary forms do not. This is particularly true of European hymn translations, which frequently assume amusing forms when the language tones are not followed. One Western hymn with the text "Awake, my soul, and with the sun . . ." was translated into Yoruba as "Ji, okan mi ba orun ji," but the language tones following the Western tune gave it the meaning of "Steal, soul of mine, steal in my sleep."[7] It has been suggested, however, that freedom from the restrictiveness of language tones has been a factor in African preferences for new styles of music and has thus opened the way for new modes of creative expression.

The development of complex and dynamic forms of musical expression depends in part upon the amount of time which musicians have to devote to their art. In contemporary Africa the popular band seems to be the easiest way of fulfilling this condition, since the musicians are supported by nightclub appearances as well as by the production of records. Although an important motivation of popular music is financial, this does not mean that it cannot contain creative musical invention. Because composers are not restricted by systems of music writing, a great degree of spontaneity and range of experimentation is possible. Consequently, this will probably be the source of the most innovative and creative musical developments in modern Africa.

The forms which African popular music has taken reflect the African musical backgrounds of the performers, the African element in Latin American music and in jazz, and the Western input into these idioms. Whereas jazz in America has not retained a great deal of the rhythmic complexity characteristic of African music, it has retained a large share of harmonic sophistication. African adaptations of jazz, on the other hand, tend to simplify the harmonic element by using only the three basic chords, but also include more rhythmic variety.

A common rhythmic structure of jazz is 4/4 time. This is often modified in Africa by playing triplets on each beat, thus making 12/8 time. Another modification, which is more common, is to treat a bar of 4/4 time as eight eighth notes of equal stress, creating a feeling of eight beats in a particular harmonic section (eight-to-the-bar). The eight-beat grouping is given emphasis in an irregular way, so that instead of the ♩♩ ♩♩ ♩♩ ♩♩ of 4/4 time, one finds rhythms of ♩♩♩ ♩♩♩ ♩♩♩ (♩ ♩ ♩) or of ♩♩♩ ♩♩ ♩♩♩ (♩ ♩ ♩) or of ♩♩ ♩♩♩ ♩♩♩ (♩ ♩ ♩) (♩ = two beats; ♩. = three beats). Such beats are usually slower than the rapid pulses of traditional African music, and also characterize such forms as rumba, samba, cakewalk, and habanera. Which of the three rhythmic types actually results depends upon the relationship of the rhythm to the harmony and the melody.

People who perform and enjoy highlife do not concern themselves with theorizing and defining what highlife is; as a result, it encompasses a wide variety of musical forms. However, its rhythm is often considered distinctive and is characterized by an offbeat pattern. Ghanaian highlife frequently has a percussive effect, such as a gong, on the beats following the harmonic change.

Gong

Main Beats

Recordings of some highlife from Nigeria show a rhythm which is not found in other popular types, a combination of the eight-beat rhythm with the playing of two notes against three. "Travellers Lodge Atomic Eight,"[8] a recording by the guitar band of Daniel (Satch) Joseph, indicates this clearly; sometimes the rhythm is ♩ ♪♩♪♩ and other times the first three beats (equal to the first two notes) are played as two equal notes (♫ ♩) , giving the rhythm of ♫♩ ♩ ♪♩ , which is not characteristic of other popular rhythm types but which does appear in a number of highlife recordings. In a recording of the Mayor's Dance Band in Port Harcourt, Nigeria,[9] this rhythm is heard in the melody played by the brass instruments. This makes a counter-rhythm, or offbeat pattern with the regular eight-beat steady rhythm:

Although popular bands in Africa have often had a preeminent place in the development of new forms of expression, in certain areas traditional musical forms are being utilized in new situations. An example of this is the Yoruba dance drama, which includes traditional Yoruba music and dance as well as newly composed interludes. Yoruba language and mythology are also incorporated in these dramas, which have been described as taking the place of traditional story-telling sessions.[10] One such play, *Oba Koso* (The King Did Not Hang) by Duro Ladipo, is based on an ancient Yoruba legend concerning the ancient king, Shango, whose followers believe he did not die but rather became a god of thunder.[11]

Conclusion

While Western theorists are concerned with questions of preserving "traditional African styles" or eliminating "banal European influence," Africans simply go ahead and make the music they like. Although musical factors are important in change, social and economic factors may be just as influential even though they may remain unrecognized. An important aspect of modernization in Africa is an increase in scale, with growing numbers of people coming into contact with one another. Music in the future will necessarily reflect this situation, with the possibility that forms of musical expression based on little-known languages and musical styles will gradually disappear unless they are incorporated into a larger scheme, such as national dance troupes, or into some national cultural awareness program.

Certain types of music are likely to disappear from use, sometimes because of passing fads and other times because of the decline of customs with which the music has always been associated. However, music can also find new uses and meanings, as in the adaptation of traditional music for modern political purposes. Music in Africa is still not seen as an art form which exists for intellectual listening, nor is it cultivated as an elitist occupation engaged in by persons who have sufficient leisure or money to do so. African music usually serves as entertainment or it fulfills requirements of ritual or social life. It derives from a rich and diverse tradition, and as it evolves it will continue to exert a significant influence on the music of the modern world.

NOTES

1. J. Clyde Mitchell, *The Kalela Dance: Aspects of Social Relationships Among Urban Africans in Northern Rhodesia* (Manchester: Manchester University Press, 1956. Rhodes-Livingstone Institute Paper No. 27).

2. H. M. Taylor, ed., *Tunes From Nyasaland* (Livingstonia Mission, Malawi: The Overtoun Institution, 1959).

3. George T. Nurse, "Popular Songs and National Identity in Malawi," *African Music* 3 (1964), 104.

4. Yvonne Huskisson, *The Bantu Composers of Southern Africa* (South African Broadcasting Corporation, 1969), p.273.

5. Edna M. Smith, "Popular Music in West Africa," *African Music* 3 (1962), 11; David Coplan, *Go To My Town, Cape Coast! Syncretic Developments in the Social and Musical History of Ghana*, in *Studies in Urban Ethnomusicology*, ed. Bruno Nettl, forthcoming (1977).

6. J. H. Kwabena Nketia, *The Music of Africa* (New York: Norton, 1974), p.10.

7. Nicholas G. J. Ballanta, "Gathering Folk Tunes in the African Country," *Musical America* 44 (September 1926), 11.

8. Phillips West African Records PEN 922.

9. Nigerphone NSF 240.

10. Oyekan Owomoyela, "Yoruba-Language Theater Draws Inspiration from Tradition," *Africa Report* 15 (June 1970), 32–33.

11. This play is recorded on Kaleidophone record set KS-2201. A synopsis of the story and an English translation are provided.

SUGGESTIONS FOR FURTHER READING

African Urban Notes, Vol. 5, No. 4, is an issue devoted to the study of music in urban Africa.

Nettl, Bruno, ed. *Studies in Urban Ethnomusicology*. Forthcoming, 1977.

Roberts, John Storm. *Black Music of Two Worlds*. New York: Praeger, 1972. Part of this book deals with the influence of Afro-American music on modern African music.

Weman, Henry. *African Music and the Church in Africa*. Uppsala: Svenska Institutet for Missionsforskning, 1960.

The following periodicals have frequent articles on modern developments in African music:

Africa Report

African Music

Gwendolen M. Carter
A Case Study of the Republic of South Africa

23 Our major task is to ensure that a white nation will prevail here. Every nation has the inalienable right to safeguard that which it has built for itself and for posterity. This then is our task. . . . but we know that this cannot be done by suppressing those entrusted to our care; neither can they be denied the opportunity to develop fully. This is a lesson that history has taught us, and which we know only too well. It is disgraceful, therefore, that the outside world associates the concept of Separate Development with oppression.—From "Crisis in World Conscience," by Prime Minister H. F. Verwoerd, September 3, 1963.

If non-White population figures had to be the decisive factor in our history, in our existence, then, surely, our White nation should have disappeared centuries ago. No, the decisive factor is to have inexorable faith in your right to a separate ethnic existence; and along with that faith one's willingness and one's readiness to grant others what one claims for oneself. . . .—Minister Marais Viljoen in the House of Assembly, February 2, 1970.

We have been through 150 years of white domination, and have been subjected to 66 years of oppression. . . . This has always been perpetrated against us in the name of Western democracy, and Christian Civilization, by White manipulation of the Houses of Parliament and members of the Assembly. . . . South Africa's malady is the refusal of the Whites to share power with Blacks. Now it is our turn to tell them that Whites in this Country can only do one thing to help themselves and they can do only one thing to help us to help them. They must be prepared to share power. . . .

The whole World must be told that we despise what some people euphemistically call "Separate Development" or "Separate Freedoms" which we know to be nothing more nor less than White *basskap*. South Africa is one Country, it has one destiny and it in fact has one economy. Those who are attempting to divide the land of our birth are attempting to stem the tide of history. . . . The majority of black people do not want to abandon their birthright. They have toiled for generations to create the wealth of South Africa. They intend to participate in the Wealth of the land.—From "A Message to South Africa from Black South Africa," Speech to Africans at the Jabulani Amphitheatre, Soweto, by Chief Gatsha Buthelezi, First Minister of Kwazulu, on March 14, 1976.

What leads one group in a country to discriminate against another? Is it difference of color, class, religion, ethnicity, sex? Is it fear, or greed, competition for political power, habit, or calculated intent? Why do groups that live together harmoniously in one country fight against each other in another? Why does discrimination become explosive at one point and not at others? What overcomes discrimination? What is the basis of a stable society?

These questions are being asked by people throughout the world. Why do Christians and Muslims fight in Lebanon after decades of peaceful living together? Why do Protestants and Catholics fight in Northern Ireland? Why did the American civil rights movement take place when it did? Why did black ghettos erupt in violence?

African countries face these questions even more acutely than do long-established independent states. Only a very few modern African nations have been independent for more than two decades, most for a shorter time. They have had to adjust quickly from subservience to an external colonial power to facing internal demands from many groups for a share in political power and wealth. There have been civil wars in Nigeria, Sudan, and Ethiopia in which distinctive ethnic groups have tried, though unsuccessfully, to detach themselves from central government control. There have been massacres, as in Burundi, of one ethnic group by another. In Angola three separate African groups, each ethnically based, fought fiercely to dominate that potentially rich country after the Portuguese declared it would become independent on November 11, 1975.

Why then does the racial discrimination in South Africa by a white minority over the black majority arouse such bitter feeling not only within Africa itself but throughout the world? Is it because it is so extensive and has lasted so long? Is it at least in part because it mirrors in a single country the long-established dominance of the predominantly white countries of Europe and North America over the peoples of the Third World? If so, what does the South African situation mean, and how should what the South Africans call "their answer" to their racial problem be evaluated?

Occupying the southern end of Africa, South Africa is the most developed, the most powerful, and the richest country on that continent. It has by far the most sophisticated military force in Africa. More than 350 American firms have subsidiaries or outlets in South Africa, while Britain has a far heavier economic stake in South African prosperity. With 70 percent of the output of gold outside the communist world, rich diamond mines, other valuable minerals, an iron and steel industry, the world's largest dynamite factory, manufacturing capacity for cars and heavy equipment, modern cities, and an international banking system, South Africa may appear invulnerable.

But South Africa's position has changed drastically since April 1974. In that month, an army coup in Portugal overthrew that country's long-existing dictatorship and established a new regime. One of the first decisions of the new government was to extend independence to Portugal's three African territories,

73. A view of Johannesburg, the largest city in South Africa.
Photo courtesy United Nations/ Frank/ nj.

Guinea-Bissau, Mozambique, and Angola. Debilitating colonial wars had been fought by local liberation movements in each of these territories for more than a decade, and these wars had, in fact, been the major cause of the collapse of the former Portuguese government. When the new Portuguese regime turned over control by 1975 to locally based movements, each with a strongly socialist or Marxist orientation, South Africa lost much of its former insulation from militant African regimes. Mozambique shares a long border with Rhodesia, and

74. A Frelimo guerrilla in Mozambique.
Photo courtesy United Nations/ Basom/ nj.

Angola is adjacent to South African-held Namibia. Moreover, Rhodesia and Namibia are themselves under pressure from liberation movements and the United Nations because Rhodesia's small white minority, numbering about a quarter of a million, has long refused to share political power with its huge African majority of some six million, while Namibia is acknowledged even by South Africa to have an international character of a former League of Nations mandated territory. In time, therefore, South Africa may be the only white-controlled state on the continent and may itself be the focus of international as well as internal militant pressures for change. Widespread and prolonged demonstrations, riots, and work stoppages organized by African and, subsequently, Coloured youth in mid-1976 and in 1977 indicate the latter pressures are already under way.

Historical Background

In the light of these developments it is particularly important to understand the character of South Africa's legally enforced discrimination based on color, and how it developed. Today, four and a quarter million whites (60 percent Afrikaners, that is descendants of the original Dutch and German settlers, and 40 percent English-speaking whose ancestors first arrived in the early nineteenth century) dominate some twenty million blacks, including more than seventeen million Africans, found all over the country, three quarter million Asians, centered mainly in Natal, and two and a quarter million Coloureds (mixed blood) living mostly in Cape Province. The constant interaction between black and white in South Africa which characterizes daily life began in that area more than three centuries ago.

The first Dutch settlers landed in 1652 at the tip of the continent near what is now Cape Town. They were a sturdy, self-reliant group embued with the Calvinist doctrine of predestination, as were the Huguenots who joined them at the end of the seventeenth century. It was not difficult for them to feel that they were an elite come to claim a new land. Though the settlement was originally intended only as a "half-way house" en route to the East Indies, settlers soon spread out beyond the colony's effective boundaries and clashed with indigenous peoples for control of the land.

The San were driven from their hunting grounds and over the next two centuries virtually exterminated. The cattle-raising Khoikhoi fought unsuccessfully to defend their grazing grounds but gradually became hangers-on and the servants of white society. One of the most decisive elements in the formation of racial attitudes was the slaves brought from the East Indies and from other parts of Africa. From the amalgam of whites, San, Khoikhoi, and slaves stemmed the Coloured. From the experience of slave owning developed a white expectation of domination that has never disappeared.

As settlers spread out along the coast, they encountered a more effective adversary: the well organized Nguni-speaking peoples, especially the Xhosa, who had been moving slowly south and southwest for centuries. The Boers and the Xhosa met and clashed along the line of the Great Fish River that today forms the western boundary of the Transkei and Ciskei; in 1781 occurred the first of the frontier wars that were to erupt intermittently for decades leaving the Xhosa militarily crushed, dispersed, and with much of their land expropriated. Later, the same was to happen with the Zulu in Natal.

The British occupied the Cape in 1795, annexed it in 1815, and a decade later, under the influence of missionaries and liberalizing trends at home, began to introduce measures to protect the position of both the Coloureds and the Africans. In 1833 slavery was abolished. Three years later the cumulative effect of what the Boers termed interference with their chosen way of life started their slow exodus north and northeast in what has been called the Great Trek. Moving into Natal, they clashed with and defeated the Zulu army led by Dingane, but their attempt to establish a separate state was thwarted by British annexation of that area in 1845. Elsewhere, Boer trekkers eventually formed two republics, the Orange Free State and the South African Republic (Transvaal), recognized by the British as independent in 1854 and 1852. Their all-white male electorates embraced the principle of no equality between blacks and whites in church and state. In contrast, the British government provided the far wealthier and more populous Cape Colony with a nonracial franchise for a representative assembly in 1853, and this provision was continued when the Cape received internal self-government in 1872.

The area that became South Africa was to be torn by conflict before Union and independence within the British Empire were achieved in 1910. Complicating all relations was the discovery of phenomenal wealth under the soil: diamonds in 1867 at Kimberley and gold in 1886 on the Witwatersrand in the heart of the Transvaal. The latter deposits were larger than any other gold field in the world but demanded sophisticated machinery to process the veins that ran deep into the ground. European capital and entrepreneurs, white diggers, and thousands of Africans were mobilized to exploit the riches.

Eastward expansion by Boer farmers, checked as the British reluctantly extended their control over what became Basutoland (now Lesotho) and Swaziland, was paralleled by spasmodic British northward expansionism. What led to conflict, however, was the clash between the Afrikaner administration in the

Transvaal, which stubbornly refused political rights to the foreigners (the Uitlanders) who were exploiting the subsoil riches, and those who sought political power in that area to complement their economic interests. In an ill-advised maneuver in which Cecil Rhodes, Prime Minister of the Cape, and the British government had a hand, an attempted coup known as the Jameson Raid failed ignominiously to take control of the Transvaal. Inflamed feelings on both sides led inevitably to the Anglo-Boer War, 1899–1902. At its end, the peace settlement went some way toward easing the strain between English and Afrikaners in South Africa, although this has never wholly disappeared. In the process of attempted reconciliation, the black majority was sacrificed.

While white settlers and administrations had jockeyed for power, Africans and Coloured had not been oblivious or uninvolved. The nonracial franchise in the Cape had given the vote to the African elite on equal terms with whites and Coloured. In 1884, the Native Electoral Association was organized by white Cape Independents with the help of John Tengo Jabavu, who the same year founded the most famous of African newspapers, *Imvo Zabantsundu* (Native Opinion). By that time, Africans numbered 47 percent of all voters in five border constituencies in the eastern Cape and over 59 percent in two of them. Their potential political influence frightened the white members of the Cape Parliament, which in 1887 began the long process of limiting and ultimately, nearly a century later, eliminating the African vote from the central electoral process. Cape Liberals fought for an extension of their own nonracial franchise to all of South Africa during the 1908–1909 all-white national convention that drew up the terms of Union; they succeeded only in having it safeguarded for their own province. The South African Act of Union in 1910 provided that only whites could be elected to the national Parliament.

On the eve of South African Union, the National Native Convention protested the exclusion of Africans from Parliament. In 1912, under the leadership of four brilliant American- and English-trained African lawyers, the South African Native (subsequently African) National Congress was formed out of political associations that had been working for African rights in all four provinces. Their long series of appeals for a common citizenship based on liberal values went unheeded. In 1913, the Native Land Act evicted squatters and limited African land rights to the reserves, 7.3 percent of the country, raised to some 13 percent in 1936, the current figure. In 1914, World War I broke out. African appeals to the British government and subsequently to the Versailles conference were no more effective than those to the South African Parliament.

In the 1920s, the Industrial and Commercial Union, led by a dynamic Nyasalander, Clements Kadalie, gained wide support with its appeal for a minimum wage. African dockworkers, and subsequently African miners, secured some wage increases through strikes. But when mineowners attempted in 1922 to cut costs by shifting jobs from unskilled whites to Africans, white unions took action that turned into a general strike. Ensuing disorders were put down by force by the government. Yet the white workers proved the ultimate victors. A coalition of Afrikaner nationalists and the largely English-speaking Labour Party won the 1924 election. They proceeded to enact legislation to protect white labor from black competition. This was looked on as a pressing need because unskilled Afrikaners were flooding off their drought-stricken farms into a crowded labor market. Thus, the key characteristic of the South African economy was established; the advancement of black labor was made dependent on the consent of white labor. As South Africa moved into an industrial revolution that has made it the strongest and richest country on the African continent, it was apparent that politics controlled economics, and the Afrikaner majority among the whites controlled politics.

While the dominant white minority remained dedicated to Western forms of democracy in its own political sphere, it used these same institutions to dominate and coerce the large black majority in the country. As part of that process, the white-controlled Parliament systematically eliminated blacks from any role in the electoral process, even though their rights had been entrenched in the Act of Union. In 1936, the nonracial franchise in Cape Province, under which all black males who could meet educational and economic qualifications could vote for the same candidates as did whites, was amended by constitutional process to remove Africans from the common roll and place them on a separate roll to elect three whites to represent them. In 1959, Africans lost even this share in parliamentary politics. The Coloured were similarly shifted to a separate roll in 1956 after an extended constitutional struggle and were subsequently also excluded from the central electoral process. Neither has accepted its exclusion, and many of the Coloured refuse to cooperate with the government until they are put back on the common roll.

Major Developments Since 1948

The black franchise is still a major issue in South Africa. The United Party, the official opposition until 1977 that was supported by most of the English-speaking community, some Afrikaners, and the business establishment, came out in support of putting the Coloured back on the common roll. The Progressive Reform Party, which provides by far the most trenchant criticisms of government policies, would not only put the Coloured back on the common roll but would also provide votes for the Africans on a qualified franchise. However, no current party yet supports the principle of "one man, one vote" as did the former Liberal Party.

The party most opposed to any sharing of political influence with blacks is the National or Nationalist Party, which is primarily representative of the Afrikaner population. Coming into office in 1948 with a bare majority of the white electorate, the Nationalists have steadily increased their share of parliamentary representation in every election and since 1961 appear to have an unassailable control of parliamentary power. The party is adamantly opposed to providing blacks, whether Coloureds, Asians, or Africans, with the right to vote in a parliamentary election.

Instead, the Nationalists uphold the principles of differentiation and separation. They maintain that the answer to South Africa's racial situation is what they call "Separate Development," that is, separate institutions for each of the black racial groups (everyone in South Africa is formally classified as White, Coloured, Asian, or African under the Population Registration Act of 1951). The Coloureds and Asians have each been given councils, which many of their members reject as badges of an inferior status. For Africans, the government went still further at the end of the 1950s by embarking officially on the establishment of the Bantustans, or homelands. Under this policy, Africans are said to have political rights only in areas that have been ethnically demarcated by the government. These areas, shown in map 27, which so far barely total the 13 percent of the land surface of South Africa which Parliament had promised Africans in 1936, are scattered around the periphery of the country. Apart from the Transkei, all the so-called homelands consist of fragmented pieces of largely undeveloped and overpopulated land. They cannot begin to support those living in them.

This policy of Separate Development or territorial *apartheid* (separation) is the most significant and controversial part of official policy. The government claims it is a generous, constructive policy through which Africans receive the rights they can never attain in white-controlled South Africa. But Chief Gatsha Buthelezi, of Kwazulu, the most populous of the homelands, has called them "rural slums." Separate Development, carried to its logical conclusion, which the white government is eager to do, means that each area which has been designated as being the "homeland" of a particular ethnic group, the Xhosa, Zulu, Tswana, etc., can graduate from its semiautonomous status, where it controls part of its own budget and policies, to independence. Chief Kaiser Matanzima, of the Transkei, which is more consolidated than other homelands and has long possessed a semirepresentative assembly, opted for independence in October

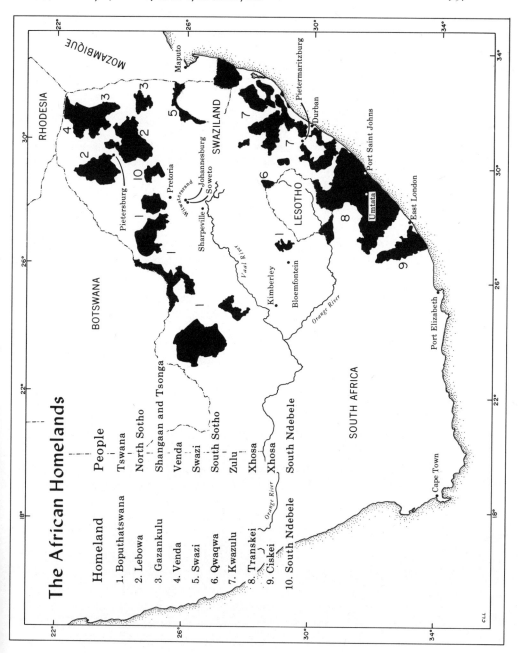

The African Homelands

Homeland	People
1. Boputhatswana	Tswana
2. Lebowa	North Sotho
3. Gazankulu	Shangaan and Tsonga
4. Venda	Venda
5. Swazi	Swazi
6. Qwaqwa	South Sotho
7. Kwazulu	Zulu
8. Transkei	Xhosa
9. Ciskei	Xhosa
10. South Ndebele	South Ndebele

MAP 27

75. Kwazulu, one of the ten South African "homelands."
Photo courtesy United Nations/ Muldoon/ pas.

1976. Chief Lucas Mangope, of Bophuthatswana, which is still composed of six separated segments of land, declares it will follow. But Chief Buthelezi rejects the process as a fraud and urges concentrating efforts on gaining rights for all Africans in South Africa.

Less than half the country's Africans have homes in the Bantustans. Moreover, a high proportion of the men from these areas between the ages of sixteen and sixty must go as migratory labor to so-called white parts of the country in order to earn what is necessary to keep themselves and their families from starvation. A complex system of labor offices in the homelands and rigid influx control permit only those approved for particular jobs to go to urban areas for employment. Once their service is completed they must return to their own homeland to await another assignment. The government favors this migratory labor system, which provides 60 percent of all male workers in the central economy. Some new employment is being created on the borders of the homelands and in so-called growth points within them, but so far it does not begin to keep up with the numbers who seek work annually on the labor market. Thus, in addition to widespread poverty, families are broken up and unhealthy conditions exist in the compounds and hostels in the cities where migrants are domiciled.

Some three and a half million Africans live in white rural areas, working on white farms or in forestry, transportation, or service jobs. Most can have their families with them, unlike the migratory laborers described above. Much of farm labor depends partially on sharecropping. There are pressures, however, to concentrate on training more skilled African labor and sending to the homelands the less-skilled and the wives and children. This process is part of a vast resettlement program devised and enforced by the government to remove to the homelands Africans from so-called black spots in white areas, even if they and their ancestors have long lived there. Between two and three million Africans have been or will be moved in this program, one of the largest forced resettlements in peacetime the world has ever known.

Some five million urban Africans live in strictly segregated townships linked to where they work by overcrowded buses and trains. The largest of these is the township of Soweto outside Johannesburg which now numbers over a million persons. Africans cannot own land in white areas, and there is a great shortage of housing and much overcrowding. In 1975, Africans were again permitted to

76. Barracks-like living quarters for African gold miners near Johannesburg.
Photo courtesy United Nations/ Pendl/ db.

have thirty-year leases on their houses, but at first only if they possessed certificates as homeland citizens. Few wished to take out such certificates for fear it would imperil their urban residence, and this restriction was removed after the June 1976 demonstrations and riots in Soweto.

All Africans outside of the homelands must carry a pass or identity paper at all times, with threat of arrest and jail for failure to do so. Nearly a million Africans are jailed every year, most of them on petty charges. Moreover, wages are low, economic mobility is limited, and African trade union organization is unrecognised under existing industrial legislation. Strikes by Africans though no longer illegal require a complicated mechanism and a time period that virtually nullify their effectiveness. Government bannings of potential leaders also inhibit the emergence of overt industrial leadership.

Sixty to seventy percent of urban Africans live below the poverty line despite some wage increases which have resulted partly from the pressure of adverse foreign publicity. Since the six to seven million Africans in the labor force are excluded by the government from the definition of "employee" in the Industrial Conciliation Act, they have virtually no share in shaping the conditions under which they work. Frequent, if sporadic, strikes have long evidenced the increasing restlessness of urban African labor over their bare subsistence wages, crowded living conditions, and inadequate and often unsafe transportation between their homes and places of work. The large disparity between black and white wages is illustrated in figure 21. Moreover, education for African youth in

FIGURE 21

Income by Racial Group

Group	Percentage of total population	Percentage of estimated income (1968)
Whites	17.5	73.4
Coloureds	9.4	5.4
Asiatics	2.9	2.4
Africans	70.2	19.8

Source: H. Adam, Modernizing Racial Domination (Berkeley: University of California Press, 1971), p.7.

their segregated schools is neither free nor compulsory, and lack of opportunities for those with educational qualifications contributes to a high dropout rate and the prevalence of tsotsi gangs that harass people in African townships that lie well outside "white" towns and cities where the Africans earn their livelihood.

Segregation, and thus discrimination, is suffered by Africans on three levels.

The first, known as petty *apartheid*, is in public and private facilities: waiting rooms, buses, trains, washrooms, ambulances, post office counters, beaches, elevators, and the like. Some of the obvious signs of discrimination at this level have recently been removed in response to internal and external pressures; for example, segregated park benches, once the distinctive hallmark of *apartheid*, are disappearing. But these are only cosmetic changes; the core of the policy remains. The second level is the segregated residential ghettos established by the Group Areas Act of 1951. The different ethnic groups—Whites, Coloured, Asians, and Africans—are rigorously restricted to segregated living areas in and

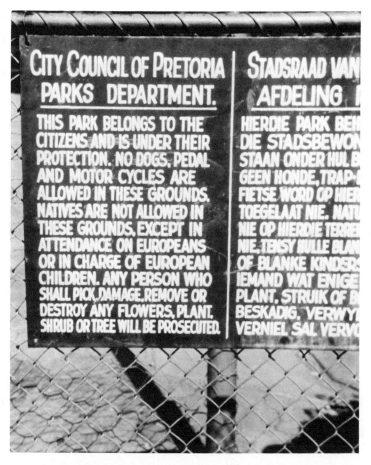

77. Sign outside a public park in South Africa which excludes Africans from the grounds.
Photo courtesy United Nations/ Boernstein/ pas.

near towns and cities. The third level of segregation, territorial or great *apart-heid*, involves the division of South Africa between those areas which are designated as African homelands and the rest of the country, so-called white South Africa.

The homeland policy is a source of bitter contention among urban Africans. The members of SASO (the Black South African Student Organization), BPC (Black Peoples Convention), and several other urban-based African movements, all of which have been subject to persistent harassment and bannings by the government, vehemently oppose the homeland policy as one that is fragmenting a country which belongs to all Africans as much as to the whites. The Black Renaissance Convention, with 300 all-African delegates, voted in December 1974 to "condemn and so reject Separate Development and all its institutions"; the proscribed African nationalist movements, the African National Congress and the Pan Africanist Congress, which continue to operate outside the country, equally reject the homeland policy. Moreover, some of the homeland leaders, notably Chief Buthelezi of Kwazulu, and Dr. Cedric Phatudi of Lebowa, also oppose the territorial and ethnic fragmentation of South Africa implicit in Separate Development and maintain that Africans must stand together to work for political and economic rights in a united country.

The Future

Africans and whites in South Africa are thus divided as to the merits of Separate Development as a means of extending rights and justice to the country's African majority. Chief Kaiser Matanzima and his supporters claim that they can do more to change *apartheid* from outside, that is after their territory becomes independent, than from inside. They insist, however, that Transkeian citizenship will be extended only to those urban-based Transkeians who wish to accept it. The central government, on the other hand, would prefer that all Transkeians, no matter where they are domiciled, be regarded as Transkeian citizens. Its aim is not only to reduce the population ratio of Africans to whites in the cities but also to relieve itself of responsibility for urban Africans with ethnic connections to any independent homeland whether or not they or their ancestors have ever lived there.

Both the Organization of African Unity and the General Assembly of the United Nations are on record as condemning Separate Development as an extension of *apartheid*. Unless the Transkei ultimately receives international recognition as an independent state, both it and the South African government will have gained little from the declaration of Transkeian independence on October 26, 1976. Apart from Bophuthatswana's Chief Mangope, other homeland leaders have pledged not to accept independence and to maintain their right to share in molding the future of South Africa. The crucial issue in South Africa remains the government's policies toward urban Africans, for they are the crucial factor in race relations within the republic. Should they be extended the economic privileges and opportunities of whites and, in time, their political rights, it might truly be said that South Africa is well on the way to providing an answer for its racial situation, particularly if such a policy were coupled with some form of constitutional relation with the largely rural homelands.

There are still a number of possibilities within the South African situation. They range all the way from an ultimate racial harmony through systematic reduction of restrictions and acceptance of the country's blacks as citizens in a common society, to ever-tightening controls on blacks and their white sympathizers as South Africa is moved by a frightened government into the *laager*, a defensive stance reinforced by military means against both internal and external pressures for change.

Not only the South Africans, both white and black, but also other countries that have close links with that Republic are concerned with the direction of change in South Africa. What influence will its African neighbors, and the governments of those Western countries like the United States and Britain, which have massive investments in South Africa, exert on the latter's government? African countries inevitably support change toward racial justice in South Africa. Will Western countries live up to their own principles of democracy and individual freedom and support change in this direction, or will economic interests and white solidarity lead them to support the *apartheid* system which publicly they deplore? It is not only the future character of southern Africa that is in balance but also relations between the West and the Third World.

A stable society is one that is free from legally enforced discrimination, a society in which individuals and groups feel they have a fair opportunity to share in resources and to improve their situation. There are not many signs that South African official policies are moving in this direction, but external and internal pressures are mounting. There is much at stake for us all; in this era, discrimination based on color is our most explosive issue.

SUGGESTIONS FOR FURTHER READING

Adam, Heribert. *Modernizing Racial Domination: South Africa's Political Dynamics.* Berkeley: University of California Press, 1971.

Benson, Mary. *South Africa: The Struggle for a Birthright.* Baltimore, Maryland: Penguin, 1966.

Carter, Gwendolen M. *American Policy and the Search for Justice and Reconcilia-*

tion in South Africa. Racine, Wisconsin: The Johnson Foundation, 1975. Available without charge.

―――――, Thomas Karis, and Newell Stultz. *South Africa's Transkei: The Politics of Domestic Colonialism*. Evanston, Illinois: Northwestern University Press, 1967.

Desmond, Cosmos. *The Discarded People*. Baltimore, Maryland: Penguin, 1971.

Hoagland, Jim. *South Africa: Civilizations in Conflict*. Boston, Massachusetts: Houghton Mifflin, 1972.

Marquard, Leo. *The Peoples and Politics of South Africa*. 4th edition, paper. London: Oxford University Press, 1969.

Thompson, Leonard, and Jeffrey Butler, eds. *Change in Contemporary South Africa*. Berkeley: University of California Press, 1975.

Walshe, Peter. *The Rise of African Nationalism in South Africa*. Berkeley: University of California Press, 1970.

J. Gus Liebenow
Africa in World Affairs

24 The emergence of Africa as an active force in world affairs has been one of the more unexpected developments following World War II. Up until 1945 the African continent was still not in the mainstream of global commercial, military, political, and cultural interaction. Although several very crucial battles of the war had been fought along the North African littoral, in the Italian-occupied Horn of Africa, and in scattered sections of the French empire, the continent was substantially regarded as a residual area. Africa provided minerals and agricultural resources needed for the war effort, it served as a source of manpower for campaigns in Europe and Asia, and it was a vital link in the supply network of the Allied forces. It was a minor pawn, however, in a larger chess game.

In addition to the white-dominated society in South Africa, there were only three African countries which were eligible for charter membership in the United Nations in 1945. None of the three—Egypt, Liberia, or Ethiopia—was considered a power of consequence at the time. British control of Suez and the Egyptian economy still made Egypt a "vassal" state; the economy of Liberia was still closely tied to American investment; and Ethiopia had only recently been liberated from its brief period of Italian domination, which had witnessed the slaughter of a great portion of its educated elite. Africa was on the international frontier, an area where non-African powers proposed and disposed of Africa's affairs.

This is not to suggest that Africa was a continent where nothing happened or that its involvement in international politics could only be considered consequential when Africans interacted with people from Europe or Asia. This would be an ethnocentric definition of international politics. Certainly, long before the so-called journeys of European discovery and exploration, the peoples of the African continent were constantly interacting with one another. As the earlier chapters of this volume have indicated, various African communities were engaged in the expansion of trade, in warfare, the spread of religion, and even cultural imperialism centuries—if not millennia—before the first Portuguese mariners began their cautious probing of the northwest coast in the middle of the fifteenth century. Obviously, international politics were going on within the continent.

In the global perspective, however, relations between peoples of Africa and those outside the continent were of a special character. Contact was, first of all, largely intermittent in nature. Ties which had been established with some vigor during one period would languish and all but cease during a subsequent era. Secondly, until well into the present century, contact with many regions of Africa was often limited to specific nodal points or to fragile lines of transportation, such as a river or a trail. This has been characteristic of centuries of Arab activity in East Africa. Similarly limited in character was the European-African interaction which took place during the period of the transatlantic slave trade. Despite the fact that over eleven million people from West and Central Africa were transported to the New World, the European presence was miniscule. Until the middle of the nineteenth century, few Europeans could be found beyond the small depots which slavers and legitimate traders had established on offshore islands or other fortified areas along the coast. The interior trade was in the hands of African middlemen, who sustained the external trade with Europe and the Americas.

The third characteristic of precolonial contact between Africa and the outside world was that in most instances it took the form of accommodation to the interests of non-African forces. While in the historical chapters of this volume there are examples of peoples who were able to influence if not control their interactions with outsiders, the predominant situation was one in which non-Africans set the terms. This tendency to react to external stimuli became most pronounced in the late nineteenth century. While there was heroic resistance to European rule, subjugation was accomplished with relatively little resort to massive organized force on the part of European powers. In a curious way, moreover, the occupation of Africa came almost as a secondary consequence of events which were occurring in Alsace-Lorraine, Indochina, and elsewhere in the world. Africa was an area of indirect accommodation for the more powerful movers in world politics and trade as they confronted each other directly in Europe. The territorial boundaries bore almost no relation to African political, economic, and cultural realities.

A fourth characteristic of the contact during the colonial era has persisted beyond the attainment of independence: the tendency for relationships within the continent and between the peoples of Africa and the outside world to be fragmented and channeled in accordance with distinct sets of colonial experiences. Thus, for example, the Wolof and other people of the colony of Senegal were encouraged by the French to relate to one another as well as to other Africans included within the French empire. Conversely, customs collectors, labor recruiters, administrative officers, missionaries, and agents of commercial companies attempted to reduce or eliminate social, economic, and political intercourse with other Africans, who by accident of diplomacy were included within British, Portuguese, or other colonial territories. Contacts by Senegalese with the outside world were monopolized by metropolitan France, which recruited them for the army, permitted some to attend schools in France, and even allowed a few to establish political or trade union links with their counterparts in Paris or Marseilles. The same situation prevailed in other colonial systems, except that the Belgians and the Portuguese positively discouraged external linkages. Inasmuch as the United States, Russia, China, and the Latin American states had no colonies in Africa, contacts between Africans and citizens of those countries were minimal.

Emergence of Africa as an Active International Force

The gradual transformation of Africa into an active force in world affairs coincided with the achievement of independence during the decade of the 1960s. The manner in which independence was achieved, however, initially had an ambivalent effect upon this transformation. On the one hand, it established a positive attitude toward internationalism as a political mode among African leaders. On the other hand, the process whereby African liberation was achieved tended to reinforce Africa's role as a marginal area in world politics. The latter statement is based on the fact that there were relatively few instances in which European colonial rule was directly terminated because of armed rebellion on the part of African groups. The Mau Mau emergency in Kenya is an obvious exception. Other examples, however, such as the guerrilla movement in Algeria and the prolonged campaign against the Portuguese in Guinea-Bissau, Mozambique, and Angola, should be noted. While the impact which armed resistance had upon changing popular attitudes and policies in Europe cannot be disputed, it was the revolutionary changes of government in France in 1958 and Portugal in 1974 that were the immediate causes of change in colonial strategy regarding Algeria and the Portuguese territories.

The general withdrawal of European colonial control, which began in the late 1950s and reached massive proportions in the following decade, can be traced to forces and situations external to Africa as much as to developments within the continent itself. External factors included the defeat of Italy as an Axis power in World War II, the problems which postwar reconstruction posed for Western Europe, the decision of Britain to withdraw from India and Pakistan, the emergence of the Cold War, the rise of the Labour Party in Britain and the socialists in Belgium, political instability within France under the Fourth Republic, and the vocal support which newly independent Asian and Arab states were giving to the cause of African independence.

Asian and Arab support was advanced most vigorously in the United Nations, which became a significant forum for African liberation despite the paucity of African membership prior to 1960. Although the Trusteeship Council of the United Nations had jurisdiction only with respect to eight of the fifty African territories (Tanganyika, Ruanda, Burundi, French and British Togoland, French and British Cameroon, and Italian Somaliland), it set high standards in holding colonial powers accountable and in demanding accelerated timetables for independence. The periodic visits by missions of the council to Africa and the hearing of African petitioners at the United Nations headquarters kept the colonial situation in the limelight. The model of accountability embodied in the trusteeship system, moreover, was ultimately extended to cover all non-self-governing territories, through a special committee of the General Assembly, where the anticolonial forces were in the majority.

In most instances the breakup of empire was accomplished with relative ease. Typically, the European power was committed to the continuation of economic development plans which had been launched in the later phases of colonial rule. The Europeans, moreover, agreed to provide services in a number of other areas where the new state had needs. Although this support later came to be recognized as a double-edged sword, at the time of independence it seemed reasonable and humane and it partially compensated for the abuses of colonial rule.

Africans in International Politics

In contrast with the situation of limited and controlled contact with the outside world during the colonial period, individual Africans have now become among the globe's most peripatetic citizens. No international conference on development, pollution, sea law, or other major issue is without its African delegation. Nigerian businessmen can regularly be seen in London, New York, or Tokyo. In their respective capacities as religious leaders a Senegalese *marabout* flies to Mecca to worship at the tomb of the Prophet, a Tanzanian cardinal attends a consistory in Rome, and a Liberian preacher chairs an international gathering of Baptists in Brazil. It is not unusual to find a very young Kenyan attending a Boy Scout jamboree in Stockholm, while his older brother prepares for an Olympic track event in Montreal. Countless thousands of young Africans are now attending universities in Moscow, Chicago, New Delhi, Peking, and Brasilia. And still other Africans each year will be attending art festivals, writers' seminars, and labor union congresses almost anywhere in the world. In this respect African participation in international affairs is much like that of other societies, with the exception of countries like Burma and many of the communist states where citizen travel abroad is still strictly limited and controlled. Yet all societies, libertarian or otherwise, set some limits upon citizen travel through currency controls, the issuing of passports, and other devices. Thus, African leaders, like government officials elsewhere, do set parameters for the legitimate participation by African individuals in international transactions. It is the state, acting through its designated representatives, that is the significant unit in international politics.

The typical African country is a relatively fragile unit in international politics, and this has consequences with respect to the way African countries relate to each other as well as to their interaction with forces external to the continent. The fragility of the African state is traceable in large measure to the manner in which the artificial boundaries were drawn on the map during the European partition in the nineteenth and early twentieth centuries. One of the more publicized aspects of this problem was the division of people like the Ewe in West Africa among as many as four colonial territories. In other instances, historic claims by one group to suzerainty with respect to neighboring communities were also ignored. Thus a series of irredenta, or claims to lost territory, were created during the colonial period. These have persisted and actually led to armed clashes among African states following independence. The efforts of the Somali to reunite with their lost brethren in Ethiopia, Kenya, and former French Somaliland is the most serious case to date, but there has been conflict between Morocco and its neighbors in the northwest and border disputes among various states in West Africa as well.

An even greater consequence of the boundary setting by European statesmen has been the inclusion of a great number and variety of ethnic groups within the borders of a single territory. In Zaire the number exceeds 40, in Tanzania there are over 120, and in Nigeria the estimate regarding distinct ethnic groupings runs close to 300. The number of political units involved actually exceeds these figures since many ethnic communities were fragmented and lacked an overarching political authority. Potentially, each ethnic group had its distinct language, economic and social system, religious values and organization, and ways of interacting with its neighbors. Some, which had sustained hostile relations over centuries before the European arrival, were compelled to maintain an uneasy truce under the umbrella of colonial rule. With independence, some of the suppressed animosity has flared into the open. In a few states the ethnic diversity is largely an inconvenience, which will erode in time. On the other hand, in Zaire, Nigeria, Sudan, Chad, Ethiopia, and Angola, major and prolonged civil wars have erupted, to which issues of ethnic, racial, or religious diversity have contributed. With the exception of a few relatively homogeneous states, such as Somalia, Lesotho, and Swaziland, Africa today consists not of some fifty nation-states, but rather of fifty states in search of fifty nations.

The immediate impact of national instability causes the diminution of the stature of an African state as a participant in the international arena. Not only are the existing resources drained in maintaining internal peace or in publishing the same government documents in different languages, but the ability of the country to extract minerals, grow export crops, and pursue other facets of modernization is seriously impeded. Instability is not limited to the country directly concerned, moreover, for it frequently has regional, continental, and even global implications. In the crisis of 1960 following the independence of Zaire, in the Biafran War of 1967-70, and again in 1976 with respect to Angola, instability in an African state invited the possibility of direct confrontation and conflict between the major non-African states or blocs who intervened in the dispute. In the process, too, the facade of African unity was destroyed as African states lined up in support of one side or another in the domestic conflict.

Although the artificial boundaries are a contributory factor to instability, most African leaders are committed to retaining them. Power has a way of perpetuating itself, and those who came to power within one political framework, no matter how artificial, are reluctant to risk losing power by redistributing territorial authority in accordance with ethnic, religious, and other factors. It is a significant fact that the only changes in the old colonial map of Africa that have been accomplished (British Togoland, French and British Cameroon, British and Italian Somaliland, Ethiopia and Eritrea, Spanish Sahara, and even the short-lived Mali Federation) took place when one or more of the group were still under colonial rule. Since independence, almost as a matter of self-preservation, African leaders have largely rejected the pursuit of irredentist claims as a never-ending problem which can only exacerbate relations among the new states. Similarly, they have tended to refuse recognition to each other's secessionist movements, since each state is vulnerable on that score. There is a realization, too, that the reconstitution of Africa along ethnic lines is all but impossible. Traditional political authority had eroded and ethnic boundaries had blurred under European rule. For better or for worse, Africans had achieved a measure of economic, cultural, and even political integration within the colonial framework. In any event, the "balkanization" of Africa into several hundred mini-states would make each of them even more vulnerable to some new form of colonial exploitation—whether from Western Europe, China, Russia, the United States, or possibly South Africa. In addition to strategic considerations, the redivision of Africa runs counter to the ideology of Pan-Africanism. This is an article of faith which envisions the ultimate political unity of all people on the African continent.

The greatest argument, however, is that the redivision of Africa would further frustrate efforts to achieve economic development. Even as presently constituted, there are few African states that possess within their own national borders even one or two of the ingredients needed for industrial growth. Given existing technology, those ingredients include oil, iron ore, coal, other forms of fuel—such as hydroelectric power or uranium—and the very essential ingredient of skilled manpower. Ironically, the few states that have the greatest prospects of industrialization are the very states which have had or are now suffering the greatest crises of national identity, racial conflict, or political instability. This includes South Africa, Nigeria, Angola, Zaire, and Rhodesia. The best that the majority of African states can hope for is the limited prosperity which comes from improvement in agricultural production and processing, or from the more vigorous exploitation of the mineral resources required by the more developed countries of the world. Either of these routes, however, is threatened by radical price fluctuation for agricultural and mineral commodities on the world market. Ghana realized this when it based too many of its development hopes on cocoa, and Zambia experienced the same fate as the price of copper drastically fell. Nevertheless, the agricultural and mineral-producing states are better off than the 30 least developed African states that are popularly referred to as members of the "Fourth World," 48 countries which, by various indices of underdevelopment, constitute the world's poorest nations (see figure 22).

FIGURE 22
"Fourth World" Countries
(African countries in italics)

Afghanistan	*Guinea-Bissau*	Nepal
Bangladesh	Guyana	*Niger*
Benin	Haiti	Pakistan
Bhutan	Honduras	*Rwanda*
Burma	India	*Senegal*
Burundi	*Ivory Coast*	*Sierra Leone*
Cameroon	*Kenya*	*Somalia*
Cape Verde Islands	Khmer Republic	Sri Lanka
Central African Republic	(Cambodia)	*Sudan*
Chad	Laos	*Tanzania*
Egypt	*Lesotho*	*Togo*
El Salvador	*Madagascar*	*Uganda*
Ethiopia	*Malawi*	*Upper Volta*
The Gambia	Maldive Islands	Western Samoa
Ghana	*Mali*	Yemen, Arab Republic
Guinea	*Mauritania*	Yemen, People's Republic
	Mozambique	

International Involvement: The Issues

Given the weaknesses of the African state system, the typical African nation finds itself at a disadvantage in dealing with the external world. This applies whether the African country is the object of friendly or hostile intervention or where it directly engages in international activities in pursuit of some desired goal. While most African states might hope to remain neutral or nonaligned with respect to such issues as the East-West conflict, the rivalry between Russia and China, and even the Israeli-Arab confrontation, they do not equate neutrality with isolationism. Despite the risks, the leaders of most African states feel compelled to involve themselves in international affairs in order to protect and expand their vital interests.

Foremost among these is the continuing assault against colonialism. African leaders assume that unless the campaign against colonialism everywhere in the world remains strident and unrelentless, there is always the possibility that it may reassert itself in the liberated areas of Africa. Leaders like Julius Nyerere and Kenneth Kaunda are prepared to sacrifice scarce resources to provide military assistance to guerrilla movements and relief to refugees from colonial oppression. In support of its ideological opposition to colonial rule in southern Africa, Zambia has been prepared to pay the higher price of having its copper shipped out through the longer and more expensive routes to the north rather than going through South Africa.

A second concern is the desire on the part of Africa's leaders to limit the direct solution of the continent's political problems to Africans themselves, unless Africans solicit external support. The efforts to establish a "Monroe Doctrine" for Africa, however, have not always been successful. There was widespread concern regarding the requested external intervention in the Congo during the 1960s, in the suppression by British and French paratroopers of army mutinies in East and West Africa during 1964, in the Biafran War of 1967-70, and in Angola during 1976. The involvement of external forces underscores the fundamental weakness of African military strength and reopens the possibility of Africa once again becoming an area of accommodation for the interests of non-African powers.

Growing out of the two preceding interests is a third major concern which transcends national boundaries in Africa. This is the desire to establish an African "presence" in global affairs and reestablish the dignity of black peoples. This has been fundamentally a reaction to the heritage of slavery. In the modern era blacks were the only people who were considered candidates for slavery in racial terms, and this went beyond the issue of the colonial experience, which Africans shared not only with other nonwhites but with whites as well. Africans in various international forums have thus become the champions of human rights, and they have urged the adoption of a "Convention to Eliminate Racial Discrimination" as a universal proposition. With regard to the continent specifically, Leopold Senghor's *Négritude* and Kwame Nkrumah's "African Personality" represent desires for acceptance of African cultural values by Africans as well as by the outside world. Pan-Africanism is the political and economic expression of the same concept.

The fourth vital interest which Africans seek to fulfill through involvement in international affairs is an improvement in their quality of life. Given the present level of economic development, most states lack the resources to cope with the problems of mass poverty, illiteracy, disease, and malnutrition which afflict the people of the continent. They seek not only direct and immediate international assistance in dealing with crisis situations, such as the sustained drought in the Sahel during the early 1970s, but long-term help as well. There are a variety of ways of approaching these problems. One method would be to achieve greater cooperation among African states themselves, so that political boundaries do not pose obstacles to the more rational utilization of the continent's resources. A second approach would be to secure technical assistance, low-interest development loans, private investment, and other forms of aid from the developed world, so that Africa's own industrial capacity could be raised. Still another approach would be to raise and stabilize the prices that the developed world has to pay for the agricultural and mineral resources needed to sustain industrialization. Commodity agreements on cocoa, copper, and other resources—similar to the arrangements achieved by OPEC (the Organization of Petroleum Exporting Countries)—could achieve a more equitable sharing of the world's wealth.

Some quality-of-life aspects of industrialization, such as pollution control and regulation of the birthrate by international action, seem not to concern many African leaders even though the problems of overpopulation, slum development, and lack of sanitation are already apparent in large cities such as Lagos. On the other hand, the United Nations Environmental Program has established its headquarters in Nairobi.

Finally, African states have involved themselves in international activities in order to deal with general problems of armed conflict. In recognition of the failure of the League of Nations to come to the rescue of Ethiopia in 1935, African states generally have supported the collective action machinery of the United Nations force. Although some African states subsequently regretted bringing the Cold War to Africa, many initially welcomed United Nations intervention in the Congo in 1960 and several provided troops to the peace-keeping effort. In addition, African states have supported proposals for disarmament, recognizing that the high cost of modern weaponry would undermine their economic development programs. Finally, African states have urged greater utilization of the International Court of Justice and other pacific means for the settlement of international disputes.

Arenas of International Relationships

The involvement of each African state in world affairs does not occur on a random basis. There are historic, economic, ideological, cultural, and other factors which contribute to the systematic patterning of international relationships. No two African states will have identical clusterings of external linkages. It is possible, however, to discern five general patterns of clustering which constitute the arena of international involvement for African states.

1. The Colonial Connection

The first of these arenas is based on the unique set of relationships which developed out of the colonial heritage. As time passes this may become an area of diminishing importance. In most cases, however, it was one of the strongest external linkages following the achievement of independence. The example of Guinea is a rarity. There, the rebuff of President Charles DeGaulle in the 1958 referendum on the French Community led to the abrupt and nearly complete rupture of ties with the metropole. Even where Africans had to fight for their independence, however, there has been a curious ambivalence in attitudes toward the former colonial power. African leaders may vilify the Europeans for the harshness of colonial rule and for the failure to develop their territory economically. Yet, there is an attachment to the European language, the educational system, the political structures, and even the culture of the colonial power.

In some countries, particularly those associated with France, the attachments are so intense that it has been frequently charged that these nations are victims of the dependency syndrome. A decade after independence, France continues to provide personnel to staff the army in Chad, run the banks in Ivory Coast, and assist in administering rural development projects in Niger and Upper Volta. The dependency syndrome is manifest by the fact that there are several times as many French technicians, businessmen, and others in Africa today as there were prior to 1960. France is still the major source of investment capital for most of its former colonies except Guinea and Mali. Typically, France buys more products from and sells more products to the former French colonies than does any other external power. While this may be neocolonialism, African leaders such as Félix Houphouet-Boigny would insist that the prosperity of Ivory Coast is proof of the wisdom of continuing to rely on this special relationship with France to secure the investment capital, technical skills, and ready markets for Ivorian products needed for modernization. What is said for the former French territories applies to a lesser degree to the relationship between Zaire and Belgium, Kenya and Britain, Ethiopia and Italy, and other states as well. Only a few, like Tanzania, have opted for a drastic reordering of their external ties.

Even the case of Tanzania, however, demonstrates the way in which the colonial legacy shapes more than the relationship between the former colony and the metropole. Independence automatically qualifies a former British territory for membership in the Commonwealth of Nations, which recognizes the British sovereign as the head of the Commonwealth. Although the white regimes of South Africa and Rhodesia have been denied admission, only Sudan among the black states of Africa has declined the option of membership in this strange association that embraces five continents. While the benefits of participation are often intangible, membership does provide the African state with a forum for voicing its opinions on international problems, with a more responsive source of assistance for economic or educational programs, with the privilege of Commonwealth preference in matters of trade among Commonwealth members, and with a number of agencies for achieving cooperation in scientific research, civil aviation, and telecommunications. Membership has also given the African states additional leverage in pressuring Britain in matters relating to South Africa and Rhodesia.

In the former French, Belgian, and Italian territories, continued association with the metropole considerably broadened their economic horizons in one area that was only belatedly open to former British territories in Africa: associate membership in the European Economic Community was accorded some African states under the Treaty of Rome (1958) and the Yaoundé Conventions (1963 and 1969). This gave these African states unique access to investment funds and markets within the West European area.

2. Relations Among African States

The colonial experience has also been a significant factor in the second arena of international activity, namely, the shaping of relations among independent African states. The most sustained contacts often take place between countries that were members of the same imperial system. This refers not only to bilateral transactions involving labor migration, educational exchange, and trade, but applies as well to multilateral and regional groupings of states. Thus most of the former French territories in Africa are loosely organized into OCAMM (*Organisation commune africaine, malgache, et mauricienne*), which achieves some cooperation in economic, military, transport, cultural, and diplomatic areas. One of the more publicized examples of regional economic cooperation in postindependence Africa is UDEAC (*Union douanière et économique de l'Afrique centrale*), which embraces Cameroon and most of the former territories in French Equatorial Africa. An even older example of sustained cooperation in the areas of transport, postal services, education, currency, customs, and scientific research involves the former British territories of Kenya, Uganda, Tanganyika, and Zanzibar. The foundations for the East African Community were laid more than a decade before independence. Unfortunately, both UDEAC and the East African Community have been weakened by ideological and nationalist differences and by the competitive industrial advantage which one of the members enjoys in each of these regional groupings.

Efforts to transcend the colonial boundaries and linkages in securing regional cooperation in economic or political matters have proved abortive. Kwame Nkrumah's plans to link Ghana with Guinea and Mali never went beyond the rhetoric stage. The Mano River Union involving Liberia and Sierra

Leone remains a paper organization. Similarly, the gesture of extending membership in the East African Community to Ethiopia, Somalia, Zaire, and Zambia was unsuccessful because of dissension among the three original members. It remains to be seen whether the Nigerian-promoted Economic Community of West African States can surmount the currency and linguistic differences or the basically competitive character of the agricultural economies of the fifteen member states.

The epitome of multilateralism in Africa, of course, is the almost universal commitment to pan-Africanism. The origin of the ideology antedates African independence by almost six decades and owes as much to West Indian and American blacks like W. E. B. DuBois and Marcus Garvey as it does to Blaise Diagne of Senegal, Kwame Nkrumah of Ghana, and other West African intellectuals. Pan-Africanism, however, is a complex ideology, and efforts to translate it into a concrete program of action have suffered from the variety of its interpreters. The desire to organize the entire continent into one political community is challenged by the counterpull of those who want to maintain extracontinental links with the former metropole. The Arab countries to the north, for example, share a far stronger set of traditions with nations of the Middle East than they do with the black African states south of the Sahara. Opinion diverges among Africans, moreover, on the question of whether economic and other forms of cooperation should precede political union, and whether efforts at regional cooperation should be a necessary prelude to continental action.

The launching of the Organization of African Unity in 1963 represented a compromise on the issues involved in pan-Africanism. It embraced the entire continent, but it was certainly not a political or economic union. Its major accomplishment thus far has been to halt the division of Africa into two hostile camps: the pro-Western states had adopted a moderate stance both on southern African liberation and on methods of achieving economic and social change; a second camp was inclined either to neutrality or to making common cause with Asian, Arab, and communist bloc countries in seeking more radical solutions to Africa's problems. The other major contribution of the OAU has been the creation of a forum where African leaders can discuss the solution of intra-African disputes. In general this has reduced external intervention, unless African states actually desire external help, as they have in the cases of Rhodesia, Namibia, and Angola. Finally, the OAU has provided its good offices in dealing with at least some of the border disputes, such as the one between Morocco and Algeria in 1963.

On the other hand, some of the difficult internal problems—Uganda and Tanzania, Somalia and its neighbors, the Biafran War, the conflict over the

Spanish Sahara, and the Angolan crisis of 1976—have found the machinery for pacific settlement of disputes to be ineffective. Indeed, public discussion of these issues has exposed the paper-thin facade of African unity. The organization, moreover, suffers from an absence of financial commitment on the part of member states. And the OAU has been less than effective in its campaign to isolate the white regime of South Africa from any kind of contact with other African states. It was unable to punish Malawi, which continued its ties with South Africa. Similarly, the OAU has not been able to prevent leaders of Ivory Coast, Liberia, and even Zambia from engaging in a policy of dialogue with South Africa.

3. *The Arena of the United Nations*

The significance of the third arena of international involvement, the United Nations, has already been noted in the discussion of African liberation. Membership in the world organization magnifies the importance of such small states as the Gambia or Botswana, which have the same vote in the General Assembly as does China or the United States. The growth of African representation from three seats in 1945 to fifty-one in 1977 has given it the largest voting bloc—roughly one-third of the General Assembly. The African bloc, in concert with

78. Angie Brooks of Liberia, President of the Twenty-fourth Session
of the General Assembly of the United Nations.
Photo courtesy United Nations/ Nagata/ jr.

the Arab and the Asian states, has had the United Nations Charter amended to give regular representation to the African bloc in the Security Council, the Economic and Social Council, the Secretariat, and the International Court of Justice. The African bloc has been fairly cohesive on issues such as colonial rule, opposition to South Africa, the need for multilateral economic assistance to the less developed countries, human rights, and disarmament. There is less cohesion, however, on other issues.

There are two areas in particular where African states still have high expectations with regard to the United Nations. The first area is the continued struggle against colonial rule in Rhodesia, Namibia, and South Africa. The earlier accomplishments of the United Nations in dealing with British, French, Belgian, and Italian colonialism in Africa have not properly prepared the organization to deal with the more intransigent white bastions in the south. The organization can take little credit for the ultimate withdrawal of the Portuguese. Similarly, a combination of factors and forces severely limited the effectiveness of the United Nations' economic boycott in dealing with the white regime in Rhodesia. The campaign against South Africa will be even more difficult, considering the peculiar character of "domestic colonialism," the size of the white dominant minority, and the industrial and other resources at its disposal. Efforts to isolate the white regime by denying it full representation in the various organs and agencies of the United Nations may have the effect of making it difficult to hold South Africa internationally accountable for its policies.

Africans also hope to secure United Nations help in the economic area. Technical assistance, development loans, and other aid given through the United Nations or its various agencies, such as the World Bank, are regarded with far greater favor than bilateral and even multilateral assistance given outside the world organization. There are fewer ideological strings attached to United Nations aid, and working through that organization gives an aura of universal support to what would otherwise appear to be purely African objectives. Unfortunately, the kind of financial support available through the United Nations' Economic Commission for Africa, the specialized agencies, and other United Nations economic groups is limited largely to what the more developed states are prepared to contribute.

4. *The Less Developed Countries*

Involvement of African states in the fourth arena, cooperation among the less developed countries of the world, takes place outside the framework of the United Nations as well as within that organization. The links of cooperation were forged during the preindependence era when Asian and Middle East states in the United Nations carried the burden of the attack against European colonialism in Africa. These bonds were sustained by such gatherings as the Bandung Conference of 1955 and the Afro-Asian Peoples' Solidarity Conference held in Cairo in 1957. The loose coalition moved beyond the attack on colonialism to a general assault on nuclear testing, Western military alliances, and the maldistribution of wealth between the industrialized societies of the West and the less developed world.

The coalition has highly diverse interests, and this has often been used to advantage in vote-swapping arrangements in the United Nations. The Arab countries, for example, have supported African states in their campaign to isolate Rhodesia and South Africa. In return, African nations have gradually broken their ties with Israel and have voted against the Israelis in the General Assembly and the specialized agencies of the United Nations. Solid support for the Arabs has been very costly for most African states, however, in the area of oil-pricing arrangements. With the exception of Nigeria, Angola, Algeria, and Libya, which are themselves significant producers of oil, most African states have found that the 500 percent increase in oil prices during the years 1973–76 has played severe havoc with all their development plans. There are other grounds as well for discord within the less developed group. India and Pakistan, for example, have been displeased with the treatment accorded Asians in Kenya and Uganda. In approaching the question of economic redistribution, moreover, the African states want to maintain their special relationship with Western Europe, while similar attachments prevail regarding Latin America and the United States, Asian countries and Japan, and the orientation of communist bloc countries to either Russia or China. Thus, the Third World is not a monolith, and many African states have found that the coalition's bargaining cards are often very weak.

Despite the internal dissension among the underdeveloped group, some progress has been made regarding the question of a more equitable sharing of the world's wealth. Starting with the meeting of the first United Nations Conference on Trade and Development (UNCTAD) in 1968, the 110 poorer countries of the world have been making a serious demand on the industrial nations. Much of their concern focuses on the fluctuation of prices for agricultural and mineral commodities which Africa, Latin America, and Asia sell to industrial countries. What they seek is the establishment of buffer stocks of key commodities, which would be financed by a common fund to which producer and user countries would contribute. When the oversupply of a commodity threatens to break the market, the excess is purchased and stored. Conversely, when prices threaten to soar, supplies are sold from the stockpile. The less developed countries would also like to abolish duties on goods manufactured in their countries so that they could capture a larger share of the world's trade. They would, furthermore, like to tie the prices of commodities exported by the less developed states to the prices of manufactured goods imported from the industrial world. They insist, too, that transfer of technology and increase in interest-free loans should be financed by the industrial powers through a lowering of the general level of military expenditures. Finally, they seek the cancellation of the international debts of the poorest countries. Since the industrial states are increasingly dependent on the nonindustrialized countries for most of their strategic raw materials, the wealthier nations may be at the point of negotiating prices more acceptable to Third World nations. In paraphrasing Abraham Lincoln, one American spokesman at UNCTAD IV in Nairobi in 1976 said: "It is clear to us all that this world cannot indefinitely endure half-rich and half-poor."

5. *Relations with the Major Powers*

The fifth arena for international involvement, bilateral and multilateral contacts with major world powers other than the West European states, is far less patterned than the preceding four. The continued dependence on former colonial powers for assistance and the reluctance of African leaders to bring the Cold War to the continent have limited the kind of contact that African states have had with the United States, the Soviet Union, and the People's Republic of China. Indeed, it has been far easier for trade, aid, and other kinds of relationships to be established with second level world powers—such as the Scandinavian states, Japan, India, West Germany, Yugoslavia, and, at least for a time, even Israel—who appear to be more neutral insofar as East-West conflict is concerned.

Despite the efforts of African states to establish a "Monroe Doctrine" for the settlement of continental crises, a number of situations have directly involved the major powers in Africa's affairs. The United States, for example, was one of the major supporters in the 1960s of the United Nations force in the Congo crisis, a situation which ultimately led to a direct confrontation with the Soviet Union. As recently as 1976, the Angola crisis once again raised the specter of a direct confrontation between American-supported groups and the Russian- and Cuban-supported government of Angola. In addition to these two crises, the Russians and the Chinese have been supplying arms to various southern African liberation movements; the Russians have established a naval base in Somalia; the United States has been training African military officers from various countries as well as maintaining until 1977 a military installation in Ethiopia and renewing a defense agreement with Liberia. Whether the allegations were true or not, at various times during the period since 1960 the Chinese were expelled from Burundi, the Russians from Guinea, and the Americans from Uganda—to name only a few instances in which the three major powers have been accused of intervention in the domestic affairs of an African state.

Unpredictable as the relationship might be, African states individually have turned to one or more of the major powers for economic, military, and other forms of assistance. The decision may be based upon several considerations. It may be the expectation that the major powers are greater sources than Western Europe for investment capital, technical personnel, and other forms of aid, particularly at a time when Western Europe is turning inward to the solution of its own problems of economic and political integration. Seeking aid from the United States or Russia may also be a symbolic act on the part of African states in an effort to break the dependency link with France, Britain, or Belgium. Finally, it may constitute an attempt to control the shape of the future by inviting in a great number of external donors so that no single power or bloc has a preponderant influence. This was the pattern that Ethiopia established after it was liberated from Italian domination, and it is one emulated by Tanzania, which has widely diversified its sources of external assistance.

The interests of the major powers in Africa are varied. Many of the raw materials needed to sustain industrial development in the United States, Russia, and China can only be obtained in suitable quantities from Africa. All three powers have an interest in obtaining ideological allies or at least the neutralization of Africa when the vital goals of the major power become the subject of debate in the United Nations or other international forums. When it comes to trade and aid agreements, however, each of the major powers is selective in deciding where it can make the most significant impact. The Chinese, through the construction of the Tan-Zam railway, for example, have established very strong ties with Tanzania. The United States has special links with Liberia, Zaire, Zambia, and Nigeria. Indeed, Nigeria in recent years has become one of the single most important suppliers of imported crude oil into the United States. Russia has had significant ideological impact in Africa through its support of African liberation movements, while the United States has suffered diplomatically because of its very strong economic links with South Africa and its importation of chrome from Rhodesia.

Conclusion

The years since 1960 have witnessed the emergence of the African continent as an area of importance in world politics, and events in Africa serve as front-page headlines in the world press. In a number of areas African political leaders have been successful: for example, in keeping alive the campaign against colonial rule in southern Africa, in efforts to restrict external intervention in Africa's affairs, and in the establishment of an African "presence" in world affairs. They seem to be making limited progress in their efforts to redress the balance between the wealthier and the poorer nations of the globe.

Participation in the multiple arena of international politics, however, has not been without its attendant costs. Colonial rule left most African states with a very limited pool of educated manpower. It has been charged that international involvement has claimed a disproportionate share of the elite's attention to the neglect of pressing domestic problems, such as economic development, the creation of stable political structures, urban planning, health care delivery, and various programs of social reform. Political instability, moreover, has led to the emergence of military regimes. The latter, in encountering the same difficulties faced by their civilian predecessors, are far more likely to turn to military adventurism as a way of diverting attention from domestic failure. The example of General Idi Amin, who has managed to antagonize most of his neighbors, may not be an isolated case. Africa could suffer the fate of Latin American continental politics by being beset with a series of never-ending border wars.

Activism in global politics is a high-risk venture. There is a great danger that African states may mistake their numerical voting strength in the United Nations for real power. Whether it be population, industrial development, military organization, mineral and agricultural resource base, or any other index of power, African states, both individually and collectively, are at the deficient end of the scale. Thus Africa's fifty-one votes may commit the United Nations to a course of action which the more powerful states are not prepared to pursue. Involvement, moreover, in the solution of other people's problems does invite reciprocity. The major powers cannot be expected to stand by passively while African leaders take activist stances contrary to positions which the major powers adopt on certain international issues. This has happened in such cases as the administration of Puerto Rico and the recognition of the nationalist regime on Taiwan by the United States and the Russian reoccupation of Czechoslovakia. Involvement in global problems may seriously weaken the success of a policy of nonalignment.

Above all, what must be kept in mind in assessing Africa's new role as an area of consequence in world affairs is that the experience is all too brief. This chapter has attempted to delineate patterns based upon little more than a decade of African participation in five different arenas of international politics. It is a dynamic situation. Thus, description of the kaleidoscopic present is only slightly less hazardous than prediction regarding the future.

SUGGESTIONS FOR FURTHER READING

Cervenka, Zkenek. *The Organisation of African Unity and Its Charter.* New York: Praeger, 1969.

El-Ayouty, Yassin, and Hugh C. Brooks, eds. *Africa and International Organization.* The Hague: Martinus Nijhoff, 1974.

Emerson, Rupert. *Africa and United States Policy.* Englewood Cliffs, New Jersey: Prentice-Hall, 1967.

Keesing's Research Report, No. 6. *Africa Independent: A Study of Political Developments.* New York: Scribner's, 1972.

Hamrell, Sven, ed. *Refugee Problems in Africa.* Uppsala: Scandinavian Institute of African Studies, 1967.

Larkin, Bruce D. *China and Africa.* Berkeley: University of California Press, 1971.

Mazrui, Ali A., and Hasu Patel. *Africa in World Affairs: The Next Thirty Years.* New York: Third Press, 1973.

Mutharika, B. W. T. *Toward Multinational Economic Cooperation in Africa.* New York: Praeger, 1972.

Nielsen, Waldemar A. *The Great Powers and Africa.* New York: Praeger, 1969.

Welch, Claude E. *Dream of Unity: Pan-Africanism and Political Unification in West Africa.* Ithaca, New York: Cornell University Press, 1966.

Widstrand, Carl Gosta. *African Boundary Problems.* Uppsala: Scandinavian Institute of African Studies, 1969.

Zartman, I. William. *International Relations in the New Africa.* Englewood Cliffs, New Jersey: Prentice-Hall, 1966.

Jean E. Meeh Gosebrink
Bibliography and Sources for African Studies

THERE IS NO NEED to be ignorant about Africa today, in view of the availability of a cumulative body of literature and data about the continent: the manuscripts written by Africans; the descriptions of travelers, missionaries, traders, colonial administrators, and other visitors to Africa; the research of anthropologists, historians, political scientists, and other scholars; the reports of government bodies and international agencies. The greatest amount of this literature has been published in the past twenty-five years. There is also an increasing amount of literature about Africa being written today by African scholars, statesmen, and poets.

The purpose of this compilation of source materials is to provide an introduction to some of the basic reference works and periodicals for African Studies and to suggest titles for further reading. This bibliography cannot attempt to be comprehensive. However, the bibliographies, guides, and periodicals listed here may be used by those who wish to find further information on specific aspects of Africa which interest them. This bibliography is arranged under topical headings which follow closely but not exactly the chapter titles in the text. The books listed for further reading include suggestions made by the authors of the preceding chapters. A variety of viewpoints is represented. It should be remembered that the study of Africa is inter-disciplinary and that subjects and disciplines may therefore overlap in many of the works listed.

For most topics, references are given for (1) bibliographies, abstracts, indexes, guides, and other reference aids; (2) major journals in the field; (3) suggestions for further reading. With a few exceptions, the works listed have been published in the past ten years, and many were in print at the time this compilation was prepared. American editions, if available, are cited and paperback editions (Pbk) are noted.

Contents

African Culture and Background

Africa is a complex cultural area, a continent marked by variety and diversity. Yet a few writers have attempted to explain the shared cultural patterns and values which they have seen in Black Africa and to present the underlying unity in African culture. Suggested for further reading for those interested in this area are:

Bohannan, Paul, and Philip D. Curtin. *Africa and Africans.* Rev. ed. Garden City, N.Y.: Published for the Museum of Natural History by the Natural History Press, 1971. Pbk.

Davidson, Basil. *The African genius: an introduction to African cultural and social history.* Boston: Little Brown, 1970. Pbk.

Diop, Cheikh Anta. *The origin of African civilization: myth or reality?* New York: Laurence Hill, 1974. Pbk.

Maquet, Jacques. *Africanity: the cultural unity of black Africa.* New York, London: Oxford University Press, 1972. Pbk.

Mazrui, Ali A. *World culture and the black experience.* Seattle: University of Washington Press, 1974. Pbk.

Sofola, Johnson O. *African culture and African personality; what makes an African person African.* Ibadan, Nigeria: African Resources Publishers, 1973.

General Reference Sources

Africa south of the Sahara. 1971–. London: Europa Publications. Annual.

An annual compendium of information, with essays on various aspects of Africa: a directory to the continent's regional organizations; country surveys, which include brief historical sketches, economic information, statistics, and directories to government, diplomatic representation, political parties, religious organizations, financial and commercial institutions, the media, educational institutions, and the like. Also featured are a "who's who," a section on primary commodities, a list of research institutes concerned with Africa, and various maps.

Area handbook series. Washington, D.C.: Government Printing Office.

These country handbooks, prepared by the Foreign Area Studies of The American University, Washington, D.C., and published by the U.S. Government Printing Office, aim to be "convenient compilations of basic facts about social, economic, political, and military institutions and practices of various countries. The emphasis is on objective description of the nation's present society and the kinds of possible or probable changes that might be expected in the future." Handbooks exist for about thirty African nations, the latest being Malawi, Guinea, and Southern Rhodesia (all 1975) and Egypt (1976). Each handbook includes an extensive bibliography.

Dickie, John, and Alan Rake. *Who's who in Africa: the political, military and business leaders of Africa*. London: African Development, 1973.

Dictionary of black African civilization. New York: Leon Amiel, 1974.

Prepared under the direction of Jacques Maquet and Georges Balandier. Entries under headings such as adornment, ancestors, fauna, games, initiation, masks; emphasis on traditional Africa; well illustrated.

MacDonald's encyclopedia of Africa. London: MacDonald, 1976.

Although as yet unseen, the periodical *West Africa* gave this reference work a good review (26 June 1976): "Aspects of the continent are covered in 'thematic' chapters: People, Economy, Social Services, Landscapes, Wildlife, Arts, Sports, History, Government . . . supplemented by three reference sections: 'A guide to Peoples and Languages of Africa' containing more than 1500 entries; a 'Gazetteer' in which the 450 entries include extended articles on each country, with shorter entries on interesting places; and a 'Who's who', with 250 entries of personalities past and present."

Nguyen, Chi-Bonnardel, Regine. *The atlas of Africa*. New York: Free Press, 1973.

Prepared by the editors of *Jeune Afrique* in Paris, this is the first comprehensive atlas of the continent to appear in twenty years. The first section of maps and explanatory content on such features as population, geology, climate, vegetation, languages, history, agriculture, communications, and so forth, is followed by a section of regional and country maps. There is a gazetteer and an index of geographical terms.

GUIDES TO AFRICAN STUDIES IN THE UNITED STATES

AF-Log: *African interests of American organizations*. Edited by the African Bibliographic Center and Development Alternatives. Washington, D.C.: African Biblographic Center, 1976. (*Its* Current reading list series, v. 11 no. 2.)

"A comprehensive and selected directory of academic institutions, nonprofit and profit-making corporations of all types with an active interest in Africa."

Directory of African and Afro-American studies in the United States. 5th ed. Compiled by Mitsue Frey and Michael Sims. Waltham, Mass.: African Studies Association, 1976.

Lists courses, faculty, library collections, financial aid, and areas of specialization for 623 principal universities and colleges with African Studies courses and about 300 subsidiary entries listing school and courses.

Duignan, Peter. *Handbook of American resources for African studies*. Stanford, Calif.: Hoover Institution, 1967.

Descriptions of 302 library, archival and museum collections.

BIBLIOGRAPHIES:

The African experience. Edited by John N. Paden and Edward W. Soja. v. IIIa: Bibliography. Evanston: Northwestern University Press, 1970. Pbk.

Contains over 4000 references under topical and country headings. Other volumes in this set include: v. I. Essays, the essays of 27 contributors, all who have taught African studies in American universities, to show the state of current research in a number of disciplines; v. II. Syllabus; v. IIIb. Guide to resources.

Duignan, Peter, ed. *Guide to research and reference works on sub-Saharan Africa.* Compiled by Helen F. Conover and Peter Duignan, with the assistance of Evelyn Boyce, Liselotte Hofmann, and Karen Fung. Stanford, Calif.: Hoover Institution, 1972. (Hoover Institution. Bibliographical series, 46.) Pbk.

Of major importance. It lists 3,127 bibliographies, guides, indexes, and other reference works, as well as essential serials and monographs, all annotated, in four sections: part I, guide to research organizations, libraries and archives, and the book trade; part II, bibliographies for Africa general; part III, subject guide in general; and part IV, area guide by former colonial power, region, and country. The *Guide* has been supplemented and expanded upon by Hans E. Panofsky's A *bibliography of Africana* (Westport, Conn.: Greenwood Press, 1975).

Hartwig, Gerald W., and William M. O'Barr. *The student Africanist's handbook: a guide to resources.* Cambridge, Mass.: Schenckman, 1974. Pbk.

A guide and bibliography especially useful for beginning students of African Studies.

CONTINUING BIBLIOGRAPHIES:

The following bibliographies are all published at regular intervals and thus give up-to-date information on new books and articles. The book reviews and lists of books currently received in many periodicals also provide another way of keeping up with new publications.

African book publishing record. 1975–. Oxford (P.O. Box 56, Oxford OX1 3EL, England). Quarterly.

Attempts to give "comprehensive coverage of new and forthcoming books published in Africa"; also articles on African publishers and publishing in Africa.

Africana journal. 1970–. New York: Africana Publishing Corp. Quarterly. (Formerly *Africana Library Journal.*)

Book reviews, bibliographic essays and longer bibliographies; current listings.

Current bibliography on African affairs. 1963–. Farmingdale, N.Y.: Baywood Publishing Co. for the African Bibliographic Center. Quarterly.

Book reviews, bibliographies, and bibliographic essays; listings under subject and country: of special interest are its listings under "African heritage studies."

International African bibliography. 1971–. London: International African In-
    stitute. Quarterly.

Coverage of books, articles, conference papers, reports, etc. The International
African Institute also has promised to reinstitute its *African abstracts* (1950–1972),
twice yearly, in 1978.

PERIODICALS:

Africa report. 1956–. New York: African-American Institute. Bimonthly.

Articles on various subjects of political, social, economic and artistic interest; frequent interviews with African statesmen, scholars, etc.; U.S.-African relations, attitudes, policies; a regular feature is "African update," a monitoring service for economic and political developments around the continent.

Africa today. 1956–. Denver: Graduate School of International Affairs, Uni-
    versity of Denver. Quarterly.

Articles analyzing current political and economic events; essays on the arts and
culture; issues are often centered on a theme, as Mozambique independence or
famine in Africa; book reviews.

African affairs. 1901–. London: Royal African Society. Quarterly. (Formerly
    Journal of the Royal African Society.)

African social, economic and political affairs; lengthy book review section; special features include a bibliography of new titles on Africa and a "Select list of articles
on Africa appearing in non-Africanist periodicals."

African studies review. 1958–. Waltham, Mass.: African Studies Association.
    (Formerly *African studies bulletin.*)

Multidisciplinary journal with scholarly articles.

Issue. 1971–. Waltham, Mass.: African Studies Association. Quarterly.

Generally concerned with matters of political and social interest, although a
number of commentaries on African literature and letters have been published.

Journal of African studies. 1974–. Los Angeles: University of California Press
    for the UCLA African Studies Center. Quarterly.

Contributions on all aspects of African Studies, especially the results of recent
research.

Présence africaine. 1947–. Paris: Présence Africaine. Quarterly.

Published in French and English since 1967; a cultural review with articles on
political, economic, and social matters, history, poetry, literature; book reviews.

Transition. 1961–. Accra: Ghana Transition Ltd., in association with the Inter-
    national Association for Cultural Freedom (c/o Standard Bank, P.O. Box
    768, Accra, Ghana). Quarterly.

Known for its provocative articles on all aspects of life in Africa; now under the
editorship of the Nigerian writer Wole Soyinka.

Ufahamu. 1970–. Los Angeles: African Activist Association, African Studies Center, UCLA. 3 x yr.

A student publication, with contributions ranging from scholarly articles, book reviews, to freelance writing, poetry, and fiction.

Statistics

The best sources of statistical information from Africa are the official statistical annuals and other statistical publications issued by individual governments. The U.N. Economic Commission for Africa, located in Addis Ababa, Ethiopia, publishes a number of statistical bulletins and reports, such as its *Statistical and economic bulletin for Africa, Economic bulletin for Africa, African statistical yearbook,* and various other publications on trade, commercial, agricultural, economic, and demographic statistics. In its annual *Summaries of economic data* series, brief pamphlets provide recent figures in a number of areas for each African country. The Commission also is the source of the *Bibliography of African statistical publications (1950–1965),* which has been updated to 1973. The *Statistical yearbook of the United Nations* and the *Unesco statistical yearbook* also remain important sources.

A comprehensive set of statistics which allow for a comparison of nations, especially the developing countries, can be found in the *World handbook of political and social indicators,* now in its second edition. Comparative statistics and data for 32 nations of Black Africa are presented in *Black Africa: a comparative handbook.*

BIBLIOGRAPHIES:

Harvey, Joan M. *Statistics Africa: sources for market research.* Beckenham, Kent, Eng.: CBD Research Ltd., 1970.

U.N. Economic Commission for Africa. Library. *Bibliography of African statistical publications, 1950–1965.* Addis Ababa; 1966. (E/CN.14/LIB/SER.C/2)

———. *Bibliography . . . 1966–1973.* Addis Ababa; 1973. (E/CN.14/LIB/SER.C/6)

Listing of statistical publications of African countries, including censuses.

SOURCES:

Black Africa: a comparative handbook. By Donald G. Morrison, Robert C.

Mitchell, John N. Paden, and Hugh M. Stevenson. New York: Free Press, 1972.

Divided into three parts: part I contains data on 172 variables, such as area, population, population increase, languages, religions, GDP, literacy rates, political regime characteristics, etc.; part II gives country profiles; part III, cross-national research on Africa.

U.N. Economic Commission for Africa. *Statistical and economic bulletin for Africa*. 1972–. Addis Ababa, Ethiopia.

————. *Economic bulletin for Africa*. 1961–. Addis Ababa, Ethiopia. Irreg.
Contains most recent statistics.

————. *African statistical yearbook*. Addis Ababa, Ethiopia. 4 pts. Annual.

U.N. Statistical Office. *Statistical yearbook*. 1948–. New York, 1949–. Annual.
Master digest of statistics for over 200 countries.

Unesco. *Unesco statistical yearbook*. 1963–. Paris. Annual.

Data on areas and populations, education, libraries and museums, book production, newspapers, media, and cultural expenditures.

World handbook of political and social indicators. By Charles L. Taylor and Michael C. Hudson. 2d. ed. New Haven: Yale University Press, 1972.

Population / Demography

The size, character, and growth of a population—its rates for births, deaths, infant mortality; its data on migratory changes and patterns—are important factors in explaining and planning for economic and social development. In Africa, despite numerous censuses, the data for population study remains uncertain.

CONTINUING BIBLIOGRAPHY:

Population index. 1935–. Princeton, N.J.: Office of Population Research. Princeton University and Population Association of America. Quarterly.
Annotated bibliography covering books, articles, and official publications.

BIBLIOGRAPHIES:

African Bibliographic Center. AFRIECON. *Population Problems in Africa*. Washington, D.C.: 1973. (*Its* Current reading list series, v. 10, no. 7.)
Resources published between 1969 and 1973, with an emphasis on attitudinal factors.

Radel, David. *Population in sub-Saharan Africa, 1965–1971*. Chapel Hill, North Carolina: Carolina Population Center, University of North Carolina, 1973.

SOURCES:

U.N. Economic Commission for Africa. *African population news.* 1970–. Addis Ababa.

———. *Demographic handbook for Africa.* 3d. ed. Addis Ababa: 1974.

U.N. Statistical Office. *Demographic yearbook.* 1948–. New York, 1949–. Annual.

SUGGESTIONS FOR FURTHER READING:

Caldwell, John C., and Chukuka Okonjo, eds. *The population of tropical Africa.* London: Longmans, 1968.

"A record of the first African Population Conference sponsored by the University of Ibadan, in co-operation with the Population Council and held at the University of Ibadan, Nigeria, 3–7 Jan. 1966."

Hance, William A., ed. *Population, migration and urbanization in Africa.* New York: Columbia University Press, 1970.

Ominde, S. H., and C. N. Ejiogu, eds. *Population growth and economic development in Africa.* London: Heinemann, in association with the Population Council, 1972.

A collection of papers presented at the Seminar on Population Growth and Economic Development held at the University of Nairobi, Kenya, from 14 to 22 December 1969.

The Population factor in African studies. Edited by R. P. Moss and R. J. A. R. Rathbone. London: University of London Press, 1975.

According to a review in *African affairs* (1976), this work "has tapped the resources of able scholars from various population-related fields . . ." ranging from historians, linguists, anthropologists, economists, to demographers and ecologists.

The African Environment

The drought of 1973–74 throughout the Sahel and eastern Africa focused the world's attention and concern on the "delicate balance between man and nature" in the African environment. One response to the drought was the establishment of an Environmental Review Unit by the International African Institute in London in order to study famine and food supply in the context of environmental change and economic development. The titles edited by Dalby and Richards, and the journal *African environment,* have been issued under its auspices. A research program and subsequent publications are also planned.

Other works are also listed, including a number of geographical overviews of the African landscape, its peoples and resources, and their relationships to one another.

CONTINUING BIBLIOGRAPHIES:

Bibliographie geographique internationale . . . Bibliographie annuelle. 1891–. Paris, 1894–. Annual. (Published since 1954 by the Centre national de Recherches scientifique.)

Current geographical publications. 1938–. New York: American Geographical Society. Monthly, except July and August.

Geo abstracts. 1966–. Norwich: University of East Anglia. 6 series, each with 6 nos. a year.

The series are: A. Landforms and the Quaternary; B. Biogeography and climatology; C. Economic geography; D. Social geography; E. Sedimentology; F. Regional and community planning.

BIBLIOGRAPHIES:

Bederman, Sanford H. *Africa, a bibliography of geography and related disciplines; a selected listing of recent literature published in the English language.* 3d ed. Atlanta: Publishing Services Division, School of Business Administration, Georgia State University, 1974.

Harmons, V. Alvin. "Land-use: a select bibliography." *Rural africana,* no. 23 (Winter 1974): 91–96.

Odimuko, C. L., and Diana Bouchard. *Urban geography of Africa.* Montreal: Centre for Developing Area Studies, McGill University, 1973.

Sommer, John W. *Bibliography of African geography, 1940–1964.* Hanover, N.H.: Dartmouth College, Dept. of Geography, 1965.

PERIODICALS:

African environment. 1975–. Dakar: Environment Training Program, in association with the International African Institute. Quarterly. (First issue entitled *Environment in Africa.*)

". . . environmental studies and regional planning bulletin"; bilingual in English and French; book reviews and bibliographies.

Cahiers d'outre-mer. 1948–. Bordeaux: Institut de Géographie, Faculté des Lettres, Université de Bordeaux. Quarterly.

Studies in human geography.

SUGGESTIONS FOR FURTHER READING:

Church, R. J. Harrison. *West Africa: a study of the environment and man's use of it.* 7th ed. London: Longman, 1974. Pbk.

Dalby, David, R. J. Harrison Church, and Fatima Bezzazz, eds. *Drought in*

Africa. London: International African Institute, 1975. (African environment special report.)

"The volume with contributions from a wide range of contributors in Africa and elsewhere, is designed to review the causes and effects of the recent Sudano-Sahelian drought . . . , the effectiveness of relief programmes and the lessons and alternatives in the future for semi-arid lands in Africa."

de Souza, Anthony R., and Philip W. Porter. *The underdevelopment and modernization of the Third World.* Washington, D.C.: Association of American Geographers, Commission on College Geography, 1974. (Resource paper, no. 28.)

Gourou, Pierre. *The tropical world: its social and economic conditions and its future status.* 4th ed. London: Longmans, 1966. Pbk: New York: Halstead Press, 1974.

Hance, William A. *The geography of modern Africa.* 2d. ed. New York: Columbia University Press, 1975.

Knight, C. Gregory. *Ecology and change: rural modernization in an African community.* New York: Academic Press, 1974.

Mabogunje, Akin. "Manufacturing and the geography of development in tropical Africa." *Economic geography,* v. 49, no. 1 (Jan. 1973): 1–20.

McNulty, Michael L. "West African urbanization." In: Berry, B. J. L., ed. *Patterns of urbanization and counterurbanization.* Beverly Hills, Calif.: Sage Publications, 1976 (Urban affairs annual review, v. X.)

Morgan, W. T. W., ed. *East Africa: its peoples and resources.* 2d. ed. Nairobi, London, New York: Oxford University Press, 1972.

Prothero, R. Mansell, ed. *Peoples and land in Africa south of the Sahara.* New York: Oxford University Press, 1972.

Richards, Paul, ed. *The African environment: problems and perspectives.* London: International African Institute, 1975. (African environment special report, 1.)

History

As John D. Fage has written, "It is only since about 1950 that historians have really begun to engage in coherent study of the history of Africa and its peoples." And it is only more recently that histories synthesizing the broad array of new knowledge and information have been attempted. To mention only two, Robin Hallett in two volumes has provided a readable, yet scholarly, treatment of African history, and the new *Cambridge history of Africa,* a multivolumed effort, with chapters written by a number of experts, promises to be a "serious appraisal of Africa's past."

CONTINUING BIBLIOGRAPHIES:

Historical abstracts: a bibliography of the world's periodical literature. 1955–. Santa Barbara, Calif.: American Bibliographic Center–Clio Press. Quarterly.

Part A: Modern history abstracts, 1775–1914; Part B: Twentieth century abstracts, 1914 to the present.

International bibliography of historical sciences. 1926–. Paris: Colin, for the International Committee of Historical Sciences. Annual.

BIBLIOGRAPHY:

Current themes in African historical studies: a selected bibliographical guide to resources for research in African history. Edited by Daniel G. Matthews. Westport, Conn.: Greenwood Press, 1970. (African Bibliographic Center. Special bibliographic series, v. 7, no. 2.)

Includes: "Toward a bibliography of medieval West Africa," by Samir M. Zoghby; "Current themes in African historical studies," by the African Bibliographic Center; "Topics on the African diaspora," by Rafael L. Cortada and Wayne A. Selcher.

PERIODICALS:

African economic history review. 1974–. Madison, Wisconsin: Department of History, University of Wisconsin. 2 x yr.

International journal of African historical studies. 1968–. New York: Africana Publishing Corp. Quarterly. (Formerly *African historical studies.*)

Journal of African history. 1960–. London: Cambridge University Press. Quarterly.

Major scholarly source for research, theory, and reviews.

Tarikh. 1965–. Ikeja, Nigeria: Published for the Historical Society of Nigeria by Longman and in the U.S.A. by Humanities Press. 2 x yr.

"Readable" journal of African history for use in schools, colleges, and universities: each issue devoted to a theme, such as independence movements, African resistance, etc.

Transafrican journal of history. 1971–. Nairobi: East African Publishing House. 2 x yr.

Articles on the history of eastern and southeastern Africa.

REFERENCE:

Fage, John D. *An atlas of African history.* London: E. Arnold, 1963. Reprint with amendments of 1958 ed.

Freeman-Grenville, G. S. P. *A modern atlas of African history.* London: Rex Collings, 1976.

SUGGESTIONS FOR FURTHER READING:

Ajayi, J. F. A., and Michael Crowder, eds. *History of West Africa.* New York: Columbia University Press, 1972–74. 2 v. Pbk. Revised ed. of vol. I published in 1976.

Atmore, Anthony, and Roland Oliver. *Africa since 1900.* 2d ed. Cambridge, Eng.: Cambridge University Press, 1972. Pbk.

Bennett, Norman R. *Africa and Europe from Roman times to the present.* New York: Africana Publishing Corp., 1975. Pbk.

Bovill, E. W. *The golden trade of the Moors.* 2d ed. London: Oxford University Press, 1968. Pbk.

Cambridge history of Africa. Edited by John D. Fage and Roland Oliver. Cambridge, Eng.: Cambridge University Press. 7 volumes expected.
   At time of writing only v. 4 has been published.

Collins, Robert O., ed. *Problems in African history.* Englewood Cliffs, N.J.: Prentice-Hall, 1968. Pbk.

Davidson, Basil. *Africa: history of a continent.* Rev. ed. New York; Macmillan, 1972.

————. *Africa in history: themes and outlines.* Rev. ed. New York; Macmillan, 1974. Pbk.

————. *A history of East and Central Africa.* Garden City, N.Y.: Doubleday Anchor, 1967. Pbk.

————. *A history of West Africa.* Garden City, N.Y.: Doubleday Anchor, 1966. Pbk.

Hallett, Robin. *Africa since 1875: a modern history.* Ann Arbor: University of Michigan Press, 1974.

————. *Africa to 1875: a modern history.* Ann Arbor: University of Michigan Press, 1970.
   Both volumes accompanied by lengthy bibliographic essays.

The Horizon history of Africa. Edited by Alvin M. Josephy. New York: American Heritage Press, 1971. 2 v.

July, Robert W. *A history of the African people.* Rev. ed. New York: Scribners, 1974. Pbk.

Murphy, E. Jefferson. *History of African civilization*. New York: Crowell, 1972.
    Pbk: New York: Dell Delta, 1974.
Ogot, Bethwell A., and J. A. Kieran, eds. *Zamani; a survey of East African his-*
    tory. New York: Humanities Press, 1968. Pbk.
Rodney, Walter. *A history of the Upper Guinea Coast, 1545–1800*. London;
    New York: Oxford University Press, 1970.
Rotberg, Robert O., and H. Neville Chittick, eds. *East Africa and the Orient;*
    cultural synthesis in pre-colonial times. New York: Africana Publishing
    Corp., 1975.

Reconstructing the African Past:
Historical Methodology in African History

With only a limited number of written records on Africa, the study of the
African past has depended more than that of other areas on unwritten evidence:
archaeology, ethnography and anthropology, linguistics, oral tradition, ethnomusicology, art, ethnomedicine, ethnobotany. Using these kinds of data, historians have been able to expand our knowledge of African history. (It should
also be noted that in the past fifteen to twenty years numerous unknown written records, mainly in Arabic script from Islamized areas of Africa, have been
discovered.) *History in Africa* is a new periodical dedicated to exploring the
uses of such methods.

PERIODICAL:

History in Africa: a journal of method. 1974–. Waltham, Mass.: African Studies
    Association. Annual.
    "Articles on source criticism and evaluation, the nature of history and historical
thought, surveys of historiography of themes and events, archival and bibliographical reports; review essays of methodological works; studies of historical problems
which are comparative in focus or approach." Includes a regular bibliography on comparative historical methodology.

SUGGESTIONS FOR FURTHER READING:

Henige, David P. *The chronology of oral tradition: quest for a chimera*. Oxford:
    Clarendon Press, 1974.
McCall, Daniel F. *Africa in time perspective: a discussion of historical recon-*
    struction from unwritten sources. Boston: Boston University Press, 1964.
    Pbk: Oxford University Press, 1969.
Reconstructing African culture history. Edited by Creigton Gabel and Norman
    R. Bennett. Boston: Boston University Press, 1967.

Vansina, Jan. *The oral tradition*. Chicago: Aldine, 1964. Pbk: Harmondsworth: Penguin.

————. *Kingdoms of the savanna*. Madison: University of Wisconsin Press, 1966. Pbk.

Prehistory

The dramatic discoveries of the Leakeys in eastern Africa indicate that Africa is the birthplace of mankind. In addition to the search for the origins of man in the Rift Valley, archaeological research has concerned itself with such questions as the interpretation of rock art, the Iron and Stone ages, the beginnings of agriculture, the contacts between Asia and Africa, and trade.

CONTINUING BIBLIOGRAPHY:

Abstracts in anthropology. 1970–. Farmingdale, N.Y.: Baywood Publishing Company. Quarterly.
    Has published separate listings on archaeology in Africa since 1973.

PERIODICALS:

Azania: journal of the British Institute in eastern Africa. 1966–. Nairobi. Annual.
    Coverage of eastern African countries.
Journal of African history. 1960–. London: Cambridge University Press. Quarterly.
    Scholarly articles; book reviews; regularly publishes articles on radiocarbon chronology of sub-Saharan Africa.
South African archaeological bulletin. 1945–. Cape Town: South African Archaeological Association.
West African journal of archaeology. 1971–. Ibadan: Oxford University Press. Annual. (Formerly *West African archaeological newsletter*.)

SUGGESTIONS FOR FURTHER READING:

Clark, J. Desmond. *The prehistory of Africa*. New York: Praeger, 1970.
————. "Africa in prehistory: peripheral or paramount?" *Man*, n.s., v. 10 (1975): 175–198.
Fagan, Brian, and Roland Oliver. *Africa in the Iron Age c. 500 to 1400 A.D.* Cambridge, Eng.: Cambridge University Press, 1975. Pbk.
Fage, John D., and Roland Oliver. *Papers in African prehistory*. Cambridge, Eng.: Cambridge University Press, 1970.

Sampson, C. Garth. *The Stone Age archaeology of southern Africa*. New York: Academic Press, 1974.

Slavery and the Slave Trade

Historians have focused on a variety of problems concerning both the trans-atlantic slave trade and the slave trade from East Africa. These have included the organization of the trade (Davidson, Mannix and Cowley), statistical assessments of its dimensions (Anstey, Curtin), and its short- and long-term effects on African societies (Alpers, Fage, Wrigley).

BIBLIOGRAPHY:

Hogg, Peter G. *The African slave trade and its suppression: a classified and annotated bibliography*. London: Cass, 1972.

DOCUMENTARY SOURCES:

Beachey, R. W., ed. *Documents: the slave trade of eastern Africa*. London: Rex Collings, 1976.

Donnan, Elizabeth, ed. *Documents illustrative of the history of the slave trade to America*. Washington, D.C.: Carnegie Institution, 1930–35. 4 v. Revised ed.: New York: Octagon Bate, 1965.
Collection of source material on trade to North America.

SUGGESTIONS FOR FURTHER READING:

Alpers, Edward A. *Ivory and slaves in east Africa*. London: Heinemann Educational Books, 1975. Pbk.

Anstey, Roger. *The Atlantic slave trade and British abolition, 1760–1810*. London: Cambridge University Press; Atlantic Highlands, N.J.: Humanities Press, 1975.

Curtin, Philip D. *The Atlantic slave trade: a census*. Madison: University of Wisconsin Press, 1969. Pbk.
An important work of statistical analysis, estimating the number of slaves brought to Europe and the Americas between 1451 and 1870 at approximately 9.5 million. Recently Curtin's computation of the number of slaves imported into the Americas has been disputed in: Inikori, J. E. "Measuring the Atlantic slave trade: an assessment of Curtin and Anstey." *Journal of African history*, v. XVII, no. 2 (1976): 197–223.

Davidson, Basil. *The African slave trade*. Boston: Little, Brown and Co. 1961. Pbk.

Fage, John D. "Slavery and the slave trade in the context of West African history." *Journal of African history,* v. X, no. 3 (1969): 393–404.

Fisher, Humphrey J., and Allan G. B. Fisher. *Slavery and Muslim society in Africa: the institution in Saharan and Sudanic Africa and the trans-Saharan trade.* London: Hurst, 1970. Pbk.

Mannix, Daniel, and Malcolm Cowley. *Black cargoes: a history of the Atlantic slave trade, 1518–1865.* New York: Viking Press, 1962. Pbk.

Wrigley, Christopher C. "Historicism in Africa: slavery and state formation." *African affairs,* v. 70 (April 1971): 113–124.

Colonialism and Independence

The place of the colonial period in African history still evokes strong feelings. As R. Hunt Davis explains, there are three prevalent positions: that the colonial regimes and their influences caused a break or cleavage with the African past (see Fanon, Suret-Canale for the debilitating effects of colonialism; Duignan and Gann for its positive side); that the colonial period, seen in retrospect, was brief and African institutions adapted to it and influenced it (see Ajayi and Crowder); that the colonial period caused major dependence on a metropole with a resulting need for revolution (see Amin and Rodney).

SUGGESTIONS FOR FURTHER READING:

Ajayi, J. F. A. "The continuity of African institutions under colonialism." In: *Emerging themes in African history: proceedings of the International Congress of African Historians held at Dar es Salaam, 1965.* Edited by T. O. Ranger. London; Nairobi: East African Publishing House; dist. in the U.S.A. by Northwestern University Press, 1968.

Amin, Samir. "Underdevelopment and dependence in Black Africa: its origins and contemporary forms." *Journal of modern African studies,* v. 10, no. 4 (1972): 503–524.

Collins, Robert O., ed. *Problems in the history of colonial Africa, 1860–1960.* Englewood Cliffs, N.J.: Prentice-Hall, 1970.

Crowder, Michael. *West Africa under colonial rule.* Evanston, Ill.: Northwestern University Press, 1968.

Davis, R. Hunt. "Interpreting the colonial period in African history." *African affairs,* v. 72 (1973): 383–400.

Fanon, Frantz. *A dying colonialism.* New York: Grove Press, 1967. Pbk.

————. *Toward the African revolution; political essays.* New York: Monthly Review Press, 1967. Pbk.

Gann, Lewis H., and Peter Duignan, eds. *Colonialism in Africa, 1870–1960.* London: Cambridge University Press, 1969–75. 5 v.

The different volumes under different editorships include: v. I. The history and politics of colonialism, 1870–1914. v. II. The history and politics of colonialism, 1914–1960. v. III. Profiles of change. v. IV. The economics of colonialism. v. V. Bibliography.

————. *Burden of empire; an appraisal of Western colonialism in Africa south of the Sahara.* New York: Praeger, 1967.

Gellar, Sheldon. "State-building and nation-building in West Africa." In: Eisenstadt, S.N., and Stein Rokan. *Building states and nations.* Beverly Hills, Calif.: Sage Publications, 1973: v. II., 384–426.

Hodgkin, Thomas. *Nationalism in colonial Africa.* New York: New York University Press, 1957. Pbk.

Rodney, Walter A. *How Europe underdeveloped Africa.* London: Bodle-L'Ouverture; New York: Panther House, 1972. Reprint: Washington, D.C.: Howard University Press, 1974.

Rotberg, Robert I., ed. *Rebellion in Black Africa,* New York: Oxford University Press, 1971. Pbk.

Suret-Canale, Jean. *French colonialism in tropical Africa. 1900–1945.* London: Hurst; New York: Universe Books, 1971.

Wallerstein, Immanuel. *Africa: the politics of independence.* New York: Vintage, 1961. Pbk.

Social Organization and the Individual

The demarcation between the social science disciplines of anthropology, sociology, and psychology is often arbitrary. In Africa-related research, they have strong links to such other disciplines as linguistics, economics, comparative politics, ethnomusicology, etc. Similar research issues are confronted by each: social and cultural change; modernization and the adaptation of traditional ways to contemporary life; urbanization; rural development; social stratification; ethnicity and the interactions of racial and religious groups; the role of women in development. The works suggested here for further reading demonstrate some trends in recent research in these disciplines.

CONTINUING BIBLIOGRAPHIES:

Abstracts in anthropology. 1970–. Farmingdale, N.Y.: Baywood Publishing Company. Quarterly.

Abstracts of articles and books on archaeology, cultural and physical anthropology, and linguistics.

Bibliographie ethnographique de l'Afrique sud-Saharienne. 1925–. Brussels.
(Title varies, 1925–1959, as *Bibliographie ethnographique du Congo belge
et des régions avoisinantes.*)

References to books and articles in all languages, although French and English
predominate, on ethnology in its wider sense, including social and cultural anthropology, sociology, linguistics, history, archaeology, the arts, education, politics, and
economics. Entries are listed alphabetically by author and annotated. A detailed and
generous index is arranged by subject, geographical location, and ethnic group.

International bibliography of social and cultural anthropology. 1955–. London:
Tavistock; Chicago: Aldine. Annual. (International bibliography of the
social sciences.)

International bibliography of sociology. 1951–. London: Tavistock; Chicago:
Aldine. Annual. (International bibliography of the social sciences.)

BIBLIOGRAPHIES:

Armer, Michael, ed. *African social psychology: a review and annotated bibliography.* New York: Africana Publishing Corp., 1974.

Bouhdiba, Adelwahab. *La sociologie du développement africaine; tendances
actuelles de la recherche et bibliographie.* La Haye: Mouton, 1971. (Current sociology, v. 17.)

Gibson, Gordon D., et al. "A bibliography of anthropological bibliographies:
Africa." *Current anthropology,* v. 10 (Dec. 1969): 527–566.

Groothues, Christine. *A bibliography of child development in Africa.* Legon,
Ghana: Institute of African Studies, University of Ghana, 1974.

Irvine, S. H., J. T. Sanders, and E. L. Klingelhofer, comps. *Human behavior in
Africa: a bibliography of psychological and related writings.* Westport,
Conn.: Greenwood Press, 1973. (African Bibliographic Center. Special
bibliographic series, v. 8, no. 2.)

Moore, Jane Ann. "Preliminary bibliography for the sociology of occupations
and professions in Africa." *A Current bibliography of African affairs,* n.s.,
v. 7, no. 1 (Winter 1974): 38–62.

PERIODICALS:

Africa: journal of the International African Institute. 1928–. London: International African Institute. Quarterly.

Research articles on anthropology, ethnology, folklore, linguistics; scholarly book
reviews; reviews of current research.

African notes. 1963–. Ibadan, Nigeria: Institute of African Studies, University
of Ibadan. 3 x yr.

Political, anthropological, and language studies, especially on Nigeria; bibliographical essays.

African social research. 1966–. Manchester, Eng.: Manchester University Press, for the Institute of Social Research, University of Zambia. Semiannual.

". . . general field of social research in Africa, especially sociology and social anthropology, psychology, economics, human geography and demography, history and political science . . ."; book reviews.

Ghana journal of sociology: a review of research on West African society. 1965–. Legon: Dept. of Sociology, University of Ghana. 2 x yr.

Man: the journal of the Royal Africa Institute. 1901–. London. Quarterly. (Absorbed the *Journal* of the Royal Anthropological Institute of Great Britain and Ireland, 1872–1965, in 1966.)

Studies in social and cultural anthropology.

Psychopathologie africaine: bulletin de la Société de Psychopathologie et d'Hygiène mentale de Dakar. 1965–. Dakar: Publiée avec le concours du Centre national de la Recherche scientifique.

Scholarly articles on the social sciences, particularly on the cultural psychology and psychopathological manifestations of African peoples; book reviews.

West African journal of sociology and political science. 1975–. Exeter, Eng.

SUGGESTIONS FOR FURTHER READING:

Balandier, Georges. *Ambiguous Africa: cultures in collision.* New York: Pantheon, 1966. Pbk: New York: Avon, 1975.

————. *The sociology of Black Africa: social dynamics in Central Africa.* New York: Praeger, 1970.

Erny, Pierre. *Childhood and cosmos; the social psychology of the black African child.* Washington, D.C.: Black Orpheus Press, 1973.

Clifford, W. *An introduction to African criminology.* Nairobi, London, New York: Oxford University Press, 1974.

Lloyd, Peter C. *Africa in social change.* New York: Praeger, 1967. Pbk: Baltimore: Penguin.

————. *Power and independence: urban Africans' perception of social inequality.* London: Routledge & Kegan Paul, 1974.

Maquet, Jacques J. *Power and society in Africa.* New York: McGraw Hill, 1971. Pbk.

Middleton, John, ed. *Black Africa; its peoples and their cultures today.* New York: Macmillan, 1970. Pbk.

Oppong, Christine. *Growing up in Dagbon.* Accra-Tema: Ghana Publishing Corporation, 1973.

Sandbrook, Richard, and Robin Cohen, eds. *The development of an African working class.* London: Longmans, 1976.

Social stratification in Africa. Edited by Arthur Tuden and Leonard Plotnicov. New York: Free Press, 1970.

Tessler, Mark A., William M. O'Barr, and David H. Spain. *Tradition and identity in changing Africa.* New York: Harper & Row, 1973. Pbk.

Turnbull, Colin, ed. *Africa and change.* New York: Knopf, distributed by Random House, 1973.

Van den Berghe, Pierre. *Africa: social problems of change and conflict.* San Francisco: Chandler Publishing Co., 1965.

Wober, Mallory. *Psychology in Africa.* London: International African Institute, 1976. Pbk.

African Peoples: Ethnographies/Field Studies

African societies and larger groupings of related African societies are described in the following works:

Case studies in cultural anthropology. This series published by Holt, Rinehart, Winston (New York) includes these titles focused on Africa:
> *Bunyoro: an African kingdom,* by John Beattie. 1960.
> *The Swazi,* by Hilda Kuper. 1963.
> *The Igbo of Southeast Nigeria,* by Victor C. Uchendu. 1965.
> *The Lugbara of Uganda,* by John Middleton. 1965.
> *The Kanuri of Bornu,* by Ronald Cohen. 1967.
> *The Qemant: a pagan-Hebraic peasantry of Ethiopia,* by Frederick G. Gamst. 1969.
> *The Yoruba of southwestern Nigeria,* by William Bascom. 1969.
> *The Barabaig: East African cattle herders,* by George J. Klima. 1970.
> *The Kaguru: a matrilineal people of East Africa,* by T. O. Beidelman. 1971.
> *The Dinka of the Sudan,* by Francis Madeng Deng. 1972.
> *Kafr El-Elow: an Egyptian village in transition,* by Hani Fakhouri. 1972.
> *Watts and Woodstock: identity and culture in the United States and South Africa,* by James O'Toole. 1973.

Ethnographic survey of Africa/Monographies ethnologiques africaines. Edited by Daryll Forde. 1950–. London: International African Institute.

Since 1950, sixty volumes, written by leading anthropologists, have been published under the direction of the International African Institute and the Musée royale de l'Afrique centrale, and in cooperation by Presses Universitaires de France, Paris. They provide a precise summary of available information on each people or group of peoples, and include bibliographies and maps. Some representative titles are: *Les Dogon*, by Montserrat Paulau Marti, 1957; *Le Groupe dit Pahouin*, by Pièrre Alexandre and Jacques Binet, 1958; *The Northern Nilo-Hamites*, by G. W. B. Huntingford, 1953; *The Benin Kingdom and the Edo-speaking peoples of Southwestern Nigeria*, by R. E. Bradbury, 1954; *Les Tribus Ba-Kuba et les peuplades apparentées*, by Jan Vansina, 1954.

Hiernaux, Jean. *The peoples of Africa*. New York: Scribner, 1975. Pbk.

Mair, Lucy. *African societies*. New York: Cambridge University Press, 1972. Pbk.

Maquet, Jacques. *Civilizations of Black Africa*. New York: Oxford University Press, 1972. Pbk.

Murdock, George P. *Africa: its peoples and their culture history*. New York: McGraw Hill, 1959.

A survey of African ethnic groups by culture area, accompanied by an index of about 5,000 ethnic names and a large folded map showing principal groups and culture areas.

Shorter, Aylward. *East African societies*. London, Boston: Routledge & Kegan Paul, 1974.

Cultural and Ethnic Pluralism

Modern African nations are pluralistic; their populations reflect a diversity in language, religion, race, and ethnicity. The relations of these various groups, whether in conflict or cooperation, have been the subject of recent studies. The following works present different theoretical viewpoints and case studies.

Bates, Robert H. *Ethnicity in contemporary Africa*. Syracuse, N.Y.: Program of Eastern African Studies, Syracuse University, 1973. (Eastern African studies, 14.)

Gluckman, Max. *Custom and conflict in Africa*. Oxford: Blackwell, 1963.

Kuper, Leo. *Race, class and power; ideology and revolutionary change in plural societies*. London: Duckworth, 1974.

Lemarchand, Rene. "Political clientelism and ethnicity in tropical Africa: competing solidarities in nation-building." *American political science review*, v. LXVI, no. 1 (March 1972): 68–90.

Olorunsola, Victor A., ed. *The politics of sub-nationalism in Africa*. New York: Doubleday Anchor, 1972. Pbk.

Analyzes ethnicity in five African states: Nigeria, Sierra Leone, Uganda, Zaire, and Kenya.

Pluralism in Africa. Edited by Leo Kuper and M. G. Smith. Berkeley: University of California Press, 1969. Pbk.

    Major theoretical discussions of pluralistic societies.

Smock, David R., and Audrey C. Smock. *The politics of pluralism: a comparative study of Lebanon and Ghana.* New York: Elsevier, 1975.

Race in Southern Africa

Much has been written on the racial policies and conditions in South Africa, Rhodesia, and Namibia. The South African Institute of Race Relations annually presents a summary review of developments and trends in education, politics, legislation, sports, government action, the opposition, etc. in its *Survey of Race Relations in South Africa.* The *Survey* has been supplemented since 1972 by *Black review,* a publication of the Black Community Programmes, which aims "to project present trends in the Black Community in order that leaders can assess these directions." A similar survey for Rhodesia has been compiled for the first time by Dorothy Keyworth Davies.

The United Nations, in its *Notes and documents* series, its periodicals *Decolonization* and *Objective: justice,* and other publications, has also reported on race relations, liberation movements, economic and social developments in southern Africa, and the relationships of South Africa and Rhodesia to other African states.

The section on Liberation Movements (pp.445–46) has references to related material.

BIBLIOGRAPHIES:

American-southern African relations: bibliographic essays. Edited by Mohammed A. El-Khawas/Francis A. Kornegay, Jr. Westport, Conn.: Greenwood Press, 1975. (African Bibliographic Center. Special bibliographic series, n.s., no. 1.)

Schapera, Isaac. *Select bibliography of South African native life and problems.* London: Oxford University Press, 1941.

    The section on modern status and conditions has been supplemented four times: Holden, M. A., and A. Jacoby. Suppl. 1: 1934–1949; Giffen, R., and J. Back. Suppl. 2: 1950–1958; Solomon, C. Suppl. 3: 1958–1963. Alman, B. A. Suppl. 4: 1964–1970.

U.N. Dept. of Political and Security Council Affairs. Unit on Apartheid. *Selective bibliography on apartheid.* New York: 1974. (Notes and documents, 10/74.)

Covers 1970–73; supplements *Apartheid: a selective bibliography on the racial policies of the Republic of South Africa.* New York: 1966. (ST/LIB/22)

PERIODICALS:

Southern Africa; a monthly survey of news & opinion. 1967–. New York: American Committee on Africa. Monthly.
Action-oriented articles; current events.

Journal of southern African studies. 1974–. London: Oxford University Press. Biannual.
Scholarly articles on the history and social analysis of southern Africa.

Decolonization. 1974–. New York: U.N. Dept. of Political Affairs, Trusteeship and Decolonization. Centre against Apartheid (formerly Unit on Apartheid).

Objective: justice. 1969–. New York: U.N. Office of Public Information. Quarterly.

Social dynamics. 1975–. Cape Town, South Africa: Faculty of Social Science, University of Cape Town. 2 x yr.
Aims "to provide a forum within South Africa for academic work in the social sciences that is relevant to the study of Southern Africa . . . an attempt to understand and document certain social processes which are especially relevant for Southern Africa."

SOURCES:

Black review. 1972–. Durban, South Africa: Black Community Programmes, 1973–. Annual.

Race relations in Rhodesia: a survey for 1972/73. Compiled by Dorothy Keyworth Davies. London: Rex Collings, 1975.

A Survey of race relations in South Africa. 1953/54–. Johannesburg: South African Institute of Race Relations. Annual.

U.N. Dept. of Political Affairs, Trusteeship and Decolonization. Centre against Apartheid (formerly Dept. of Political and Security Council Affairs. Unit on Apartheid). *Notes and documents* series, 1969–.

DOCUMENTARY SOURCES:

From protest to challenge; a documentary history of African politics in South Africa, 1882–1964. Edited by Thomas Karis and Gwendolen M. Carter. Stanford, Calif.: Hoover Institution Press, 1972–77. 4 v.

The Rhodesian problem: a documentary record. 1923–73. Edited by Elaine Windrich. London, Boston: Routledge & Kegan Paul, 1975.

SUGGESTIONS FOR FURTHER READING:

Adam, Heribert. *Modernizing racial domination: South Africa's political dynamics.* Berkeley: University of California Press, 1971. Pbk.

Bowman, Larry. *Politics in Rhodesia: white power in an African state.* Cambridge, Mass.: Harvard University Press, 1973.

Desmond, Cosmos. *The discarded people.* Baltimore: Penguin, 1971. Pbk.

Hoagland, Jim. *South Africa: civilizations in conflict.* Boston: Houghton Mifflin, 1972.

O'Meara, Patrick. *Rhodesia: racial conflict or co-existence?* Ithaca, N.Y.: Cornell University Press, 1975.

Thompson, Leonard, and Jeffrey Butler, eds. *Change in contemporary South Africa.* Berkeley: University of California Press, 1975. Pbk.

African Women

Research on African women is still meager, but there is a growing interest in studying the roles they have played in the history of Africa, in traditional life, as well as their place in development and modernization. Recently issues of the *Canadian Journal of African studies*, the *African studies review*, and *Ufahamu* were devoted to articles about women throughout Africa. The number of new studies on African women is increasing and more are expected.

BIBLIOGRAPHIES:

African Bibliographic Center. *Contemporary African women: an introductory bibliographical overview and a guide to women's organizations, 1960–1967.* New York: Negro Universities Press, 1969. (African Bibliographic Center. Special bibliographic series, v. 6, no. 2.)

Dobert, Margarita. "Women in French-speaking West Africa: a selected guide to civic and political participation in Guinea, Dahomey and Mauritania." *A current bibliography on African affairs,* n.s., v. 3, no. 3 (September 1970): 5–21.

Kratochvil, Laura, and Shauna Shaw., comps. *African women; a select bibliography . . .,* with an introductory essay by Karen Reidy. Cambridge, Eng.: African Studies Centre (Sidgwick Ave., Cambridge CB3 9DA), 1974.

Perlman, M., and M. P. Moal. "Analytical bibliography." In: Paulme, Denise, ed. *Women of tropical Africa.* See below.

Westfall, Gloria. "Nigerian women: a bibliographical essay." *Africana journal,* v. 2, no. 2 (1974): 99–138.

SUGGESTIONS FOR FURTHER READING:

"African women today and other issues." *Ufahamu*, v. VI, no. 1 (1976).
An issue "designed exclusively to carry articles on the role and position of women in contemporary Africa."

Bay, Edna G., and Nancy J. Hafkin, eds. *Women in Africa: studies in social and economic change.* Stanford, Calif.: Stanford University Press, 1976.

Little, Kenneth L. *African women in towns; an aspect of Africa's social revolution.* London, New York: Cambridge University Press, 1973.

Paulme, Denise, ed. *Women of tropical Africa.* Berkeley: University of California Press, 1963. Pbk.

"The roles of African women: past, present and future." *Canadian journal of African studies*, v. 6, no. 2 (1972).

"Women in Africa." *African studies review*, v. XVIII, no. 3 (December 1975).
The majority of the articles focus on development-related issues.

Rural/Urban Studies

While the urban-rural dichotomy is a central problem for analysis in a number of social science disciplines, including anthropology, political science, and sociology, it is also of importance in several other fields, such as art history, ethnomusicology, and linguistics.

BIBLIOGRAPHIES:

Ajaegbu, Hyacinth I. *African urbanization: a bibliography.* London: International African Institute, 1972.

Dejene, Tekola, and Scott E. Smith. *Experiences in rural development: a selected, annotated bibliography of planning, implementing and evaluating rural development in Africa.* Washington, D.C.: Overseas Liaison Committee, American Council on Education, 1973.

Rhett, Anita. *Rural development in Africa.* Washington, D.C.: African Bibliographic Center, 1972. (*Its* current reading list series, v. 9, no. 2.)

PERIODICALS:

African urban notes. 1966–1971; ser. B. 1975–. East Lansing, Mich.: African Studies Center, Michigan State University. Irregular.
Presents current research, information on conferences, courses taught, and other activities pertaining to African urban life; some issues focus on special topics, others are general; bibliographies often included.

Rural Africana. 1967–. East Lansing, Mich.: African Studies Center, Michigan State University. 3 x yr.

". . . devoted to current research in the social sciences exploring the problems of social and economic development in rural Africa, south of the Sahara. Each issue is focused on a specific problem or area of research presenting papers selected by a guest editor. . . . A comprehensive bibliography is provided in each issue, as well as news of new publications, projects, and individual research. . . ." Issues have focused on such topics as rural geography, ethnohistory, rural land use, traditional healers, and the like.

SUGGESTIONS FOR FURTHER READING:

Chambers, Robert. *Managing rural development: ideas and experiences from East Africa.* Uppsala: Scandinavian Institute of African Studies, 1974.

Duvignaud, Jean. *Change at Shebika; report from a North African village.* New York: Pantheon Books, 1970.

Hanna, William J., and Judith L. Hanna. *Urban dynamics in Black Africa: an interdisciplinary reader.* Chicago: Aldine, 1971.

Little, Kenneth L. *Urbanization as social process: an essay on movement and changes in contemporary Africa.* London, Boston: Routledge & Kegan Paul, 1974.

Mabogunje, Akin L. *Urbanization in Nigeria.* New York: Africana Publishing Corp., 1969.

Skinner, Elliott P. *African urban life: the transformation of Ouagadougou.* Princeton, N.J.: Princeton University Press, 1974.

Smock, David R., and Audrey C. Smock. *Cultural and political aspects of rural transformation; a case study of eastern Nigeria.* New York: Praeger, 1972.

Political Science/Government

An overview of the major concerns of political science regarding Africa is given in *An introduction to African politics: a continental approach,* by Leslie Rubin and Brian Weinstein. Its bibliography and an appendix, "African states, 1973," though somewhat altered by the independence of Angola, Mozambique, and Guine Bissau, and changes of heads of states and names of countries (Dahomey officially changed its name to Benin in December 1975), remain useful.

For documentation as well as sophisticated analysis of the events of the preceding year, see *Africa contemporary record: annual survey and documents.* Each volume includes a section on current issues with essays by authorities in the field; a country by country review of the past year; a section of documents; and a section on social and economic developments. Other documentary collections of interest are *African aims and attitudes, Basic documents on African affairs,* and *Africa independent: a study of political developments.*

CONTINUING BIBLIOGRAPHIES:

International bibliography of political science. 1952–. London: Tavistock; Chicago: Aldine. Annual. (International bibliography of the social sciences.)

International political science abstracts. 1951–. Oxford: Blackwell. Quarterly. Abstracts journal articles only.

Public Affairs Information Service (PAIS). *Bulletin.* 1915–. New York. Weekly.
Indexes books, articles, reports, government publications published in English throughout the world. *P.A.I.S. foreign language index* covers publications in French, German, Italian, Portuguese, and Spanish.

"Current Africana." In: *Review of African political economy.* v. 1–, 1974–.
Continues the bibliography "Radical Africana" and lists publications of relevance to the study of contemporary African political economy.

BIBLIOGRAPHIES:

Alderfer, Harold F. *A. bibliography of African government, 1950–1966.* 2d. rev. ed. Lincoln University, Pa.: Lincoln University Press, 1967.

Doro, Marion. "Bibliographic essay on the role of the military in African states." *A Current bibliography on African affairs,* n.s., v. 4, no. 3 (May 1971): 190–197.

Jumba-Masagazi, A. H. K. *African socialism: a bibliography and short summary.* Nairobi: East African Research Information Centre, 1970.

McGowan, Patrick J. *African politics; a guide to research resources, methods and literature.* Syracuse, N.Y.: Program of Eastern African Studies, Syracuse University, 1970. (Occasional paper, 55.)

Shaw, Robert B., and Richard L. Sklar. *A bibliography for the study of African politics.* Los Angeles: African Studies Center, University of California, 1973. (Occasional paper, no. 9.)

Turner, Thomas. "The study of local politics in rural Black Africa." *Rural Africana,* no. 18 (Fall 1972): 97–103.

PERIODICALS:

African review. 1971–. Nairobi: East African Literature Bureau. Quarterly.
"A journal of African politics, development and international affairs."

American political science review. 1906–. Washington, D.C.: American Political Science Association. Quarterly.

Journal of Commonwealth and comparative politics. 1961–. London: Cass. 3 no. a yr. (Formerly *Journal of Commonwealth political studies.*)

Journal of modern African studies. 1963–. London: Cambridge University Press. Quarterly.

"A quarterly survey of politics, economics and related topics in contemporary Africa," with scholarly articles, research reports in its "Africana" section, reviews and review articles.

Review of African political economy. 1974–. London: Merlin Press. Quarterly.

Articles generally have radical slant; features include "Briefings" (current news), "Debate" and the bibliography "Current Africana."

See also: *African affairs, Africa report, Africa today, West African journal of sociology and political science,* listed elsewhere.

DOCUMENTARY SOURCES:

Africa contemporary record: annual survey and documents. Edited by Colin Legum. 1968–. New York: Africana Publishing Co. Annual.

Africa independent: a study of political developments. New York: Scribners, 1972. (Keesings research report, no. 6.)

Brownlie, Ian, comp. *Basic documents on African affairs.* Oxford: Clarendon Press, 1971.

Minogue, Martin, and Judith Molloy, eds. *African aims and attitudes: selected documents.* London, New York: Cambridge University Press, 1974. Pbk.

Selections from the political writings and speeches of African politicians and intellectuals.

SUGGESTIONS FOR FURTHER READING:

Bereket, H. Selassie. *The executive in African governments.* London: Heinemann, 1974. Pbk.

Gutteridge, William F. *Military regimes in Africa.* London: Methuen, 1975. Pbk.

Decalo, Samuel. *Coups and army rule in Africa: studies in military style.* New Haven, Conn.: Yale University Press, 1976.

Hopkins, Nicholas S. *Popular government in an African town.* Chicago: University of Chicago Press, 1972.

Local government in Kita, Mali.

Lofchie, Michael, F., ed. *The state of the nations: constraints on development in independent Africa.* Berkeley: University of California Press, 1971. Pbk.

Potholm, Christian P. *Four African political systems.* Englewood Cliffs, N.J.: Prentice Hall, 1970.

Case studies and comparisons of the governments of South Africa, Tanzania, Somalia, and Ivory Coast.

Rubin, Leslie, and Brian Weinstein. *Introduction to African politics: a continental approach.* New York: Praeger, 1974. Pbk.

Traditional Political Systems

The traditional political systems of Africa range from decentralized forms of authority based on kinship ties to large centralized empires. In some instances specific works are entirely devoted to an analysis of traditional forms of government (Fortes and Evans-Pritchard, Middleton and Tait). However, it is also necessary to consult general ethnographic studies which will include chapters on political systems (for example, *Case studies in cultural anthropology* and *Ethnographic survey of Africa*, see pp.435–36).

BIBLIOGRAPHIES:

Hertefelt, Marcel d'. *African governmental systems in static and changing conditions: a bibliographic contribution to political anthropology*. Tervuren: Musée royale de l'Afrique centrale, 1968.

Lewis, Herbert. "African political systems: a bibliographical inventory of anthropological writings." *Behavior science notes*, Part I: v. 7, no. 3 (1972): 209–235; Part II: v. 7, no. 4 (1972): 331–347.

SUGGESTIONS FOR FURTHER READING:

Fortes, Meyer, and E. E. Evans-Pritchards, eds. *African political systems*. London: Oxford University Press, for the International African Institute, 1940. Pbk.

Gluckman, Max. *Order and rebellion in tribal Africa*. New York: Free Press, 1963.

Mair, Lucy. *Primitive government*. Rev. ed. Bloomington: Indiana University Press, 1977. Pbk.

Middleton, John, and David Tait, eds. *Tribes without rulers: studies in African segmentary systems*. London: Routledge & Kegan Paul, 1958.

Schapera, Isaac. *Government and politics in tribal societies*. London: Watts, 1956. Pbk: New York: Schocken, 1967.

Whitaker, Cleophus Sylvester, Jr. *The politics of tradition; continuity and change in Northern Nigeria, 1946–1966*. Princeton, N.J.: Published for the Center for International Studies by the Princeton University Press, 1970. Study of how traditional political systems adapt to contemporary politics.

International Relations

The relationships of African states with each other, with former colonial rulers, with the major world powers, and with other nations of the Third World, the regulation of their international affairs through international and regional agencies, and the political realities of such relationships are explored in the works listed below.

PERIODICALS:

African international perspective: the African review of international affairs. 1975/76–. Monrovia, Liberia: African Publishing House. Monthly.

The monitoring of the international activities of African states can be found in such other periodicals as the *African research bulletins, Africa report,* and others listed under current events. Articles on international relations are also frequently published in *African affairs, African review, Africa today,* and the *Journal of modern African studies.*

DOCUMENTARY SOURCES:

Sohn, Louis B., comp. *Basic documents of African regional organizations.* Dobbs Ferry, N.Y.: Oceana, 1971–72. 2 v.

Also *Africa contemporary record* and Brownlie's *Basic documents on African affairs.*

SUGGESTIONS FOR FURTHER READING:

Cervenka, Zdenek. *The Organization of African Unity and its charter.* New York: Praeger, 1969.

El-Ayouty, Yassin, and Hugh C. Brooks, eds. *Africa and international organization.* The Hague: Martinus Nijhoff, 1972.

Ingham, Kenneth, ed. *Foreign relations of the African states.* London: Butterworths, 1974.

Larkin, Bruce D. *China and Africa, 1949–1970; the foreign policy of the People's Republic of China.* Berkeley: University of California Press, 1971. Pbk.

McLane, Charles B. *Soviet-African relations.* London: Central Asian Research Centre, 1974.

Nielsen, Waldemar A. *The great powers and Africa.* New York: Published for the Council on Foreign Relations by Praeger, 1969.

Widstrand, Carl Gosta, ed. *African boundary problems.* Uppsala, Sweden: Scandinavian Institute of African Studies, 1969.

Howe, Russell Warren. *Along the Afric shore: an historic review of two centuries of U.S.-African relations.* New York: Barnes & Noble, 1975.

Liberation Movements

Studies of insurgency and counterinsurgency in white-ruled southern Africa, the former Portuguese colonies, and other places in Africa are listed below.

BIBLIOGRAPHY:

Smaldone, Joseph P. *African liberation movements: an interim bibliography.*
Waltham, Mass.: African Studies Association, Brandeis University, 1974.
References to books and articles as well as a listing of periodicals issued by libera-
tion groups and their special interest lobbies.

For other recent studies, see the journals, *Southern Africa, Journal of modern
African studies*, and the annual *Africa contemporary record.*

SUGGESTIONS FOR FURTHER READING:

Gibson, Richard. *African liberation movements: contemporary struggles against
white minority rule.* London, New York: Oxford University Press, 1972.
Pbk.

Grundy, Kenneth W. *Confrontation and accommodation in southern Africa:
the limits of independence.* Berkeley: University of California Press, 1973.
(Perspectives in southern Africa.)

————. *Guerrilla struggle in Africa: an analysis and preview.* New York: Gross-
man, 1971.

Maxey, Kees. *The fight for Rhodesia: the armed conflict in Southern Rhodesia
since UDI.* London: Rex Collings, 1975.

Current Events

Newspapers, particularly African newspapers, provide the best method of
keeping informed about African opinions and social, political and economic
events. However, subscriptions to African newspapers are expensive and few
libraries have extensive collections. Universities which are members of the Foreign Newspaper Project of the Center for Research Libraries in Chicago may
borrow a number of newspapers from Nigeria, South Africa, Kenya, Zaire,
Senegal, and other countries through interlibrary loan. Microfilm copies of
newspapers are sometimes available, though by the time that they are filmed
they usually are two or more years behind the date of publication. *The New
York Times*, the *Christian Science Monitor*, and the *Times* of London (with
comprehensive and current indexes), *The Economist* and *Le Monde*, also pub-
lish a substantial amount of news from and about Africa.

Of major importance is *Africa contemporary record* (described elsewhere in
this bibliography), which appears annually and gives a breakdown of events for
the past year by country and topic. A number of periodicals which present news
and analysis of current political, economic, and social developments are listed
below.

DIRECTORIES TO NEWSPAPERS:

Feuereisen, Fritz, and Ernst Schmacke, comps. *Die Presse in Afrika; ein Hand-buch fuer Wirtschaft und Werbung. The press in Africa; a handbook for economics and advertising.* 2d ed. Munich: Verlag Dokumentation, 1973.

U.S. Library of Congress. Catalog Publications Division. *Newspapers in micro-form: foreign countries, 1948–1972.* Washington, 1973–.

PERIODICALS:

Africa; an international business, economics and political monthly. 1971–. London: Africa Journal Ltd. Monthly.

Africa confidential. 1960–. London. 25 issues per yr.
   Brief "insider" commentaries.

Africa currents. 1975–. London: Africa Publications Trust.
   ". . . aims to provide a deeper insight into topical issues"; political comment and analysis culled primarily from the African press.

Africa diary: weekly diary of African events with index. 1961–. New Delhi, India. Weekly.

Africa report. 1956–. New York: African-American Institute. Bimonthly.
   See its regular "African update . . . monitoring economic and political developments around the continent."

Africa research bulletin: economic, financial and technical series, and *Africa research bulletin: political, social and cultural series.* 19–. London: Africa Research Ltd.
   "Facts on file" format, with detailed accounts of events; news taken from African newspapers and magazines; well indexed.

Afriscope; an indigenous monthly on Africa's social economic development. 1971–. Yaba, Nigeria: Pan Afriscope Publications. Monthly.

Jeune-Afrique. 1960–. Paris: Jeune Afrique. Weekly.

West Africa. 1917–. London: West Africa Publishing Co. Ltd.
   Feature articles, columns, book reviews, economic and business news; "Dateline Africa."

Economics/Development

The study of economics in Africa has been dominated by the theories of development and accommodation to a world market. Representative works by Kamarck, Arkhurst, and Seidman are listed. A more recent radical trend looks more skeptically at the bases of industrial growth and stresses the problems caused by outwardly-directed development, dependence on the West, and class differences. It takes on an historical Marxian perspective. Examples are the titles by Davidson, Arrighi and Saul, and Rodney. Samir Amin's works, recently translated into English, provide some of the theoretical bases of this view.

The statistical data used for economic comparisons can be found in the publications of the U.N. Economic Commission for Africa: its *Economic survey of Africa* and *Economic bulletin for Africa*. It also issues a regular bibliography, *Africa index: selected articles on socio-economic development*. Other sources for economic data are the *Quarterly economic reviews* published by the Economic Intelligence Unit, London, and the *Surveys of African economies* of the International Monetary Fund.

CONTINUING BIBLIOGRAPHIES:

Economic abstracts: semi-monthly review of abstracts of economics, trade, finance and industry, management and labor. 1953–. The Hague: Nijhoff. Semimonthly.
    Emphasis on economic policy and applied problems.
International Bibliography of economics. 1952–. London: Tavistock; Chicago: Aldine. Annual. (International bibliography of the social sciences.)
U.N. Economic Commission for Africa. Library. *Africa index: selected articles on socio-economic development*. 1–, April 1971–. New York.
Continuing bibliographies on development are regular features of the periodicals *Cultures et développement* (Paris, 1968–   ), the *Journal of developing areas* (Macomb, Ill., 1966–   ), and *Review of African political economy*.

BIBLIOGRAPHIES:

Aronson, Jonathan D. "The multinational corporation, the nation-state, and the international system: a bibliography." *A Current bibliography on African affairs*, n.s., v. 7, no. 4 (Fall 1974): 378–436.
Erb, Guy F. "Research on foreign investment in Africa." *A Current bibliography on African affairs*, n.s., v. 6, no. 3 (Summer 1973): 345–354.
Molnos, Angela. *Development in Africa: planning and implementation. A bibliography (1946–1969) and outline with emphasis on Kenya, Tanzania and Uganda*. Nairobi: East African Research Information Centre, 1970.
Mortimer, Delores H., Gita Rao, and Sandra Ann Howell. *Economic cooperation and regional integration in Africa*. Washington, D.C.: African Bibliographic Center, 1973. (*Its* Current reading list series, v. 10, no. 6.)
————. *Implementation and administration of development activities in Africa*. Washington, D.C.: African Bibliographic Center, 1973. (*Its* Current reading list series, v. 10, no. 8.)
Rhett, Anita. *Income and employment generation in Africa*. Washington,

D.C.: African Bibliographic Center, 1973. (*Its* Current reading list series, v. 10, no. 5.)

Smith, John G. *Regional economic cooperation and integration in Africa: some bibliographic references*. Montreal: Centre for Developing Area Studies, McGill University, 1973.

U.N. Economic Commission for Africa. *Bibliography: economic and social development plans of African countries*. Addis Ababa? 1969.

PERIODICALS:

African development. 1966–. London. 6 no. yr.

    News magazine focusing on economic development and finance; features detailed economic surveys of African countries.

Eastern Africa economic review. 1969–. Nairobi: East African Literature Bureau. 2 x yr. (Formerly *East Africa economic review*.)

    Articles on theoretical and applied economics, for eastern Africa.

Journal of developing areas. 1966–. Macomb, Ill.: Western Illinois University. Quarterly.

    ". . . descriptive, theoretical and comparative study of regional development, past and present . . ."

Manpower and unemployment research in Africa. 1969–. Montreal: Centre for Developing Area Studies, McGill University. 2 x yr.

    Future issues to be devoted to "specific themes" such as trade unionism, land use, marginal participants, transnational corporations.

Quarterly economic reviews (of the various countries and regions of Africa). London: Economic Intelligence Unit.

South African journal of economics. 1933–. Johannesburg: Economic Society of South Africa. Quarterly.

    Covers Africa as a whole, though articles mainly concern South Africa; theoretical and applied economics.

REFERENCE SOURCES:

Surveys of African economies. Washington, D.C.: International Monetary Fund.

    Contents: v. I. Cameroon, Central African Republic, Chad, Congo (Brazzaville), Gabon. 1968. v. II. Kenya, Tanzania, Uganda, Somalia. 1969. v. III. Dahomey, Ivory Coast, Mauritania, Niger, Senegal, Togo, Upper Volta. 1970. v. IV. Zaire, Malagasy Republic, Malawi, Mauritius, Zambia. 1971. v. V. Botswana, Lesotho, Swaziland, Burundi, Equatorial Guinea, Rwanda. 1973. v. VI. The Gambia, Ghana, Liberia, Nigeria, Sierra Leone. 1975.

U.N. Economic Commission for Africa. *Economic bulletin for Africa*. 1961–. Addis Ababa.

————. *Economic survey of Africa.* Addis Ababa, Ethiopia.

SUGGESTIONS FOR FURTHER READING:

Amin, Samir. *Accumulation on a world scale: a critique of the theory of under-development.* New York: Monthly Review Press, 1974. 2 v.

————. *Neo-colonialism in West Africa.* New York: Monthly Review Press, 1975. Pbk.

Arkhurst, Frederick S., ed. *Africa in the seventies and eighties: issues in development.* New York: Praeger, 1970.

Arrighi, Giovanni, and John S. Saul. *Essays on the political economy of Africa.* New York: Monthly Review Press, 1973. Pbk.

Berry, Sara S. *Cocoa, custom and socio-economic change in rural western Nigeria.* London, New York: Oxford University Press, 1975.

Davidson, Basil. *Can Africa survive? Arguments against growth without development.* New York: Atlantic Monthly Press, 1974. Pbk: Boston: Little Brown.

Ghai, Dharam P., ed. *Economic independence in Africa.* Nairobi; East African Literature Bureau, 1973.

Kamarck, Andrew M. *The economics of development.* Rev. ed. New York: Praeger, 1971.

Lele, Uma J. *The design of rural development: lessons from Africa.* Baltimore: Published for the World Bank by Johns Hopkins University Press, 1975. Pbk.

Leys, Colin. *Underdevelopment in Kenya: the political economy of neo-colonialism.* Berkeley: University of California Press, 1975. Pbk.

Multinational firms in Africa. Edited by Carl Gosta Widstrand, with an introduction by Samir Amin. Uppsala, Sweden: Scandinavian Institute of African Studies, 1975.

Onyemelukwe, Clement C. *Economic underdevelopment: an inside view.* New York: Longman, 1974. Pbk.

The political economy of contemporary Africa. Edited by Peter G. W. Gutkind and Immanuel Wallerstein. Beverly Hills, Calif.: Sage Publications, 1976.

Seidman, Ann W. *An economics textbook for Africa.* 2d. ed. New York: Praeger, 1974.

————. *Planning for development in sub-Saharan Africa.* New York: Praeger, 1974.

Uppal, J. S., and L. R. Salkever, eds. *Africa: problems in economic development.* New York: Free Press, 1972.

Traditional Economic Systems

There are basically two schools of thought in the study of African economic organization, and it is useful to know which "camp" an anthropologist or economist belongs to before reading his or her work. The substantivists (Bohannan and Dalton) argue "that the values and motivation of pre-industrial societies differ in kind rather than degree from those of industrial societies" (Hopkins, p. 6). The formalists (Hill, Schneider) argue that Africans, like everyone else, are "economic men" who have the same kind of economic responses to situations as do other peoples regardless of time or place.

BIBLIOGRAPHY

Pas, H. T. van der. *Economic anthropology, 1940–1972: an annotated bibliography.* Oosterhout, Netherlands: Anthropological Publications, 1973.

SUGGESTIONS FOR FURTHER READING:

Bohannan, Paul, and George Dalton, eds. *Markets in Africa.* Evanston: Northwestern University Press, 1962. Pbk: Garden City, N.Y.: Doubleday Anchor, 1965.

The development of indigenous trade and markets in West Africa. Edited by Claude Meillassoux. London: Oxford University Press for the International African Institute, 1971.

Hill, Polly. *Rural Hausa, a village and a setting.* Cambridge, Eng.: Cambridge University Press, 1972.

———. *Studies in rural capitalism in West Africa.* Cambridge, Eng.: Cambridge University Press, 1970.

Hopkins, Anthony G. *An economic history of West Africa.* New York: Columbia University Press, 1973. Pbk.

Schneider, Harold K. *The Wahi Wanyaturu: economics in an African society.* Chicago: Aldine, 1970.

The Arts

Visual Art/Architecture/Decorative Arts

African art can be seen in all aspects of African life, and therefore studies have focused on the rich variety of visual and plastic expression: masks and figures and their uses in ritual and social occasions, architecture, textiles, leather and metal work, pottery, basketry, house decoration, dress, body decoration and hairstyles, and even objects made for the tourist trade. Studies of African art fall into three categories: broad studies that present fairly sweeping surveys of the arts of all or nearly all of the subcontinent; more specific studies of a particular area or group or time; and studies, often in the form of collected essays or symposia, on particular problems. There are only two journals dedicated exclusively to articles on African art. Museum catalogues often contain very useful material but quickly become unavailable.

BIBLIOGRAPHIES:

Eicher, Joanne B. *African dress: a select and annotated bibliography on sub-Saharan countries.* East Lansing, Mich.: Center for International Programs, African Studies Center, Michigan State University, 1969.

Gaskin, Lionel J. *A bibliography of African art.* London: International African Institute, 1965.

Hartwig, Gerald W. "East African plastic art tradition—a discussion of the literature." *Geneve-Afrique,* v. 7 (1968): 31–52.

Prussin, Labelle, and David Lee. "Architecture in Africa: an annotated bibliography." *Africana library journal,* v. IV, no. 3 (Autumn 1973): 2–32.

Western, Dominique C. *A bibliography of the arts of Africa.* Waltham, Mass.: African Studies Association, 1975.
    Sections on art, architecture, oral literature, music, and dance.

PERIODICALS:

African arts. 1967–. Los Angeles: African Studies Center, UCLA. Quarterly.
    Scholarly and popular articles on the arts, particularly visual arts, and their functioning; richly illustrated; book reviews.

Arts d'Afrique noire. 1972–. Villiers-le-Bel, France (24 rue de Draguignan, 95400 Arnouville, France). Quarterly.

SUGGESTIONS FOR FURTHER READING:

Beier, Ulli. *Contemporary art in Africa.* New York: Praeger, 1968.

Bravmann, René. *Open frontiers: the mobility of art in Black Africa.* Seattle: Published for the Henry Art Gallery by the University of Washington Press, 1973.
    Catalog for a show.

————. "An urban way of death." *African arts,* v. 8, no. 3 (Spring 1975): 42–47; 62–64; 90.

————. *Islam and tribal art in West Africa*. London, New York: Cambridge University Press, 1974.

Crowley, Daniel J. "The West African art market revisited." *African arts*, v. 7, no. 4 (Autumn 1974): 54–59.

Delange, Jacqueline. *The art and peoples of black Africa*. New York: Dutton, 1974. Pbk.

Elisofon, Eliot, and William Fagg. *The sculpture of Africa*. New York: Praeger, 1958.

Fraser, D. and H. Cole, eds. *African art and leadership*, Madison: University of Wisconsin Press, 1972.

Gardi, Rene. *African crafts and craftsmen*. New York: Van Nostrand-Reinhold, 1970.

————. *Indigenous African architecture*. New York: Van Nostrand-Reinhold, 1974.

Gwatkin, Nina W. *Yoruba hairstyles: a selection of hairstyles from southern Nigeria*. Lagos, Nigeria: Craft Centre, National Museum Compound, 1971.

Mount, Marshall. *African art: the years since 1920*. Bloomington: Indiana University Press, 1973.

Prussin, Labelle. *Architecture in northern Ghana: a study of forms and functions*. Berkeley: University of California Press, 1969.

Sieber, Roy. *African textiles and decorative arts*. New York: Museum of Modern Art; distributed by New York Graphic Society, Greenwich, Conn., 1972. Pbk.

Thompson, Robert F. *African art in motion: icon and act* . . . Los Angeles: University of California Press, 1974.
   Catalog for an exhibition.

Trowell, Margaret. *African design*. 3d. ed. New York: Praeger, 1971.

Wahlman, Maude. *Contemporary African arts*. Chicago: Field Museum of Natural History, 1974.

Willett, Frank. *African art: an introduction*. New York: Praeger, 1971. Pbk.

————. *Ife in the history of West African sculpture*. New York: McGraw, 1967.

Music/Dance

Two new books on African music (Bebey and Nketia) provide broad surveys of the field, dealing with its historical, social, and cultural background, and include discussions of musical instruments, melody, polyphony, rhythm, the relations of music to speech and to dance, and African musical convention. Both contain discographies and indicate commercial sources and distributors for recordings.

One of the major collections of phonorecordings, both field recordings and commercially made recordings, is Indiana University's Archives of Traditional Music. Its catalog of phonorecords and oral data is now available in book form. The survey of African field recordings of music and oral data, conducted at the Archives, has also recently been published (Stone and Gillis). It indexes the holdings of the Archives, of similar centers such as at the Library of Congress, Columbia University, and the Institute of Ethnomusicology at UCLA, and of individual collectors.

BIBLIOGRAPHIES:

Drewal, Margaret Thompson, and Glorianne Jackson. *Sources on African and African-related dance.* New York: American Dance Guild, 1974. Pbk.

Gaskin, Lionel J. *A select bibliography of music in Africa.* Compiled . . . under the direction of K. P. Wachsmann. London: International African Institute, 1965.

Hanna, Judith Lynne. *The anthropology of dance: a selected bibliography.* Richardson, Texas: School of Arts and Humanities, University of Texas at Dallas, 1976. Available from the author, P.O. 1062, Englewood Cliffs, New Jersey.

Merriam, Alan P. *African music on LP: an annotated bibliography.* Evanston: Northwestern University Press, 1970.

Indiana University. Archives of Traditional Music and Oral Data. *Catalog of phonorecords of music and oral data held by the Archives of Traditional Music.* Boston: G. K. Hall, 1975.

Stone, Ruth M., and Frank J. Gillis. *African music and oral data: a catalog of field recordings, 1902–1975.* Bloomington, London: Indiana University Press, 1976.

PERIODICALS:

African music. 1954–. Roodepoort, Transvaal, South Africa: African Music Society. Quarterly.
Articles, reviews, notes and news.

Ethnomusicology. 1953–. Ann Arbor.: The Society for Ethnomusicology, Inc. 3 x yr.
Features a "current bibliography and discography," book and record reviews, as

well as original articles. The Society's *S.E.M. Newsletter* functions as a vehicle for the exchange of ideas, news, and information.

SUGGESTIONS FOR FURTHER READING:

African urban notes, v. 5, no. 4 (1970).

Entire issue devoted to the study of music in urban Africa.

Bebey, Francis. *African music: a people's art.* New York: Lawrence Hill, 1975. Pbk.

Blacking, John. *Venda children's songs.* Johannesburg, South Africa: Witwatersrand University Press, 1967.

Blum, Odette. "Dance in Ghana." *Dance perspectives*, v. 56 (Winter 1973).

Hanna, Judith Lynne. *The highlife: a West African urban dance.* New York: CORD, 1973. (Dance research monograph, 1.)

Imperato, Pascal James. "The dance of the Tyi Wara." *African arts*, v. 4, no. 1 (1970): 8–13, 71–80.

Nketia, J. H. Kwabena. *The music of Africa.* New York: Norton, 1974. Pbk.

Roberts, John S. *Black music of two worlds.* New York: Praeger, 1972. Pbk: New York: Morrow, 1974.

Deals with the influence of Afro-American music on modern African music.

Tracey, Hugh. *Chopi musicians: their music, poetry and instruments.* London: Oxford University Press for the International African Institute, 1948. Revised ed. 1971.

Wachsmann, Klaus P., ed. *Essays on music and history in Africa.* Evanston: Northwestern University Press, 1971.

Folklore/Oral Literature

The study of folklore in Africa, which has usually concentrated on verbal expression (tales, songs, proverbs, riddles, narratives), overlaps with studies in literature and drama, anthropology and linguistics, history, and religious expressions and beliefs. Additional references may be found under those headings.

BIBLIOGRAPHIES:

Görög, Veronika. "Bibliographie analytique sélective sur la littérature orale africaine." *Cahiers d'études africaines*, v. 8, no. 3 (1968): 453–501; "Littérature orale africaine: Bibliographie analytique (Périodiques)." *Cahiers d'études africaines*, v. 9, no. 4 (1969): 641–666; v. 10, no. 4 (1970): 583–631; v. 12, no. 4 (1972): 174–192.

Scheub, Harold. *Bibliography of African oral narratives.* Madison, Wisconsin:

African Studies Program, University of Wisconsin, 1971.

Western, Dominique C. *A bibliography of the arts of Africa*. Waltham, Mass.: African Studies Association, 1975.

See the section on "oral literature."

PERIODICALS:

Many articles on African folklore are published in *Africa* (International African Institute, London), *African studies* (Johannesburg), and *Research in African literatures and the arts* (Austin, Texas), all described under other headings.

SUGGESTIONS FOR FURTHER READING:

Courlander, Harold. *Tales of Yoruba gods and heroes*. New York: Crown, 1972. Pbk.

————. *A treasury of African folklore: the oral literature, traditions, myths, legends, epics, tales, recollections, wisdom, sayings and humor of Africa.* New York: Crown, 1975.

Dorson, Richard M., ed. *African folklore*. Bloomington: Indiana University Press, 1972. Pbk: Garden City, N.Y.: Doubleday Anchor, 1972.

Papers given at a conference at Indiana University are introduced by Professor Dorson and complemented by verbal texts.

Finnegan, Ruth H. *Oral literature in Africa*. London: Clarendon Press, 1970.

Liyong, Taban lo. *Popular culture of East Africa: oral literature*. Nairobi: Longmans, 1972. Pbk.

Literature

One of the most effective ways of achieving an in-depth understanding of Africa is to read novels by African writers. Many titles have appeared in the last two decades; however, no attempt has been made to list them below since the major ones have already been cited and discussed in the context of Emil Snyder's chapter. Other titles are listed in the bibliographies.

CONTINUING BIBLIOGRAPHIES:

These can be found in the *Journal of Commonwealth literature* and *African literature today*, both described below.

BIBLIOGRAPHIES:

Baratte-Eno Belinga, Thérèse. *Bibliographie, auteurs africaines et malgaches de langue française.* 3d. ed. Paris: O.R.T.F. (Office de Radiodiffusion television française; 38, rue Saint Sulpice, 75006) 1972. Pbk.

East, N. B. *African theatre; a checklist of critical materials.* New York: Africana Publishing Corp., 1970. Pbk.

Herdeck, Donald E. *African authors: a companion to Black African writing, 1300–1973.* Contributors: Abiola Irele, Lilyan Kesteloot, Gideon Mangoaela. Washington, D.C.: Black Orpheus Press, 1973–.

Short biographies for 594 authors, followed by systematic listing of their works, critical commentaries; extensive appendices; critical essays; authors by chronological period; authors by country of origin; authors writing in African languages; authors writing in European languages; women authors; publishers; journals; bibliographies; critical studies; and anthologies. Continuation seems to be promised.

Jahn, Janheinz, and Claus Peter Dressler. *Bibliography of creative African writing.* Nendeln, Liechtenstein: Kraus-Thomson, 1971.

An attempt at a comprehensive list of all black African writing (excluding works in Arabic and Amharic) before 1900 and creative writing after 1900; secondary works and criticism also listed.

Zell, Hans M., and Helene Silver. *A reader's guide to African literature.* New York: Africana Publishing Corp., 1971. Pbk.

Lists over 800 works by black African authors writing in English and French; also sections on critical works, reference materials, anthologies. Other features include sections on children's books by African authors; politically-committed literature; select articles on creative African literature; biographies of some major authors; annotated lists of periodicals; publishers and book sellers.

PERIODICALS:

African literature today: a journal of explanatory criticism. 1968–. Oxford, Eng.: Heinemann Educational. 2 x yr. (Formerly *Bulletin* of the Association for African Literature in English.)

Features a current bibliography on new African literature including books and periodical articles; book reviews; articles analyzing the works of African authors.

The Conch. 1969–. New Paltz, N.Y.: Dept. of African Studies, State University of New York, New Paltz. Biannual.

"A sociological journal of African cultures and literature."

Dhana. 1971–. Nairobi: East African Literature Bureau. 2 no. a yr.

"The Makerere University, Dept. of Literature journal of creative writing,"– featuring short stories, poetry, plays, and book reviews.

Journal of Commonwealth literature. 1965–. London: Heinemann Educational and the University of Leeds. Semiannual.

Critical reviews and book reviews on English language writing; annual bibliography of Commonwealth literature in the January number.

Research in African literatures. 1970–. Austin, Texas: African and Afro-American Research Institute, University of Texas at Austin. Semiannual.

Emphasis on theoretical, historical, and biographical articles; bibliographies and bibliographical essays, research, discographies, filmographies.

Journal of the new African literature and the arts. 1966–1972. New York: Third Press.

Creative works, reviews, criticism on African literature, music, fine arts, dance, and other aspects of African culture.

Présence africaine. 1947–. English and bilingual editions, 1967–. Paris.

Early champion of Negritude, with articles on literature, the arts, history and African culture; also prose, poetry, and drama featured.

Umma. 1971–. Nairobi: East African Literature Bureau. 2 x yr.

Journal of creative writing from the Literature Dept. of the University of Dar-es-Salaam.

World literature today. 1927–. Norman, Oklahoma: University of Oklahoma Press. Quarterly. (Formerly *Books abroad.*)

Reviews African books.

SUGGESTIONS FOR FURTHER READING:

Awoonor, Kofi. *The breast of the earth: a survey of the history, culture and literature of Africa south of the Sahara.* Garden City, N.Y.: Doubleday, 1975. Pbk.

Dalhousie review, v. 53 (Winter 1973–74).

Special issue on African literature.

Dathorne, O. R. *The black mind: a history of African literature.* Minneapolis: University of Minnesota Press, 1974.

Gérard, Albert S. *Four African literatures: Xhosa, Sotho, Zulu, Amharic.* Berkeley: University of California Press, 1971.

Graham-White, Anthony. *The drama of Black Africa.* New York, London: Samuel French, 1975.

Hamilton, Russell. *Voices from an empire: a history of Afro-Portuguese literature.* Minneapolis: University of Minnesota Press, 1975.

Kesteloot, Lilyan. *Intellectual origins of the African revolution.* Washington, D.C.: Black Orpheus Press, 1972.

Larson, Charles R. *The emergence of African fiction.* Bloomington: Indiana University Press, 1972. Pbk.

Mphalele, Ezekiel. *The African image.* New York: Praeger, 1974. Pbk.

Mutiso, Gideon C. M. *Socio-political thought in African literature: weusi?* New York: Barnes & Noble, 1974.

Traoré, Bakary. *The black African theatre and its social functions.* Ibadan, Nigeria: Ibadan University Press, 1972.

ANTHOLOGIES:

Moore, Gerald, and Ulli Beier, eds. *Modern poetry from Africa.* Rev. ed. Harmondsworth, Eng.: Penguin, 1966. Pbk.

Collins, Marie. *Black poets in French.* New York: Scribners, 1972. Pbk.

The negritude poets: an anthology of black poetry. Translated from the French by Ellen Kennedy. New York: Viking Press, 1975.

Larson, Charles R., ed. *African short stories.* New York: Collier Macmillan, 1970. Pbk.

Shores, Herbert L., and Megchelina Shore-Bos, eds. *Come back Africa.* New York: International Publishing Co., 1968. Pbk.

Languages and Literacy

Four main areas of concern under this heading are the classification of African languages (Greenberg), the study of African languages (Blass, Johnson, and Gage), the problem of literacy (Goody, Unesco publications), and the role of language in the development of African nations (Whiteley).

CONTINUING BIBLIOGRAPHIES:

Permanent International Committee of Linguists, *Bibliographie linguistique des années . . .* 1939–. Utrecht. Annual.

BIBLIOGRAPHIES:

Blass, Birgit, Dora E. Johnson, and William W. Gage. *A provisional survey of materials for the study of neglected languages.* Washington, D.C.: Center for Applied Linguistics, 1969.

Bibliography of dictionaries, grammars, and other teaching aids for a number of African languages.

Der-Houssikian, Haig. *A bibliography of African linguistics.* Edmonton, Canada; Champaign, Ill.: Linguistic Research, 1972.

Molnos, Angela. *Language problems in Africa, a bibliography (1946–1967) and summary of the present situation, with special reference to Kenya, Tanzania and Uganda.* Nairobi: East African Research Information Centre, 1969.

Murphy, John D., and Harry Goff. *A bibliography of African languages and linguistics.* Washington, D.C.: Catholic University of America Press, 1969.

PERIODICALS:

African languages/Langues africaines. 1975–. London: International African Institute. Annual.

A new journal, concerned with educational, literary, cultural, historical, and sociolinguistic aspects of African languages, as well as with descriptive and comparative studies.

African studies. 1941–. Johannesburg, South Africa: Witwatersrand University Press. Quarterly. (Formerly *Bantu studies.*)

Articles on linguistics, social aspects of African languages, as well as anthropology, folklore, government.

Journal of West African languages. Ibadan, Nigeria: Published by the West African Linguistic Society at the Ibadan University Press. Semiannual.

Kiswahili. 1930–. Dar-es-Salaam, Tanzania: Institute of Swahili Research, University of Dar-es-Salaam. 2 x yr.

Articles on the language, literature, and linguistic studies of Swahili; reviews of literature in Swahili.

Studies in African linguistics. 1969–. Los Angeles: Dept. of Linguistics and African Studies Center, UCLA. 3 x yr.

Linguistic studies.

SUGGESTIONS FOR FURTHER READING:

Alexandre, Pierre. *Languages and language in Black Africa.* Evanston, Ill.: Northwestern University Press, 1972.

Goody, John R., ed. *Literacy in traditional societies.* Cambridge, Eng.: Cambridge University Press, 1968.

Case studies on how "writing" affects essentially nonliterate societies and changes societies who adopt literacy.

Greenberg, Joseph H. *The languages of Africa.* 3d. ed. Bloomington: Indiana University Research Center for Language Sciences, 1970.

Linguistics in sub-Saharan Africa. Leiden: Brill, 1972. (Current trends in linguistics, v. 7.)

Language use and social change: problems of multilingualism with special reference to eastern Africa. . . . Edited by W. H. Whiteley. London: Published for the International African Institute by Oxford University Press, 1971.

Unesco. *The experimental world literacy programmes: a critical assessment.* Paris: Unesco Press with UNDP, 1976.

————. *Practical guide to functional literacy; a method of training for development.* Paris: 1973.

Unesco. *Educational studies and documents series.* 1970–. Paris. No. 5. *Literacy for working: functional literacy in rural Tanzania.* By Margo Viscusi. 1971. No. 10. *Functional literacy in Mali: training for development.* By Bernard Dumont. 1973.

Whiteley, Wilfred H. *Swahili: the rise of a national language.* London: Methuen, 1969. (Studies in African history, 3.)

Worldview: Religion/Philosophy

In the past, religious studies have either been written by Christian missionaries in Africa or by anthropologists who have leaned toward a functional interpretation. Many of the recent works have been written by Africans (Idowu, Mbiti) who are concerned with establishing an African theological focus. This section includes sources for the study of Islam and Christianity, as well as for traditional religions.

CONTINUING BIBLIOGRAPHY:

International bibliography of the history of religion. 1952–. Leiden: Brill, 1954–. Annual.

BIBLIOGRAPHIES:

Ofori, Patrick E. *Black African traditional religions and philosophy: a select bibliographic survey of sources from the earliest times to 1974.* Nendeln, Liechtenstein: Kraus-Thomson Organization, 1975.

————. *Christianity in tropical Africa: a selective annotated bibliography.* Nendeln, Liechtenstein: KTO Press, 1977.

————. *Islam in Africa south of the Sahara: a select bibliographic guide.* Nendeln, Liechtenstein: KTO Press, 1977.

Turner, Harold W. *New religious movements in primal societies,* v. 1: *Black Africa.* Boston: G. K. Hall, 1977.

PERIODICALS:

AFER: *African ecclesiastical review.* 1959–. Eldoret, Kenya (P.O. Box 908): AMECEA Pastoral Institute (Gaba). Bimonthly.

Articles on Christianity (especially Catholicism) in Africa; occasional articles on traditional religions.

Cahiers des religions africaines. 1967–. Kinshasa, Zaire: Centre d'Études des Religions africaines, Université Nationale du Zaire.

Bilingual; scholarly articles and bibliographies.

Cahiers philosophiques africaines. 1972–. Lubumbashi, Zaire: Département de Philosophie, Université Nationale du Zaire. Irreg.

Bilingual; regular bibliography on philosophy in Africa.

Journal of religion in Africa. 1967–. Leiden: Brill, 3 x yr.

". . . devoted to the scientific study of the forms and history of religion" in Africa; features articles, short notes, reports and news items, bibliographic material, reviews.

Orita: Ibadan journal of religious studies. 1967–. Ibadan, Nigeria: Dept. of Religious Studies, University of Ibadan. Biannual.

". . . aims at an interpretation and understanding of African tribal religion, Christianity and Islam . . ."; Orita in Yoruba means "where the ways meet."

Second order: an African journal of philosophy. 1972–. Ile-Ife, Nigeria: University of Ife Press. Semiannual.

Thought and practice: the journal of the Philosophical Association of Kenya. 1974–. Nairobi: East African Literature Bureau. 2 x yr.

SUGGESTIONS FOR FURTHER READING:

Ajayi, J. F. A., and E. A. Ayandele. "Emerging themes in Nigerian and West African religious history." *Journal of African studies,* v. 1, no. 1 (Spring 1974): 1–39.

Christianity in tropical Africa. Edited by C. G. Baeta. London: Oxford University Press, 1968.

Horton, Robin. "African traditional thought and Western science." *Africa* (London), v. 37, no. 1-2 (1967): 50–71, 155–187.

———. "The Kalabari world view; an outline and an interpretation." *Africa* (London), v. 32, no. 3 (1962): 197–219.

Idowu, E. Bolaji. *African traditional religion: a definition.* Maryknoll, N.Y.: Orbis Books, 1973.

King, Noel Q. *Christian and Muslim in Africa.* New York: Harper & Row, 1971.

———. *Religions of Africa: a pilgrimage into traditional religions.* New York: Harper & Row, 1970.

Islam in tropical Africa. Edited by I. M. Lewis. London: Oxford University Press, 1966.

Lewis, William H., and James Kritzeck, eds. *Islam in Africa.* New York: Van Nostrand-Reinhold, 1969.

Mbiti, John S. *African religions and philosophy.* New York: Praeger, 1970. Pbk: Garden City, N.Y.: Doubleday Anchor, 1970.

———. *African traditional prayers.* Garden City, N.Y.: Doubleday Anchor, 1975. Pbk.

———. *Introduction to African religion.* New York: Praeger, 1975.

Mugo, Erasto. *African response to western Christian religion: a sociological analysis of African separatist religions and political movements in East Africa.* Nairobi, Kenya: East African Literature Bureau, 1975. Pbk.

"This book is a study of the interaction between Africans in East Africa and the

European missionaries in a colonial situation and after independence."

Ranger, Terence O., and Isaria Kimambo, eds. *The historical study of African religion.* Berkeley: University of California Press, 1972.

Ranger, Terence O., and John Weller, eds. *Themes in the Christian history of Central Africa.* Berkeley: University of California Press, 1975.

Ray, Benjamin. *African religions: symbol, ritual and community.* Englewood Cliffs, N.J.: Prentice-Hall, 1976.

Shorter, Aylward. *African Christian theology—adaptation or incarnation?* London: Chapman, 1975.

————. *African culture and the Christian Church: an introduction to social and pastoral anthropology.* London: Chapman, 1975.

Taylor, John Vernon. *The primal vision: Christian presence amid African religion.* London: SCM Press; Philadelphia: Fortress Press, 1963.

Trimingham, John S. *The influence of Islam upon Africa.* London: Harlow, 1968.

Films

In the colonial period, films made about Africa were usually Eurocentric and often appeared to reinforce the worst stereotypes of the "Dark Continent." Some of these films can still be used, however, as documentaries which show the colonialists' view of Africa. Since independence, many new films that are dynamic statements about the African experience have been made. In particular, films by African producers, such as the Senegalese Ousmane Sembene, give new perspectives and insights.

FILMOGRAPHIES:

Africa from real to reel: an African filmography. Compiled by Steven Ohrn and Rebecca Riley. Waltham, Mass.: African Studies Association, 1976.

The most comprehensive listing of films on Africa available; approximately 1,300 16mm films distributed in the U.S. and Canada, with the following information: title, date, producer and filmmaker, location, distributors, synopsis; bibliography.

Films on Africa: an educator's guide to 16mm films available in the Midwest. Compiled by the African Studies Program, University of Wisconsin-Madison, Wisc.: African Studies Program, University of Wisconsin (1450 Van Hise Hall, 1220 Linden Drive, Madison, Wisc.), 1974.

List of films available in the midwestern United States, with descriptions provided by distributors; also recommendations by category from other U.S. Africanists; suggested age levels of usage also included.

Hennebelle, Guy. *Les cinémas africains en 1972.* Dakar, Senegal: Société africaine d'Édition, 1972. (L'Afrique littéraire et artistique, 20.)

Study of African filmmakers which includes filmographies and bibliographies of reviews.

Miller, Norman N. *Teaching African development with film.* Hanover, N.H.: American Universities Field Staff, 1971. (Fieldstaff reports: Africa; East Africa series, v. 10, no. 1.)

Travel

For those lucky enough to travel in Africa, or for the armchair traveler, travel guides can be useful and interesting. The books listed here generally give some useful advice and impressions, although prices may be higher with inflation, a few restaurants and hotels may no longer be in business, and some new ones may open.

The African American Institute's Educators to Africa Association (833 United Nations Plaza, New York, N.Y. 10017) and several colleges and universities offer low-cost trips to African countries. Sometimes these also include the opportunity to take courses at an African university.

SUGGESTIONS FOR FURTHER READING:

Allen, Philip S., and Aaron Segal. *The traveler's Africa.* New York: Scribners, 1975.

Blumenthal, Susan. *Bright continent: a shoestring guide to sub-Saharan Africa.* Garden City, N.Y.: Doubleday Anchor, 1974. Pbk.

Boone, Sylvia. *West African travels: a guide to people and places.* New York: Random House, 1974.

Traveller's guide to Africa, 1974. Colin Legum, editor-in-chief. London: African Development; New York: distributed by Rand McNally, c1974.

Cookbooks

The following list will allow gourmets to broaden their culinary horizons. Some cookbooks give Western equivalents for African ingredients which are difficult to obtain, and the book by Hachten has a selected list of stores in the United States that carry the ingredients for African recipes.

Hachten, Harva. *Kitchen safaris: a gourmet's tour of Africa.* New York: Atheneum, 1970.

Oka, Monica O. *Black Academy cookbook: a collection of authentic African recipes.* Buffalo, N.Y.: Black Academy Press, 1972.

Sandler, Bea. *The African cookbook.* New York: Crowell, 1972.

Van der Post, Laurens. *African cooking.* New York: Time-Life Books, 1970. (Foods of the World.)

Wilson, Ellen Gibson. *A West African cookbook: an introduction to good food in Ghana, Liberia, Nigeria and Sierra Leone.* New York: Evans; distributed by Lippincott, Philadelphia, 1971. Pbk: New York: Avon.

Instruction

The following works are guides for teaching about Africa at the elementary, secondary, and college levels.

Africa: teaching perspectives and approaches. Editor: John E. Willmer. Tualatin, Oregon: Geographic and Area Study Publications, 1975.

Introduced by 13 essays by Africanists, this work has sections on resources and materials, approaches to teaching about Africa, and teaching strategies.

The African experience, edited by John N. Paden and Edward W. Soja. Evanston, Ill.: Northwestern University Press, 1970. 4 v. Pbk.

Volume II provides a syllabus for college teaching; other volumes include essays, bibliography, and a guide to resources.

Murphy, E. Jefferson, and Harry Stein. *Teaching Africa today: a handbook for teachers and curriculum planners.* New York: Citation Press, 1973. Pbk.

Other Sources

African American Institute, 833 United Nations Plaza, New York, N.Y. 10017. (212) 661-0800

A private organization whose purpose is to further African development and strengthen understanding between the United States and Africa. Its programs bring African students to U.S. universities and African leaders, specialists, and educators for short-term study and travel. Other programs are the Educators to Africa Association, offering low-cost travel plans to Africa; American Study in Africa; Africa Policy Information Center; and its School Services Division.

Publications: *Africa report;* various teaching materials.

African Studies Association, 218 Shiffman Center, Brandeis University, Waltham, Massachusetts 02154. (617) 899-3079

Professional association for Africanists in the United States. Attempts to promote, integrate, and facilitate research on Africa; gathers and distributes data and research on Africa, informs researchers of research regulations and priorities of various African countries; annual meeting.

Publications: *African studies newsletter; African studies review; Issue; History in Africa; ASA review of books;* bibliographies and reference guides to African studies in the U.S. and current research.

Index